The Changing Faces of Citizenship

THE CHANGING FACES OF CITIZENSHIP

Integration and Mobilization among Ethnic Minorities in Germany

Joyce Marie Mushaben

Berghahn Books
New York • Oxford

Published in 2008 by
Berghahn Books
www.berghahnbooks.com

Library of Congress Cataloging-in-Publication Data

Mushaben, Joyce Marie, 1952–
  The changing faces of citizenship : social integration and political
mobilization among ethnic minorities in Germany / Joyce Marie Mushaben.
    p. cm. — (Monographs in German history ; vol. 21)
  Includes bibliographical references and index.
  ISBN 978-1-84545-453-1 (hardback : alk. paper) — ISBN 978-1-84545-468-5
(pbk. : alk. paper)
  1. Citizenship—Germany. 2. Germany—Ethnic relations. 3. Assimilation
(Sociology)—Germany. 4. Minorities—Germany—Political activity.
5. Immigrants—Legal status, laws, etc.—Germany. I. Title.
  JN3774.M87 2008
  305.9'069120943—dc22   2008020325

British Library Cataloguing in Publication Data

A catalogue record for this book is available from the British Library

Printed in the United States on acid-free paper

ISBN 978-1-84545-453-1 Hardback

For all the kids "with migration background" who have been unwittingly herded into German Hauptschulen *and* Sonderschulen, *despite their parents' efforts to give them a better life. May the Federal Republic of Germany come to realize, sooner rather than later, that your future is its future.*

To Joshua and Moritz, who have understood the power of speaking a second language and shared the fun of cross-cultural friendship "ever since they were born."

CONTENTS

TABLES

ACKNOWLEDGMENTS

It takes a village—not only to educate generations of migrant offspring, but also to write books like this. The individuals who assisted me in "coming to terms" with the changing nature of German citizenship are spread across many cities and countries, reflecting the globalized times in which we live.

I am deeply grateful to Gisela Janetzke and Manfred Osten at the Alexander von Humboldt Foundation as well as to the University of Missouri–St. Louis for the generous financial support that enabled me to conduct extensive field-work in 2002. Thanks are also extended to Rainer Münz, Rainer Ohliger, Antje Schiedler, and Frau Zeiske for the professional hospitality I enjoyed during my six months as a guest professor at the Institut für Bevölkerungswissenschaft/ Humboldt University. Berlin's veteran Commissioner for Foreigners Barbara John contributed more than she will ever know, having graciously consented to four interviews over a span of twenty years. District integration commissioners Doris Nahawandi and Karin Korte, along with Stuttgart commissioners Gari Pavkovic and Isabel Lavadihno were likewise generous with their time and materials. Özcan Mutlu (Berlin Abgeordnetenhaus) and Steffen Angenendt (German Council on Foreign Affairs) supplied interview contacts along with invitations to dinner and lunch. I also learned a lot from Werner Schiffauer (Europa Universität Viadrina), Ruud Koopmans (Wissenschaftszentrum Berlin), and Klaus Bade (Universität Osnabrück), all of whom provided "tons" of insightful reading material. This is only the tip of the iceberg, of course; many more interview partners shared qualitative insights and quantitative data, as gratefully acknowledged in subsequent chapters.

Others contributed to this project by way of their personal encouragement and collegial support. Publisher Marion Berghahn and her daughter Vivian have long counted among my favorite dinner partners at annual German Stud-ies Association meetings, but I appreciate their professionalism, competence, and kindness all the more as this work goes to press. Asiye Kaya introduced me to new dimensions of "women and Islam," as well as to unfamiliar sections of Kreuzberg and Neukölln. Having shared many bottles of wine, *Kopftuch* articles, and gender-mainstreaming books with me over the last five years, Gabriele Abels not only kept me up to date but also intellectually sane in Missouri, the home state of John Ashcroft. Rejected by Show-Me State voters in 2000, Ashcroft moved on to the post of Attorney General, eliminating fundamental freedoms for hundreds of thousands of innocent migrants, refugees, and tourists across the USA after September 11th. Most of the criticisms I raise regarding German asylum and "temporary migration" policies now apply to my home country as well.

My "charming husband" Harry deserves honorable mention for accepting my extended stays in Berlin as well as frequent German occupations of our St. Louis guestroom as normal components of our dialectical family life. I am also deeply indebted to Nikki Doughty, my loyal friend, office therapist, website wizard, and administrative assistant at the Institute for Women's and Gender Studies at UM–St. Louis, who worked as hard as I did through the final months of writing. The last year there was a life-transforming experience for both of us. Leesa Althen provided the index assistance and help with proofreading.

Finally, I hail my son Joshua for his sense of humor, his love of ICE trains, his enthusiastic embrace of FC Schalke 04 and FIFA soccer, as well as his valiant efforts to master, in Mark Twain's words, "the awful German language." The quality time we spent together eating döner, riding the U-Bahn, commenting on *Kopftuch* variations, and otherwise musing over the new look in German *Staatsbürgerschaft* counted among the high points of my research leave.

EXPLAINING THE PARADIGM SHIFT IN GERMAN CITIZENSHIP LAW

In 1985, I began to explore the contours of national identity in the Federal Republic, based on the belief that generational change had played a compelling role in the democratization of German political culture after 1945. Few of my interview partners at the time believed that they possessed a West German identity, as Theo Sommer of *Die Zeit* confessed to me in 1992. In fact, I discovered a wide assortment of "FRG" identities, rooted in generational change.[1]

I secured funding for a parallel study of East German identity in 1988 but was unable to start that project until 1989. Few GDR citizens I knew up to that point willingly admitted to possessing an East German identity, although several grudgingly conceded that such feelings arose when they compared themselves to distant relatives on the other side of the border. Less than a year later, the Berlin Wall had collapsed, the D-Mark emerged as the coin of the realm, and unification was scheduled for 3 October 1990. By that point, Eastern residents had embraced the motto "We are one people!" Confronted with unity and its costs as a fait accompli, Westerners responded: "So are we!" One critic, reviewing my work, insisted that it was an exaggeration to refer to different East and West German mentalities. By the time my monograph rolled off the press, analyzing *ostdeutsche Identität* had become a growth industry.[2]

Notes for this section begin on page 9.

The fact that blood lineage, shared borders, and a common currency do not a unified citizenry make became quite obvious over the next five years. By 1996, 62 percent of the easterners felt that Germans had grown further apart (up from 48 percent), 30 percent among westerners.[3] The Old *Länder* emerged as the ostensible winners of unification, due to Western-dominated production and reconstruction booms. New *Länder* residents saw themselves as the losers: The national jobless rate stood at 10.7 percent by 2002; the Eastern average ran 18 percent, and as high as 20–35 percent in certain regions. Although 90 percent of all GDR women age fifteen to sixty had engaged in paid labor prior to unity, they were disproportionately excluded from the job market due to biases built into the Western system.[4]

Although they experienced the same history prior to 1945, residents of both states were taught to interpret Nazi atrocities and national division in very different ways over a forty-year period. They do however share a sense of what being German could *not* mean after 1945.[5] By 1990 I had yet to discover a text beyond the Basic Law explaining what it *should* mean to be German in a positive sense. Easterners certainly did not think it meant doing everything the Western way when they called for a united fatherland; by 1998 they were even less persuaded that *Besserwessis* (know-it-all westerners) had all the answers to pressing social problems.[6]

This brings me to real losers of unification, given the events that followed: the so-called *Ausländer* (foreigners). A majority of Germany's seven million alien residents have lived there for twenty to thirty years; indeed, 1.5 million were born there. Social-cultural biases have always outweighed the legal and economic barriers to their integration, and are further used to justify their political exclusion.[7] Prior to 1990, most aliens who met the formal requirements for naturalization could still be rejected at the discretion of bureaucrats as being "not in the best interest of German culture." Additional discretionary criteria imposed by local or state actors lead to big incorporation gaps among the *Länder*, and from one *Bezirk* (district) to another.

The wave of xenophobic attacks that washed across Germany following unification coincided with a mass migration of "co-ethnics" from Eastern Europe and the Soviet Union, along with thousands of Yugoslav refugees. While it did not cause ultranationalist violence, unification served as a catalyst for violence in Germany, especially among young, disadvantaged males. The first year of unity saw 1,483 physical attacks against foreigners, ranging from gang assaults in subways to firebombings of temporary asylum quarters (tents, container ships, and community centers). Of the 2,368 xenophobic incidents reported in 1991, five hundred occurred between September and October; three-fourths of the arson attacks took place in the Old *Länder*. The Office of Constitutional Protection registered a 54 percent increase in 1992, resulting in seventeen deaths—nine in the West, eight in the East; 1993 saw 1,814 acts of violence and eight more fatalities.[8] Attacks occurred in towns stretching from Aalen (Westphalia) to Zwickau

(Saxony). The more sensational cases in Hoyerswerda, Rostock, Mölln, and Solingen led to copycat actions among youth in other cities.

Marginalization, stigmatization, and intolerance toward foreigners owes much to the lack of a positive identity among Federal Republicans themselves. I have long wondered how one could expect Turkish guestworkers to "assimilate," given the reluctance of postwar citizens to specify the contours of their own Germanness. Even the *Leitkultur* (leading or guiding culture) debate invoked by conservatives in 1999 provides few clues.[9] For three decades politicians and pundits have erroneously referred to a lack of effective integration as *das Ausländerproblem*, the "foreigner problem." The national-identity conundrum, coupled with a refusal to adopt proactive policies, sooner renders it a "German problem."

Legal codes and political rhetoric have failed to keep pace with social realities in the FRG. The value of citizenship ought to derive from "its capacity to confer a minimum of social dignity."[10] Germany's adherence to a *jus sanguinis* paradigm is increasingly at odds with its own needs as a democratic polity. Its economic competitiveness, not to mention the solvency of its pension system, is intricately connected to migration and integration—past, present, and future.

My book on postwar generations exhorted FRG policymakers to jettison the myth that Germany was "not a land of immigration" and to adopt a bona fide *Einwanderungsgesetz* (immigration law), enabling persons not subject to persecution to acquire admission and residency rights. It likewise called for educational reforms stressing the national benefits inherent in a multicultural society. The 1998 election of an SPD-Green coalition made the first step of the reform process possible (though its motives were neither altruistic nor "leftist radical," as charged). In spring 2002, CDU/CSU Bundesrat members rejected the second step, a real Immigration and Integration Law, despite the fact that conservatives like the Saarland's Peter Müller and ex-Bundestag president Rita Süssmuth had worked intensely on a bipartisan bill.

I argue throughout subsequent chapters that multicultural identities have taken root in the Federal Republic and that their contributions to the dominant political culture have been positive and democratic, even though Germany still does not perceive itself as a multicultural society. This book is the logical corollary to my earlier studies on postwar identity and generational change, with special emphasis on the significance of citizenship reform for women and youth.

German Citizenship in Transition

Since 1913, Germany has relied on a concept of *citizenship* grounded in organic conceptualizations of *the nation*, the lessons of two World Wars notwithstanding. The last fifteen years have witnessed not one but two historical breaks with the past regarding its understanding of what it means to be German. The first major break, effected in grand style in 1989–1990, was territorial in nature; longer in the making, the second shift can be described as generational in character. These two changes combined have precipitated a paradigm shift in public discourse over citizenship in the nation united.

The legal manifestation of this shift is the revised Citizenship/Naturalization Law, adopted by parliament in 1999. Enacted on 1 January 2000, the new statute provides an important launching point for assessing Germany's relation to a complex array of foreigners in the new millennium. Its rational counterpart, the Law on Immigration and Integration was promulgated under controversial circumstances in 2002, then rejected on procedural grounds by the Constitutional Court.[11] A radically revised version finally passed in both chambers in 2004.

As to the first break, the fall of the Berlin Wall and the opening of Central/East Europe significantly undermined Germany's insistence on ethnonational citizenship. Codified in the 1913 *Reichs- und Staatsangehörigkeitsgesetz*, the idea of an organic national community (*das deutsche Volk*) was reinforced by the Preamble to the 1949 Basic Law and Article 116 GG. Adherence to *jus sanguinis* throughout the Cold War supplied the fledgling Republic with new sources of political legitimacy along several axes. Above all, it rendered the idea of German division provisional, obliging lawmakers to work toward unification, as reinforced by the Constitutional Court's 1973 judgment on the Treaty on Basic Relations between the FRG and the GDR. Secondly, the assertion that East and West Germans remained blood brothers and sisters justified foreign policy mechanisms used to undermine the existential legitimacy of the other German state. Outstanding examples were the Hallstein Doctrine and the FRG's insistence that it alone represented all Germans (*Alleinvertretungsanspruch*). Last but not least, *jus sanguinis* could be used to keep open the question of Germany's final boundaries by way of ties to ethnic Germans dispersed throughout Eastern territories. Negotiations geared toward improving the life conditions of these diaspora Germans served as the thin edge of the wedge for effecting slow changes in domains that otherwise would have been deemed domestic affairs and thus off limits to would-be international meddlers.

Unification turned millions of GDR "resettlers" into everyday citizens, despite post-unity perceptions that they were treated as second-class Germans. Known as the Two Plus Four Agreement, the Treaty on Final Settlement (September 1990), coupled with the German-Polish Treaty (November 1990), drew a definitive line at the Oder-Neisse River, settling the border question once and for all. However, the end to direct claims on the Eastern Territories did not resolve the problem of ever more people, labeled *AussiedlerInnen*, pouring into the country to reactivate their citizenship, even if most were several cohorts removed from personal experience with the German nation.

The second break with historical notions of German citizenship will carry us well into the new millennium. This break is predominantly generational in nature. My core argument here is that "Long Marchers" who assumed national power in 1998 mark the final stage in the changing of the guard, bringing closure to fifty years of political reeducation. Schooled in the street politics of the late 1960s involving many Third-World struggles, then professionalized by way of grassroots participation in new social movements, these Germans have seen their radical aims legitimated by way of transnational human-rights agreements, beginning with the 1975 Helsinki Accords. This numerically strong group of citizen activists has come to embrace the Federal Republic as a *Staat der Gegenwart*, "state of the present," rather than as a nation whose future rests primarily with the past.[12] "States of the present" are characterized as those redefining their national interests in accordance with changing global conditions. Modern and pluralistic in orientation, they rely primarily on *jus soli* to establish the parameters of membership in the polity. They accept as citizens any and all willing to embrace core political values, who share a sense of national-qua-community purpose and follow the rules of the larger economic game. *Staaten der Vergangenheit*, "states of the past," fixate on the more exclusive *jus sanguinis* as the defining element of citizenship, reinforcing their own identity conundrums by imposing unmasterable historical burdens on all blood relations who follow.

The FRG is currently home to more foreigners than any other European country, 7.3 million, equivalent to 9 percent of the population. Obviously these people did "wander in" from somewhere, even without the benefits of a formal *Einwanderungsgesetz*. Though many fluctuations occur across specific groups (guestworkers, repatriates, refugees), the influx has been continuous since 1949. Official policies affirming the rule that "Germany is not a land of immigration," treating millions of foreigners as exceptions, are completely out of sync with national facts of life. This school is represented by conservative politicians like Jürgen Rutgers who seek limits on immigration by calling for *Kinder statt Inder*, "children, not Indians." They insist that Germany's shortage of high-tech workers is a simple demographic problem, sooner remedied by way of pronatalism than by means of a selective, skills-oriented migration policy (the Green Card approach).[13] Others, such as Friedrich Merz, maintain that real Germans must reassert their privileged position as the *Leitkultur*, the imperatives of globalization and democratic pluralism notwithstanding. What is really at issue here are the terms under which individuals, families, students, workers, professionals, or refugees can, do, or should enter the country.

The liberalized naturalization law, coupled with "provisional" dual citizenship for newborns, is the logical outgrowth of a long process of learning to live with difference. This national learning process suggests that the host state is finally committed to becoming a land of integration, despite the disingenuous protestations of hardliners that it is not a land of immigration; as anyone who visits the cities of Berlin, Frankfurt/Main, Cologne, or Stuttgart can attest, the Federal Republic is already both.

Theoretical and Empirical Parameters of the Study

My work on East German transformation processes taught me that to prove stable in the long run, democratic institutions not only need to represent citizens in a territorial sense; they must also respond to more deep-seated identity needs.[14] Studying the reformation of intermediary associations in the young *Länder*, I found that citizens who cultivate intersubjective ties to emerging organizations not only internalize democratic values more quickly, they also establish effective channels for advancing their own interests. Such ties, known as *social capital*, give a democratizing society the coherence it needs to adapt to new institutions and values in hard transitional times and to create spaces for previously unorganized interests and citizens within new power structures. Social capital nonetheless presupposes the existence of a positive group identity, a subject that has triggered many contentious debates in unified Germany since 1991.

The more I reflected on Easterners' efforts to draw on parts of their old GDR identity in order to cultivate a new one grounded in united Germany, the more I began to see parallels among the FRG's foreign populations. It is not only natural, it is in many respects necessary for Turkish workers, Greek exiles, Italian migrants, Russian Jews, repatriates from Kazakhstan, Bosnian refugees, and Iranian dissidents to build on ties to their own cultures, to develop organizational skills and practice democracy in familiar settings (e.g., in ethnic associations), in order to forge a new identification with the host country. Community action and informal networking lie at the heart of civil society. Ethnic minorities capable of simply forgetting their own past—by divorcing themselves from their languages, customs, and cuisines—will find it hard to understand why Germans hang on to theirs, even when it runs counter to national interests. Thus this work also explores the role of social capital and local community in interest mobilization among minority populations.

A further point of contention entails the processes by which new arrivals should come to enjoy the full range of citizenship rights. Although millions have lived in Germany for nearly two decades, enjoy substantial socioeconomic benefits and even permanent residency, foreigners lack the participatory rights associated with a democratic polity. Here one could fault the European Union, especially the Maastricht Treaty, for carving up citizenship into four distinct status categories: viz., legal, political, economic, and social citizenship, subject to varying degrees of local, national, and supranational regulation. Each construct carries its own set of benefits, duties, and ties to the national community, the likes of which have been explored by scholars ranging from Karl Deutsch and T. H. Marshall to Gerard Delanty and Elizabeth Meehan, inter alia.[15] As Delanty writes, "Citizenship is no longer a coherent discourse fixed in a particular framework. In short, it has suffered the fate of other 'meta-narratives' and is consequently open to new definitions: its core components—rights, duties, participation and identity—have become disjointed."[16]

I argue that the key stumbling block to effective integration rests with the public's tendency to overemphasize the costs associated with asylum seekers and refugees while ignoring the contributions of long-term migrant workers who comprise the majority, despite clear legal distinctions between the two groups. Germany's generous embrace of victims of political oppression ended in 1993 as the result of a constitutional amendment (Article 116) and the new purposes accorded the 1990 Schengen Agreement. Beyond its disturbing normative implications, the negative political rhetoric fueling the asylum debate led alienated youth to believe that their acts of xenophobic violence mirrored the will of the people. The riots directed against an asylum hostel in Rostock are conflated in the public mind with the arson deaths of Turkish families in Mölln and Solingen—although the latter were property-owning, permanent legal residents. The new Immigration Law is an attempt to un-blur the lines between "deserving" and "undeserving" foreigners.

Last but not least, this book stresses the reciprocal nature of lifestyle changes effected by the presence of foreign "co-citizens," one result being the gradual elimination of negative character traits long deemed typically German. Most Germans have acquired multicultural tastes that should make it easier for subsequent generations to believe that they are normal. Unfortunately, frequent reiterations of the mantra "Germany is not a country of immigration" have impeded processes of self-identification along these lines. In short, the more politicians espouse exclusive images of Germanness, the more they force average citizens to deny their own enlightened tendencies toward inclusiveness, and the more they misjudge the critical need for deeper socioeconomic reforms in *Modell Deutschland*. The Green Card's failure to generate the expected tidal wave of super-competent, Information Technology specialists eager to uproot their families, relegate their wage-earning spouses to unpaid care work, learn fluent German, pay outrageous rents, and then go back home after five years of rescuing the national economy from educational stagnation has helped to demonstrate the FRG's uncanny ability to hoist itself by its own petard regarding migration policy.

The book begins with a discussion of changing conceptualizations of citizenship, as well as theories of integration mirrored in German reform debates, summarizing the legal classifications that informed official policy from 1949 to 1989: i.e., *Vertriebene, Einsiedler, Aussiedler, Um-* and/or *Übersiedler* (expellee, first-time settler, ethnic resettler, and persons settling-over from the GDR).

These categories were reconfigured following the territorial break with the past witnessed in 1989–1990. Ironically, co-ethnics do not comprise the largest pool to have taken up residence as of the 1960s, despite being viewed as the most legitimate arrivals. The *Gastarbeiter*, profiled in chapter 2, actually built the bridge to a new concept of *Staatsangehörigkeit* following the generational break of 1998–1999. Chapter 3 addresses integration dynamics among German reset-tlers from Central Eastern Europe and post-Soviet states, followed by the exclu-sionary treatment of refugees and asylum seekers since 1990 in chapter 4.

Chapter 5 shifts our attention to the multicultural metropolis of Berlin, serv-ing as a national laboratory for overcoming East-West differences, given its sta-tus as divided city-turned-capital. Berlin has functioned as an enlarged petri dish for ethnic-identity projects and integration experiments for nearly three decades, due to the extraordinary efforts of its first *Ausländerbeauftragte*, Dr. Barbara John (1982–2002). I describe basic patterns of incorporation among core migrant groups most likely to bestow a new look to German citizenship in the decades ahead. Chapter 6 returns to the linkages between identity, natural-ization, interest organization, and political rights among second and third gen-eration *Inländer*, awkwardly labelled "residents of non-German heritage." The concluding chapter assesses the role of Islam in urban life, the paradigm shift in citizenship law, and possible complications at the EU level. Ethnic minorities may yet emerge as winners now that Germany has, at least legislatively, crossed that bridge to the twenty-first century.

Methodological Framework(s)

This study analyzes the interactive effects of official integration strategies and emerging patterns of practical-communitarian or mobile-transactional activity among Germany's minority residents. I develop case studies rooted in established enclaves in Berlin, supplemented by evidence from other cities with large ethnic populations, e.g., Stuttgart and Amsterdam. In addition to refining my inter-disciplinary skills, my earlier research on German identity taught me the value of participant observation and ethnomethodology, otherwise known as "living among the natives." I spent January to July 2002 conducting field research as a guest scholar at the Humboldt University and the tricultural Europa Universität Viadrina in Frankfurt/Oder. I returned to Berlin in 2003 and 2004 to update earlier findings.

In addition to reviewing official documents, statistical data, expert recommen-dations, and media accounts and reports commissioned by federal ministries, I conducted open-ended interviews with representatives of ethnic interest associa-tions and integration commissioners in Berlin and Stuttgart, providing qualitative indicators of social integration and political mobilization among those entities. I processed many a survey executed by colleagues at the Institut für Bevölkerungswissenschaft, the Wissenschaftszentrum Berlin, the IMS-Osnabrück, the Zentrum für Türkeistudien, and Berlin's *Ausländerbeauftragte*. All translations from German texts are my own.

A note regarding the masculine nature of the German terms used here: the frequent exclusion of (feminist) *Innen* forms throughout parts of the text is deliberate. The standards used to recruit foreign workers, to ensure "the free flow of persons" in the single European market, to extend legal protections, welfare benefits, and permanent residency status, as well as the criteria used to accord asylum rights, have been far from gender neutral. Disaggregated data assessing the plight of foreign women and youth were hard to come by through the 1980s and 1990s; to compensate, I have incorporated gender-specific treatments in most chapters.

The *Aussiedler* were likewise underrepresented, or missing entirely from most studies directly comparing different migrant groups (e.g., criminality, unemployment), since they are absorbed into German statistics shortly after arrival. There is now a growing awareness among policymakers that recent arrivals from the former Soviet Union, the so-called *Spätaussiedler*, face the same problems of acculturation and integration seen among many Third World migrants. In 2002 the Berlin Government extended the powers of Commissioner Barbara John to attend to the needs of this group as well. Even more encouraging, the job title itself has been changed. Dr. John's successor, Günter Piening, is now the commissioner for integration and migration. His counterparts in Frankfurt/Main and Stuttgart adopted comparable proactive titles several years ago: a paradigm shift indeed.

Notes

1. Joyce Marie Mushaben, *From Post-War to Post-Wall Generations: Changing Attitudes towards the National Question and NATO in the Federal Republic of Germany* (Boulder, CO: Westview, 1998).
2. Joyce Marie Mushaben, *Identity without a Hinterland? Continuity and Change in National Consciousness in the German Democratic Republic, 1949–1989* (Washington, DC: AICGS/Johns Hopkins University, 1993).
3. "Umfrage: Daumen runter," *Der Spiegel*, no. 9 (26 February 1996): 49.
4. East Germans have good reasons for seeing themselves as second-class citizens in the nation they helped to unite, despite the fact that they have benefited from billions in transfer funds. See Heidrun Abromeit, "Zum Für und Wider einer Ost-Partei," *Gegenwartskunde* 4 (1992): 445; further, "Die 'Vertretungslücke': Probleme im neuen deutschen Bundesstaat," *Gegenwartskunde* 3 (1993): 281–292. Also, Peter Kirnich, "Forscher fördern langfristiges

Konzept für Aufbau Ost," *Berliner Zeitung*, 19 June 2002; Jens Blankennagel, "Nur noch Schlafdörfer für Rentner," *Berliner Zeitung*, 29 May 2002.

5. Mushaben, *From Post-War to Post-Wall Generations*, chap. 3.

6. Reinhard Höppner, Rede auf dem Rechtspolitischen Kongreß der Friedrich Ebert Stiftung am 20. April 1997, Rheingoldhalle-Mainz. Also, Eckhard Priller, *Ein Suchen und Sichfinden im Gestern und Heute: Verändern die Ostdeutschen ihre Einstellungen und Haltungen zur Demokratie und gesellschaftlichen Mitwirkung?* Working Paper FS III 97–411, Wissenschaftszentrum Berlin (December 1997).

7. Joyce Marie Mushaben, "A Crisis of Culture: Social Isolation and Integration among Turkish Guestworkers in the German Federal Republic," in Ilyan Basgöz and Norman Furniss, eds., *Turkish Workers in Europe: A Multidisciplinary Study* (Bloomington: Indiana University Press, 1985), 125–150.

8. Mushaben, *From Post-War to Post-Wall Generations*, chap. 7.

9. I also criticized the inflammatory rhetoric used by Helmut Kohl's advisors: for example, Edmund Stoiber's declaration that a "flashflood" of immigrants would produce a "multinational society on German soil"—*durchmischt und durchrasst*—of mixed, and by implication inferior, races.

10. Judith N. Shklar, *American Citizenship: The Quest for Inclusion* (Cambridge, MA: Harvard University Press, 1991), 2.

11. Andrea Beyerlein, "Der Ja-Sager und der Nein-Sager," *Berliner Zeitung*, 20 March 2002; "Eklat im Bundesrat: Union wirft Wowereit Verfassungsbruch vor," *Berliner Zeitung*, 23–24 March 2002; Werner Kolhoff, "Urteilsverkündung," *Berliner Zeitung*, 21 June 2002.

12. On the Green Card, see Rita Süssmuth et al. (ICI), *Structuring Immigration, Fostering Integration*, report by the Independent Commission on Migration to Germany (Zuwanderungsbericht), (Berlin: 4 July 2001), 63ff.

13. Joyce Marie Mushaben, "*Die Lehrjahre sind vorbei!* Re-Forming Democratic Interest Groups in Eastern Germany," *Democratization* 8, no. 4 (Winter 2001): 95–133.

14. See Karl W. Deutsch, *Nationalism and Social Communication: An Inquiry into the Foundations of Nationality* (Cambridge, MA: MIT Press, 1966); T. H. Marshall, *Class, Citizenship and Social Development* (Garden City, NJ: Doubleday, 1964); Gerard Delanty, "Models of Citizenship: Defining European Identity and Citizenship," *Citizenship Studies* 1, no. 3 (1997): 285–303; and Elizabeth Meehan, *Citizenship and the European Union* (London: Sage, 1993).

15. Delanty, "Models of Citizenship," 295.

16. Ibid., 295.

CHAPTER 1

CITIZENSHIP, NATIONALITY, IDENTITY

Community Interfacing Reconsidered

Germany: the country with 6.5 million foreigners and no immigrants.

—Jane Kramer (1993)

Tell me what paragraph you came in under, and I will tell you who you are.

—Yugoslav refugee, interviewed by Harald Balder

Riding the Number 148 bus along Potsdamer Street to the new *Staatsbibliothek* near the Wall, I started to notice dramatic changes in the neighborhoods I passed through daily during my two years at the Free University of Berlin (1977–1979). In 1983 I wrote an article on problems of sociocultural integration among "guestworkers" in Germany but moved on to research a burgeoning anti-nuclear movement. I found the article in a basement file cabinet when I returned to St. Louis in 2002, following six months of field research in Berlin. The essay stressed the German Catch-22 of migration, applied to anyone trying to enter the country in search of economic opportunity: working permits were only granted in conjunction with residency permits, which, in turn, depended on stable employment status.

Notes for this section begin on page 39.

Germany has countless laws applying to foreigners on its soil; until 1999, however, it refused to adopt one allowing people to enter on a permanent basis unless they had been politically persecuted. My article stressed the spurious connection between the utilization of migrant workers and the high unemployment afflicting Germany during the 1980s.[1] I described problems of language acquisition among second-generation foreigners born in Germany or arriving by way of family unification after 1973. I grumbled further about the difficult lot of Turkish females, caught between arcane understandings of family honor and feminist demands for sexual liberation.

That 1983 essay provides strong empirical support for the adage, "the more things change, the more they stay the same." As noted then, the Federal Republic refused to recognize "that integration . . . is a developmental process, not a set of policy prescriptions. It is a process requiring openness—not exactly a German character trait—and engagement based on a measure of equality of contribution." I concluded: "One thing is certain . . . two questions, what does integration mean, and how will it be achieved, have supplanted the more rhetorical query, 'to integrate or not to integrate?'" With statistical updating and a few new sources, I could probably publish the same article again. This time it would draw a larger audience, given the many migration research institutes now focusing on these problems.

The *greening* of Germany, viz., the political realignment wrought by a changing of the generational guard in 1998, simultaneously attests to the *greying* of Germany: a rapidly aging population has failed to reproduce itself sufficiently to ensure a steady stream of skilled laborers to finance an eroding social security system. This chapter describes Germany's looming demographic deficit, linking recent debates over immigration and integration to processes of democratization, globalization, and social change. It draws heavily on expert evaluations compiled for the Independent Commission on Immigration (ICI), established in 2001 as a prelude to legislative reforms.[2]

I also address competing theoretical approaches to the collective incorporation of foreigners into German political and economic life. My sources deliberately exclude widely cited American writings on immigration for three reasons. First, having traveled back and forth for thirty years, I am astounded at the extent to which American discourses and methodologies dominate research in Germany, despite their exceptional character. Recognizing the context-specific nature of power, I prefer to analyze my research subjects in terms they use to define themselves. Secondly, the "automatic" extension of citizenship to persons born on US soil affords immigrants a fundamentally different political opportunity structure than the one confronting *Outlanders* in the Federal Republic. North American theories depicting the steady incorporation of second- and third-generation offspring hold little relevance for 1.6 million foreigners born in Germany who speak the language and contribute economically yet still lack political rights. Thirdly, while FRG scholars are well-versed in classical theories advanced by "the Chicago School," their own analyses are rooted in German historical experiences. Their commissioned evaluations have shaped recent changes in citizenship/immigration legislation to an unprecedented degree— even if the final package has been subjected to cutting and pasting by political hardliners.[3]

We then turn to a process I label *community interfacing*, deriving from my studies of social capital and East German inclusion into FRG life. As argued throughout this book, the social integration of non-nationals cannot be mandated in top-down fashion; it occurs instead through day-to-day interactions with the host society. Integration is a reciprocal process, best measured by changing behaviors on the part of Germans themselves. As comparisons with other EU states show, it is not inherent elements of Turkish culture that inhibit full participation in German society but rather intentional legal barriers that thwart minority efforts to embrace new (trans)national values and loyalties. We then briefly explore neglected dynamics of gender and generational change, and their increasing salience in German debates over multicultural identity. Finally, I outline the paradigm shift in citizenship and immigration law marking the new millennium. We begin with the "demographic deficit" and its implications for *Standort Deutschland* (as a desirable business location).

Demographics, Globalization, and Competitiveness

The Federal Republic has changed a great deal since the 1980s as a function of unification, European integration, and economic globalization. Instead of triggering a democratic collapse predicted by hardliners in 1998, the presence of once-radical, fashionably attired *'68ers* (1968 activists) in government highlighted an imminent welfare crisis more than Helmut Kohl's verbal assaults against "Amusement-Park Germany" ever could.[4] Were it not for the so-called foreigners, the social security system would hardly survive beyond 2015, yet even they are failing to reproduce themselves fast enough to rescue the pension system and counter a looming labor shortage: guestworkers are also crossing the retirement threshold.

Between 1960 and 1990, Germany's total population increased from 73 million to 82 million residents; 16 million Easterners entered by way of unification, 9 million via migration. The death rate already exceeds the national birth rate: by 2010, 300,000 more Germans will exit rather than enter this world, despite increasing life expectancies—eighty for women, seventy-four for men. Nearly 22 percent of all Germans are over sixty; by 2035, half will be older than fifty; the number of benefit-dependent octogenarians will quadruple, and the population could decrease by 23 million through 2050.[5]

By the new millennium, Germany had become home to 7.3 million foreigners (8.9 percent), 5.8 million of whom physically moved there. Another 1.66 million (22.5 percent) were born in the FRG, that is, 68 percent of all foreigners under age eighteen.[6] Concentrated in urban-industrial areas, 40 percent have lived in Germany for more than fifteen years, 50 percent for over a decade. Their distribution (3 percent of Eastern residents, 10 percent among Westerners) reflects differences in GDR and FRG labor policies across forty years of division. Only 190,000 foreigners served as GDR contract laborers in 1989. Eastern leaders met a pressing need for qualified workers by pushing women into paid labor after 1950; Western authorities chose to import foreigners. Urban concentrations range from a high of 29 percent in Frankfurt/Main, 24 percent in Stuttgart, 24 percent in Munich, and 14 percent in Berlin, to 5.5 percent in Leipzig, and 2.8 percent in Dresden.[7]

The statistical picture is nonetheless distorted by record-keeping anomalies: FRG data do not differentiate between "nationality" and "foreign-born" status, in contrast to US Census figures. Prior to 1999, officials maintained no records on parentage, e.g., whether children stem from German parents, parents who naturalized, or benefit from the retroactive application of the 1999 Citizenship Law (encompassing those born after 1991). Many are dual nationals, although lawmakers insist this is "exceptional." Once naturalized, individuals are subsumed under the category "German." This blurring of ethnic lines is quite problematic with regard to "repatriates" admitted after decades in former Eastern territories under Soviet rule. Though classified as Germans, these families from Russia, Kazakhstan, and other Central Asian republics face many crises of adjustment. As later chapters reveal, the *Aussiedler* are the least well integrated of all foreigners, despite the special benefits they receive upon entry. New rules adopted since 1993 (quotas and language tests) have dramatically reduced the influx.

There is also incongruity between national statistics and data supplied by branch offices responsible for residency permits. While local agencies claimed to admit 592,233 (asylum seekers, family members, migrant workers, Jewish admissions, EU nationals), national head counters reported 605,500 in 2001. The number "reunified" with families may be higher insofar as the Foreign Ministry only began registering them in 1996. Nor are foreign students included in general assessments. The *Länder* evince dramatic differences regarding naturalization criteria, despite the federal nature of citizenship law. Under the amended Foreigner Law of 1993, dual-nationality rates in Berlin (46.6 percent) were almost quadruple those in Bavaria (12.7 percent); rates for North Rhine-Westphalia and the FRG as a whole were 32.9 percent and 31 percent, respectively.[8]

Nor does the Federal Republic regularly report on foreigners who leave each year, leading to over-inflated perceptions of "drains" on the welfare system. Prior to 1970, more than half of all entrants hailed from EEC/EU states. Over 737,000

Greeks, Italians, Spaniards, and Portuguese entered in the 1950s but returned home in waves during the 1970s due to the collapse of military dictatorships and improved economic conditions. In 1999, 137,284 entered from EU territory, while 138,245 departed. Ralf Ulrich estimates that 50 million people have crossed the border since the 1960s. Some waves resulted in net losses: in 1967, 200,000 fewer people came than went. Roughly thirty-one million entered between 1954 and 1999, while twenty-two million moved out.[9]

The period between 1968 and 1973 saw an average annual admission rate of more than 388,000. The freeze on labor importation triggered a drop in net migration: the number of entrants fell from 869,000 in 1973, to 366,000 in 1975; the average "loss" stood at 108,000 per year from 1974 to 1977. The balance shifted again in 1978 due to liberalized family unification rules. The number of Yugoslavs admitted from 1968 to 1973 averaged 88,000 per year, but returnees exceeded residents by the mid 1980s. Another recession caused admissions to plunge across the board. Figures shot up again in the early 1990s due to war in Yugoslavia coupled with a major influx of *Aussiedler* from the post-Soviet republics. Over 1.2 million entered in 1992, but 500,000 Bosnian refugees returned—or were returned—to their homeland by 1997–1998.[10] Germany has clearly become a land of active immigration *and* emigration.

Turkish males between the ages of twenty and thirty comprised the majority of new arrivals after 1970. First-wave migrants often arrived with little more than a primary-school education. Political asylum seekers and Jewish "refugees" constitute the exception, since intellectuals and professionals are the first to flee militaristic or fundamentalist governments. Family unification policies brought a major shift in group composition: once women and children arrived the Turkish population naturally grew. The rise of fundamentalism and a 1980 coup triggered waves of Turkish and Kurdish refugees for a thirty-year average of 30,000 per annum.[11] Two million residents of Turkish descent account for 28 percent of the non-German population; 53 percent have lived there for over fifteen years, although merely 470,000 naturalized by 2001. Among the total alien population, 945,600 have acquired German citizenship since 1974.[12]

The "foreign" population is projected to grow to 13 percent by 2030, not including offspring eligible for citizenship under the 1999 reform. The Federal Republic will require a net immigration of 17.8 million by 2050 to keep its population stable. The age-dependency ratio stands at 26 percent, meaning there are four people working for every individual age sixty-five and older. To maintain a stable ratio Germany will need millions of new workers. Without them economic growth will cease, given a projected decline in gainfully employed persons from forty-one million to twenty-six million by 2035.[13]

German birth rates dropped precipitously after the 1960s with the advent of the Pill. Given the Western fertility rate, 1.3–1.4 per woman, births will drop by one-third for each subsequent generation; the Eastern rate plunged from 1.9

to 0.8 in the early 1990s. Despite decades of pro-natalist rhetoric, the FRG did little to help women reconcile family and career. The GDR provided substantial infrastructural support for working mothers by the early 1970s; as a result 90 percent of the Eastern women engaged in paid labor *and* produced children. At present, female employment rates are 61.7 percent in the West, 73.5 percent in the East.[14] Germany united continues to rely on a half-day school system, now blamed for a measurable deterioration in educational outcomes even among the natives.

Despite cutbacks in insurance coverage for contraceptives, and a 1993 Court ruling declaring abortion "illegal but unpunishable," only 2 percent of the existing care facilities accept children under age three. Parents can take three years of subsidized leave, but once a woman drops out of the paid workforce for three years, her average salary lags behind by DM 3.50 ($2) per hour for the rest of her working life. Experts also stress the costs of child rearing, amounting to a "loss" of DM 380,000–DM 576,000 in lifetime disposable income. These factors explain why 40 percent of the best-qualified women remain childless, and why hopes that increasing female employment will ease future labor shortages are illusory.[15]

Beyond a pension crisis, economists predict that a scarcity of skilled workers will trigger wage-push inflation, rising debt, and infrastructural stagnation. The problem is rendered more complex by the rapidly shifting needs of the New Economy. Praised for its quality production and economic discipline since 1949, Model Germany finds itself unable to meet the challenges posed by technological innovation and "the competition for the best brains." Since 1998, the government has had a difficult time persuading voters that, despite high unemployment, the FRG can only secure its long-term prosperity by increasing migration.

According to the ICI, 38.5 million eligible workers hold jobs, but the remaining 3.9 million are not an easily deployable group: 36 percent lacked employment for over a year, 38 percent had no vocational training as of 2000, while another 800,000 were age fifty-five or older. Structural change eliminated 1.4 million jobs between 1970 and 1990, disproportionately affecting migrants in heavy industry; unemployment among the latter runs 16.4 percent, compared to a German rate of 8.8 percent (9 percent West, 17 percent East). Joblessness among repatriated *Aussiedler* is even worse at 20 percent.[16] The 3.7 million jobs created since unification rest largely in the service sector, where net wages close to Social Assistance offer few incentives to work. Unemployment payouts exceeded DM 166 billion in 1997. The federal government spent DM 42.4 billion on "proactive policies" and DM 18.5 billion on training for 2 million persons in 2000; the *Länder* contributed another DM 3.7 billion.[17]

The ICI noted that 580,000 to 1.5 million positions remained unfilled in 2000–2001 (90 percent located in the East).[18] Vacancies are difficult to fill, due to "precise" selection criteria and a dearth of technically qualified applicants. Germany lags behind on several educational axes, despite the privileged position of students (free tuition) and professors (highly paid, flanked by scientific assistants). Despite dramatically expanded academic capacities, only 28 percent of German youth move on to the university (OECD average: 40 percent); the demand for graduates will rise by 16 percent over the next decade.[19] Only 130 academics from non-EU states regularly teach/research at German universities, although 23,000 foreigners entered for "further training." Until 2004, the law denied these graduates permanent residency and employment, even though they disproportionately pursued degrees in engineering and "hard sciences," the areas of greatest need.

Small and medium size enterprises, likely to generate new jobs, face the most critical shortages. The majority of startups are undertaken by those age thirty to fifty, an under-populated category. Among 2.82 million alien jobholders, 263,000 (9.3 percent) are self-employed, compared to German rates of 9.5 percent in the West, 8.2 percent in the East (1999). Among Turkish residents the number of self-employed rose from 22,000 in 1985 to 59,500 in 2000, a growth rate of 170 percent. One in five is female; the majority has lived in Germany for twenty-two years. Non-national status poses a competitive disadvantage vis-à-vis Turks in other EU countries, accounting for higher naturalization rates among would-be entrepreneurs.[20] Another 342,000 aliens have entered the country since 2000, many limited to ninety-day permits. The official quota for contract workers was initially set at 65,000. Access to the regular labor market remains inextricably intertwined with residency rights.

Enter the *Green Card*, the "thin edge of the wedge" introduced by the first SPD-Green government in hopes of redefining the migration framework. Equivalent to the US H-1B visa, the Green Card foresees the temporary employment of information and communications technology (IT) experts through 2008. Applicants must hold formal academic degrees, or earn a minimum salary of €50,000, to be recognized as specialists. Successful applicants may change jobs in Germany, but family members must wait a year before working (for pay). Card holders are limited to five years in Germany, hardly an enticement for families with two wage earners and school-age children.

When the Green Card was introduced in July 1999, the Alliance for Labor, Training and Competitiveness hoped to attract 250,000 workers. Between August 2000 and April 2001, authorities received 45,000 inquiries. Nearly 7,000 work permits were pledged: 1,500 for Hesse, 1,300 in Baden-Württemberg, 1,000 in North Rhine-Westphalia, and 2,000 for Bavaria. Not to be outfoxed by a Red-Green government, Bavaria promptly introduced its own Blue Card, though it has fought to restrict other forms of migration. Among the initial wave, 1,400 workers came from India and 3,000 from Central/Eastern European states. At least 1,000 of those approved had studied in Germany, ensuring the requisite language qualifications (although the global IT language is English). Roughly 12 percent earn €50,000 or more; two-thirds work for companies employing less than one hundred.[21] The Green Card system is a guestworker program *mit Niveau*, catering to groups already privileged by globalization.

Despite its sophisticated analysis of Germany's current demographic dilemmas and economic imperatives, the Independent Commission saw its recommendations pushed aside by partisan politics. It concluded in 2001 that "existing law does not meet the requirements of modern labor market oriented immigration and intimidates the potential immigrants Germany so desperately needs," yet the driving principle behind parliamentary debates remains "prohibition subject to possible granting of permission."[22] What Germany purportedly needs is "a flexible migration system that takes quantitative and qualitative supply-demand trends into account." They propose to do so, however, by restricting the number of entrants more "systematically," through use of points and quotas. Although they insist that "the boat is full," the truth is that policymakers are missing the boat that will move German society into the twenty-first century.

Concepts of Incorporation

The term *Mitbürger* (co-citizen), used by Chancellor Kohl during his sixteen-year administration, contains the germs of three types of citizenship: political-legal citizenship, economic citizenship, and social citizenship. Theorists ranging from Karl Deutsch, Gerard Delanty, and Rogers Brubaker, to Elisabeth Meehan, Rainer Bauböck, and Catherine Hoskins, inter alia, do not always distinguish among the three types.[23] Many of the rights, duties, and opportunities for participation traditionally associated with citizenship already transcend the spatial domain. Under the rubric of post-national membership, rights have assumed a multilayered quality; they can be exercised exclusively or in various combinations at the local, regional, national, or even supranational level.

Popularized by SPD-parliamentarian Freimut Duwe in the 1980s, the term *post-national* does not do justice to the increasingly disjointed or newly conjoined dimensions inherent in our understanding of political "belonging." Residential foreigners enjoy local voting rights in Sweden and Demark, but the German High Court struck down such rights in Schleswig-Holstein. The ethno- versus civic-nationalism distinctions drawn by Christian Joppke do not encompass critical distinctions found in real life: constitutional rights do not apply in equal measure to women and men.[24] Despite EU "free-movement" clauses, the residency rights of foreign females depend on their marital attachment to bread-winning males. Their ability to seek legal employment, and thus economic independence, is also restricted by marriage status. Non-national women in Germany are subject to all abortion constraints but do not enjoy equal protection in other gender-specific domains. Differences persist in cases of domestic abuse or abandonment, although the 2004 Immigration Law recognizes women-specific grounds for asylum.

Patterns of incorporation differ from country to country but also from one ethnic group to another, necessitating different self-integration strategies across various levels. The larger question posed by this chapter is whether social integration begins or ends with formal political citizenship. One reason why post-national theories become irrelevant at the grassroots level is because they conflate means and ends: citizenship can serve as a dependent or independent variable, contingent on the context. Open societies like the United States, Sweden, and the Netherlands accord citizenship within a five-year framework as a means to other ends, assuming that minorities will make a good-faith effort to adjust to their new homeland once they enjoy participatory rights. Other forms of linguistic, social, and economic integration are expected to follow. Germany presumes that citizenship is an end in itself, a prize accorded for years of self-integration, when, in fact, legal insecurity makes foreigners unwilling to give up their original state identification. Although the Basic Law prohibits the deprivation of citizenship that became common practice under the Nazis, recent legislation inferring that "dual nationals" can be stripped of German citizenship at age twenty-three puts a willingness to naturalize back on hold.

My own readings on "integration theory" include many authors who call for a reassessment of one concept or another; yet the more they reassess, the more they blur the lines among four basic patterns of incorporation.[25] As one ICI evaluator writes, "*Structural assimilation*, that is, *social integration* in the form of placement in central positions within the host society, is the condition for attaining *all other forms of social integration*. . . . And it is . . . in the long run, an indispensable part of *system integration* within society" (emphasis added).[26] My analysis relies on the following definitions and frameworks.

The most restrictive approach to incorporation, *assimilation,* correlates directly with *jus sanguinis,* a standard implying a "sameness" in values, behaviors, and perhaps even appearance. Assimilation imposes a standard that Turkish, African, or Asian migrants would find hard to meet, regardless of generational status. One anomaly of postwar German identity is that few citizens describe their emotional ties to the country in positive terms, as Marielouise Janssen-Jurreit's book (*Lieben Sie Deutschland?*) demonstrated. Most natives are quick to assert what it can *not* mean to be a German: ultranationalistic, war-mongering, anti-Semitic, or subservient to an authoritarian state; nor are they particularly disciplined or punctual these days. Ethnic minorities, paradoxically, are supposed to recreate themselves in a national image few indigenous souls are especially "proud" to embody.[27] Their inability to do so becomes the justification for their economic marginalization and social exclusion.

The second incorporation strategy, *acculturation*, implies a one-way process of adaptation that many German politicians mistakenly identify as "integration." A contradiction in terms, the 1977 Naturalization Guidelines explicitly stated that Germany "is not a land of integration," nor does it "strive to increase the number of its citizens through naturalization."[28] A 1990 reform changed the letter but not the spirit of the law. It declared "integration . . . a prime objective of the German government's policy on aliens" but encouraged foreigners "to become German citizens and *integrate themselves* not only into Germany's economic life, but also into the social, cultural and political texture of their adopted country. In doing so the government *does not propagate a multi-cultural society.* Instead it expects those foreigners, *irrespective of their cultural traditions* and private religious beliefs, to accept the basic ethical, legal and cultural principles that govern public life in Germany" (emphasis added).[29] Insofar as these expectations are imposed irrespective of cultural ties (as if the latter merit no recognition), acculturation also posits sameness. This approach best characterizes mistaken assumptions that East Germans would simply abandon their old ways after unification and become carbon copies of Federal Republicans, give or take a few *(n)ostalgic* remnants. Yet younger Easterners are no more willing than older ones to abandon all features of their former identity in the name of "internalized unity" (*innere Einheit*), as the renewed popularity of GDR products and practices shows, e.g., the *Jugendweihe* (the GDR's coming-of-age ritual).[30]

Integration refers to a process of mutual cultural adjustment, a kind of "change through drawing closer" (*Wandel durch Annäherung*) that finds both sides moving toward common ground on core values, e.g., supporting the free-democratic order, but allowing for reinterpretation of others, based on the contributions of new entrants. It's one thing to expect persons living within German borders to accept constitutional principles like gender equality and religious freedom, or to abide by criminal statutes against "honor killings." It is quite another to presume that one must embrace only "German" business practices, musical tastes, eating habits, modes of dress, and child-rearing patterns to ensure national order. Integration is not a one-way street. It entails ongoing processes, formal and informal, covering the entire population.

Multiculturalization is yet another approach, offering a mosaic of self-defined identities that exist separately but enjoy mutual respect, and equal access to educational-qua-occupational opportunity. Its common political expression is interest-group pluralism. "Separateness" is decided upon by the group, not imposed by the dominant culture in ways that trigger marginalization and stigmatization. Multiculturalization need not lead to the formation of parallel societies, or to an "anything goes" orientation feared by some pundits. Nor should individuals be required to identify with a particular ethnic group in order to take advantage of equal opportunities, as occurs under state-enforced multiculturalism in Singapore, for example.[31]

Debates over citizenship likewise encompass a broad spectrum of ideological frameworks. The *liberal-individual orientation*, embodied by the United States and Britain, focuses on extending formal rights to political participation based on objective criteria, e.g., a set residency period, language competency, and knowledge regarding key features of government. Its primary task is to eliminate legal barriers to participation; the rest is up to the individual. Quite progressive in earlier centuries as Europeans sought collective freedom from absolutist states, this approach overestimates an individual's ability to exercise such rights as we "cross that bridge to the 21st century." The extension of voting rights is a necessary but not sufficient condition for integrating foreign residents into public life. As I remind students, homeless persons cannot vote in the United States, even if age eighteen and native born; without the benefits of social citizenship, implying a right to a regular roof over one's head, most cannot register. Given the extraordinary decline in electoral participation across many states, voting is apparently not the main thing that holds a national community together.

The *conservative-organic approach*, favored under *jus sanguinis*, projects a heavy dose of "duties to the state," along with a belief in one's absolute identification with a particular "homeland." CDU/CSU officials reject dual citizenship, based on the argument that Turkish males can't be trusted to serve two Fatherlands. Some countries insist that men complete military conscription before being "released" from their initial citizenship. According to organic notions of identity, "foreigners" born in Germany lack the deeper emotional loyalty necessary to defend the Federal Republic. Ironically, critics of this ilk overlook possible NATO conscription, which would serve both Turkish and German defense interests. The premise that the dutiful citizen is an obedient person who does not ask "what the state can do for him but what he can do for the state" ignores the fact that 25 percent of West German males invoke conscientious-objector status. East German men serve the (new) *Vaterland* at higher rates, owing not to deeper national attachments but to dismal employment prospects in their home *Länder*.[32]

The *radical-democratic position* is articulated by Third World/human-rights activists and some Greens who see themselves as "citizens of the world." Scholars like Marlies Galenkamp and Ruth Rubio-Marin argue from the perspective of universal personhood.[33] The idea that medium- to long-term residents should be entitled to vote wherever they work undermines the legitimacy of the nation-state, or at least anticipates its imminent demise. Perpetual wrangling within the European Union over asylum, immigration, and "internal order" refutes any notion that the nation-state is dead, however, or so infirm that it doesn't care who is included in setting Member-State priorities.

The *practical-communitarian approach* is implicit in discussions of dual citizenship, though I have not heard experts call it by this name. The logic here derives from a stress on civil society, in particular, the role of social capital in sustaining the trust, reciprocity, and connectedness needed to "make democracy work." Social capital inheres in "the structure of relations between actors and among actors," meaning it is lodged neither in specific actors nor "in the physical implements of production."[34] Difficult to measure, social capital combines with other resources—human, cultural, and financial—to promote community action and shared outcomes for individuals with divergent interests. Participatory rights make more sense among people who share a stake in day-to-day conditions than among imagined communities grounded merely in ethnic descent. This approach recognizes socioeconomic contributions to the local environment yet lends itself to constitutional patriotism while according respect for cultural differences. The civil-society framework, implicit in urban citizenship, recognizes that the place most non-nationals "come from" is not necessarily where they want to be.

Last but not least, there is an emerging *mobile-transnational orientation* toward the exercise of citizenship rights. The SEA/Maastricht Treaties prescribe this approach for EU nationals, though both accords posit political engagement as a second-order concern in their pursuit of free markets. At the higher end of the food chain, jet-setting technicians, managers, and professionals—predominantly well-educated white males—often find their welfare benefits warranted by the multinational corporations for which they work, rather than by any single welfare state; pension schemes, profit sharing, and even one's tax status may no longer depend on nationality.

Although the German Green Card appeals directly to this group, political rights are clearly excluded from the overall package, raising normative questions about the relationship between free markets and citizen democracies. One exceptional individual who uses his transnational status to the political max is French-'68-protester turned Frankfurt-multiculturalist turned Euro-politician Daniel Cohn-Bendit. The abysmal turnout for European Parliament elections (under 46 percent in 2004) suggests that persons most likely to benefit from transnational rights do not accord high priority to political participation. It will take more than a common currency to push European identity beyond the status of an imagined community, espoused primarily by an elite group of EU commissioners.

The barriers to integration, as well as the benefits a minority can expect to derive differ significantly from one ethnic group to another in Germany. As Hartmut Esser noted in 2001, identification with the host society can only be expected "when belonging to it is also experienced as beneficial, especially in comparison to other alternatives. An important prerequisite for this is embeddedness in social connections that are perceived as happy and otherwise interesting. . . . The key to every sustainable [case of] social integration, even with regard to interaction and identification, is the location of actors in relatively central positions that would be attractive to all actors and that stand in reciprocal relationship to binding culturation."[35]

Here it is useful to distinguish between system integration and social integration. System integration emerges as a function of institutional regulation, constitutional norms, and defined administrative practices. Formal integration draws on state authority, but "markets and the media can provide for systemic integration that was not planned" by lowering the transaction costs for all who would participate in public life. Labor contracts requiring employers to provide equal pay, meet national health and safety standards, and guarantee disability/pension benefits fit into this category. Social integration begins with guaranteed rights but presumes a personal ability to take advantage of educational and occupational opportunities, interethnic friendships, and participation in public life, fostering emotional identification with the host country. The emphasis falls on subjective, individual needs rather than on the interests of the host country.

Esser characterizes the *Bundesrepublik* through 1967 as "a system-integrated, ethnically homogeneous society," which is not to say it lacked migration (over twelve million war refugees) or regional differentiation.[36] Thereafter it witnessed a process of ethnic stratification, that is, "the systematic co-variation of ethnic groups with typical positions in the system of vertical social inequality."[37] Drawn along functional lines, this segmentation reduces social mobility for individuals, and leads to cultural "distance" between groups. This, in turn, may lead to the construction of parallel societies, as minorities become physically isolated from the indigenous population, e.g., through housing segregation. Small groups have few alternatives to assimilation, while larger ones can facilitate or impede their own integration through the creation of self-sufficient enclaves. System integration assumes subservience, or at best, deference: "By virtue of obvious inequalities," Esser writes, "the dominant group has the possibility but not the motivation to bring about a transformation in this social construction; for the subgroup, the reverse holds true."[38] Persistent experience as a member of a subclass hardly fosters loyalty to the host society. Some may turn to fundamentalism or even re-ethnicization; younger residents, especially, wind up with split identities.[39]

The debate over a German *Leitkultur* implies a need for heavy-handed integration standards defined in anachronistic national terms.[40] If globalization constitutes a major challenge to the FRG economy, then a renewed emphasis on a "leading" national culture is clearly a step in the wrong direction:

> Because the different component-systems of modern society—given its progressive functional specialization (or differentiation)—increasingly cannot afford the functionally diffuse inequalities or non-functional considerations inherent in the random positioning (of certain groups), the acquisition of special, functional qualifications

for locating individuals in central positions becomes ever more pressing. Whoever falls just a little short or comes just a little late will be punished over the long run by the self-generating rules of the system, often enough with total exclusion and marginalization, for instance, with long-term unemployment, or homelessness. This is especially true in relation to education, which is becoming more and more of a necessity but less and less a sufficient condition for assuming such positions, especially as pertains to the labor market.[41]

The problem is not new. Children stemming from the first guestworker wave had little access to higher education, though this era coincided with an equal-opportunity push for German working-class children.[42] With the exception of a few comprehensive schools (*Gesamtschulen*) created during this period, little changed in terms of elite school culture. The special linguistic, religious, and social needs of ethnic children were simply ignored, based on the presumption that Turkish families would eventually "go home." The second generation enjoyed better educational access than the first, but the inequalities among school types have grown over time. Whether unequal opportunity results from direct or indirect discrimination is irrelevant: ethnic concentration in the classroom, coupled with self-perpetuating housing segregation, impedes language acquisition, "the key to all other integration processes, an investment that leads to the ability to take advantage of an opening opportunity structure."[43]

If the dominant culture is reluctant to interact regularly with minorities, there may be conflicts but few opportunities to develop shared values, a hallmark of pluralist democracy. Finding ways to reconnect these groups in a society characterized by new interdependencies, like European integration, is no easy task, as post-unity tensions between East and West Germans have demonstrated.[44] The ability to deal effectively with globalization depends on diverse forms of cultural capital or intercultural competence. Correspondingly, the ability to maintain a national-qua-democratic community in the face of centrifugal forces is rooted in social capital, as unification has further shown.[45] Here I concur with Esser: "It is hardly possible to eliminate prejudices solely through contacts between groups. Only when problematic situations exist for both sides among persons with the same status, who then experience sustainable patterns of shared problem-solving, do contacts lead to a change in the negative stereotypes and make room for sympathetic feelings."[46]

Generational succession establishes greater opportunity for "sympathetic feelings," access to education and interethnic friendships indicative of social integration. Social integration ensues not only because of enhanced language skills but also because younger cohorts evince weaker emotional ties to the country of origin. Increasing human capital also leads to the cultivation of social capital, first within ethnic neighborhoods and then in relation to the host community, as my case studies illustrate. This triggers the first of many *Tocquevillean paradoxes*: "It is not when the inequalities are most intense that the conflicts break out, but rather when the lot of the subordinated group begins to improve and the groups on all sides begin to accumulate power."[47] Social capital depends on face-to-face relations, forged most easily at the grassroots level. Let us now consider the ways in which local communities can contribute, first, to citizen consciousness and then to citizenship acquisition in Germany.

Thinking Globally, Integrating Locally

Tocqueville's nineteenth-century reflections on the role of voluntary associations in fostering democratic participation have experienced a cross-national comeback, thanks to Robert Putnam's focus on declining social capital in the United States.[48] Curiously, the literature on "citizen efficacy" has rarely been applied to groups with the greatest stake in becoming democratic insiders, namely, resident *Outlanders*. Most integration theorists focus on the national and transnational levels, as well as on the degree to which ethnic organizations mirror associational patterns in the host country. Yasemin Soysal is one oft-cited representative of this school, although her research along these lines was conducted before the collapse of the Iron Curtain, revisions to the Schengen Agreement, enactment of the Maastricht Treaty, and tighter EU asylum policies. Many of the rights she took for granted became subject to new restrictions.

Scholars at the Institute for Migration and Ethnic Studies in the Netherlands, the Berlin Science Center, and the Center for Turkish Studies infer that post-national analyses are "high on inflationary rhetoric and rather low on critical theoretical reflection and systematic empirical evidence."[49] Macro analyses of the post-national sort, by definition, presume substantial acculturation on the part of ethnic elites. Unable to take accommodation for granted, field researchers note the importance of social capital, coupled with extraordinary intra- and interorganizational diversity among ethnic minorities at local levels. They further refute essentialist arguments advanced by *jus sanguinis* proponents who insist that Islamic cultures are inherently incapable of integration. Their studies prove that "homeland influences or primordial attachments to ethnic, national, religious, or racial 'transnational communities,' are relatively marginal to understanding patterns of migrant claims-making."[50]

My framing of ethnic integration processes has been reinforced by Meindert Fennema, Jean Tillie, Ruud Koopmans, Claudia Diehl, and Ertekin Özcan. These scholars stress that, next to structural-legal mechanisms promoting or inhibiting naturalization, the most critical variable defining integration prospects is the mobilization of ethnic groups themselves. Koopmans and Statham argue, it is not so much the [supranational] transformation of the basis of citizenship which is eroding the capacity of nation-states to politically shape migrants in their national image, but the de facto behaviour of migrants. . . . We expect migrants to be more inclined to make claims regarding their situation in the country of settlement where the state provides opportunities for them and their organizations to do so. Perhaps the most important factor here is whether migrants have the right to vote (which largely depends on them holding citizenship), but in addition such factors as the existence of equal opportunity and anti-discrimination legislation, state subvention and consultation of migrant organizations, or the availability of cultural group rights in domains such as education and the media will play a role.[51]

In short, national citizenship regimes shape the ability and willingness of migrants to identify with and participate in the host culture. In 1994, the ratio of aliens to natives in Germany was 85 per thousand, 51 per thousand in the Netherlands, and 35 per thousand in Great Britain; their naturalization rates stood at 1.5 percent, 7 percent, and 4.2 percent, respectively. While 12 percent of all Turks in the Netherlands became citizens in 1994, only 7.6 percent successfully completed the process in the FRG. The German case is further complicated by the discretion accorded state and local officials in implementing citizenship law. Bavaria continues to treat long-term Turkish residents as temporary. State officials there provide Islamic and mother-tongue instruction using teachers sent by the Turkish Ministry of Religion, insisting their children must be prepared for a return to the "homeland." Not coincidentally, it evinces the lowest naturalization rate among sixteen *Länder*: In 1993, Berlin's naturalization rate was four times that of Bavaria.[52]

Migrants are forced to develop identities along lines imposed by the host culture. In Germany most remain "foreigners," even if the only time spent in the homeland consists of a few weeks of vacation each year. The FRG accords special status to Jews but views religion as a barrier to integration when it comes to Muslims. The United Kingdom relegates migrants according to racial categories (Blacks or Asians); this ignores major cultural or religious differences (Muslim, Hindu, Sikh) but allows for active anti-discrimination policies under the Commission for Racial Equality. Since 1983, Dutch law has shifted from a post-colonial "guestworker hangover" to a focus on ethnic minorities; Turks, Surinamese, and others may also be classified according to religion (Muslim, Hindu, or Christian). Recognizing its own "permanent multicultural character," the Netherlands sees the preservation of minority cultures as an effective vehicle for social integration; extending *pillarization* to these groups leads to self-confident sub-structures, capable of participating in public life.

Writing in the 1930s, Karl Deutsch stressed the importance of communication in fostering a sense of national union. Drawing on the metaphor of communications engineering, he characterized *society* as an entity rendered interdependent by a particular division of labor tied to the production of goods and services. *Culture* was grounded in a unique configuration of value preferences, while *community* rested on "the observable ability of certain groups of men and women to share with each other a wide range of whatever might be on their minds . . . both society and community are developed by social learning . . . a community consists of people who have learned to communicate with each other and to understand each other well beyond the mere interchange of goods and services. . . . *A larger group of persons linked by such complementary habits and facilities of communication* we may call *a people*" (emphasis in original).[53] Witness to the barbarity of two World Wars sparked by ethnonationalism, Deutsch rejected the idea that modern nations rely on organic foundations. Membership rests in complementarity, "the ability to communicate more effectively, and over a wider range of subjects, with members of one large group than with outsiders." This trait "differs from the old attempts to specify nationality in terms of some particular ingredient. . . . People are held together 'from within' by this communicative efficiency," acquired by all members.[54]

Fennema and Tillie likewise assert that democratic nations depend more "on the need for cohesive networks of communication rather than on shared values," although values must be shared to a degree in order to make communication meaningful.[55] The purpose of communication is to resolve conflicts that arise over the authoritative allocation of values, as well as the day-to-day distribution of goods in societies shaped by diversity and self-interest. "Making democracy work" requires the articulation, aggregation, and mediation of diverse societal needs. Making competing claims upon the state relies, in turn, on self-organization, institutional trust, and a belief in one's ability to contribute to social change.

Democratic theorists ranging from Tocqueville to Putnam stress a positive correlation between active engagement in intermediary associations and subjective political competence. "Discovering" *civic culture,* Gabriel Almond and Sidney Verba found, "if the citizen is a member of some voluntary organization, he [*sic*] is involved in the broader social world but is less dependent upon and less controlled by his political system. The association of which he is a member can represent his needs and demands before the government. It would make the government more chary of engaging in activities that would harm the individual."[56]

As East German experiences show, it takes more than "a vote" to push government to work as an agent for diverse citizen groups.[57] The more competent citizens feel, the less likely they are to leave government to its own devices, thus raising overall political accountability and legitimacy. Scholars agree that voluntary organizations "are a hotbed for civic competence, and moreover appear to promote good governance." Empirical tests focus on national-mainstream groups, though the more sensational "citizen initiatives" in recent years have been transnational in nature, e.g., Amnesty International, Doctors without Borders, and Greenpeace.[58]

The logic of voluntary associations and community participation should also apply to ethnic groups intent on "integrating themselves" into the host society. German politicians who insist that aliens demonstrate "loyalty to the nation" as a prerequisite to formal citizenship ignore the wisdom of nation-building further espoused by Reinhard Bendix, Carole Pateman, and Ralf Dahrendorf.[59] Germany, of all places, proved after 1949 that what makes democracy sustainable is not the precept "my country, right or wrong" but rather effective channels of communication and participation open to all with a stake in the community.

Non-national residents have induced changes in German political culture over the last three decades; at the same time their own identities have been altered by day-to-day encounters with the host culture. Still, the political opportunity structure is shaped by official integration policies (or lack thereof), which, in turn, "are crucial determinants of how migration changes the receiving society, for better or worse." Drawing on sixteen studies executed in eight *Länder*, three city-states, and five large cities, Koopmans and his colleagues provide compelling evidence that migrants in Germany and Switzerland

> hardly participate in the political process of the country of residence, partly because the receiving society defines them as foreigners and offers them few political rights and opportunities, partly—and as a consequence of the former—because migrants in these countries continue to identify themselves with the national and ethnic categories of their homelands. This identification, in turn, leads to a strong preoccupation with—often violent—conflicts 'imported' from migrants' countries of origin . . . [thus] the restrictive citizenship regime in these two countries produced exactly the ethnic 'parallel societies' that the proponents of such exclusive policies say they seek to avoid.[60]

Exclusionary approaches employed by German and Swiss officials stand in stark contrast to the Netherlands, where ethnic minorities were accorded formal political rights in 1985. Lo and behold, Turkish residents are not only more likely to participate but also display greater trust in state institutions than Christian, Dutch-speaking ex-colonials, e.g., the Surinamese. Minorities seeking participatory opportunities need not give up their cultural identities in order to find their way into host institutions; ethnic organizations provide "low thresholds for joining and thus can trigger the emancipation of the group through intermediary roles"[61] Still, political participation can fall short of advancing socioeconomic equality, as the African American experience demonstrates.

More than twenty million migrants live within EU boundaries; 65 percent lack host-state citizenship, denying them the minimal voting rights ensured by Article 8 of the Maastricht Treaty. Over 25 percent of Germany's foreigners are EU nationals, with Italians comprising the largest group (33 percent of the EU total). In city-states like Bremen, Hamburg, Berlin, and Vienna, EU nationals are unable to vote for "municipal"-qua-state parliaments. While their ethnic counterparts can vote in Munich or Paderborn, these aliens lack such rights in national capitals where they are likely to congregate. Correspondingly, 20–25 percent of all residents in Frankfurt/Main, Stuttgart, Munich, and Cologne are unable to influence the allocation of scarce resources, the distribution of job opportunities, educational policies, neighborhood revitalization plans, or regulation of their own behavior in places they have lived for decades.

Rainer Bauböck draws on the increasing "transnational connectivity" between cities to argue for a practical brand of urban citizenship that would guarantee equal participatory rights at the local level, regardless of nationality. Nation-states, Saskia Sassen observes, are dependent on strategic decisions driven by global markets, transnational corporations, and international financial organizations. However, "these new agencies of power do not operate only in virtual space. They have their headquarters in global cities and their operations depend on material infrastructure provided by city governments and on services provided by city populations."[62] Cities become the contested territory upon which ethnic groups are compelled to "define their identities, stake their claims, wage their battles and articulate citizenship rights and obligations."[63] Local authorities determine the flow of opportunity, operating neighborhood schools and sponsoring cultural events. In addition to maintaining deficit-ridden public housing and transportation systems, urban centers bear the social costs (substance abuse, domestic violence, gang activity) for those whose welfare eligibility has run out at other levels. Migrants are drawn to job opportunities, ethnic enclaves, and integration programs afforded by metropolitan areas. Modern cities, Werner Schiffauer observes, provide *diversity of access* as well as *access to diversity.*[64]

Acquiring urban citizenship, Bauböck contends, does not entail formal processes requiring passports or other local documents. I counter that German cities have become part of the legal machine allocating citizenship rights. Guaranteed a degree of autonomy under the Basic Law, communal authorities exercise exclusionary discretion concerning naturalization criteria. Local governments are empowered to grant or deny residency permits, work permits, housing allocations, and social assistance. Vulnerable to "open admission and easy exit," cities are the place where social integration succeeds or fails. Despite the Constitutional Court's rejection of communitarian voter rights, I share Bauböck's conclusion that urban citizenship is the "homebase" of multicultural democracy: "The restriction of the quintessential right of political membership, the franchise, is imposed on local governments by national constitutions. . . . The restriction of urban citizenship to nationals of the state is unjustifiable [whether limited by national constitution or adopted by the local government per se] . . . cities are political communities of a different kind and they can assert this by granting full local citizenship to all residents within their jurisdiction. This . . . could still allow for a reasonable grading of rights according to length of residence."[65] Given the Amsterdam Treaty's explicit protection against discrimination based on race, sex, religion, national origin, and sexual orientation, I believe that EU policies will eventually impel Germany to reverse its rejection of voting rights for resident foreigners. Non-citizens are as essential to the well-being of major cities as nationals, and just as likely to rely on its services: "As workers, taxpayers, consumers, neighbors, they are persons who constitute part of the life of the (nationally bounded) political community—the very community that citizenship in its internal mode considers the proper domain of concern."[66]

Migrants do develop local identities. Urban citizenship based on a specified residency period neither implies onerous national duties—e.g., conscription—nor requires one to renounce higher order loyalties. It matters not because "it would provide an alternative basis to territorial federation," but because "it could *transform national identities and nationalist ideologies from below and from within* . . . provide an alternative model of membership that could eventually help to overcome some of the exclusionary features of national citizenship" (emphasis added).[67]

If civic participation promotes social capital and trust among the natives, strong ethnic organizations and subaltern networks might also foster integration and participation among migrants. Instead, the specter of parallel societies overshadows the naturalization process: "When migrants apply for German citizenship, they are asked if they are active in ethnic organisations. If they answer in the affirmative on this question, it surely isn't beneficial for the chances that they will see their application granted."[68] These fears have not been borne out by ethnic associational patterns since September 11th. Muslim residents were more attracted to fundamentalist groups at a time when they were "the only game in town," controlled by outside governments and forced to focus on developments in the country of origin.

As subsequent chapters show, local involvement in ethnic organizations does not preclude participation in German associational life. In fact, ethnic organizations fulfill an important "bridge function." Active engagement in the Turkish Parents Association supplies the same kind of learning experience Putnam attributes to PTOs across the United States: The role ethnic communities play in fostering political integration "can definitely not be described as a zero-sum game."[69] Persons active in ethnic associations possess more German acquaintances, participate more in German organizations, and evince a deeper interest in FRG politics (72 percent among men, 61 percent for women) than persons outside country-of-origin organizations.[70]

A November 2001 survey showed that "residents of non-German heritage" display, in some cases, even greater support for democratic values than average citizens. Drawing on 1,500 Turks, Italians, and Russian ethnics, along with a German control group, Koopmans et al. found, contrary to prevailing stereotypes, that most aliens feel more closely tied to Berlin than to their purported countries of origin.[71] A Konrad Adenauer Foundation poll countered that strong local identification existed "only in a few cities and states"—but that is exactly where ethnics are concentrated. Their political activities focus on developments in Germany and Berlin, rather than on the country of origin. Most do not see peaceful coexistence among their respective cultures endangered by the events of September 11th.

Paradigm Shifts: Citizenship Reform, 1999–2005

From 1949 to 1993, the Basic Law featured two key articles establishing the parameters of *citizenship*. Article 116 extended a "right of return" to persons compelled to renounce their citizenship under Nazi rule, defining as *German* any person displaced by forced resettlement or by borders redrawn after conditionless surrender (using 1937 boundaries as a baseline). Article 73 renders migration regulation a task of the central government; implementation falls to state and local authorities, however. Article 16 granted an unqualified right to political asylum in 1949, recognizing many peoples persecuted by Nazis, as well as Germans who had perished for lack of refuge after 1933. Article 116 further delineated persons relocating to West Germany after 1949, warranting different political and financial benefits for each group. An individual might be classified as a refugee (*Flüchtling*), an expellee (*Vertriebener*), or as an ethnic resettler. The latter were classified as *Umsiedler* if entering from areas subject to Soviet Military Administration, or as *Aussiedler* if relocating from outside occupational boundaries. Persons fleeing political persecution from other regions were categorized as asylum-seekers (*Asyl-Bewerber*). The striking thing about the categories routinely used by officials through 1999 was that the list never included the term immigrant (*Einwanderer*). Until 2004, there was no "law of entry" allowing the systematic admission of non-EU nationals, accounting for the "abuse" erroneously associated with the asylum guarantee.

The presence of millions of guestworkers after 1955 triggered laws regulating migrant behavior, demanded by the Federal Interior Ministry and *Land*-level ministers responsible for policing and registration functions; the former were continuously at odds with ministries focusing on economic growth, humanitarian aid, and relations with the "recruitment" states. State efforts to require the rotation of workers after a maximum three-year period clashed with broader needs to uphold the free-movement and family-unification rights of EEC

Table 1.1 Legal Bases of German Citizenship or Dual Nationality

Acquisition	German Citizenship	Dual Nationality (German/Foreign)
By birth (*jus sanguinis*; birthright citizenship)	Children of German parents (at least one German parent)	Children of bi-national couples Children of dual citizen parents
By ethnic descent (constitutional right, legal claim)	Ethnic German expellees (*Vertriebene*) of 1944–48 without German citizenship (collectively naturalized in 1949)	Ethnic German immigrants (*Aussiedler*) from central and eastern Europe (individually naturalized upon arrival in Germany since 1950)
	Ethnic German immigrants (*Aussiedler*) who came since 1990 and were not forced to relinquish their original citizenship	Ethnic German immigrants (*Aussiedler*) who successfully reclaimed their original citizenship
By ethnic descent (constitutional right, legal claim)	Former German citizens (stateless) who were expatriated and successfully reclaimed their original citizenship	Former German citizens (meanwhile naturalized by another country) who were expatriated and successfully reclaimed their original citizenship
		Citizens of other countries who were naturalized by Nazi authorities (predominantly *Volksliste* III +IV) and successfully reclaimed German citizenship; children of this group of people.
By fulfilling residency requirements in Germany (legal claim, discretion of local authorities)	Foreigners (regardless of birthplace) who relinquished their original citizenship upon naturalization in Germany	Foreigners (regardless of place of birth) who are naturalized in Germany while maintain or (claming) their original citizenship

(continued)

Table 1.1 Legal Bases of German Citizenship or Dual Nationality *(continued)*

Acquisition	German Citizenship	Dual Nationality (German/Foreign)
By place of birth (*jus soli*; birth-right citizenship)		Conditional *jus soli* (After 1 January 2000): children born in Germany to legal foreign residents; option to become a German citizen or to remain German by renouncing other nationalities between the age of eighteen and twenty-three

Sources: Basic Law (1949), Reich- and State Citizenship Law (1913), Aliens Act (1990), Citizenship Reform Law (1999), compiled by Rainer Münz and Ralf Ulrich, "Immigration and Citizenship in Germany," *German Politics and Society* 17, no. 4 (Winter 1999): 9.

nationals from Italy, as well as with employers' reluctance to retrain new arrivals. The Interior Ministry was the first to articulate the precept "Germany is not a land of immigration," although the phrase was unfamiliar to the Bundestag when it passed the 1965 Aliens Act.[72]

This statute, complemented by refugee and expellee acts, specified the rights and duties of foreigners already inside the country. Amended in 1976 and again in 1978, the *Ausländergesetz* "clarified" residency issues (table 1.2). Changes regarding visas for children over the age of sixteen took effect after 1981, as did decrees involving housing. In 1982, the new Kohl Government introduced a repatriation campaign, including an early payout of accumulated pension funds in 1983, but no integration assistance for those who stayed. To pursue citizenship, an applicant had to live on FRG soil for at least ten years (five if married to a German) and enjoy full legal standing (excluding minors). She had to possess an "unblemished character," occupy her own dwelling, and prove capable of supporting herself and all eventual dependents. Family application costs ran as high as DM 5,000. Yet even after meeting rigid, objective "qualification" requirements, applicants faced the ultimate hurdle of bureaucratic discretion. The civil servant processing the case decided whether the naturalization of each individual was desirable "from a general political, economic, and cultural viewpoint." Candidates lacking a *Bekenntnis zum Deutschtum* (commitment to Germanness) faced certain rejection—even if Germans themselves were unwilling or unable to sing the national anthem![73]

Revised again in 1990, the Aliens Act introduced two "generational" modifications. Drawing on a new Framework Law for Ethnic Resettlers (*Aussiedler-aufnahmegesetz*), it curbed the inheritable nature of return rights for would-be "repatriates" and liberalized naturalization rules for guestworker children born in Germany. Minors between the ages of sixteen and twenty-three could

Table 1.2 Types of Residency Permits in Germany

The Aliens Act provides for different types of residence status according to the purpose of the stay:

* A *residence title for specific purposes* makes a person's stay conditional upon the reason for which it is issued. The holder must always leave Germany when the reason for his or her stay expires. For example, foreign students allowed to study in Germany under development aid schemes can apply for a residence title for their studies and, if granted one, may not remain in Germany for any other purpose.

* A *limited residence permit* establishes a basis for permanent residence. The holder's residence status becomes more secure the longer he or she stays.

* An *unlimited residence permit* is the first step towards secure residence status. Holders of a limited residence permit can apply for an unlimited one after five years provided that they satisfy certain other criteria.

* A *right of unlimited residence* is the best and most secure residence status under the Aliens Act. Holders of a residence permit can apply for a right of unlimited residence after eight years provided that they satisfy certain other criteria.

* A *residence title for exceptional purposes* is usually granted on humanitarian grounds. In practice it is mostly granted to civil war refugees. It can only be renewed if the humanitarian grounds for its issue still obtain, though holders may apply for a right of unlimited residence after eight years.

* A *temporary suspension of deportation* is not a residence permit. It merely means that the state has abstained from deporting the person concerned. It may be granted on application when a foreigner is legally obliged to leave the country but there are legal or factual reasons against deportation (for example, the person's own country refuses entry or the person faces the death sentence there).

* *Permission to reside* is separate from the various types of residence status provided for in the *Aliens Act*. It is the status accorded to an asylum seeker whose application is being processed. Asylum seekers who are granted asylum under the Basic Law receive an unlimited residence permit; those granted asylum under the Geneva Convention on Refugees receive a residence title for exceptional purposes.

* Foreigners with a *residence title for exceptional purposes* under Section 30 of the *Aliens Act* usually have the intention to remain in Germany. Unlike a temporary suspension of deportation, the residence title for exceptional purposes, which was granted on humanitarian grounds, can lead to a more secure residence status.

Source: Federal Commissioner for Foreigners' Issues, *Facts and Figures on the Situation of Foreigners in the Federal Republic of Germany* (Berlin: October 2000).

attain citizenship independent of parental status after eight years of residency and six years of schooling, provided they renounced their original citizenship and held no criminal record. Instead of ten years of consecutive residence for adults, the law foresaw fifteen years, raising the application fee to DM 100 for each family member while reducing the "discretionary-citizenship" fee to DM 500. Most importantly, it accorded applicants an automatic right (*Anspruch*) to citizenship once they met all objective conditions, rather than leaving decisions up to the bureaucrat processing the case.

Following failed efforts to introduce a bona fide immigration law after 1990, the Greens pushed the issue again as members of the new coalition in 1998. The main catalyst nonetheless came from Chancellor Schröder, who announced plans for an American-style "Green Card" at Hannover's CeBit Computer Fair in February 2000. Schröder's remarks unleashed pent-up demands for a new approach to migration. Employers welcomed the opening of the labor market but insisted the plan did not go far enough; restricted to a specific class of specialists, the visas would be valid for five years, maximum. Churches and humanitarian groups protested that the elite-guestworker model would not remedy the pressing problems facing refugees, denied residency permits that would render them economically self-sufficient. Business owners claimed that Bosnian refugees hired on a "temporary" basis had become indispensable to their operations. Demographers offered dire prognoses for the pension system, based on low fertility and rapid aging among the natives.

Interior Minister Otto Schily (SPD) declared that an immigration law allowing for dual nationality would "change our whole understanding of the state if we no longer connect belonging to the legal community of ethnic descent but rather with the acceptance of our constitution and laws."[74] He convened an Independent Commission on Immigration (ICI) in September 2002. Bavaria and Lower Saxony (Niedersachsen) established their own task forces on migration, while the CDU countered with its own commission, chaired by Saarland's minister-president, Peter Müller. Not to be swayed by national "expert" commissions, the CSU published its own views, which (predictably) became the hard-line position as the parliamentary debate unfolded.

Chaired by Rita Süssmuth (CDU), the ICI concluded unequivocally that "Germany needs immigrants" to ensure its economic prosperity and to meet (inter)national humanitarian obligations. The Commission called for objective application criteria, active recruitment in areas of need, transparent asylum procedures, and a systematic approach to integration. Schily jumped the gun, issuing a draft law before Commission findings were issued on 4 July 2001; his version was criticized by the Greens, the churches, and the CDU/CSU. Despite comparable recommendations from the Müller Commission, conservatives objected that the ICI (headed by one of their own) wanted to expand rather than limit immigration. By September 11th, the immigration question would be redefined by security and terrorist concerns.

The Cabinet approved a revised law in tune with ICI proposals in November, adopted by the Bundestag on 1 March 2002. The Bundesrat pulled the brakes on 22 March, after a staged split vote by Brandenburg (SPD Minister-President

Stolpe for, CDU-Minister Schönbohm against) was counted as majority support. The "procedure" was scrutinized by the High Court and overturned on 18 December 2002. The Union demanded ninety-one changes, then 130 after winning two state elections. Disagreement centered on the link between migration and unemployment, creation of a point system, and lowering the maximum age at which children can rejoin families. Usually fixated on "family values," CDU / CSU hardliners insisted that children over twelve cannot integrate successfully—an absurd proposition: thousands of foreign students want to stay after completing degrees, only to be denied work permits. Employers are just as anxious to hire them. My participant observations suggest that the failure to "integrate" owes more to abysmal school conditions, an obsolete vocational-tracking system, and the exclusionary rhetoric of politicians than to age. Hardliners also reject Green efforts to recognize new family types.

The core difference between pro- and anti-immigration activists is an ideological one: opponents have skillfully blurred the lines among migrant groups, between imported labor and unemployment, despite employer testimonies to the contrary. In 2003, 250 prominent economists, hardly flaming radicals, urged lawmakers in an open letter to pass the desperately needed act, struck down by "political trickery."[75] Ironically, the more hardliners try to block the undesirable hordes they claim will enter under reforms, the less acceptable they render Germany to the cream-of-the-crop IT specialists they think the country deserves—clearly demonstrated by the Green Card program. Following the first howls that Germany needed "integration not immigration" and *Kinder statt Inder* (though Union policies inhibit both), parliament allowed for twenty thousand special visas. In early 2003, only 13,566 Green Cards had been issued, 19 percent to Indians, 44 percent to Central/Eastern Europe specialists. By June, no one was talking about renewal.

After an eleven-month stalemate, Schröder reached an agreement with the CDU and FDP in May 2004 on the Immigration Law parameters; Greens were excluded from the negotiations. The temporary disappearance of a radical Islamist, Metin Caplan, in Cologne, led Conservatives to pull the brake again, insisting that the *Zuwanderungsgesetz* lacked tough passages allowing for the rapid deportation of criminal or terrorist elements. The law enacted in January 2005 reduces residency-permit types from five to two, tied to purposes of the stay: a limited *Aufenthaltserlaubnis*, and an unlimited *Niederlassungserlaubnis* (settlement permit). This eliminates the need for separate work permits, under stricter criteria. A new Federal Office for Migration and Refugees will sponsor integration courses, maintain a central registry, coordinate information exchanges between state/local labor and consular offices, as well as sponsor migration research. The federal government will provide €188 million per year to finance obligatory language courses, along with orientation classes (€76 million) on culture, history, and the constitutional order for those with less than six years of residency. The emphasis on *sustainable integration* for new arrivals comes at the expense of long-term residents. New migrants who fail to participate in authorized courses will face residency/welfare sanctions.

Highly qualified workers with advanced degrees (or salaries over €83,700 per year) can apply for permanent settlement at the outset; family members can also pursue paid employment. Self-employed entrepreneurs who invest at least €1 million and create ten jobs can qualify for limited (!) residency. The point system proposed in 2002 has been dropped. Semi-skilled, unskilled, and certain skilled workers are still subject to a recruitment freeze. Students who complete degrees may work for only one year afterward. One must ask: What are they thinking? Sending entrepreneurs and experienced graduates "back home" after a certain period defeats the purpose of trying to shore up the expert-labor supply.

Children up to the age of eighteen will be admitted in recognized asylum cases when joining an extended family evincing German language skills or otherwise offering "a positive integration prognosis"; for the rest, sixteen is the cut-off point.[76] Family members who accompany Late Repatriates must also demonstrate language competence. The law recognizes non-state and gender-specific grounds for asylum, but *toleration* has been retained as an "instrument for fine tuning." States may create their own commissions to judge "hardship cases." Persons accorded "little asylum" can engage in paid labor and apply for residency after three years if they meet other criteria, or if conditions have not improved in the homeland.

Commensurate with a new Counter-Terrorism Act, the law permits deportation in light of "factual evidence of a potential threat," unless the individual faces torture or capital punishment, in which case authorities can restrict freedom of movement and ban communication to enhance security. Human smuggling comprises a "new and compelling" basis for expulsion, as does supporting an organization promoting terrorism. Persons who incite hatred or violence, "such as agitators in mosques," are subject to discretionary expulsion. A law desperately needed for labor migration and integration purposes has thus been redefined as a vehicle for national security policing. Legislatively speaking, Germany has nonetheless become both a land of immigration and integration. Finally.

The Argument: Citizenship Equals What?

This study analyzing ethnic minorities in the Federal Republic emphasizes a practical-communitarian approach to integration. According to the logic used by German policymakers since 1949—namely, that *citizenship equals*

ethnicity—each group investigated here should fall into one of the incorporation patterns outlined above. A look at their daily lives nonetheless leads to
some surprising findings. Eastern Germans should have proved most capable
of assimilation under the *jus sanguinis* paradigm; fifteen years' worth of data
nonetheless shows that many still do not enjoy the economic opportunities or
political influence they expected to flow automatically from unification, thus
perceiving themselves as "second-class citizens." The next group to meet formal
lineage requirements consists of the *Aussiedler*; co-ethnics who have "returned"
since 1990 constitute the least well integrated of the resident minorities, despite
the special benefits they receive. They are also the least inclined to exercise the
political rights they immediately possess once they migrate.

EU nationals, especially Italians, Greeks, and Spaniards, are expected to
undergo a process of acculturation. They can pick and choose from an array of
employment opportunities and educational settings without reconfiguring their
identities. Although they are entitled to participate in local and EU elections,
based on the Maastricht premise that *citizenship equals legal status*, few actually
do. Nor do they keep in touch with homeland developments via ethnic organizations. Their relationships are largely anomic, yet average citizens rarely think
of this group when they hear the term *Ausländer*. When I asked for a list of
Italian organizations in Berlin in 2002, Commissioner Barbara John's secretary
responded: "Ach, the Italians? They're not foreigners. We hardly notice them!"

Ostensibly the least "assimilatable" but also most actively mobilizing migrants
in Germany are long-term Turkish residents, who have made substantial progress regarding integration, albeit not in ways anticipated by national policymakers. Against all odds, Turkish residents have established broad community ties
promoting incorporation in the face of generational change. Their experiences
demonstrate that it is neither "blood," nor the precept *citizenship equals religion*, but rather day-to-day social interaction that fosters integration. To borrow
from James Carville, trying to mobilize voters in the 1990s, "it's the economy,
stupid!" The Turkish community has relied on economic enclaves to build a
participatory base denied it by virtue of German citizenship laws. A comparison
with the participatory patterns of Turks in the Netherlands moreover suggests,
"it's the legal structure, stupid!" that comprises the main impediment to identification with the new homeland.

I moreover evaluate the status of new-EU members, Polish migrants, who
enjoy special status along guestworker lines. One notes a definitive split
between the integration experiences of early and recent arrivals. Long-term
Polish residents seem well acculturated, though few are politically active; the
first wave treated here entered Germany in the 1970s and 1980s as ethnic
repatriates or as recognized asylum seekers, following martial law in Poland.
The second wave, whose border-hopping activities parallel those of Mexican
workers in the United States, does not yet enjoy protections granted regular

EU laborers, and thus remains concentrated in the least desirable, often illegal sectors of the market. Difficult to organize, they lack an effective ethnic lobby due to their "temporary" status. Relations are often tense among border communities, despite modest EU investments in these areas: lower-paid Polish workers undercut perceived employment opportunities for East Germans, to the benefit of West German firms.

Last but not least, I consider the destinies of ethnic women, refuting the thesis that the quest for citizenship is inherently male. Young Turkish women account for a higher share of all naturalizations in Germany. They lead the rest in establishing themselves as independent economic actors and elected representatives.

While students may find this chapter pretty abstract, integration theories do shape national policies—even when they are wrong. Since most of us are not affected by immigration law, we are usually oblivious to the contradictory nature of policies that are supposed to "control" human movement. Many citizens would be deeply troubled by the devastating impact legalities can have on real people—if only they knew. The following chapters "put a human face" on the migrants portrayed here, assuming that many criticisms of Germany also apply to the ever-harsher treatment of foreigners in the US.

Furthermore, most scholars specialize in a particular group (e.g., studying Latinos, Turks, migrant workers, refugees), depriving them of the big picture and obscuring policy gaps that result in "failed integration." Although it is a very complicated task, I attempt to portray all groups in a single frame, to show that arcane legal structures and labor regulations—not culture, ethnic origin, religion, family practices, sex roles, or homeland attachments—lie at the root of Germany's demographic, socioeconomic, and national-identity crises. We will "visit" each group in its own legal, ethnic, and urban neighborhood in subsequent chapters. These case studies prove that while hardliners tried to block passage of a real *Einwanderungsgesetz* for thirty years—debating whether Germany should become "a land of immigration"—citizens without passports were busy at the grassroots level, reshaping it into "a land of integration." It is to their stories that we now turn.

Notes

1. Joyce Marie Mushaben, "A Crisis of Culture: Social Isolation and Integration among Turkish Guestworkers in the German Federal Republic," in Ilyan Basgöz and Norman Furniss, eds., *Turkish Workers in Europe: A Multidisciplinary Study* (Bloomington: Indiana University Press, 1985), 125–150.

2. Rita Süssmuth et al. (ICI), *Structuring Immigration, Fostering Integration*, Report by the Independent Commission on Migration to Germany (*Zuwanderungsbericht*), (Berlin: 4 July 2001), 27–28.

3. All expert opinions can be accessed via the Federal Ministry of the Interior website (www. bmi.bund.de) under *Gutachten/Unabhängige Kommission*.

4. Kohl referred to *Freizeitpark Deutschland* in conjunction with the 1996 Savings Package, scaling back on welfare, pension, and health care costs, as unions lobbied against the elimination of certain paid holidays.

5. Ralf E. Ulrich, "Die zukünftige Bevölkerungsstruktur Deutschlands nach Staatsangehörigkeit, Geburtsort und ethnischer Herkunft: Modellrechnung bis 2050," Gutachten für die Unabhängige Kommission "Zuwanderung" (Berlin/Windhoek: April 2001).

6. ICI, *Structuring Immigration, Fostering Integration*, 14; Federal Commissioner for Foreigners, "Facts and Figures on the Situation of Foreigners in the Federal Republic of Germany" (Berlin: October 2000).

7. ICI, *Structuring Immigration, Fostering Integration*, 15ff.

8. Dietrich Thränhardt, "Die Reform der Einbürgerung in Deutschland," Friedrich Ebert Stiftung: Digitale Bibliothek (www.fes.de/fulltext/asfo/ 00229003.htm).

9. Ulrich, "Die zukünftige Bevölkerungsstruktur Deutschlands," 19–20; ICI, *Structuring Immigration, Fostering Integration*, 29.

10. Bavaria was very quick to declare parts of Yugoslavia "safe," sending back refugees ahead of all other states. Alan Cowell, "Bavaria, Acting Alone, Begins Ousting Bosnian Refugees," *New York Times*, 9 October 1996.

11. Zentrum für Türkeistudien, *Die ökonomische Dimension der türkischen Selbständigen in Deutschland und in der Europäische Union* (Essen: June 2001), 4–5.

12. ICI, *Structuring Immigration, Fostering Integration*, 66–67, 69.

13. Ibid., 26–28.

14. Ibid., 34–35.

15. The Euro was first introduced in 2002, but it took two years for reports to catch up with currency developments. ICI, *Structuring Immigration, Fostering Integration*, 53; reports since 2006 fault "childless academics" for negative population growth.

16. Ibid., 37–39.

17. Ibid., 48–49.

18. Ibid., 39.

19. Ibid., 43, 54.

20. Zentrum für Türkeistudien, *Die ökonomische Dimension*, 9.

21. ICI, *Structuring Immigration, Fostering Integration*, 63.

22. Ibid., 58, 62. The FRG often chooses means inconsistent with its migration goals; marketed as liberalizations, the 1986 and 1990 Foreigners Acts tightened requirements but overrode bureaucratic discretion with legal entitlement. State "quotas" for redistributing asylum seekers backfired due to xenophobic violence; the 1993 Asylum Compromise was undermined by wars in Yugoslavia, Afghanistan, and the Persian Gulf.

23. T. H. Marshall does in *Class, Citizenship and Social Development* (Garden City, NJ: Doubleday, 1964) but defines the terms differently than applied here. Further, Karl W. Deutsch, *Nationalism and Social Communication: An Inquiry into the Foundations of Nationality* (Cambridge, MA: MIT Press, 1966); William Rogers Brubaker, *Citizenship and Nationhood in France and Germany* (Cambridge: Harvard University Press, 1992); Yasemin N. Soysal, *The Limits of Citizenship: Migrants and Postnational Membership in Europe* (Chicago: University of Chicago Press, 1994); Gerard Delanty, "Models of Citizenship: Defining European Identity and Citizenship," *Citizenship Studies* 1, no. 3 (1997): 285–303; Elizabeth Meehan, *Citizenship and the European Union* (London:

Sage, 1993); Rainer Bauböck, "Reinventing Urban Citizenship," *Citizenship Studies* 7, no. 2 (2003): 139–160.

24. Christian Joppke and Steven Lukes, eds., *Multicultural Questions* (Oxford: Oxford University Press, 2000). Ruud Koopmans and Paul Statham offer different ideal types: Ethno-cultural assimilationism (Germany); ethno-cultural pluralism (Switzerland); civic assimilationism (France); and civic pluralism (Britain, Sweden, Netherlands). See Koopmans and Statham, "How National Citizenship Shapes Transnationalism," in Christian Joppke and Ewa Moravska, eds., *Integrating Immigrants in Liberal Nation-States: From Postnational to Transnational* (Berkeley, CA: University of California Press, 2002). The definitional possibilities are endless, hence my decision to stick with four simplified, non-interchangeable categories of incorporation.

25. See Richard Alba and Victor Nee, "Rethinking Assimilation Theory for a New Era of Immigration," *International Migration Review* 31, no. 4 (1997): 826–874; Mikael Hjerm, "Multiculturalism Reassessed," *Citizenship Studies* 4, no. 3 (2000): 357–381. Also, Josh DeWind and Philip Kasinitz, "Everything Old is New Again? Processes and Theories of Immigrant Incorporation," *International Migration Review* 31, no. 4 (1997): 1096–1111.

26. Hartmut Esser, *Integration und ethnische Schichtung*, Gutachten für die Unabhängige Kommission "Zuwanderung" (Mannheim, 2001), 57.

27. Mushaben, *From Post-War to Post-Wall Generations*.

28. *1977 Einbürgerungsrichtlinien*, issued by the Federal Ministry of the Interior.

29. German Information Center, *Foreigners in Germany: Guestworkers, Asylum-Seekers, Refugees and Ethnic Germans* (New York: November 1991), 2–3.

30. Joyce Marie Mushaben, "Ost-West Identitäten: Generationen zwischen Wende und Wandel," *Berliner Debatte INITIAL* 12, no. 3 (2001): 74–87; and *"Auferstanden aus Ruinen*: Social Capital and Democratic Identity in the New Länder," *German Politics and Society* 14, no. 4 (1997): 79–101.

31. Warwick Neville, "Singapore, Ethnic Diversity in the Interventionist Milieu," in Curtis Roseman, Hans Dieter Laux, and Günther Thieme, eds., *EthniCity: Geographic Perspectives on Ethnic Change in Modern Cities* (London: Rowman & Littlefield, 1996).

32. Mushaben, *From Post-War to Post-Wall Generations*.

33. Marlies Galenkamp, "Do We Need Special Collective Rights for Immigrants and Refugees in Western Europe?" *Citizenship Studies* 2, no. 3 (1998): 501–517. Also, Ruth Rubio-Marin, *Immigration and the Democratic Challenge: Citizenship and Inclusion in Germany and the United States* (Cambridge: Cambridge University Press, 2000).

34. James Coleman, "Social Capital in the Creation of Human Capital," *American Journal of Sociology* 94 (1988): 98.

35. Esser, *Integration und ethnische Schichtung*, 16.

36. Ibid., 28.

37. Ibid., 31.

38. Ibid., 38.

39. Werner Schiffauer, *Islam in the Diaspora: The Fascination of Political Islam among Second Generation German-Turks*, WPTC-99–06 (Viadrina). Also, Zentrum für Türkeistudien, *Intergeneratives Verhalten und (Selbst) Ethnisierung von türkischen Zuwanderern* (Essen, 2001).

40. Oliver Tomlein, ed., *Leitkultur: Besonderes Kennzeichen D. Wahre Deutsche Staatsbürger zweiter Klasse und die unsichtbaren Dritten* (Hamburg: Konkret, 2001).

41. Esser, *Integration und ethnische Schichtung*, 37.

42. Mushaben, "A Crisis of Culture."

43. Esser, *Integration und ethnische Schichtung*, 22.

44. Mushaben, *"Auferstanden aus Ruinen."*

45. Joyce Marie Mushaben, "*Die Lehrjahre sind vobei!* Re-Forming Democratic Interest Groups in Eastern Germany," *Democratization* 8, no. 4 (2001): 95–133.

46. Esser, *Integration und ethnische Schichtung*, 34.

47. Ibid., 38.

48. Robert D. Putnam, "Bowling Alone: America's Declining Social Capital," *Journal of Democracy* 6, no. 1 (1995): 65–78.

49. Koopmans and Statham, "How National Citizenship Shapes Transnationalism," 38.

50. Ibid., 38.

51. Ibid., 7.

52. Thränhardt, "Die Reform der Einbürgerung in Deutschland."

53. Deutsch, *Nationalism and Social Communication*, 91, 96.

54. Ibid., 97–98.

55. Meindert Fennema and Jean Tillie, "Ethnic Associations, Political Trust and Political Participation," Working Paper 3A UNESCO-MPMC Project, Multicultural Policies and Modes of Citizenship in European Cities, 5.

56. Gabriel A. Almond and Sidney Verba, *The Civic Culture* (Boston: Brown & Little, 1965), 245.

57. Mushaben, "*Die Lehrjahre sind vorbei!*"; Heidrun Abromeit, "Die 'Vertretungslücke': Probleme im neuen deutschen Bundesstaat," *Gegenwartskunde* 3/1993: 281–292.

58. Fennema and Tillie, "Ethnic Associations," 4.

59. Ralf Dahrendorf, *Society and Democracy in Germany* (Garden City, NY: Doubleday, 1967).

60. Ruud Koopmans, "Migrant Participation, Citizenship and Democracy: National and Local Perspectives" (paper presented at the WZB Workshop on Strategies of Integration: The Multiethnic Society and Local Government, Essen, 24–25 September 2001), 12.

61. Fennema and Tillie, "Ethnic Associations," 22ff.

62. Sassen, cited in Bauböck, "Reinventing Urban Citizenship," 156; further, William W. Goldsmith, "The Metropolis and Globalization: The Dialectics of Racial Discrimination, Deregulation and Urban Reform," *American Behavioral Scientist* 41, no. 3 (1997): 299–310.

63. Engin Isin, cited in Bauböck, "Reinventing Urban Citizenship," 50.

64. Werner Schiffauer, *Fremde in der Stadt: Zehn Essays über Kultur und Differenz* (Frankfurt/Main: Suhrkamp, 1997), 93.

65. Bauböck, "Reinventing Urban Citizenship," 139, 150.

66. Linda Bosniak, cited in Kim Rubenstein, "The Centrality of Migration to Citizenship," *Citizenship Studies* 7, no. 2 (2003): 262.

67. Bauböck, "Reinventing Urban Citizenship," 157.

68. Klaus Bade, cited in Maria Berger, Christian Galonska, and Ruud Koopmans, "Not a Zero-Sum Game: Ethnic Communities and Political Integration of Migrants in Berlin" (paper presented at a workshop on Political Participation of Immigrants and their Descendants [*sic*] in Post-War Western Europe, Turin, Italy, 22–27 March 2002), 28.

69. Ibid., 28.

70. Jürgen Fijalkowski and Helmut Gilmeister, *Ausländervereine: Ein Forschungsbericht* (Berlin: Hitit, 1997), 147–148.

71. Ruud Koopmans, "Zuwanderer in Berlin unterstützen demokratische Werte: Umfrage zeigt, daß weder Parallelgesellschaft noch Kulturkampf zu befürchten sind," WZB Pressemitteilung, 14 January 2002.

72. Karin Schönwälder, "Zukunftsblindheit oder Steuerungsversage? Zur Ausländerpolitik der Bundesregierungen der 1960er und frühen 1970er Jahre," in Jochen Oltmer, ed., *Migration steuern und verwalten: Deutschland vom späten 19. Jahrhundert bis zur Gegenwart* (Osnabrück: Universitätsverlag, 2003), 131ff.

73. Klaus J. Bade, "From Emigration to Immigration: The German Experience in the Nineteenth and Twentieth Century," in Bade and Myron Weiner, eds., *Migration Past, Migration Future: Germany and the United States*, 21.

74. "Den Reformaufbruch wagen! Aufruf von 250 ökonomen an die politischen Entscheidungsträger," *Frankfurter Allgemeine Zeitung*, 31 May 2003. Schily has played a curious role in the debate, given his eclectic political biography: as founding member of the Greens and a defense lawyer for radical groups, he switched to the SPD in the late 1980s, and counted as Schröder's most conservative Cabinet member.

75. Ibid.

76. General criteria apply: the family member already living in Germany has a residence or settlement permit; sufficient living space is available; the member has sufficient means to support him- or herself without recourse to public funds, and no grounds for expulsion exist.

CHAPTER 2

THE INVISIBLE MAN (AND WOMAN)

Permanently Provisional Guestworkers

They called for workers and there came human beings.
—Max Frisch

I'm not the black man
I'm not the white man
I'm just the type between them
I'm a Turkish man in a foreign land
—Rap-verse by a "Turkish Power Boy"

It wasn't all that long ago that Turkish street-fighters took on neo-Nazis, soccer hooligans, and other "power boys" after unification to assert their manhood, demonstrate ethnic solidarity, and exercise a bit of neighborhood control. The last decade has seen new street clashes and a societal race to the bottom among Turkish, Arab, and post-Soviet "repatriate" youth. Used to occupying the last rung on the social-mobility ladder, Turkish gangs claim it's their turn for special treatment, now that East Germans have gotten a piece of the pie. Despite questionable tactics, their claims seem justifiable, given their long residency, consumer habits, and language skills that render them much more acculturated than youth arriving from Russia, Kazakhstan, and the Ukraine since 1994.

Street-level violence between German-Turks and Russian-Germans, added to high crime rates among maladjusted adolescents, testify to the "two-faced history of German migration policies," noted by Klaus Bade. The guestworker population gave way to "a real immigrant population [consisting] of 'domestic foreigners', 'foreign inlanders', or 'Germans with foreign passports', while ethnic Germans from the East, as 'foreign Germans', are the real immigrants with German citizenship."[1] The Federal Republic's ethnonational orientation has resulted in "a consistent political denial and a belated acceptance of social realities in immigration, a corresponding lack of clear and comprehensive legal conceptions, as well as [a lack of] long-term perspectives needed for immigration management."[2]

Ethnic subcultures have become constituitive elements of pluralist democracies. Only integration allows ethnic minorities to preserve and reconfigure elements of their own identity while building bridges to the dominant culture. In a 2001 study of intergenerational transfer, Bernhard Nauck and Anja Steinbach traced patterns of social- and cultural-capital formation. Sampling four hundred parent-child dyads, they found that social relations follow family rather than ethnic lines.[3] They reached the not-so-surprising conclusion that the more time parents spend with children, the higher their level of educational attainment qua human capital.

Ethnic minorities face a unique structural dilemma, however: group cohesion can provide the community with substantial social capital, but it may be the wrong kind for the next generation. Though it builds on factors such as age of entry, gender, parental status, and language skills, integration requires social capital linked to the dominant culture. Ethnic networks buffer successor cohorts against negative experiences with the dominant group, but they also trigger new conflicts between mothers, daughters, fathers, and sons. The skills needed to function in the new homeland are ones that migrant parents cannot provide; correspondingly, the cultural/religious ties their offspring draw on to weather discrimination may be rejected by the host society as "barriers to integration."

Identity formation is not an all-or-nothing proposition. Nauck and colleagues admit that "when migrants master the German language, know how to prepare bread-dumplings, regularly read German magazines and own music cassettes by Udo Lindenberg, [this doesn't mean] that they shouldn't know Orhan Gencebay, should not be fluent in Turkish, should lose their taste for *raki* and *ayran,* and prove incapable of following a Turkish video-film."[4] Never mind the fact that only people over the age of fifty remember Udo and that videos have yielded to DVDs. These authors are willing to create space for Turkish habits and tastes, yet they focus on food, music, and media consumption, not on religious attire, ritual slaughter (*halal*), and other identity variables more likely to clash with traditional German images of "good neighbors and citizens."

This chapter addresses three stages of migration—*arrival, settlement,* and *securing a place* in mainstream culture—based on the experiences of Germany's Turkish community. It examines changing patterns of identification with the host state across three generations, drawing on ethnographic studies. I argue that guestworkers' early hopes of returning home in the 1960s ceased to be a motivating force for Turkish mobilization by the late 1970s; instead, the latter became a vehicle for preserving select elements of Turkish identity to counter marginalization by the host country. The belief that imported workers would "go home" developed a mythical quality of its own among lawmakers, despite all statistical evidence to the contrary. Refusal to adopt active integration policies gave rise to the very ethnic segregation, fundamentalist tendencies, and youth alienation leaders claimed they wanted to avoid.

The 1990s bring to the fore a new generation as well as a paradigm shift in the orientations of community activists willing to confront Germany with a plethora of integration demands. Drawing on Berlin surveys, I assess the "integration potential" of second- and third-generation Turks in the capital city, showing that structural factors, not immutable cultural differences, comprise the main barrier to their incorporation as citizens.

Arrival: Strangers in a Strange Land, 1955–1972

The plan, according to policymakers of the 1950s, was to import an expendable work force commensurate with the needs of a "miraculously" recovering economy. Foreign labor recruits faced strict selection criteria and rigorous medical examinations, only to be subjected to the dirtiest, most dangerous forms of shift work and assembly-line production shunned by the natives. Less than a decade removed from Nazi slave labor, officials justified the temporary utilization of alien workers as foreign assistance: recruiting the best and the brightest by way of state-to-state agreements, politicians claimed the rotation system would outfit recruits with technical skills needed for homeland development, while supplying remittances to families left behind. The fact that the monies sent served the purposes of dictatorial regimes in Greece, Portugal, Turkey, Spain, and Yugoslavia was never debated.

The first recruitment campaign did not stem from a clear labor shortage, as often presumed: 900,000 Germans were unemployed at the time. The catalyst was provided by farmer confederations in Baden-Württemberg, seeking an alternative workforce to locals inclined to shun hard labor. A real shortage arose in 1961, once the Berlin Wall made it impossible for Western businesses to rely on Eastern commuters. The GDR economy had been hard hit by the hundreds of thousands who had "voted with their feet": 194,000 proletarians headed west in 1960. Another 103,000 fled during the first six months of 1961, rising to 50,000 per week by 13 August. The Wall presented FRG leaders with a golden opportunity to reaffirm their commitment to *jus sanguinis,* as well as to bolster claims that they alone legitimately represented all-German citizens. The FRG's immediate economic loss became its long-term political gain. The flip side of an historical event (*Mauerbau*) that brought in millions of foreigners, and fostered their economic inclusion, would provide a core justification (*Mauerfall*) for their sociopolitical exclusion.

The number of indigenous workers declined by 2.3 million from 1960 to 1972, as well-paid jobs (textile production) moved to low-wage countries while the share of alien laborers rose from 1.3 percent to 11.9 percent. The need for women in service industries grew so quickly that men could submit the names of family members for direct hire. By 1966, 16 percent of the Turkish males lived with their wives in the FRG.[5] Viewed by businesses as a "labor-policy" decision, this exemption initiated family reunification from 1962 to 1967. Rotation plans were declared dead on arrival, given employers' unwillingness to reinvest in training new cohorts; potential social consequences were ignored.

In practice, guestworker policy amounted to "development economics in reverse." The training costs for one German worker ran as high as DM 150,000 in 1970, compared to the Turkish average of DM 100,000; Özcan reports that 40 percent of the males and 25 percent of the female workers completed occupational training in Turkey prior to migration. Thus the human capital transfer from Turkey to Germany (612,000 workers) added up to DM 61.2 billion; further, 75 percent of the monies remitted to Turkey (DM 2.5 billion) flowed back to the host country through the import of automobiles and household appliances.[6] Faruk Sen estimates that Turkish deposits in German banks, available for domestic investment, rose to DM 30 billion by the early 1980s.[7]

Settlement, Family Reunion, and the Myth of Return, 1973–1982

Ray Rist observed that guestworkers embarked on "a migration not of conviction, but of expediency," yet many changed their minds after settling in.[8] The fact that new jobs are constantly opening up at the lower end of the status hierarchy feeds migration even in times of economic stagnation. Mass unemployment led the government to halt recruitment (*Anwerbestopp*) in 1973, resulting in a sharp decline from 2,595,000 migrants in 1973, to 1,840,500, rising again to 2,015,600 after 1978 despite the freeze. According to one report, "the 'oil price shock' of 1973 was less a real cause than a welcome opportunity to halt recruitment and to adopt restrictions on immigration, as Switzerland and Sweden had already begun to do in 1970 and 1972."[9] Italian workers undermined the ban by traveling back and forth as jobs grew scarce or plentiful, since EEC membership entitled them to free movement denied other national groups. In 1964, 212,087 Italians entered Germany, while another 165,925 left; the first recession in 1966 saw 240,225 arrive and 220,263 depart. The Italian total fell by 50 percent from 1973 to 1974, but the returnees also dropped below 85,000 in 1976.[10] Migrants from Spain, Portugal, and Greece headed home once dictatorships crumbled in those countries.

More important than those who left were those who stayed. Although the guestworker total fell to 786,000 between 1973 and 1982, the foreign population reached a new high of 4,667,000 in 1982. While 80 percent of all migrants held jobs in 1961, this segment declined from 65 percent in 1973, to 41 percent in 1980, and 36 percent in 1985. The share of Turkish residents who had stayed ten or more years rose from 16.2 percent in 1972, to 37.8 percent in 1980, to 47.5 percent in 1982, and 58.9 percent by 1985.[11] Those under age eighteen grew from 788,147 (out of 4.12 million) in 1974, to 1,050,495 in 1979, to 1,183,203 (among 4.7 million) by 1982.[12] Workers who feared they would not be readmitted once economic conditions improved took advantage of curiously inconsistent family policies to bring in dependents before it was too late.

In 1974, for example, the Brandt Government decreed that youth arriving after November would no longer receive work permits and tightened eligibility for aliens already there. When the deadline was extended through December 1976, many rushed to relocate older children. That system was replaced with a "waiting period" in 1980: youth became eligible for permits after two years, spouses after four years. Germans themselves thus reinforced the stay-at-home status of foreign women.

In January 1975, officials amended rules for monthly child subsidies, declaring they would only be paid out to minors in Germany; guestworkers hastened to bring over offspring under grandma's care back home. Household formation rendered Turkish residents visible, since families require more services than men confined to company hostels: e.g., grocery stores, doctors, schools, and playgrounds. They also intensified competition for "affordable housing with an indoor toilet," a scarce commodity that triggered a rowdy squatters' movement in the early 1980s. In April 1975, local authorities began to prohibit foreigners from moving into neighborhoods with more than a 12 percent concentration, doing nothing to meliorate discrimination by landlords in other districts. SPD chancellor-candidate Hans-Jochen Vogel captured the emotional intensity, if not the political complexity surrounding the "ghetto" issue with his 1982 assessment: "In ten years we will have our San Salvador in Kreuzberg."[13] Even this policy contradicted the mobility demands of business and was therefore rescinded in 1977, except for a "small ban" for Berlin, not as dependent on heavy industry.

In 1976–1977, a federal-state commission recommended a "temporary integration" approach that would have liberalized rules for unlimited residency permits (eight years for an *Aufenthaltsbereichtigung*). The 1979 Kuhn Memorandum favored a ban on labor imports but called for active integration measures. The new "consolidation" strategy called for the inclusion of foreign children in preschools and occupational training programs. Second- and third-generation youth were not to be alienated from their cultures of origin but could take advantage of intensified social services. The commission recommended liberalizing naturalization rules for children after six years. Instead, policymakers reduced the eligible-entry age from twenty-one to eighteen.

Table 2.1 Foreigners in the Federal Republic, 1960–2003

Year	Foreign Population[1]	Foreign Women	Foreign Population (% of Total)	Socially Insured Laborers
1960	686,200	—	1.2	279,400
1968	1,924,200	—	3.2	1,014,800
1969	2,381,100	—	3.9	1,372,100
1970	2,976,500	—	4.9	1,838,900
1971	3,438,700	—	5.	2,168,800
1972	3,526,600	—	5.7	2,317,000
1973	3,966,200	—	6.4	—
1974	4,127,400	—	6.7	2,150,600
1975	4,089,600	—	6.6	1,932,600
1976	3,948,300	—	6.4	1,873,800
1977	3,948,300	—	6.4	1,833,500
1978	3,981,100	—	6.5	1,862,200
1979	4,143,800	—	6.7	1,965,800
1980*	4,453,300	1,834,100	7.2	1,925,600
1981	4,629,700	1,919,500	7.5	1,832,200
1982	4,666,900	1,957,900	7.6	1,709,500
1983	4,534,900	1,925,300	7.4	1,640,600
1984	4,363,600	1,864,100	7.1	1,552,600
1985	4,378,900	1,874,100	7.2	1,536,000
1986	4,512,700	1,936,000	7.4	1,544,700

(continued)

Table 2.1 Foreigners in the Federal Republic, 1960–2003 *(continued)*

Year	Foreign Population[1]	Foreign Women	Foreign Population (% of Total)	Socially Insured Laborers
1987	4,240,500	1,898,600	6.9	1,557,000
1988	4,489,100	2,022,100	7.3	1,607,100
1989	4,845,900	2,179,100	7.7	1,683,800
1990	5,342,500	2,330,700	8.4	1,793,400
1991**	5,882,300	2,541,400	7.3	1,908,700
1992	6,495,800	2,776,100	8.0	2,119,600
1993	6,878,100	2,956,600	8.5	2,150,100
1994	6,990,500	3,045,500	8.6	2,109,700
1995	7,173,900	3,149,500	8.8	2,094,000
1996	7,314,000	3,235,800	8.9	2,050,500
1997	7,365,800	3,288,900	9.0	1,997,800
1998	7,319,600	3,293,700	8.9	2,023,800
1999	7,343,600	3,331,700	8.9	1,915,200
2000	7,296,800	3,337,500	8.9	1,974,000
2001	7,318,600	3,370,200	8.9	1,979,300
2002	7,335,600	3,408,900	8.9	1,860,411
2003	7,334,800	3,440,100	8.9	1,796,489

* Sex-disaggregated data not available prior to 1980
** Figures as of 1991 refer to united Germany
— not available
Source: Statistisches Bundesamt/Bundesanstalt für Arbeit

Another upsurge in unemployment evoked a rapid reversal of official thinking. In 1980 the Schmidt Government rejected communal voting rights, ignoring the needs of workers who had contributed to *Modell Deutschland* at great personal cost. In Özcan's words, "since the first 'foreigner generation' had already fulfilled its labor market tasks, it could now simply be ignored and excluded from consideration by the new resolutions regarding policies towards foreigners."[14] The *Fortress Germany* orientation refined by Schmidt's successor Helmut Kohl had the effect of producing another "lost generation" by the late 1980s.

Despite insistence that Germany was "not a land of immigration," most guestworkers were economically integrated by the late 1970s. According to

German Trade Union Confederation (DGB) estimates, nearly 49 percent of all Turkish laborers were union members by 1979; the proportion of Turkish metal-workers in IG Metall rose from 48 percent in 1972 to 65 percent by 1982.[15] They enjoyed collectively bargained salaries and benefits, although permanent residency remained problematic. Given its commodified welfare state (tying benefits to earnings and years of employment), Germany fostered the economic incorporation of migrant laborers by way of the social security system. The Sixth Family Report of 2000 found that "in many ways, inclusion in the welfare state led to assimilation and integration . . . involving migrant families who stayed in Germany despite their [legal] status-relegation oriented towards the principle of blood-descent."[16] State-subsidized welfare organizations divided up clients among themselves—Catholic *Caritas* for the Italians and Croatians, the social-democratic *Arbeiterwohlfahrt* for the Turks—leading them to become advocates for these groups.

Although deliberately excluded from political participation, Turkish residents had already formed rudimentary political associations, limited to a focus on homeland politics. Turkish Student Federations in Munich (1954) and Berlin (1957) banded together with others in 1962; by 1963 there were nineteen Turkish Workers' Associations. These interest constellations were the first to address the treatment of foreigners in Germany and repressive policies in the homeland.[17] Several party-political groups were formed after 1967, polarizing the ethnic community as Turkey moved toward another military coup in 1980. This orientation would change dramatically by the mid 1980s.

Subject to greater social marginalization than Greek or Italian migrants, Turkish workers helped to diversify German culture through the establishment of private mosques and the ever more popular döner kebab—"the food that changed the Republic"—as early as 1969.[18] It was a combination of German and Turkish orientations that posed the most formidable barrier to deeper integration: namely, hopes among first-generation guestworkers that they could go home some day (though 40 percent of a 1980 Labor Ministry sample had no intention of doing so), coupled with a German insistence that they should.[19]

Self-Mobilization and Social Integration, 1983–1998

Treated like invisible men and women through the 1970s, Turks became the targets of restrictive "foreigner policies" and politically exploited hostility (*Ausländerfeindlichkeit*) in the 1980s. The phrase *time-bomb guestworkers* entered the political discourse. By mid decade, structural changes in the economy would wipe out half-a-million jobs once filled by migrants, invoking claims that foreigners "were taking away jobs" and imposing undue burdens on the welfare state. An influx of 40,900 East Germans in 1984, added to rising numbers of expatriates from Soviet-bloc countries, were exempted from such charges, although both groups enjoyed significantly more integration assistance.

An ever more unpopular SPD-FDP coalition introduced new family visa requirements in October 1980 (targeting Turkish visitors), and proposed lowering the entry age for children from eighteen to six. CDU-governed states adopted their own "foreigner ordinances" in 1981, embraced by the new Kohl Government. They blocked entry for family members from non-EC states, including children over age sixteen, those with one parent living abroad, and spouses dwelling in Germany for less than eight years, or married for less than a year.

A commission established by new Interior Minister Zimmermann (CSU) after Schmidt's 1982 resignation proposed denying residency-permit renewal to "undesirable" (suddenly unemployed) migrants. It sought to ban political activities by "extremist" migrant organizations (two years after a coup in Turkey) and to designate receipt of unemployment aid and social assistance grounds for deportation. Zimmermann declared in the Bundestag: "We will bring decisiveness to policies regarding foreigners, recommend and also execute solutions that do justice to the interest of the German people . . . the ability to live together free of conflict will only be possible when the number of foreigners who live among us is limited and reduced in the longer run, especially in relation to large national groups like the Turks." Green-parliamentarian Joschka Fischer responded: "If comparable actions were pursued elsewhere against German minorities . . . you would label them the same way I label policies directed against our Turkish compatriates here: that is, expulsion [*Vertreibung*]."[20]

Elected in March 1983, Helmut Kohl quickly introduced a repatriation program, offering a lump sum of DM 10,500 and DM 1,500 per child (reduced for each month of unemployment or layoff) if foreigners departed by September 1984. Only 171,000 left, 82,000 of whom received early pension payouts; "employer contributions" (DM 3–4 billion) remained in German insurance accounts, subsidizing indigenous workers.[21] Hailed as a success, the campaign "had the concrete effect that was hardly more than the cash-and-carry outcome many had feared" for those who had already planned to leave. Some money was saved in terms of child subsidies and unemployment insurance benefits.[22] An open confrontation between Interior Minister Zimmerman and Foreigner Commissioner Funcke over reducing the age of entry from sixteen to six led the latter to resign in protest.

By 1985, 22,000 Turks were self-employed, and 100,000 had established *Bausparverträge* (building loans) with local savings banks, indicating they did not plan to depart soon. They were also the proud owners of life-insurance policies, cars, washing machines, refrigerators, stereos, and other durable goods.[23] With non-German pupils exceeding 700,000, conservatives reluctantly began to rethink their "foreigner policies" in 1988. The government first denied, then confirmed the existence of a draft "integration" law but withdrew it in response to "the sharpest protests from the public," viz., churches, labor unions, academic researchers, and human-rights activists, over its highly exclusionary mechanisms.[24] Wolfgang Schäuble replaced Zimmermann as interior minister after a Cabinet shake-up. Early 1989 triggered public shock waves as right-radical parties assumed seats in the Berlin Assembly and city governments in Hesse.

Another migrant wave during the late 1980s consisted of groups who were technically Germans. Resident *Aussiedler* increased from 42,788 in 1986, to 86,000 in 1987, to 202,673 in 1988, and then 377,055 in 1989. The number of GDR citizens allowed to emigrate rose as well; from November 1989 through January 1990 they arrived at the rate of 2,500–3,000 per day. By mid decade, nearly 55 percent of the Turkish residents had lived in Germany for over ten years, though the total had declined from 1,552,300 in 1983 to 1,434,300 in 1986.[25] Foreigners accounted for 10 percent of the births in 1983, reaching 13.2 percent in 1997.[26]

Under the circumstances, the Turkish community had no choice but to pursue social integration as a local do-it-yourself project. The 1980 military coup, along with intensified persecution of Kurds and Alevis, polarized right and left parties in Turkey; these developments did not lower interest in homeland events but did impel many to turn away from associations in Germany caught up in those struggles. By 1987, 4.5 million foreigners could choose among three thousand different political, cultural, and social service–oriented organizations, sports and leisure clubs, youth, or women's groups, business and professional entities; they evinced higher levels of associational activity than Germans at the time.[27]

A majority of right-wing organizations took shape between 1965 and 1981, many subsidized by the Turkish government, including Islamic groups. The same pattern applied to left-wing associations; the Turkish Socialist Society and the European Federation of Turkish Socialists, created in 1967–1968, overlapped with the rise of the German SDS. After 1980, new organizations focused on interest representation in the host country, the largest of which were the religious/conservative Turkish Community in Berlin (Türkische Gemeinde, or TGB) and the social-democratic Turkish Union in Berlin West (Türkischer Bund, now the Turkish Union Berlin-Brandenburg, or TBB). Established in 1985, the Turkish Parents Organization sought to mediate tensions between parents and schools, as well as to improve local facilities.[28]

A 1986 press declaration issued by the Association for Turkish Migrants in Hamburg summarizes the key goals and motives of most ethnic organizations created during a period of prolonged economic crisis. H. Keskin proclaimed on 5 November:

Nowadays we are called "co-citizens." The majority of us have lived and worked here in Hamburg for more than 10, 15 and 20 years. Many of our children were born as Hamburg-dwellers. We have long been present in the factories, schools, child-care centers and in the residential areas as an established part of this city's population. We fulfill all of the duties of citizens (except for military service):

—We pay taxes.

—We pay pension, unemployment, health care and social insurance premiums.

—We make important contributions to the state, the economy and society with our labor and our consumption.

Why are we not allowed to vote on November 9th like our work colleagues and our neighbors? Why are we not even allowed to help shape and co-determine the policies that affect us most directly in our own residential zones, regarding nurseries, schools, parking and traffic problems?[29]

It was no coincidence that these associations emerged during a period of publically manipulated "hostility towards foreigners." Renewed self-mobilization was managed largely by the second generation, young adults who had been raised, if not born in Germany, already starting families of their own.

I disagree with Esser's contention that Turkish residents have experienced a slower "assimilation tempo" than other minorities, due to the presence of well-developed enclaves.[30] The German refusal to promote active structural integration left the Turkish community no choice but to create its own networks, in contrast to migrant experiences in the Netherlands and Sweden. Further, FRG politicians consistently look for integration in all the wrong places. Over 58 percent of all non-German residents live in cities of half a million or more; another 22 percent live in towns with 100,000–500,000 residents. Integration occurs not at the abstract level of national identification but rather at the real existing metropolitan level. National identity matters more to politicians in search of hot electoral issues than it does to average citizens struggling to balance work and family life on a daily basis.

Next, there is the German tendency to focus on "ethnic differences" rather than on family similarities (US politicians, by contrast, overestimate commonalities among "the" American people, ignoring gender, race, and class disparities). Nauck et al. discovered the strongest in-group contacts among Turkish mothers (75 percent), and the least contact with relatives among Turkish sons (12 percent); 81.7 percent of the second generation, but only 8.5 percent of the oldest cohorts, enjoy external contacts with Germans.[31] My experiences in Hamburg, Bonn, Stuttgart, Frankfurt, Berlin, and Erfurt suggest that in-group/out-group patterns are not that different. What German grandmother regularly combs the streets for friends of a different race or class? How many indigenous couples regularly invite non-family members into their homes? Most I know would rather eat out at restaurants run by "their" Italians.

Policymakers stress the strength of intraethnic ties among Turks as an indicator of "failed" integration, despite minorities' explicit desire for more cross-cultural ties. The federal report on foreign families held that 77 percent preferred integrated neighborhoods. Experts claim that the significance of spatially concentrated ethnic communities is overestimated as a barrier to integration; the relation between group concentration in given areas and actual contact frequency is "very weak." True, more than 90 percent of migrant families with relatives in the host society, and 99 percent with relatives in the vicinity maintained regular contacts; 39 percent of the Italians and 34 percent of the Turks visited "daily or multiple times per week." However, only 34 percent among Turkish fathers and 14 percent among mothers contacted at least one non-related co-ethnic of the same sex.[32]

It is thus "a matter of ethnocentric misunderstanding, to conclude from the frequent appearance of 'visible' foreigners in particular living quarters that these persons must have intensive connections with each other."[33] If Germans spend less time with their families, it is because the age gap between the generations is usually greater (given delayed child bearing), because extended families have shrunk dramatically, and because they enjoy preferential access to other social venues, due to language and income.[34] Policies requiring *Aussiedler* and refugees to live in specially designated areas for three years, or face a loss of special benefits, have produced similar spatial concentrations denounced by integration experts. Anti-immigration authorities conflate cause with effect: discriminatory housing practices continually isolate and marginalize foreigners who are then accused of failing to "integrate themselves."

The 1980s witnessed a great deal of self-organization, along with efforts to enter the broader political community. Identity formation included but was not limited to processes of self-ethnicization. As Özcan determined, most formal Turkish organizations created between 1960 and 1980 displayed a clear right-wing or left-wing orientation; those established after 1980 were committed to interest representation, community development, and associational networking. Among the more prominent ones arising during this decade were the Initiative for Equal Rights in Integration (IGI), the Turkish Community in Berlin and the Union of Turkish Immigrants in Hamburg (both known by the initials TGB), the Turkish Union of Equal Rights in Berlin West (BTT), and the Turkish Parents Organization.

Older entities like the TGD and the TBB would later blossom into national roof organizations. They took up direct contact with federal ministries, the Bundestag, political parties, and welfare organizations. Though lacking grassroots legitimation, they all began to "make claims" focusing on living conditions in Germany and moved to democratize their own structures. Four of twelve TBB Executive Board members are female; the director's wife, Dilek Kolat, is a member of the Berlin Assembly. By the 1990s, they would be joined by rapidly growing economic entities like the Association of Turkish-German Entrepreneurs. The name refers to (second generation) Turkish-German employers, not to a federation of Turkish actors and their native-born counterparts.

Beyond the introduction of yet another law regulating the behavior of "foreigners" already in the country, the Kohl Government did little to recognize immigration as a fact of German life. Indeed, the chancellor failed to take decisive action against sensational xenophobic and neo-Nazi violence after unification. The first year of unity gave rise to 2,368 "xenophobic" incidents and 1,483 "physical attacks." Three-fourths of the arson attacks occurred in the old *Länder*, despite the tendency to fault "the communist legacy" for skinhead violence in the East.[35] The Office of Constitutional Protection registered a 54 percent increase in 1992: 2,584 physical attacks (7,121 right-wing acts), resulting in seventeen deaths—nine in the West, eight in the East. 1993 brought 8,109 rightwing crimes but "only" 1,814 acts of violence against foreigners, Jews, and other "political opponents" (8 fatalities). Among 11,515 individuals indicted for rightwing offenses, 60 percent were minors, 95 percent male. Attacks occurred in towns stretching from Aalen to Zwickau, the most sensational of which were seen in Hoyerswerda (1991), Rostock (1992), Mölln (1992), and Solingen (1993).[36] Following riots in Rostock, Kohl declared in a television interview, "xenophobia is a disgrace for our country." On the second anniversary of unification, he decried the forces "of right and left-extremism [that] had caused so much suffering" to Germans, and criticized disruptive elements who demonstrated against the violence in Berlin. Protestors' willingness to besmirch Germany's image in the eyes of the world was "the real crime."[37]

An arson attack on a private home in Mölln on 22 November 1992 killed a Turkish grandmother and two children and injured nine others. Bahide Arslan (age fifty-one) had lived in Germany for more than a decade; her granddaughter Yeliz Arslan (ten) had been born in Mölln, while her niece Ayse Yilmaz (fourteen) was visiting for the first time. Nearly ten thousand residents participated in a memorial service, accompanied by demonstrations in more than twelve cities, before the victims were flown back to Turkey for burial. The chancellor (who did not attend) described the arson deaths in Mölln as "a particularly depressing example of the increase in crime in Germany," with no specific reference to the nationalistic nature of the attack.[38]

During a 1993 visit to Turkey, Kohl extended a verbal guarantee that the Mölln tragedy would never be repeated. Less than two weeks later, the town of Solingen in prosperous North Rhine-Westphalia was rocked by more arson-related deaths. At 1:38 am on 29 May, four neo-Nazi youths set fire to a three-story house owned by the Genc Family. Trapped on the second floor, Kamil Genc's two sisters Hatice (age eighteen) and Gürsun (twenty-seven), his niece Gülüstan (twelve), and daughters Hülya (nine) and Saime (four) perished in the blaze; nine more were seriously injured, including a six-month-old infant and a fifteen-year-old boy. Arriving in 1970, the family had purchased their house in 1981. Urged to participate in the memorial ceremony, Kohl declared that he had no intention of becoming a "Chancellor of Funerals."

While some officials rushed to visit the injured, politicians of all persuasions called for dual citizenship, with the exception of Kohl. Two days of turbulence ensued, as three thousand radical Turkish demonstrators visited the arson site. Some attacked police cars, smashed windows, and hurled Molotov cocktails; sixty-two were arrested. State Interior Minister Herbert Schnoor deployed fourteen hundred police from the special Federal G-9 Anti-Terrorist Unit, threatening immediate deportation of all who engaged in violence.[39] President Richard von Weizsäcker spoke at a memorial service attracting six thousand participants in Cologne on 4 June. By late 1993, the count stood at 2,232 acts of right-extremist violence. Kohl called for "the utmost legal firmness" in cases of demonstrated hostility to foreigners, at the same time the vehement debate over constitutional protection for asylum seekers added legitimacy to extremist claims that "Germany belongs to the Germans."

Migration as a Family Project

Given their attachment to a myth of return consciously cultivated for three decades, hardliners remain pessimistic as to the integration potential of ethnic-Turkish residents. Migration theorists, by contrast, are too optimistic as to the integration that is likely to occur "naturally" as a function of generational change. Politicians pay verbal homage to an environment increasingly shaped by transnational forces but pretend that globalization is unrelated to developments in their own backyard; they search in vain for evidence of an emotional if not organic attachment to the German nation that even most of the natives lack. Cem Özdemir (born 1965 in Bad Urbach), the first "Turkish" compatriate to enter the Bundestag, described his own naturalization process as a "long march *against* the institutions." He celebrated the day he finally received his German passport with a costume party where "several friends just couldn't comprehend it: Why should any one be happy about the fact that he's now a German? They found it just terrible: Everyone inside the enlightened left-liberal spectrum was ashamed of being German, and this guy was happy!"[40]

Optimistic projections of generationally driven integration stem from a heavy reliance on theoretical models grounded in the US-American experience. The "Chicago School" model erroneously assumed that there was such a thing as *the* American experience. In fact, the migration histories of African-Americans, Mexican-Americans, Chinese-Americans, and Japanese-Americans differed from those of European, Puerto Rican, and even Philippine immigrants in fundamental legal, political, and economic ways. Gender, race, and class first became respectable components of migration discourse following changes in US law mandated by the 1964 Civil Rights Act.[41]

R. E. Park and E. W. Burgess defined *assimilation* in the 1920s as "a process of interpenetration and fusion in which persons and groups acquire the memories, sentiments, and attitudes of other persons and groups and, by sharing their experience and history, are incorporated with them in a common cultural life." This process was deemed inevitable, progressive, and "irreversible."[42] Drawing on an idealized melting-pot image, "straight-line assimilationists" held that new groups required three generations to run the gamut of integration. The model posits that the first cohorts to arrive comprise an internally homogenous, cohesive group; the second bears the brunt of cultural conflicts and identity crises, caught between parental and host-society norms. The third set, enjoying greater language competence and residential mobility, purportedly dissolves into mainstream culture. Each generation encounters "a distinctive set of issues in its relationship to the larger society and the ethnic group, and their resolution brings about distinctive patterns of accommodation."[43]

Although Chicago still comprises one of the most residentially segregated cities in the US, these scholars overlooked deliberate patterns of racial exclusion as late as the 1950s.[44] Few considered the possibility of re-ethnicization, as in the case of the Black and Red Power movements (well beyond the "third" generation) in the late 1960s. Challenging the inevitability of assimilation, M. L. Hansen deemed possible ethnic revival "the problem of the third generation." Successive cohorts may reawaken to "homeland" culture, especially under continuing marginalization and discrimination. The more limited the external contact, the greater the prospect of self-ethnicization, especially among youths denied a positive identity by the dominant culture. Hansen construed ethnic revival as part of a cultural transformation that contributed to the "symbolic complex" of a minority subculture. He did not recognize it as a process that could lead marginalized citizens to reject the host culture and even pray for its collapse, as witnessed literally among the fundamentalist followers of Cemaleddin Kaplan (the "Khomeini of Cologne"), and his son Mehtin Kaplan, for example.[45]

Richard Alba and Victor Nee understand the incorporation process as a sequential one: each generation embodies a new stage of adjustment to the host society and another step away from an ethnic "ground zero," as minority-enclave members enter primary groups and forge relationships with the dominant culture. Still embracing generations as the motor for change, Alba and Nee admit that the process is not necessarily linear. According to their "bumpy-line" theory of ethnicity, "there is a generational dynamic behind ethnic change" that "moves, perhaps with tangents, in the general direction of assimilation."[46] Concentrating on structural and spatial integration, these scholars note demographic changes that can alter a minority's potential for influence; as the relative size of the group expands, power shifts become more likely and the probability of "chance meetings," a decline in social distance (at school or work), a rise in self-consciousness, and even the prospect of group protest increases.

Problems of terminology aside, US theorists presume that a second generation will enjoy formal rights of citizenship by virtue of *jus soli*, a condition that did not apply to German-Turks prior to 1999. Their emphasis on intermarriage as an indicator of assimilation also misses the mark in Germany, where these statistics can refer to a union between two persons of Turkish descent, one of whom is a naturalized citizen, rather than between a "foreigner" and a native German—Helmut Kohl's son nothwithstanding. As noted in the Sixth Family Report of 2000, "an increase in the number of German-Turkish marriages is not necessarily an indicator for a coming-together. . . . The number of marriages in which the partners have two different passports but the same ethnic-cultural heritage is growing as fast as the number of marriages in which naturalization means that the partners hold identical citizenship, even though their ethnic-cultural background differs substantially."[47] An example of the latter is a union between a newly arrived *Aussiedlerin* from Kazhakstan and a native-born male—the former is automatically registered as "German."

Table 2.2 Frequent Nationalities for German-Foreigner Marriages (1997)

German men marrying women from...		*German women marrying men from...*	
Absolute number		Absolute Number	
Poland	5,230	Yugoslavia	5,858
Russian Federation	1,886	Turkey	3,934
Thailand	1,617	Italy	1,772
Yugoslavia	1,260	United States	1,220
Turkey	1,073	Austria	934
Austria	919	Poland	780
Italy	815	Great Britain	776
Czech Republic	766	Netherlands	730
Philippines	672	Russian Federation	560
France	595	Greece	524

Source: Adapted from *Sechster Familienbericht*, Deutscher Bundestag, Drucksache 14/4357, October 2000, 81ff.

Advances in information technologies have "reduced the search costs for migration opportunities and changes in transportation technologies have reduced the economic costs of migration, but the social costs have remained essentially unchanged."[48] The Sixth Family Report stressed that human capital imports not only induce cumulative, interactive changes in the host society but also in the countries left behind. Migration reshapes the intergenerational learning process as well as family cycles, altering the balance between individual identity and family identification. Family dynamics are moreover situated in a much larger, rapidly changing socioeconomic context, with significant consequences for child development.

Whereas the first generation had to learn German to "keep up with current events" through local radio, television, and newspaper reports, the Internet and satellite technology give migrants immediate access to breaking news and entertainment in their mother tongue. This reinforces feelings of cutural affinity with the country of origin, and also makes it less compelling for imported brides or children to learn German before the latter start school. The ability to stay connected to the old country, however, does not mean that migrants lack an affinity for their new one. Turkish retirees returning to the land of their birth often discover that they no longer fit in, or that they prefer the creature comforts and generous health care found in Germany. One of the fastest growing groups of "border hoppers" consists of pensioners who spend winters in one country and summers in another.[49] The number of elderly migrants doubled between 1987 and 1997.

My studies of generational asymmetries among Eastern and Western Germans compel me to view comparable changes among Turkish residents in a larger context.[50] Plunging fertility rates among the natives over the last two decades, coupled with the imminent retirement of Baby Boomers, comprise one driving force behind the paradigm shift in German citizenship and immigration policies. Another is a major break with traditional notions of what constitutes a proper German family, to the chagrin of those politicians who preferred the days when men were breadwinners, women were homemakers, and the world was "in order," i.e., securing male opportunities at female expense. Germany's reluctance to reconfigure key structures—its half-day schools, its quasi-feudal universities, its rigid labor-permit system, and breadwinner-dependent welfare policies, just for starters—renders it unprepared to meet the demands of the "new order world order."

Germany is now home to families of all sorts. One finds lots of cohabitation without the benefit of holy matrimony, families consisting of same-sex partners, single parents, and blended households. By 1993, 8 percent of all German families had at least one foreign citizen in their midst. The irony is that foreigners are most likely to adhere to the traditional model preferred by politicians espousing family values, if only because spouses are precluded from entering the paid labor force in anything other than a house-cleaning capacity. Claiming they could lose their "culture" as a result of alien child-rearing practices, nativists fail to recognize that outdated social structures generate much higher levels of dissatisfaction among educated German women, to the detriment of national fertility rates.

Presenting Germany as a progressive, child-friendly place, the Sixth Family Report claims that "the normative picture of the German majority-society is increasingly determined by a life-long responsibility of parents for their children and a strengthening of child-rights, whereby material goods and services are transferred almost exclusively in an intergenerational way from the parental to the child generation (while transfers from younger to older cohorts take place indirectly over the collective social security system)." It continues, "generational relationships among other cultures frequently rely on children's life-long obligation to their parents that begin quite early and leads to comparatively strong parental rights."[51]

What German children? National birthrates have plunged since the 1970s for the very reason that millions of adults are simply not willing to make the material sacrifices the system requires. The cost of raising a child for eighteen years is estimated at €450,000. Fertility rates were much higher among East Germans (90 percent) facing chronic material shortages than among wealthy Westerners (60 percent) prior to unity. Families with children evince higher poverty rates than those without. As late as 1998, childless households in which the wife did not engage in paid labor derived greater tax advantages than families with children and/or an employed mother. The tax structure and the insurance system support marriage in and of itself, despite the special protection accorded mothers and children by Article 6 GG.[52] Families of foreign origin quickly modify their collective behavior according to demands imposed by the host society: Between 1975 and 1985, births among women from the "recruitment nations" fell by one-third to one-half (2.08 among Turkish females by 2000).[53]

Migration is a family project, affected by personal as well as public cycles of opportunity. Families of ethnic origin differ substantially from one another in terms of their integration opportunities, however. Minorities experience varying degrees of acceptance, enjoy diverse residency rights and socioeconomic benefits. They differ significantly in terms of normative family orientations (generational obligations, household division of labor, gender roles, expectations on the state, etc.). Some become minorities *within* the minority, e.g., Kurds among Turks. Viewing long-term residents, temporary refugees, recognized asylum-seekers, "Russian" resettlers and illegal workers as a single *Ausländerproblem*, Germans assume that every nationality constitutes a closed group desirous of intense contacts and social relations among members.

This misperception derives from the urban/geographic concentration of ethnic groups, whereby a select segment of a nationality is deemed "representative" of the whole. Average citizens assume that residential concentration is a matter of choice, despite evidence of housing discrimination. During a June 2003 interview, Karin Korte, migration commissioner for Neukölln, pointed out that even within the four zones comprising one of Berlin's most "multicultural" districts (Neukölln, Britz, Buckow, Rudow), Turks had troubles with "the Arabs" (Lebanese, Palestinians) in the northern quarter, who, in turn, had little use for ex-Yugoslavians, who also disliked *Aussiedler* youth in the "southern" part of the *Kiez* (the 'hood). Knowing very little about Attaturk's forced secularization of Turkish society in the 1920s, Germans presume that migrants' religious orientations predetermine other social relationships, although most Turkish adults are not overtly pious.[54]

From *Ausländer* to *Inländer*: Generational Dynamics

A closer look at generational change among Germany's Turkish community testifies to critical linkages between education and employment, on the one hand, social integration and mobility, on the other. These links serve as concrete indicators of systemic or structural integration. Early guestworker experiences show that changes in the economic system tied to technological advances often afford migrants, legal or illegal, new competitive advantages that render them indispensable to employers. The high physical demands of postwar manufacturing produced countless opportunities for skilled and unskilled laborers during a period of unprecedented expansion. By the late 1970s, foreigners were disproportionately concentrated in the sectors subject to automation, structural adjustment, and industry transfers to less-developed countries They witnessed a dramatic decrease in the "value" of their crucial structural position, e.g., in coal and steel production, without a commensurate increase in their access to new market sectors.

A family's decision to invest in childhood education qua occupational training depends on its long-term settlement plans. Permanent residents apply different criteria than laborers repeatedly urged to "go home." Formal qualifications geared to a highly regulated, career-tracked labor market may prove of little use in a less developed country of origin. The myth of return led many parents through the early 1980s to push for the kind of job training that would "transfer back" to Turkey.

The first guestworkers—members of the Pioneer Generation—consisted predominantly of males born in Turkey between 1935 and 1955. Chain migration rendered this group the most homogeneous of the three generations, though there were noticeable differences between Turks who settled in the Ruhrpot from the northern mountains or east Anatolia, and those who gravitated to Berlin or Frankfurt from Kurdish areas or the southeast. Although 40 percent

(25 percent among women) arrived with occupational certification, the German labor market did not offer jobs commensurate with their training.[55] Contractual agreements confined them to workers' barracks short on creature comforts, like familiar cuisine and music. Evincing few language skills enabling them to interact with the host society, they established soccer teams and private "mosques" (usually a single room in a run-down tenement) to overcome the intense isolation that fueled a desire to earn money quickly and go home.[56]

When employers extended their contracts, younger men rented apartments, usually without central heating or bathrooms, bringing over wives and children between 1965 and 1975.[57] Social advances among the Pioneer Generation "were seldom tied to career mobility but were connected to extensive labor activity coupled with high savings and investment activity (mostly through property acquisition and entrepreneurship in the homeland) as well as through a shift to self-employment."[58] These years marked the Economic-Miracle phase, yet guestworkers engaged in limited consumption. Self-imposed poverty in the host country—in favor of accumulated wealth, and proving one's success back in the village—often led to inferiority complexes among the offspring, anxious to emulate the "material girl and boy" consumption of their German peers.

Hermann Tertilt describes one adolescent, "Nurettin," who winds up as a violent gang member, acting out humiliation and resentment that he dare not express to his father, a sanitation worker. His mother, who arrived first, worked for a large cleaning firm. For years, ten family members were forced to share a three-room apartment, seventy square meters, in a run-down section of Frankfurt/Main. Tertil writes:

> "To feel big," "to have money," "to have power," "to wear good clothes," to break out of his petty and confining family life—these are all motives that run through Nurettin's life like a red thread. . . . His father has invested all of his savings over the years in the home town of Eskisehir, to fulfill his dream of building a house. But half of the village people . . . have already abandoned the town and moved into larger Turkish cities or emigrated to Europe. . . . The five story house that his father had built, he called it "his villa," is quite large, with six rooms per floor and very spacious . . . for each [married sibling's] family, a whole floor. . . . Up to now the house is only being used once a year, when they meet with uncles and aunts [living in Belgium, France and Germany] during their vacation trip to Turkey. Then everyone's return is celebrated and they regularly slaughter a sheep. . . . Instead of doing justice to his responsibility as head of the family and reducing the hardships they face in the host country, [his father] invests in an illusion: the unforeseeable return home.[59]

Widespread housing discrimination complicated and delayed processes of family unification. Roughly half of the original guestworker offspring, characterized here as the *Ausländer* or Outlander Generation, were born between 1955 and 1975 in Turkey, where they are labelled *Deutschländer*. Many entered the country as children, providing varying degrees of exposure to German schools. They were in their teens/twenties when recruitment halted in 1973.

This group developed a different sensitivity to persistent discrimination, due to gradually rising educational qualifications and a lack of emotional identification with the "homeland," along with exposure to New Left movements of the 1960s and 1970s. Political consciousness was bolstered by an influx of Turkish intellectuals after the 1980 military coup but also fractured by the fundamentalist revolution in Iran and human rights violations against Kurds in Turkey and Iraq. Children were quick to acquire language skills at school, leading them to challenge the authority of parents who depended on them when visiting doctors, service agencies, and registration bureaus. This is not to argue that all were fluent in German or even proficient in the "mother tongue." The only places offering formal instruction were the Koran schools financed by the Turkish, Saudi Arabian, and Iranian governments.

Among the second generation, "it is partly a considerable increase in higher level school certification (still lagging behind the gains of German working-class children) that leads to clear intergenerational status mobility among families of foreign origin."[60] "Politically accepted and partially supported," school-aged youth did not face as much legal uncertainty concerning residency, but lawmakers' refusal to promote active integration solidified indirect patterns of discrimination.[61] Economic restructuring did not offer equivalent earning opportunities, rendering the successor generation in many ways more vulnerable. This compounded family-based educational deficits: parents could neither help with homework nor grasp the complicated nature of the dual system of vocational training. Facing prejudice and language problems, Turkish children were disproportionately channeled into the dead-end elementary school (*Hauptschule*) ending in ninth grade. While the overall number of "learning-impaired children" declined nearly 50 percent between 1976 and 1990, the share of migrant children assigned to special-education schools rose to 4.3 percent; the rates were 1.6 percent in Berlin, 3 percent in Bavaria, and 5.8 percent in Baden Württemberg, reflecting different educational "standards."[62]

Wolfgang Seifert compares the incorporation experiences of 16 to 25-year-olds who sought to enter the paid-labor force between 1984 and 1989. First and second generation youth differed in terms of socioeconomic mobility, access to higher schooling, vocational training, German language skills, interethnic contacts, ethnic identification, and occupational prestige. Based on Socio-Economic Panel (SOEP) data, 81 percent rated their own language skills as "good/very good" in 1989, yet only 14 percent felt "German."[63] Women identified more strongly with the host culture, perhaps because it afforded them more education and role diversity (albeit less occupational choice and lower pay than males). Age of entry affected access to the secondary labor market, resulting in less security, lower pay, and tougher working conditions. Three-fourths of the first-time job seekers in 1984 wound up as un-/semiskilled workers, compared to 58 percent in 1989.[64] Both cohorts were under-represented in the tertiary sector, less than 10 percent. As families learned to navigate the system, the share of foreign apprentices (age fifteen to eighteen) rose from 27 percent (1987) to 40 percent (1992), versus 70–80 percent among indigenous adolescents. Young *Ausländer* were over-represented in less future-oriented branches, as welders, auto-mechanics, grocery clerks, and beauticians.[65]

Members of this Outlander Generation integrated themselves at the lower end of the food chain or career ladder during a period of stagflation and mass unemployment. They were often urged to enter the labor force quickly, to "save" for the return home, or to pursue occupations that would foster their reintegration in Turkey. They learned that "although the ethnic economy is an important institutional arrangement for immigrants, by no means does it provide the main route for their economic advancement."[66] Initially confined to döner stands, kiosks, restaurants, grocery stores, and small retail outlets, the fledgling ethnic economy did provide new jobs as mining and construction work declined, but takers also faced lower wages, benefits, and promotional ceilings, restricting future mobility. Ethnic youth enjoyed better access to education, but the inequalities among types of schools increased rapidly over time.

Even males who followed in their fathers' occupational footsteps saw more downward than upward mobility. The jobless rate among Turkish workers rose from 4.2 percent in 1979, to 14.8 percent in 1985, dropping to 10 percent in 1990 but more than doubling to 24 percent in 1997; the latter figure clearly encompasses Turkish youth schooled in Germany.[67] Old barriers, such as temporary work permits and lack of education or language skills, were replaced by new ones connected to infrastructures and select forms of social capital, that is, ties to autochthonous feeder institutions. Career choices for the second generation were limited by mechanisms other than birthplace ("pre-selection" criteria), shielding natives from competition. Esser notes: "Despite all intensified efforts in the educational domain, migrant children are quite obviously the losers in the context of ever increasing competition and the further expansion of the educational system. Since education constitutes a central career resource for labor market positioning, indirect become direct disadvantages, largely due to segregation dynamics."[68] By 2000, 40 percent of all "foreign" students at tertiary institutions had attended German schools; 77 percent of these *Bildungsinländer* stem from working class families, only 7 percent from families of high social standing.[69]

Youth of Turkish descent are unable to reap the presumed benefits of higher education, owing to strict but subtle applications of the merit principle. Social mobility not only depends on formal diplomas; one's chances of moving up the

Table 2.3 German and Foreign "School-Leavers," 1994–1999 (percent)

Type of School	German Youth			Foreign Youth		
	1994	1997	1999	1994	1997	1999
Without lower Secondary Certificate	7.8	7.7	5.7	20.4	19.4	15.1
With lower Secondary Certificate (*Hauptschulabschluss*)	25.4	25.2	20.9	43.5	42.7	40.0
With Intermediate School Certificate (*Realschulabschluss*)	41.0	40.9	43.3	28.5	28.1	32.7
With Certificate of aptitude for specialized higher schools (*Fachhochschulreife*)	0.8	0.7	1.1	0.7	0.8	1.3
With Certificate of aptitude For University (*Abitur*)	25.0	25.5	29.0	8.9	9.0	10.9

Source: *Structuring Immigration, Fostering Integration*. Report by the Independent Commission on Migration to Germany (Berlin: July 2001): 211.

career ladder in white-collar domains are grounded in subjective qualities, like a perceived "ability to get along." Michael Bommes argues that ethnic minorities are unable to access positions in the new economy due to a lack of appropriate organizational ties. Income distribution and promotional resources are predetermined through core associations, memberships that structure expectations and specify the costs of "entry and exit."[70] In a highly regulated market, jobs are distributed not on the basis of fairness but by way of contacts, guilds, agencies, and professional groups that serve as "feeders" and/or gatekeepers. Associational structures thus possess a formal power to exclude; if they did not distinguish between insiders and outsiders, there would be no reason for their existence.

Migrant connections outside the ethnic community are still inferior to those of nationals, reproducing occupational inequalities. The same ethnic networks that promote a sense of belonging, along with day-to-day access to identity-confirming goods among first-wave cohorts (vegetable markets, bakeries, soccer clubs) can limit the occupational choices of subsequent waves. Attempting to carve out a space for themselves in the industrial domain, members of the Pioneer Generation built their own networks to ensure that offspring had a chance to "inherit" the jobs once held by fathers. Community-internal groups offered few chances, at that juncture, for building bridges to the dominant culture. They remained shut out of public and political processes, since lawmakers continued to delude themselves that most would eventually "go home."

Even plant-internal seniority principles in manufacturing were delineated according to ethnic roots. Companies, by law, enjoy the power to define their own recruitment structures: "The formal, career related rules for inclusion, interacting with prescribed company recruitment mechanisms, stabilize the ever more established inclusion and distribution structures, and with that, the systematic disadvantages that affect the inclusion of migrant laborers and their children—largely without any recourse to a complicated, explicit ethnically defined repertoire of attributes."[71] Thus, successor cohorts were allowed in but were also confined to the same production sectors as their fathers, despite union claims that all workers were being drawn into works councils and continuing education programs. Minority status within company and union structures reinforces and is reinforced by minority status in society at large.[72] Having been designated "foreigners" in other contexts, German-educated Turks (*Bildungsinländer*) remain outsiders through all walks of life.

Members of the second generation continued the pattern of marrying and bearing children earlier than average West Germans. Comprising the *Inländer* Generation, born between 1975 and 1995, these offspring are not as homogenous as presumed, due to the ongoing practice of bride or groom importation.[73] Nearly all were born in Germany; at least one parent enjoys language fluency and permanent-resident status. Yet according to the 1996 microcensus, 56 percent of German-Turkish youth and 50 percent of Italian parentage did not even finish the *Hauptschule*, suggesting a worsening of educational outcomes among the third generation.[74]

In terms of social integration, the youngest cohorts are doing quite well. Members of the *Inländer* Generation possess an intercultural competence that could contribute significantly to the national economy in the face of EU enlargement. They switch casually back and forth between languages in stores and in the subway; they confidently admonish Germans who make disparaging remarks (thinking they won't understand) to "mind their manners"; they eat at Burger King, wear short skirts, baggy jeans, platform shoes, and anything else comprising the fashion du jour, sometimes combined with a headscarf. They pick and choose among elements of German culture, just as they identify selectively, consciously, and self-confidently with the traditions of their parents and grandparents.

Missing Links: Gender and Generational Change

Although Turkish women are regularly portrayed as either exotic or oppressed, their experiences in Germany reflect a paradox noted in the BMFFJ report on foreign families: "It is exactly the population groups with the greatest collective orientation and the strongest group ties involving ethnic counterparts . . . that have shown themselves to be most mobile in regional and status terms, and whose life styles have tended to diverge the most from their original social-cultural heritage."[75]

Family unification, part of the strategy to block labor migration in the 1980s, soon led to population growth. In North Rhine-Westphalia, 14 percent of the Turkish residents entered as guestworkers, 57 percent under family unification; 21.6 percent were born in Germany.[76] New bans on spouse employment imposed through 1979 mandated a three-year waiting period for Turkish partners, four years for the rest. The Foreigners Act of 1990 eliminated the waiting period for those joining spouses with unlimited residence permits. Women lost residency rights (deportation within eighteen months) and other breadwinner-dependent benefits if the marriage dissolved before a specified number of years (not repealed until 1997). Rules for same-sex partners were even more restrictive until 1998. Turkish migration rose, on average, by thirty-five thousand per year from 1986 to 1991, and by twenty-one thousand from 1992 to 1999.

Even researchers advocating foreigner-friendly integration policies ignore the disparate opportunity structures open to women of non-national origin, shaped by divergent national legal frameworks. Esser claims that the "assimilation tempo" among Germany's Turks lags far behind other ethnicities, owing to their well developed enclaves and community associations in major cities. I challenge this on two counts. First, the "lag" rests not with aliens but rather with German citizenship rules: in 2002, more than sixteen thousand naturalization applications were sitting unprocessed on bureaucrats' desks in the Berlin districts of Neukölln and Kreuzberg alone. The number accorded citizenship rose from 580 in 1982, 1,713 in 1989 (bureaucratic discretion), and 7,377 in 1992 (automatic entitlement), to 59,664 in 1998.[77] Naturalization by way of entitlement has increased eightfold, while discretionary naturalizations "merely" tripled between 1988 and 1998. Structure and access are issues that must be addressed by the host society.

Turkish women possess different participatory rights depending on the host country. They are most restricted in Germany (where more reside than in any other EU state) but enjoy liberal citizenship policies in the Netherlands, Denmark, and France. Comprising a much smaller group in the UK, they are classified as white.[78] The Federal Institute for Population Research reports that Turkish women seeking naturalization exceeded males by 14 percent in 2000; females age eighteen to thirty-five are twice as likely to become citizens, albeit many as newly imported marriage partners.[79] Naturalizations jumped with each liberalization, from 3,529 in 1991 to 12,915 in 1993 to 59,664 in 1998; 103,900 filed for new passports under the 1999 Citizenship Law (41 percent of the total); 35,871 were issued to Turkish children younger than eighteen.[80]

Secondly, authorities refuse to address the tricky problem of "bride imports," much less their impact on language acquisition among youth. Privacy laws prevented the Foreign Ministry from collecting data on family unification prior to 1996. New arrivals from Turkey rose from 55,886 in 1996 to 75,888 in 2000. The importation of cousins as marriage partners is a taboo topic. The Basic Law (Article 6) accords special protection to families, though forced marriages are illegal. Despite near parity between women and men, 20–40 percent of Germany's Turkish couples landed in arranged marriages involving a relative. In Berlin, 41 percent of the 30 to 39-year-olds polled (64 percent of the males) "found" a spouse in Turkey.[81] Medical researchers have registered increasing rates of congenital illness and birth defects among the local Turkish population, attributed to intermarriage among close relatives.[82]

What consequences do spouse imports hold for "lagging" integration? Intricately connected, gender relations and generational change shape prospects for socioeconomic integration. One byproduct is re-ethnicization. Instead of decreasing over time, as younger cohorts acquire citizenship, make German friends, and embrace "dual identities," marriage migration has grown since the 1990s. Conservatively raised males of Turkish origin are reluctant to form unions with "emancipated" women of non-homeland origin. Lacking adequate human capital, their limited social mobility intensifies low self-esteem, producing a *Trotz* ("I'll show you") reaction. They, in turn, seek wives who will not outshine them and are prepared to restrict their consumption. They also prefer to marry younger, to ensure a comfortable home environment for themselves—a trend that finds its parallel among German men seeking "brides" from Thailand or Russia.

Enter the Turkish bride from the home village: Rural women marry younger, have less schooling, help the family to control its economic resources, and know little about host-country culture. Nor do they speak German. Once they arrive, women as young as sixteen are quite isolated, restricted to the company of comparable females. Waiting periods and the paucity of day-care failities confine them to maternal roles; children who spend all day at home in ethnically concentrated neighborhoods are unlikely to learn German. Nearly 75 percent do not attend preschools and thus fall prey to educational path dependency; 91 percent of all preschoolers move on to intermediate schools, but only 67 percent without this background do. The dearth of preschool places is a function of neighborhood concentration—reflecting decades of housing discrimination. Local mosques (where headscarves are not a problem) also offer childcare. Merely 7 percent claim in surveys that they have no desire to learn German; many turn to mosques for language courses, or rely on Turkish media for what Germans fail to provide. Foreign offspring account for 70–90 percent of the enrollees at the schools these children eventually attend.

So why can't these kids speak fluent German as members of the "third generation"? Such youngsters do not constitute a third generation, born of second-generation parents socialized in Germany by way of six to thirteen years of formal schooling. Rather, children born of arranged marriages repeat the experiences of first-wave imported children. The social isolation of the mothers feeds the marginalization of ethnic youth. Politicians pushed to limit entry to children age twelve or younger, as if this step would supply teachers with the skills needed to impart German as a second language. The problem remains that too many children born in Germany have limited access to native speakers until well beyond the age where they can absorb vocabulary and complex grammar rules. Turkish women are thus the linchpin of integration: Instruct the mother, in order to "educate the village."

Based on the assumption that "men produce, women reproduce," female migrants remain subject to stereotypes involving excessive breeding. Ethnic family structures have nonetheless changed dramatically as a function of mandatory schooling and dual-wage households. Turkish-German women outpace males in formal education. Besides delaying marriage for two to five years in order to advance their studies or careers, they are reluctant to marry "Turkish macho-men from Kreuzberg," says Green parliamentarian Özcan Mutlu. They speak better German than Turkish, rendering family communication "Babylonic." Sociologist Asiye Kaya uses German with her sister but only passively understood her mother's Zusa dialect; she considers Turkish her third language, followed by English.

Although "foreign" women age twenty to thirty-nine account for two-thirds of all live births in the FRG, they have adapted to smaller families and higher living costs in the host state. The average fertility rate for German women is 1.5, 2.3 for Turkish women in the FRG, and 2.6 children for families back in Turkey.[83] Even the better educated among them resort to stay-at-home Turkish moms for childcare or local centers populated largely by ethnic offspring, given Germany's chronic lack of places. Highlighting generational changes in her own family, Turkish-German writer Naila Minai observes: "My Turkish-Tartar grandmother was educated at home, married a polygamist man and did not take off her veil even on journeys abroad. . . . My mother never wore a veil, she went to local schools and eventually became a housewife in a monogamous marriage. I left my family to study in the United States and Europe [and] hitchhiked from country to country."[84]

No wonder authorities ignore the pivotal role of gender relations in fostering integration: the Independent Commission consisted of two women (both retired) and twenty-four men (one of whom was foreign-born). Not one of the eighteen studies commissioned by the ICI addressed gender relations; indeed, only one of 25 persons credited with authorship was female. A new Federal Council on Immigration, established by Interior Minister Schily in May 2003, consisted of Chair Rita Süssmuth (CDU) and five men, before it was abruptly dissolved in December 2004.

Werner Schiffauer likewise finds that "growing up in Germany" effectively throws young Turks "back into the group they wanted to break away from."[85] Men of the first generation, with limited formal education, turned to Islam for comfort, especially after turning forty. As the September 11th attacks revealed, younger men pursuing Islam, fundamentalist or not, are often university educated; they study Arabic and the Koran, using intellectual tools acquired in Germany. They argue their cases based on Enlightenment concepts like human rights, religious freedom, and human dignity, pushing the host country to make space for Islamic practices. For mobility-savvy individuals, the rediscovery of Islamic identity and the pursuit of "an ethnically and denominationally cohesive community" grants "young Turks who feel at home in both the German and Turkish context, a chance to advance swiftly into key positions as self-confident representatives of the interest of their minority vis-à-vis the host society."[86]

Schiffauer presents cases of Turkish teens who tried to challenge traditional family authority, emulate pop culture and clothing tastes—hoping to "integrate themselves"—only to be branded *Turkish* during a critical stage of masculine identity formation. "Seyfullah," the youngest brother of a counter-Caliph, was one of six children born in Germany in 1976. He joined the Kaplan community in Cologne in 1981 at age fifteen, describing himself as "a Turkish skateboarder, with lots of German friends but no internal peace"; encountering problems at school, he started hanging out with other troubled types. In Berlin, he found his brother's apartment full of Islamic materials; now he "can't stop reading."[87] Self-ethnicization offers a life raft for youths who have been told the German boat is full.

The strategy of self-outing or re-ethnicization through religion enables marginalized youth to turn a stigmatized attribute into a strength, allowing them to demand recognition instead of begging for it. In turning to groups linked to the right-radical *Milli Görüs* organization, some third-generation youth reach an "Archemedian point" enabling them to do three things: to "articulate opposition and loyalty simultaneously with the Turkish community and parents, find intellectual satisfaction in a diasporic identity, and cultivate more effective strategies for facing regular discrimination in FRG."[88] Schiffauer warns that the ethnic revival strategy may be "too good" at creating autonomous identities: "divine truth" brings self-empowerment, but it can also generate intolerance and self-righteousness.

Insofar as education constitutes a key resource for labor market positioning, children of migrant origin suffer multiple disadvantages. They are least likely to reap benefits when opportunity levels rise, due to subjective applications of the merit principle, determining who can be trusted to "fit in." Here migration logic takes an interesting twist: the benefits of inclusion for first-generation workers (family or village ties) have become a roadblock for successor cohorts. Turkish fathers who were modestly successful in semi-skilled, working-class jobs (avoided by Germans) persuaded their sons to pursue similar occupations that would prove useful upon "return" to Turkey. These jobs have disappeared into the vortex of structural unemployment; 5,286 Turks were used to mine German coal in 1963; by 1968, 78 mines (54 percent) had been shut down, but Turks accounted for 85 percent of 23,600 foreigners left in this sector by 1975.[89] Very few mines function today; those who found jobs elsewhere are subject to low glass ceilings within the ethnic economy.

The Outlanders-turned-Inlanders have actively lobbied for better education for their own children, overwhelmingly born in Germany. As late as 2001, however, Turkish and Italian children still had the worst grades at mid-levels; Yugoslavs and *Aussiedler* pupils do better but lag behind Germans. Only one-third of the former are channeled into *Hauptschulen* (40 percent among *Aussiedler*), compared to three-fourths of all Turkish children, and four-fifths of the Italians. Their grades for German language arts and math differ significantly, limiting their transfer from fourth grade to a *Realschule* or *Gymnasium*, based on a study of six elementary schools in Mannheim. Between 1995 and 1998, the share of apprenticeships filled by "foreigners" sank from 41.1 percent to 37.8 percent, while rising from 63.8 percent to 65 percent among nationals. In 1998–1999, 89 percent of nearly one million ethnic children left school without certification.[90]

Only pupils of Spanish descent have improved their position over time; Greeks maintain separate national schools that ensure fluency in both languages. Urban parents are now pushing for dual-language instruction, based on the successful *Europa School* model. President of the Turkish Parents Organization Eretkin Özcan stressed in a June 2003 interview that educators are finally recognizing the importance of mother-tongue instruction in solidifying the cognitive skills necessary to learn further languages. English is a regular requirement for virtually all pupils; there is no good reason for denying children of foreign descent a chance to learn Turkish in place of French or Spanish as a third language. There are only stubborn, reality-challenged, German-national reasons for not allowing this to happen.

Kenan Kolat, head of the Turkish Association of Berlin-Brandenburg (TBB), would replace reactive foreigner policies (*Ausländerpolitik*) with proactive equal opportunity policies (*Gleichstellungspolitik*), first pursued by feminists. Kolat would have Germany define itself as "an ethnically pluralistic (polyethnic) civil society . . . that should integrate minority protection into its constitution in such as way as to no longer appear as minority protection."[91] Reflecting a practical-communitarian orientation, the TBB spokesperson contends that "the sole criterion for the acquisition of German citizenship, without the abdication of original citizenship, should be the duration of residence or birthplace."[92] He would add protections that combine the EU's Copenhagen Criteria (for would-be applicant Turkey): the right to mother tongue and cultural instruction, to religious diversity, equal treatment, affirmative action programs, and codified anti-discrimination policies. A fusion of gender and minority concerns led to significant advances for both groups in the United States after the 1960s.

Many of the rights Yasemin Nuhoglu Soysal and other post-nationalists deemed "inalienable" are increasingly subject to revocation; reliance on welfare is used to deny naturalization in many parts of Germany, even though structural unemployment has hit foreigners hardest. The Federal Republic needs to invest in the human capital of its "hyphenated-German" children now, to ensure enough caretakers and workers to replace its aging Baby Boomers. Child-development research in Germany has made little effort to incorporate migrant offspring, as the state admitted in its Sixth Family Report. Authorities claim they lack knowledge of childhood socialization under different cultures but then exclude "a major portion of children's real-life experiences" from their analyses because they are not citizens. The only way to get the expertise necessary to configure appropriate neighborhood activities for intercultural education is to incorporate the parents of these children, as voting members, into the policy making process.

Ready, Willing, and Able:
Integration and Identity among "Berlin Turks"

Berlin is hardly typical of FRG cities. Its experiences as a city occupied by WWII powers rendered it more cosmopolitan than most. Male residents were exempt from military conscription, attracting many leftists and asylum seekers in the late 1960s. The absorptive capacities of its universities not only laid the foundation for vehement protest movements but also for countless Third World and human rights campaigns. Even without the industrial hinterland that brought droves of guestworkers to *Restdeutschland*, Berlin became home to disproportionate numbers of *Übersiedler, Aussiedler*, asylum seekers, and "permanently provisional" migrants.

In 1981, Mayor Richard von Weizsäcker appointed Dr. Barbara John (CDU) to serve as Berlin's first commissioner for foreigners, a post she occupied until her formal retirement in 2002. In addition to learning Turkish, Dr. John sponsored representative surveys that offer critical insights into integration processes among ethnic migrants between 1983 and 2002. Twelve studies draw directly on Turkish samples; six additional polls probe the attitudes of local Germans toward "their" foreigners, while two more focus on the city's Polish residents (1995) or compare Turkish and Yugoslav youth (1986, 1988).[93] The responses testify to increasing Turkish identification with a new homeland in reference to education/employment, citizenship acquisition, religious secularization, and social interaction with the natives. What follows is a composite of significant trends gleaned from several surveys, graciously supplied by Dr. John.[94]

This book began with the premise that foreigners were the primary "losers" of unification for the first few years. A majority of Germans (68 percent) admitted in 1992 that unity had made life more difficult for foreigners, citing mass unemployment, rising xenophobia, escalating living costs, an exacerbated housing shortage, and higher taxes all around. Still, 60 percent of the nationals felt that unification had positively affected their own lives in 1993.

Their Turkish counterparts present a much bleaker picture: 88 percent saw no positive consequences for themselves emerging out of unity, despite lower expectations regarding state benefits. Outspoken trust in government declined by 9 percent, relative to 1989. Half voiced skepticism as to their "future prospects," 47.5 percent among youth. Four-fifths were generally satisfied with their occupations, though satisfaction is relative given an exponential increase in joblessness: 7 percent of the youth sample was unemployed in 1991, rising to nearly 18 percent in 1997. Unemployment among all Turkish nationals in Berlin stood at 37 percent in 2001.

Their deeper concerns are rooted in other post-unity developments, however. Berliners overwhelmingly rejected the anti-foreigner behaviors unleashing two-years of xenophobic violence; 89 percent of the locals—compared to 43 percent in a national poll before, and 69 percent after Mölln—renounced such slogans as "Germany for the Germans!" and "Foreigners out!" Reacting to sensational cases at the time, 70 percent opposed the deportation of "Turkish" youth born and/or raised in Berlin, following criminal convictions. By 1993, Turkish women (41 percent) and youth (47 percent) felt especially threatened by violence; it speaks for the city, however, that 92 percent saw no direct threat, nor did 84 percent notice a deterioration in native-foreigner relations in their own neighborhoods.

Despite countless media reports on the rise of ethnic gangs, 88 percent denounced any effort to "arm themselves" for revenge or self-defense. While 61 percent of Turkish youth rejected violent means in 1991 (pre-Mölln), 81 percent did so in 1993, rising to 96 percent in 1997; 90 percent welcomed a local decision to recruit more Turkish-Germans into police ranks. 81 percent had not experienced "anti-foreigner hostility," although 76 percent had visited Eastern neighborhoods a few times (where certain S-Bahn stations are known for neo-Nazi attacks). Indeed, 22 percent either attended school or worked there—perhaps owing to district reforms that joined Kreuzberg with Friedrichshain, and Neukölln with Treptow.

Fears regarding hostility toward foreigners (66 percent) were compounded by economic difficulties stressed by 42 percent, although expectations are on the rise: 4.4 percent of those polled in 1991 attended university, in contrast to 7 percent in 1997; only 11 percent want to be workers (20 percent in 1991) and

12.6 percent aspired to become civil servants by 1997. Third-generation Turks reported experiences with workplace discrimination (42 percent), or during job searches (37 percent), explaining why 67.5 percent among males, 54 percent among females would prefer self-employment. Discrimination also factored into housing searches (33 percent) and dealings with police (22 percent) in 1993.

Comprising the "most strongly integrated population group," youth experience sharper demarcation than their parents because they participate more actively in public life and grasp more subtle references to their origins/nationality. Three-fourths feel they would be well served by formal anti-discrimination laws (still pending in 2006). The 1997 survey found males (55.5 percent) more sensitive to discrimination than females (42 percent). Socialization research indicates that girls internalize failure (assuming they "are not good enough") while boys blame others for their lack of expected success. The points of discrimination ranged from bureaucratic offices (32 percent), to school (28 percent), work (22 percent), and "on the streets" (20 percent). Perceived "hatred of foreigners" declined from 32.8 percent to 18.6 percent.

Greater sensitivity to discrimination also derives from youth reliance on German media, as a function of enhanced language skills. Television, especially, perpetuates negative stereotypes, while at the same time glitzy advertising fosters a sense of relative deprivation. Elderly Turks rely more heavily on Turkish newspapers and broadcasts, easily accessible thanks to cable and other technological advances. The middle generation draws on both language sources; in the 1990s, 54 percent of the readers under 35 used both print media, 63 percent German and Turkish TV. The 1997 survey found that 72 percent watch German television, 69 percent utilize Turkish channels. About 60 percent read German newspapers, 44 percent listen to Turkish radio stations; 67 percent tune in to Metropol FM and Berlin's "Radio MultiKulti." Another sign of positive integration: while a quarter find sitcoms and public performances featuring Turkish/ethnic jokes "discriminatory," 58 percent see this as part of "normal society." In 2001, 76 percent of the sample relied on Turkish, 68 percent on German media. Indeed, in 2007 public television (ARD) introduced a very popular, award-winning comedy series call "Turkish for Beginners," closely resembling an equally popular Canadian series, "Little Mosque on the Prairie."

Language skills have improved dramatically. While 40 percent of the 1985 interviews were conducted in Turkish, 83 percent of the males, 73 percent females responded to the 1997 survey in fluent German. Yet "whoever expects the Turks to deliberately turn away from their own culturally rooted lifestyles or to renounce the language of origin and the family language absolutely demands too much." The real problem is a lack of language instruction for imported brides; about 3,000 spouses arrive from Turkey each year (Table 3.5). Three-fourths want local authorities to increase nursery-school facilities (*Kitas*) to

Table 2.4 Country of Origin for Turkish Spouses, 1991–1997

	1991			1993			1997			1999		
	Total	*Male*	*Female*	*Total*	*Male*	*Female*	*Total*	*Male*	*Female*	*Total*	*Male*	*Female*
Turkey	31.1	50.9	19.6	48.8	54.6	42.4	38.6	57.6	25.5	35.6	42.4	27.5
Germany	57.9	46.6	80.4	51.2	45.4	47.6	59.7	39.8	73.4	64.4	57.6	72.5
Elsewhere	1.0	2.8	-	-	-	-	1.7	2.6	1.1	-	-	-

Source: Surveys provided by Berlin's Commissioner for Foreigners.

ensure childhood language absorption, though only 24 percent supported the idea of all-day schools in 2001.

Household size among Turkish residents has decreased, even though these Berliners remain more "marriage- and child-friendly" than their German counterparts. The share of four-person families rose from 29 percent (1993) to 34 percent (1999); households with five or more decreased from 36 percent to 29 percent to 23 percent by 2001. 1997 found 60 percent of those born in Berlin already married. The 2001 multi-cohort sample reported that 64 percent (men) and 41 percent (women) age thirty to thirty-nine had spouses; yet 47 percent of all 18 to 25 year olds were single. More women (80 percent) seek partners raised in Germany. By 1997, nearly 70 percent of male and 42 percent of female youth nonetheless said they could "imagine marrying a German."

By the late 1990s, third-generation youth differed from their parents regarding religion (43 percent), the opposite sex (55 percent), family (42 percent), and politics (60 percent). Nearly 49 percent had school-age children in 1999; 97 percent want their sons and daughters to complete their education and occupational training; only 2 percent thought it was more important for their sons. They have few qualms about social mixing: In 1993, 44 percent often spent their free time with Germans, though women were twice likely to have no such contacts. By 2000, 80.5 percent younger than thirty had German friends, with 70 percent (2001) disinclined to pull back into ethnic sports, shopping, or recreational niches.

Only 38 percent of young Turkish men, 8 percent among women, belong to clubs or organizations, which may owe to family obligations rather than to anti-integration feelings; 82 percent were involved with sports clubs, 16 percent with religious groups, and 6 percent with political organizations; indeed, 71 percent were oblivious to ethnic-interest organizations; only 17 percent knew about the *Türkische Gemeinde*. A fifth think that relations between Germans/foreigners have improved in the affluent Western neighborhoods of Charlottenberg, Wilmersdorf, and Zehlendorf, but few (8 percent) saw positive change in Spandau, Tempelhof, and Steglitz; 205 felt relations had deteriorated in Wedding,

Neukölln, and Reinickendorf since 1993, explained by tensions among Turkish, Bosnian, Russian, and Arab youth gangs.

Germans appear responsible for non-interaction between natives and foreigners, though Easterners with no foreigner contact fell from 62 percent (1990) to 44 percent (1992), from 41 percent to 22 percent among West Berliners; still, over 80 percent in both sectors said they'd be willing to "drink a beer with a foreigner in a local bar"—unaware that most Muslims eschew alcohol (Allensbach used to pose the same question to *Wessis* regarding GDR citizens they might meet on vacation). Four-fifths of the Germans admitted that "many things have to change in Berlin" to accommodate globalization but more mentioned traffic problems (38 percent) than ending intolerance/discrimination (26 percent).

Nationals overwhelmingly favored construction of a central mosque for Berlin's 160,000 Muslims—81 percent of Westerners, 74 percent among Easterners (despite "godless communism"), versus 67 percent among Turks themselves. In 1993, 16 percent of migrant parents sent their children to Koran schools, 20 percent in 2000. Two-thirds want Islamic instruction offered in public schools, taught in German by locally trained teachers. A majority (53 percent) would enroll their children even if it were sponsored by the Islamic Federation; parents want moral education preparing their children for the society in which they live—if Germans do not provide it, they will turn to other sources.[95] The number professing a "close relationship to religion" fell from 19 percent in 1989 to 11 percent by 1997; "very close" responses declined from 16.5 percent to 10.7 percent for men, from 22 percent to 11.7 percent for women. One-third (primarily men) regularly attend mosques, holding steady since 1993. Their understanding of Islam is "more enlightened and critical"; 77 percent welcome more dialogue between Muslims/non-Muslims. While one-fourth have reservations about Muslim women wearing headscarves in a non-Muslim country, 70 percent said it was "not a problem" in 2001.

Over 48,000 Turkish-Berliners became citizens between 1945 and 2000 as a function of liberalized requirements and generational change. While 61 percent were prepared to naturalize in 1988 (provided they could keep Turkish passports), the figure rose to 74 percent in 1991. In 1992, 71 percent among Germans supported dual citizenship, 53 percent favored reducing the residency rule from ten to five years. A whopping 94 percent thought that children born in Germany should be enfranchised if one parent had been born there. Few Turks (12 percent) rejected automatic citizenship based on *jus soli*. By 1997, 59 percent (63 percent among women) were prepared to naturalize even if it meant renouncing Turkish citizenship.

Since 1995, males can be released from Turkish citizenship, while still retaining the right to work and to inherit in their country of origin. By 1999, 24 percent had applied, compared to 17.7 percent in 1993; another 37 percent intended to apply (28 percent in 1993). Those rejecting the idea fell from 54 percent to 34 percent. Women who had already applied exceeded men by 3–4 percent in both years; 83 percent of the males and almost 92 percent of the females agreed that newly admitted family members should be required to take integration courses.

While 15 percent see the new Citizenship Law as an improvement, the ban on dual nationality continues to be a stumbling block for 57 percent; 40 percent cite new language-test requirements as a further hindrance. By 2001, 36 percent of all respondents had initiated/completed the naturalization process. The proportion who "want to stay" rose from 9 percent (1985), to 22 percent (1988), to 79 percent (1997), though they no longer "need" citizenship: 90 percent have secure residency status, having lived there for more than fifteen years. Still, 70 percent think their circumstances would improve with anti-discrimination laws.

Local surveys documenting stability, satisfaction, and identification with the host society are clearly at odds with Wilhelm Heitmeyer's sensationalized 1995 study and the 1997 *Spiegel* issue ("Time-Bomb in the Suburbs") stressing disintegration, a "return" to fundamentalist values, and youth violence. Berlin has become the focal point of existence for most Turkish residents: by the late 1990s, 63 percent viewed themselves as "part of German society." By 2001, only 22 percent owned a house in Turkey (39 percent in 1993). The number who return at least once each year dropped from 66 percent to 56 percent; those who only visit every other year rose from 22 percent (1993) to 36 percent (1999). About half would not retire in Turkey, because their children live in Berlin (48 percent) or because they "feel at home" in Germany (37 percent). Only 11.6 percent noted higher living standards. Four-fifths feel good/very good about their lives in the capital city; half who don't cite unemployment. When troubles arise, they turn to local organizations or to the integration commissioner, not to the Turkish Embassy. As one interviewee declared, "These are not foreigner problems, they are integration problems!"

From Marginal to Metropolitan to Minority Status

Initiated by CDU Family Minister Claudia Nolte in 1996 and issued by a Red-Green government in 2000, the first national study on the life circumstances of ethnic families in Germany offers an important corrective to "problems" emphasized by politicians, sooner rooted in stereotypes than in the daily needs of co-citizens. An artifact of the last century, the German *Leitkultur* needs to take its place "next to the bronze ax and the spinning wheel." Ethnic minorities are neither blind to modern educational opportunities, nor resistant to social change. In fact, successor cohorts are so acculturated that Turkish homosexuals have joined the pantheon of ethnic organizations. Gays and Lesbians from Turkey (GLADT), dating back to 1996, held their first national conference in 2003; the *Türk-Gay* association holds memberships in the Lesbian and Gay Union of Germany (LSVD) and the LSV Berlin-Brandenburg. GLADT has also coalesced with the TBB to establish an anti-discrimination network. This ethnic coming-out would have been unthinkable ten years ago. Turks in Berlin have created their own Turkish Day (17 May) celebration, complete with parades, street-fairs, and tribunals full of local politicians.

Although the United States offers little public assistance to migrants, it applies the same statutory framework to all legal arrivals, enabling them to qualify for citizenship in five years (notwithstanding post-2001 exceptions in the name of "homeland security"). Germany has repeatedly moved the bar for would-be citizens: first by requiring ten, then fifteen, then eight years of residence; by raising application costs and demanding professions of "Germanness" to "preserve its cultural interest"; by requiring language cum "personal-belief" tests; and, lately, by raising the threshold for "economic self-sufficiency" based on fluctuations in the national economy. Not surprisingly, these policy swings have shaped the reluctance of successive cohorts to shift their allegiance to the FRG in exchange for membership. Highly complex residency rules, added to local differences in naturalization criteria, foster perceptions of legal insecurity among aliens, limiting "permanent" resettlement. The 2004 reforms simplify the structural parameters but do not stop unequal treatment at *Land* and local levels.

In retrospect, as migrant generations sought to participate in the host society, FRG lawmakers changed the rules of the game, then used their own shifts in course to fault foreigners for not "integrating themselves." Accommodation came at a very high cost to the Pioneer Generation, both in terms of physical health and psychological isolation. Guestworkers entered a country still viewed with suspicion by the international community. Germany had hardly come to terms with its shameful exploitation of slave laborers across Europe; indeed, it would not compensate the last of those victims until the new millennium.[96] Marginalized in every sense, imported laborers responded by forming enclaves that sustained Turkish identity, necessary in case of an eventual return. Ethnic enclaves met a broad range of sociocultural needs, offering religious instruction, holiday activities, child-care and mother-tongue instruction; like enterprises everywhere, they developed their own dynamic.

Ever more metropolitan in outlook, physically concentrated in urban areas and focused on local conditions, the Outlander Generation learned to use the streets as a political stage (e.g., Kurdish protests), just like their FRG counterparts. This group paid a high price of a different kind: it lost out on crucial educational advances and professional mobility—due to the myth of return—during a period when German youth secured equal opportunity. Like the natives, Turkish successor cohorts pursued individualistic strategies and identities. Their concrete contact with the homeland, limited to vacation travel, actually undermined feelings of Turkish identity.

"Hyrattin," born 1975 in Frankfurt, summarizes the identity conflict faced by this generation, based on one trip back to Hopa:

> *Alamanci—Deutschlander!* They cursed me with these names. . . . Try to imagine: when you live in Germany, you only live among people who share your conditions, only among Turks. Being German, that is something completely different. There are also Germans there, but you don't have any contact. You live among Turks, the Germans are just as strange for me as the Turks are for the Germans. It's the same relationship back there. Try to imagine: you always travel to Turkey for your vacation, and you think—What kind of a country is this? And there are people who say, these are your brothers. The others have brothers here [in Germany], or grandparents. The German kids get to say, this is my grandpa here, my grandpa there. My grandpa was never here. Why not? That makes you start to think.[97]

"In the beginning," Hyrattin continues, "I didn't even know what an *Ausländer* was." He then relates his experience working in a supermarket at age seventeen: "I do my job there just like a normal worker. I do the work for somebody who treats me like a personal slave. And then this racism. Do you have any idea how many racists there are among people shopping there? They come up and say to your face: 'You are a shitty Turk.'"[98] Born in Turkey in 1968 but a Kreuzberger since 1973, Berlin Assembly member Özcan Mutlu (Greens) relays a less painful lesson regarding his split identity, discovered while spending a year as an exchange student in Nebraska. It was bizarre, he told me during a June 2002 panel for exchange students in Berlin: "when I got to Omaha I felt like a German for the first time in my life. . . . The minute I got out of the plane at the Frankfurt airport, I was Turk again." For the third generation, the ability to keep in touch with the metaphorical homeland through technology is producing transnational identities, distinct from the split-identity model associated with the myth of return.

Greater differentiation within the community (Kurds, Alevis, dissident intellectuals) at first led to major left-right polarization, but like the German Baby Boomers, second generation activists turned to domestic issues. The host society opened itself to their "differences," largely because its own offspring became part of an evolving human rights culture (Helsinki 1975), embracing *Ostpolitik*, non-violence, Green causes, disarmament, and women's rights, in line with Willy Brandt's exhortation to "dare more democracy." The metropolitan qua cosmopolitan approach adopted by the second generation makes sense, given the concrete needs of migrant families. The day-to-day costs of integration are borne by local authorities who have no voice in national or global policymaking, as underlined in the Sixth Family Report: "While the causes of migration are usually found at the level of internationally disparate living conditions, the living conditions of migrant families are most directly influenced in the strongest ways by the possibilities for shaping communal policies and by the procedures of local bureaucracies. Here it is usually a question of redistributing the costs from the large to the small political actors, that is, local and regional authorities have to bear the (ecological and financial) costs of globalization processes."[99]

As of February 2002, over 8,600 applications for naturalization were sitting in Neukölln offices, waiting for "4.5" district bureaucrats to process them; there were 9,700 more in Berlin-Mitte and 3,700 awaiting decisions in Friedrichshain-Kreuzberg.[100] By May 2004, 6,600 Berlin residents had received their new passports; another thirty thousand applications filed since January may take two to three years to process. If citizenship signifies national belonging, why are there disparate local prerequisites, and why isn't processing a federal responsibility? Not a single local commissioner I interviewed could answer that question.

I find striking parallels among ethnic youth and their FRG counterparts. Lacking any personal or direct experiences with the Nazi period or the height of the Cold War conflict, native-German twenty-somethings perceive their identification with a democratic Federal Republic as "no big deal." Being German or Turkish-German implies an instrumental relationship for the youngest cohorts, not a sentimental one rooted in organic *völkish* traditions. Because they have other positive sources of identity, grounded in education, travel opportunities, consumption, and language skills, they feel at home in multiple contexts.

My German sample of the early 1990s moreover encompassed rowdy "No Future" segments analogous to Turkish adolescents who have fallen between the cracks. Macho-Turkish gangs and Islamic fundamentalist youth are the ethnic equivalent of German neo-Nazis and skinheads. These groups search for their identities at the extremes, because their marginalized position in the system (poorly educated, jobless) leaves them nowhere else to look. Both groups turn to re-ethnicization ("Germany for the Germans!"), hyper-masculinity, and aggressive behavior to defend what little turf they have, usually vis-à-vis those who possess even less.

German policymakers need to stop attributing a "lack of integration" to cultural differences and recognize that structural factors hold enormous consequences for societal incorporation. Higher crime and delinquency rates are not a function of culture but evidence that many ethnic youth are denied access to quality education and job training. If these groups appear to be more violent, it is because spatial concentration makes their aggression easier to observe, and because they have already experienced more violence by way of parents, police, or other hostile youth. Barbara Dietz and Heike Roll asked German and *Aussiedler* youth whether they could "imagine any personal conflicts that just have to be settled with violence?" Nearly 27 percent of the post-Soviet emigres concurred, as did 20 percent among native-born adolescents.[101] It's not surprising that kids who previously experienced authoritarian regimes, ethnic strife, and economic collapse are disposed toward violent behavior. The bigger question is why so many born into a country as wealthy, orderly, and democratic as Germany likewise view violence as an acceptable mode of conflict resolution.

The system clearly needs an overhaul. I concluded in 2004 that Germany ought to eliminate its *Hauptschulen*, little more than an institutional dumping ground for children no one wants to educate, irrespective of national origin. In fact, four Eastern states, Rheinland-Pfalz, and the Saarland have already done so. A spring 2006 scandal regarding conditions at the Rütli-School in Neukölln (72 percent of non-German descent) may finally force educational authorities to rethink the system.[102]

Turkish compatriots want to participate in German society and are willing to assume responsibility for "the good, the bad, and the ugly" in their country of settlement. They understand the reciprocal nature of integration as a process requiring "fusion in which persons and groups acquire the memories, sentiments, and attitudes" of the host society; "by sharing their experience and history, [they] are incorporated with them in a common cultural life," as Park and Burgess observed.[103] In exchange for official recognition as a national minority, they are prepared to embrace constitutional values, as affirmed in the 2002 Islamic Charter issued by the Central Council of Muslims in Germany.[104] Some even see a need to accept the Holocaust as part of "their" German history, in order to participate in future struggles against racism and anti-Semitism.[105] Commemorating the tenth anniversary of the arson deaths in Mölln, Safter Çinar, speaker for the TBB, cited a poem by Heiner Feldhoff (my translation) reflecting the nexus between the past and present:

> I would like
> after Auschwitz
> to write poetry
> only I do not know
> the exact address
> So I had better write
> to Rostock
> there
> I am certain
> the receiver has not moved
> without a forwarding address.

Fifty years of shared memories include one further event that has rendered Turkish community concerns central to the Berlin Republic: the fall of the Wall on 9 November 1989. In a television interview, one Turkish-German writer was clearly frustrated when he was only asked to comment on the *Ausländerproblem*, although he had published an essay on the dramatic 1989 Turn-Around. He was questioned repeatedly: "But why are you interested in the Wall? That's a German topic!" Having lived in Kreuzberg for years—which ran directly along the Wall, from Kochstrasse and "Checkpoint Charlie" at the northern end of the district, down to the last Western subway stop at Neukölln, across from the GDR-stop *Grenzallee*—-the author insisted, "it was my Wall too!"[106]

When the Wall collapsed, what had been one of the most run-down, peripheral parts of the city, inhabited only by foreigners, students, squatters, and more radical Greens, suddenly became prime real estate. One now rides through multiculti neighborhoods en route to government ministries. Ethnic businesses have spread across combined Eastern and Western districts like Friedrichshain-Kreuzberg and Mitte-Wedding, rendering the döner kebab the national fast-food favorite. Turkish entrepreneurial "know-how" offers a template for new arrivals, and unemployed natives, seeking economic autonomy (see chapter 5). The Turkish community now finds itself bridging a broader "cultural gap" between *Ossies* and *Wessies* in the long divided city, not least of all by pushing debates over long-overdue educational reforms. It has, in essence, "arrived" in Germany for good.

Notes

1. Klaus J. Bade, "Immigration, Naturalization, and Ethno-national Traditions in Germany: From the Citizenship Law of 1913 to the Law of 1999," in Larry E. Jones, ed., *Crossing Boundaries, German and American Experiences with the Exclusion and Inclusion of Minorities* (Providence: Berghahn Books, 2001), 45, 43.
2. Ibid., 44.
3. Bernhard Nauck, Annette Kohlmann, and Heike Diefenbach, "Familiäre Netzwerke, intergenerative Transmission und Assimilationsprozesse bei türkischen Migrantenfamilien," *Kölner Zeitschrift für Soziologie und Sozialpsychologie* 49 (1997): 477–499; Berhard Nauck and Anja Steinbach, *Intergeneratives Verhalten und Selbstethnisierung von Zuwanderern.* Expertise für die Unabhängige Kommission "Zuwanderung" (Chemnitz: March 2001).
4. Nauck, Kohlmann, and Deifenbach, "Familiäre Netzwerke."
5. Karin Schönwälder, "Zukunftsblindheit oder Steuerungsversagen? Zur Ausländerpolitik der Bundesregierung der 1960er und frühen 1970er Jahre," in Jochen Oltmer, ed., *Migration steuern und verwalten* (Göttingen: V & R Unipress, 2003), 129; Bundesministerium für Familie, Frauen und Jugend, *Sechster Familienbericht, Familien ausländischer Herkunft in Deutschland: Leistungen—Belastungen—Herausforderung und Stellungnahmen der Bundesregierung,* 18 October 2003 (Deutscher Bundestag, Drucksache 14/4357), 36.
6. Ertekin Özcan, *Türkische Immigrantenorganisationen in der Bundesrepublik Deutschland* (Berlin: Hitit, 1992), 42–43.
7. Cited in ibid., 42.

8. Ray Rist, *Guestworkers in Germany: The Prospects for Pluralism* (New York: Praeger, 1978).

9. Bundesministerium für Familie, Frauen und Jugend (BMFFJ), *Sechster Familienbericht*, 38.

10. Sonja Haug, *Soziales Kapital und Kettenmigration: Italienische Migranten in Deutschland*, Bundesinstitut für Bevölkerungsforschung (Opladen: Leske & Budrich, 2000) 177ff., 304.

11. Özcan, *Türkische Immigrantenorganisationen*, 33, 35.

12. Bundesminister des Innern, ed., Bericht der Kommission "Ausländerpolitik" (Bonn: 24 February 1983), 6–7.

13. Nina Grünenberg, "Was tun mit den Türken?" *Die Zeit*, 6 February 1978; "Die Politiker müssen Farbe bekennen," *Die Zeit*, 12 February 1982.

14. Özcan, *Türkische Immigrantenorganisationen*, 49.

15. Ibid., 23.

16. Bundesministerium für Familie, Frauen und Jugend, *Sechster Familienbericht*, 19; also, Friedrich Heckmann, Wolfgang Bosswick, and Veit Bronnenmeyer, *Integrationsmassnahmen der Wohlfahrtsverbände*, Europäisches Forum für Migrationsstudien (Bamberg: 2000).

17. Özcan, *Türkische Immigrantenorganisationen*, 79ff.

18. Eberhard Seidel-Pielen, *Aufgespeisst! Wie der Döner über die Deutschen kam,* (Berlin: Rotbuch, 1996).

19. Özcan, *Türkische Immigrantenorganisationen*, 35.

20. Ibid., 56.

21. Ibid., 43.

22. Bundesministerium für Familie, Frauen und Jugend, *Sechster Familienbericht*, 40.

23. Özcan, *Türkische Immigrantenorganisationen*, 35; Faruk Sen, "Wer hier sein Haus baut, will auch hier bleiben," *Vorwarts* 3 (August 1985): 16.

24. Bundesministerium für Familie, Frauen und Jugend, *Sechster Familienbericht*, 41.

25. Joyce Marie Mushaben, *From Post-War to Post-Wall Generations* (Boulder, CO: Westview, 1998), 318; Özcan, *Türkische Immigrantenorganisationen,* 32.

26. Bundesministerium für Familie, Frauen und Jugend, *Sechster Familienbericht*, 70.

27. Özcan, *Türkische Immigrantenorganisationen*, 176, 223.

28. Robert D. Putnam, "Bowling Alone: America's Declining Social Capital," *Journal of Democracy* 6, no. 1 (January 1995): 65–78.

29. Özcan, *Türkische Immigrantenorganisationen*, 325–326.

30. Hartmut Esser, *Integration und ethnische Schichtung*, Gutachten für die Unabhängige Kommission "Zuwanderung" (Mannheim: 2001), 40.

31. Nauck et al., cited in Bundesministerium für Familie, Frauen und Jugend, *Sechster Familienbericht*, 113.

32. Ibid., 113.

33. Ibid., 112.

34. There are comparable gaps among Germans: GDR women gave birth, on average, to two children by the age 19–23; FRG women bore one by 27–30. Joyce Marie Mushaben, "Ost-West Identitäten: Generationen zwischen Wende und Wandel," *Berliner Debatte INITIAL* 12, no. 3 (2001): 74–87.

35. Joyce Marie Mushaben, "Asylum Law misses Point," *The Christian Science Monitor*, 15 December 1992; Mushaben, "Germany's Rising Nationalism: Everybody Deserves Some Blame," *Christian Science Monitor*, 21 October 1992; Mushaben "Behind the German Neo-Nazi Phenonmenon," *Christian Science Monitor*, 18 November 1991; Mushaben, "Germany's Immigrants," *Christian Science Monitor*, 19 November 1991; further, Wilfried Schubarth, "Fremden als Sündenbock," in *Das Profil der Deutschen: Was sie eint, was sie trennt* (Hamburg: Spiegel Verlag, 1991).

36. For a detailed description, see Mushaben, *From Post-War to Post-Wall Generations*, chap. 7.

37. Kohl, cited in Jürgen Habermas, "Die zweite Lebenslüge der Bundesrepublik: Wir sind wieder 'normal' geworden," *Die Zeit*, 18 December 1992.

38. *The Week in Germany*, German Information Center (New York), 27 November 1992.

39. "Krawalle und Blockaden in vielen Städten: Politiker drohen mit harten Maßnahmen," *Süddeutsche Zeitung*, 2 June 1993.

40. Cem Özdemir, *Ich bin Inländer: Ein anatolischer Schwabe im Bundestag* (Munich: Deutscher Taschenbuch Verlag, 1999), 59.

41. Teresa Amott and Julie Matthei, *Race, Gender and Work: A Multi-Cultural Economic History of Women in the United States* (Boston: South End Press, 1996).

42. R. E. Park, *Race and Culture* (Glencoe, IL: Free Press, 1950); also, Richard Alba and Victor Nee, "Rethinking Assimilation Theory for a New Era of Immigration," *International Migration Review* 31, no. 4 (1997): 826–874.

43. M. L. Hansen, *The Problem of the Third Generation Immigrant* (Rock Island, IL: Augustana Historical Society Publications, 1938); further, Bernhard Nauck and Anja Steinbach, "Intergeneratives Verhalten und Selbstethnisierung von Zuwanderern," Expertise for the Independent Commission on Immigration (Chemnitz: March 2001) .

44. Chicago is described as a case of "hypersegregation." See Erich Howenstein, "Ethnic Change and Segregation in Chicago," in Curtis Roseman, Hans Dieter Laux, and Günther Thieme, eds., *EthniCity: Geographic Perspectives on Ethnic Change in Modern Cities* (Lanham, MD: Rowman & Littlefield, 1996), 31–50.

45. Werner Schiffauer, *Die Gottesmänner: Türkische Islamisten in Deutschland* (Frankfurt/Main: Suhrkamp, 2000).

46. Alba and Nee, "Rethinking Assimilation Theory," 833.

47. Bundesministerium für Familie, Frauen und Jugend, *Sechster Familienbericht*, 79.

48. Ibid., 22.

49. Zentrum für Türkeistudien, *Ältere Migranten in Deutschland*, *Zft-aktuell*, no. 76 (August 1999).

50. Joyce Marie Mushaben, "Ost-West Identitäten: Generationen zwischen Wende und Wandel," *Berliner Debatte INITIAL* 12, no. 3 (2001): 74–87.

51. Bundesministerium für Familie, Frauen und Jugend, *Sechster Familienbericht*, 9.

52. Joyce Marie Mushaben, "Challenging the Maternalist Presumption: Welfare Reform in Germany and the United States," in Nancy J. Hirschman and Ulrike Liebert, eds., *Women & Welfare: Feminist Perspectives on the Welfare State in the U.S. and Europe* (New Brunswick, NJ: Rutgers University Press, 2000), 193–214.

53. Ibid., 27.

54. Ahmet Akgündüz, "Migration to and from Turkey, 1783–1960: Types, Numbers and Ethno-religious dimensions," *Journal of Ethnic and Migration Studies* 24, no. 1 (January 1998): 97–120; Deutscher Bundestag, *Islam in Deutschland* (Drucksache 14/4530), 8 November 2002.

55. Özcan, *Türkische Immigrantenorganisationen*, 31.

56. Gerdien Jonker and Andreas Kapphan, eds., *Moscheen und islamisches Leben in Berlin* (Berlin: Ausländerbeauftragte des Senats, 1999); Martin Greve and Tülay Çinar, eds., *Das Türkische Berlin* (Berlin: Ausländerbeauftragte des Senats, 1998); and Werner Schiffauer, *Die Migranten aus Subay: Türken in Deutschland. Eine Ethnographie* (Stuttgart: Klett-Cotta, 1991).

57. I have lived in a few such places myself! Students installed plastic shower booths in their kitchens, hooked up to hot-water heaters over the sink.

58. Bundesministerium für Familie, Frauen und Jugend, *Sechster Familienbericht*, 15.

59. Hermann Tertlit, *Turkish Power Boys: Ethnographie einer Jugendbande* (Frankfurt/Main: Suhrkamp, 1996), 117–119.

60. Bundesministerium für Familie, Frauen und Jugend, *Sechster Familienbericht*, 15.

61. Schönwälder, "Zukunftsblindheit oder Steuerungsversage?"

62. Bundesministerium für Familie, Frauen und Jugend, *Sechster Familienbericht*, 176, 180–181.

63. Wolfgang Seifert, *Berufliche Integration von Zuwanderern in Deutschland*, Gutachten für die Unabhängige Kommission "Zuwanderung" (Berlin: 2002); Seifert, "Die zweite Aus-ländergeneration in der Bundesrepublik: Eine Längsschnittbeobachtungen in der Beruf-seinstiegsphase," *Kölner Zeitschrift für Soziologie und Sozialpsychologie* 44, no. 4 (1992): 677–696.

64. Michael Bommes, "Probleme der beruflichen Eingliederung von Zuwanderern Migranten in Organisationen," in *Integration und Integrationsförderung in der Einwanderungsgesellschaft* (Bonn: Forschungsinstitut der Friedrich Ebert Stiftung, 1999).

65. Ibid., 29.

66. Alba and Nee, "Rethinking Assimilation Theory," 853.

67. Zentrum für Türkeistudien, *Jahrbuch 2001* (Essen), 395.

68. Esser, *Integration und ethnische Schichtung*.

69. Bundesministerium für Familie, Frauen und Jugend, *Sechster Familienbericht*.

70. Bommes, "Probleme der beruflichen Eingliederung." Further, Nan Dirk De Graaf and Hendrick Derk Flap,"'With a Little Help from My Friends': Social Resources as an Explana-tion of Occupational Status and Income in West Germany, the Netherlands, and the United States," *Social Forces* 67, no. 2 (December 1988): 452–472.

71. Bommes, "Probleme der beruflichen Eingliederung," 14; Esser, *Integration und ethnische Schichtung*, 43.

72. Rosabeth Moss Kanter makes a similar argument in "Some Effects of Proportion in Group Life: Skewed Sex Ratios and Responses to Token Women," *American Journal of Sociology* 82, no. 5 (1977): 965ff.

73. Zentrum für Türkeistudien, *Bestandsaufnahme und Situationsanalyse von nachreisenden Ehepartnern aus der Türkei* (Essen: January 2003).

74. Bommes, "Probleme der beruflichen Eingliederung," 12.

75. Bundesministerium für Familie, Frauen und Jugend, *Sechster Familienbericht*, 25.

76. Zentrum für Türkeistudien, eds., *Türkei-Jahrbuch* (Münster: LIT, 2001), 123.

77. Faruk Sen, Martina Sauer, and Dirk Halm, *Intergeneratives Verhalten und (Selbst-)Ethnisier-ung von türkischen Zuwanderern*, Gutachten für die Unabhängige Kommission "Zuwander-ung" (Essen: 2001).

78. Eleonore Kofman, "Female 'Birds of Passage' a Decade Later: Gender and Immigration in the European Union," *International Migration Review* 33, no. 2 (1999): 271.

79. Claudia Diehl, "Wer wird Deutsche/r und warum? Bestimmungsfaktoren der Einbürger-ung türkischer- und italienischstämmiger junger Erwachsenen," (January 2003), 18, 26.

80. Zentrum für Türkeistudien, *ZTS Jahrbuch 2001*, 395, 382; BMI (Federal Interior Minis-try), press release of 5 July 2001.

81. Susanne Vieth-Entus, "Wenn Cousins Cousinen heiraten," *Der Tagesspiegel*, 20 May 2003; further, Ausländerbeauftragte des Senats von Berlin, eds., *Repräsentivumfrage zur Lebens-situation türkischer Berlinerinnen und Berliner* (Berlin: 15 January 2002), 4.

82. Eva K. Ostergaard-Nielsen, "The Politics of Migrants: Transnational Political Practices" (paper presented at a conference on Transnational Migration: Comparative Perspectives, Princeton University, 30 June–1 July 2001); Susanne Vieth-Entus, "Verwandte Eltern ver-erben doppeltes Gesundheitsrisiko," *Der Tagesspiegel*, 20 May 2003.

83. Ulrich, "Die zukünftige Bevölkerungsstruktur Deutschlands," 11.

84. Naila Minai, cited in Sabine Fischer and Moray McGowan, "From *Pappkoffer* to Pluralism: On the Development of Migrant Writing in the German Federal Republic," in David Hor-rocks and Eva Kolinsky, eds., *Turkish Culture in German Society Today* (Providence/Lon-don: Berghahn Books, 1996), 15.

85. Werner Schiffauer, "Islam in the Diaspora: The Fascination of Political Islam Among Second Generation German Turks" (WPTC-99–06 Viadrina), 10; also, Sen, Sauer, Halm, *Intergeneratives Verhalten und (Selbst-)Ethnisierung von türkischen Zuwanderern*

86. Yasemin Karakasoglu, "Turkish Cultural Orientations in Germany and the Role of Islam," in Horrocks and Kolinsky, eds., *Turkish Culture in German Society Today*, 173.

87. Schiffauer, "Islam in the Diaspora," 5.

88. Ibid., 18.

89. Dilek Zaptciogluc, *Türken und Deutsche, Nachdenken über eine Freundschaft* (Frankfurt/Main: Brandees & Apsel, 2005), 105.

90. Data from the Federal Commissioner for Migration, Refugees and Integration website.

91. Kenan Kolat, "Gleichstellungspolitik statt Auslanderpolitik," in *Integration und Integrationsförderung in der Einwanderungsgesellschaft* (Bonn: Forschungsinstitut der Friedrich Ebert Stiftung, 1999).

92. Ibid.

93. Turkish residents were surveyed in 1983, 1985 through 1989, 1991, 1993, 1994, 1997, 2000, and 2002; East and West Germans or other ethnic groups were sampled in 1990, 1992, 1993, 1995, 1998, and 2000, respectively.

94. I rely on six surveys reflecting generational changes: "Berlinerinnen und Berliner -Deutsche Wohnbevölkerung geschlossen gegen Ausländer-raus Parolen" (1,800 East and West Germans), October/November 1992; "Türkischer Berliner halten trotz widriger Umstände an der Integration fest" (1,522 Turkish residents, age 18 and older) March 1994; "Berliner Jugendliche türkischer Herkunft" (1,000 Turkish youth, 16–25), October 1997, compared with 1991, 1985–1989; "Türkische Berlinnerinnen und Berliner" (560 Turks over 18, in Western districts where 97 percent reside), December 2000; "Repräsentativumfrage zur Lebenssituation türkischer Berlinerinnen und Berliner" (1,003 persons over 18), November/December 2001. All studies involved telephone interviews conducted by inTrend-Gesellschaft für Markt, Media- und Sozialforschung.

95. CDU–Family Minister Ursula Van der Leyen has called for "value education" beginning in kindergarten, but only the heads of Christian churches were invited into the advisory circle as of April 2006.

96. Joyce Marie Mushaben, "Memory and the Holocaust: Processing the Past through a Gendered Lens," *History of the Human Sciences* 17, no. 2/3, special issue, Paul Roth and Mark Spaner, eds. (2004): 147–185.

97. Tertlit, *Turkish Power Boys*, 98–99.

98. Ibid., 106.

99. Bundesministerium für Familie, Frauen und Jugend, *Sechster Familienbericht*, 22.

100. Stefan Strauss, "Langes Warten auf den deutschen Pass," *Berliner Zeitung*, 16–17 February 2002.

101. Barbara Dietz and Heike Roll, *Jugendliche Aussiedler—Porträt einer Zuwanderungsgeneration* (Frankfurt: Campus, 1998), 123. Further, Dirk Enzmann and Peter Wetzels, "Gewaltkriminalität junger Deutscher und Ausländer. Brisante Befunde die irritieren," *Kölner Zeitschrift für Soziologie und Sozialpsychologie* 52, Heft a (2000): 142–176.

102. Susanne Vieth-Entus, "Kriseneinsatz auf dem Pausenhof," *Berliner Zeitung*; Christine Richter, "Schlechte Noten für den Schulsenator," *Berliner Zeitung*, 19 April 2006.

103. Park and Burgess, cited in Alba and Nee, "Rethinking Assimilation Theory," 828.

104. Kerstin Krupp, "Deutsche Muslime bekennen sich zum Grundgesetz," *Berliner Zeitung*, 21 February 2002.

105. Ethnic activists in Frankfurt/Main have taken this step, as have groups in Berlin.

106. This incident was recounted to me during a forum on migration and identity sponsored by the TBB in June 2003. Yada Kara's novel, *Selam Berlin*, recreates these connections as well (Zurich: Diogenes, 2005).

CHAPTER 3

BLOOD VERSUS BIRTHPLACE

Ethnic-German "Resettlers" from East/Central Europe

Yeah, what should I say, for Russians I was a German, for Germans here I'm a Russian. I don't know what I am.

—A male, adolescent Spätaussiedler

I marry not only the man but the whole country as well.

—Russian-born female Aussiedlerin

When someone has a need for praise, then for common sense, for knowledge, for a friendly nature, for a good heart. The fool reveals himself for bragging about his lineage.

—Hazreti Ali

Since 1949, the Federal Republic has adhered to a concept of citizenship grounded in not one but two myths of return. The first, based on the assumption that guestworkers would return to their countries of origin once their labor was no longer needed, is actually the more recent of the two. Older still is the belief

---

that a common German heritage, rooted primarily in language, would sustain a strong organic bond among peoples separated, inter alia, by two world wars.[1] Since its founding, the Federal Republic has admitted three distinct waves of co-ethnic migrants. These three groups have differed significantly from each other in terms of their knowledge of and commitment to an obscure German state of being (*Deutschtum*). Each wave has moreover brought a motley assortment of dialects, religious dispositions, occupational skills, economic preferences and political orientations, usually at odds with those of the indigenous population.

Focusing on the experiences of GDR *Übersiedler*, East European *Aussiedler*, and post-Soviet *Spätaussiedler*, this chapter tests the effectiveness of the conservative-organic approach to citizenship favored under *jus sanguinis*, equating lineage with the quality of one's identification with a particular "homeland." I contend that the effective integration of countless co-ethnics prior to the 1990s owed more to Germany's willingness to accept historical responsibility for WWII victims and its desire for reconciliation with neighboring states than to the binding influences of a unique *Kulturnation*. Dating back to 1949, the latent citizenship status enjoyed by German resettlers across three periods—classified as *Vertriebene, Aussiedler*, and *Spätaussiedler*—guaranteed privileged access to housing, work permits, and welfare benefits as soon as they entered the country. Their special legal status was a function of Article 116 of the Basic Law until 1993, when mounting concerns about Germany's absorptive capacity induced a profound change of heart regarding "repatriates." New policies permitting unlimited exit from the countries of settlement, especially the former Soviet Union, triggered concrete limits to entry under revised asylum rules and EU migration policies.

The first wave consisted of an uncontrollable flow of war refugees and expellees through 1949, many of whom first found shelter in barracks used for former slave laborers. Between 1939 and 1944, roughly one million *Volksdeutsche* came "home to the Reich" from annexed territories. Another 12–14 million (experts disagree on the totals) fled the advancing Soviet Army, or were expelled during "the wild driving-out" of summer 1945.[2] The second wave, consisting of cohorts who might have experienced WWII but were spared expulsion, benefited from the Eastern Treaties initiated by Chancellor Willy Brandt in the early 1970s. The FRG extended trade relations, financial investment, and cultural partnerships in exchange for liberalized emigration rules and less discrimination against German minorities throughout the Soviet bloc. Continuing into the Gorbachev years, this wave consisted of Polish, Romanian, and Soviet residents; nearly 616,032 "returned" 1976–1987, added to the 803,941 admitted 1950–1975.[3] The fall of the Wall and regime collapse throughout Eastern Europe triggered another wave; admissions rose from 78,498 in 1987, to 377,042 in 1989 and 397, 067 in 1990. By 1998, the post-Wall exodus would exceed 2.5 million.[4]

Following unification, the Federal Republic shifted to a strategy of improving relations for minorities in the settlement states. The German-Soviet Treaty on Good Neighborly Relations, Partnership and Cooperation, signed on the first anniversary of the Wall's collapse, tried to strengthen minority rights by expanding German language instruction, media access, cultural facilities, and school exchanges. Comparable agreements were signed with Poland, Romania, the Czech Republic, and Hungary over the next three years.[5] The FRG agreed to accept two thousand Russian guestworkers per year; it also implemented policies "returning" less desirable migrants, e.g., Romanians (who had also suffered Nazi persecution). Average Polish citizens didn't wait for a formal treaty; they merely began moving back and forth across the border as day laborers, "undocumented" traders, and goods transporters.

Although these treaties generated little public debate at the time, they are extremely significant for the larger immigration/integration debate that ensued after 1998.[6] First, they marked the end of an unlimited "right of return" and formal melioration of "war consequences," as reflected in subsequent constitutional amendments. Secondly, they were signed by Unity Chancellor Helmut Kohl, dispelling for good the myth of an eventual return to pre-1937 borders among conservatives. They also effectively terminated the CDU/CSU issue monopoly relative to the German nation.[7] Third, the new accords undermined the FRG's exclusive reliance on *jus sanguinis* as the primary basis of citizenship, a wedge to be utilized by a new generation of Red-Green leaders after 1998. Last but not least, these agreements unwittingly bound the FRG to a concept of minority rights (enforced through EU enlargement criteria) that is compelling foot-dragging politicians to adopt anti-discrimination laws to protect other states' "minorities" within German boundaries. Language rights, freedom of religion, and the right to cultural preservation will feature ever more prominently in integration debates involving its Turkish population.

The chapter begins with historical background on the right of return accorded ethnic Germans who migrated to Russia and East/Central Europe decades, if not centuries, ago; this principle was enshrined in the Basic Law to atone for the deportation and displacement of Germans abroad avenging Nazi atrocities. Next I describe the effective integration of co-ethnic refugees and deportees from the Eastern Territories through the 1950s and 1960s, and the ways in which their success story solidified West German attachment to *jus sanguinis* as a foundation for postwar citizenship. This is followed by an analysis of new adjustment problems faced by immigrants during the 1970s and 1980s, as tensions eased between Germany and its eastern neighbors. The term *Aussiedler* becomes a household word during this period, as does *Ausländer* in reference to all other aliens. I then turn to the "resettlers" of the 1990s, families stemming primarily from the former Soviet Union whose transition to the German way of life has been far from smooth. Finally, I explore the special plight of two groups with "more to lose than their chains"—women and youth—before noting broader lessons about ethnic identity in Germany.

The Right of Return: Integration Successes of the 1950s and 1960s

Historian Klaus Bade maintains that the cultural identity of Germans never existed in the pure, homogeneous form traditionally espoused by officials. It emerged out of an extended evolutionary process, blending native and foreign elements. Characterizing the term *Aussiedler* as "a euphemistic masquerade," Bade is not alone in claiming that ethnic resettlers seem more foreign to most citizens than *ausländische Inländer* (alien residents) raised in Germany.[8] Their crises of adjustment stem from a lack of knowledge about postwar Germany, false expectations regarding ethnic solidarity, official emphasis on their "group status," and a need to a break with their internalized cultures.

Early enclaves of "external co-ethnics" date back to the sixteenth century when Russia invited thousands of German craftsmen; they quickly created their own neighborhoods and established the first Lutheran church in Moscow in 1576.[9] "Invitation manifestos" issued by Katherina II and Alexander I between 1760 and 1804 granted Germans the right to settle as "free farmers," to acquire land at no cost, eschew taxes and military service, and to use their language in schools and local administration. By 1769, 23,000 colonists had settled along the banks of the Volga; another 100,000 moved to the Black Sea region by the 1850s; 170,000 more resided in Volynya a decade later. Totaling 1.8 million, Germans comprised the eighth largest nationality in Russia by 1887.[10] Smaller groups established themselves in Silesia, Carpathia, and Vojvodina starting in the eighteenth century. Adopted in 1871, the first Reich Emigration Law came too late to stop an outpouring of Germans to the United States, and generally left migration processes up to the *Länder*. Prussia applied the principle of *jus sanguinis*, but ethnic descent first applied to all with the 1913 Reich Citizenship Law.

The Russian Revolution marked the first turn for the worse; land-owning migrants faced persecution as *Kulaks,* though Stalin allowed for autonomous German republics in the Volga region in 1924, as well as in Siberia, the Ukraine, the Caucasus region, and along the Black Sea. Forced collectivization after 1928–1929 brought new trauma and terror, however: administrators, professors, and teachers were caught up in the Great Purges of the 1930s, and the German *rayons* were abolished in 1939. The Volga Republic officially ceased to exist in August 1941, by which point tens of thousands were facing expropriation, deportation, forced labor, or even execution as "ethnic collaborators" with the Nazis. Following surrender, over 12.5 million entered the territory that later constituted the West and East German states. That figure included 3.2 million from Silesia, 2.9 million from the Sudetenland, and 1.9 million from Prussia and the Oder-Neisse area (the new Polish border). Another 2 million perished.[11] An estimated 4 million remained in old settlement areas after expulsions ceased (see table 3.1).

Though designated a "transitional passage," Article 116 GG ordained that even the second and third-generation offspring of former citizens or expellees

Table 3.1 Ethnic Resettlers and Expellees, 1940–2002

Point of Origin	Resettlers[1] 1940-1944	Expellees[1] 1945-1949	Resettlers[2] 1950-2002
Poland		6,198,000	1,444,045
Interwar Poland		672,000	
Former Soviet Union	1,500,000	65,000	2,077,334
German regions		1,000,000	—
Romania	200,000	100,000	429,849
(ex) Czechoslovakia		2,921,000	105,086
Hungary		206,000	21,403
Yugoslavia	36,000	287,000	90, 358[3]
Baltic States	77,000	25,000	
Other Regions			55,716
TOTAL	1,878,000	11,409,000	4,314,382

Source: 1) Data from Rainer Münz and Rainer Ohliger, "Long Distance Citizens," in *Paths to Inclusion*. Eds. Peter Schuck and Rainer Munz (New York/Oxford: Berghahn Books, 1998): 157.
2) Federal Ministry of the Interior (BMI), June 2003.
3) Excludes war refugees.

are entitled to protected status as citizen refugees. If a forty-something American whose German parents were forced to emigrate to the United States during the Nazi era moved back to the Federal Republic, she had run the gamut of naturalization requirements, even if married to a German; accelerated naturalization processes for spouses were not introduced until 1999. Yet the grandchildren and great-grandchildren of Eastward-driven co-ethnics who have never been outside Kazakhstan or Siberia and display limited command of the "mother tongue" need only reactivate their citizenship: They are German by definition. Recent laws now exclude anyone born after 31 December 1992 from that status.

Volker Ronge argues that campaigns by settlement countries to punish and discriminate on the basis of ethnicity during WWII and thereafter "resulted in the identification, classification, and, from a sociological point of view, perhaps even the re-creation (re-ethnicization) of German minorities."[12] It also moved postwar politicians to offer protection to the diaspora through *jus sanguinis*. The right of return (Article 116) was intended "to compensate co-ethnics for losses they experienced . . . as a result of the war that Germany had provoked."[13]

The conditions for re-entry, and the automatic restoration of German citizenship, fell outside normal immigration rules (or the lack thereof). No caps were imposed for the first forty years, though return was little more than a theoretical option, given the Iron Curtain. Until 1987, socialist governments restricted exit authorizations, "rigidly set in the context of foreign relations with individual emigrant-receiving countries."[14] The FRG engaged in a symbolic "equalization of burdens" by actively receiving the relatively small numbers who managed to get out. Migration policy required a delicate balance between complex foreign and domestic policy concerns under conditions of national division.

By 1950, co-ethnic refugees comprised 16 percent of the Western population. While most Germans were compelled by the combined effects of conditionless surrender, the Nuremburg Trials and the specter of communist expansion to renounce nationalism per se, persons who had suffered tremendously due to their ethnic status might have opted for nationalist vindication. Heightened Cold War tensions, the pressures of reconstruction, and millions of war prisoners interned abroad left the FRG's first chancellor, Konrad Adenauer, little choice but to push for rapid political incorporation of potentially radical elements. Refugees quickly mobilized national interest associations; thirty organizations joined together in August 1950 to issue a "Charter of German Expellees" renouncing violence but delineating special rights and demands.

The largest single group, the Federation of Homeland Expellees and the Disenfranchised (*Bund der Heimatvertriebenen und Entrechteten*), secured 5.6 percent, representing 1.6 million voters in the 1953 elections. The Federation of Expellees (*Bund der Vertriebene* or BdV) served as a roof organization for twenty-one ethnic-territorial organizations (*Landsmannschaften*), encompassing a reported 1.7 million members.[15] Major parties eager to cultivate support established internal refugee committees. Adenauer appointed a minister for refugee affairs to his first Cabinet, and began offering partial compensation to the "unjustly" expropriated under the 1952 Equalization of Burdens Act and the 1953 Federal Expellees Act, shoring up support for the fledgling state.

The influx of co-ethnics ranged from 5,537 in 1952 to a high of 129,660 in 1958; in 1961 the Berlin Wall brought closure, literally and figuratively, to the war-refugee era. While the FRG's founding narrative infers a process of rapid, successful integration of co-ethnics, historians attest that resettlers faced serious acculturation problems well into the 1950s. Neither lineage nor "professions of Germanness" but rather the leveling effects of war, the common subordination to occupational authorities, economic opportunities afforded by reconstruction, and the Economic Miracle facilitated the integration of a very diverse refugee population. The Pommeranians, Schlesiens, East-Prussians, Sudeten-Germans, and Russian repatriates differed as much from each other as they did from the natives—in terms of their histories, mentalities, languages, religious orientations, and the physical traumas they had endured en route to the German homeland. *Jus sanguinis* posited a cultural universality rarely reflected in empirical studies of these groups.

Hannelore Oberpenning relates the story of one notably "successful" integration experiment in the town of Espelkamp, located in eastern North Rhine-Westphalia (1990 population: 28,000). Although nearly a third of the refugees poured into Schleswig-Holstein, North Rhine-Westphalia soon became a major receiving point; by 1948, 1.4 million refugees comprised 10 percent of its population. British occupation forces blocked certain routes, channeling a steady stream of displaced persons into peripheral areas; they accounted for 19.4 percent of the Detmold residents, and 16 percent around Espelkamp by 1950.[16]

Established as a model town for refugee integration, Espelkamp was to serve as a symbol for "Christian reconstruction" as well as a "bulwark against Bolshevism" in Germany.[17] Key actors assembled in October 1948, realizing the urgent need for housing and job creation. Authorities feared that hordes of traumatically uprooted, socially declassed persons from the East would embody social-revolutionary potential. One synod official warned, "Millions of people among the Germans are turning into asocial types; they don't belong anywhere."[18] The Churches intervened to prevent destruction of a *Wehrmacht* munitions institute covering 250 hectars. One supporter was Max Ilger, a former IG-Farben manager.

Despite tensions between Catholic and Protestant interests, supporters formed the Reconstruction Association Espelkamp, Inc. in July 1949, with state and church sharing equal responsibility. The plan was hotly debated at the ecumenical refugee conference in Hamburg run through the World Council of Churches in February 1949 and, months later, at the World Exhibition for Urban Planning in Lisbon. Marshall Fund authorities deemed this effort to combine a commercial production center with social-housing construction and human services "the biggest thing in Germany today in the field of relief and reconstruction."[19] The model gave rise to similar settlements in Bavaria and Hessen.

One striking feature of the Espelkamp model was the extent to which integration was seen to require carefully planned, locally interactive services covering a broad array of daily needs. Supporters pushed for labor-intensive, small- and medium-sized businesses (e.g., lumber, cigar, and linen production; later, ironwork, mechanical processes, and chemistry). The distribution of jobs and housing was centrally controlled, with a built-in incentive system: residency permits were tied to the workplace under the motto, "first a job, then a dwelling." Authorities used a point system based on functional criteria as a basis for selecting workers.[20] The settlement included youth services, children's homes, rehabilitation and recreation centers from the outset; it added schools, language courses, and job training programs. Leaders stressed the need to cultivate a sense of neighborhood and belonging:

Collective self-help, cooperative self-initiative and forming a solidarity community became the most important unwritten social-political guidelines in the mastering of great need and the shaping of the incorporation process. Belonging to this was the creation of social networks, communication structures, information services, specialized interest agencies, organization of neighborhood meetings and task forces as well as cultural events and exchanges that transcended single-ethnicity groups, to promote shared togetherness, the emergence of community with the broadest possible foundation and reciprocal integration processes.[21]

By 1950, refugees accounted for 85 percent of Espelkamp's population, non-displaced persons only 15 percent; they were soon joined by a wave of mission-izing Mennonites from the US. Despite twelve years of propaganda devoted to German *Blut und Boden*, racial superiority, and the organic ties binding *das deutsche Volk*, Old-Espelkampers rejected the eastern co-ethnics from the beginning; they were perceived not as long-lost relatives but as threatening, disruptive, "dangerous hobos" whom they were "forced to take on as workers" by various authorities. Oberpenning writes: "The cultural-regional discrepancies between the receiving society and the refugee groups in every day life and material culture, in psychological and religious thought processes and behavioral patterns, in life-style, housing culture, work-rhythms, in clothing and cuisine were initially perceived to a high degree as 'foreign.' This applies to the same degree to perceptions of various migrant groups held among the refugees, deportees and resettlers themselves."[22]

This mirrors the reception experienced by other deportees, like the Germans of Upper Silesia. The wide assortment of acquired ethnicities, dialects, religious, cultural, and occupational differences could not be mitigated merely by bringing them under the cover of a single national-language—although contemporary discourse also posits this as the key to integrating Turks, Vietnamese, and Russian Jews. Integration succeeded in Espelkamp because "the self-distancing, culturally specific identities and developments were quickly broken down not least of all because of the multi-dimensional concept of integration that was used to build a 'we feeling' among refugees and expellees. This served, in turn, as a motor for local integration for solidifying this 'community of destiny', randomly assembled but pushed together and allowing for common if new socio-cultural traditions."[23]

The recently dispossessed built a positive identification with the settlement, rendering them so proud of their accomplishments that they tried to sustain Espelkamp's reputation as a "refugee city."[24] Occasional conflicts were directed not toward each other but against surrounding communities. This was made possible, to use modern parlance, through the promotion of civil society and voluntary organizations across ethnic lines. The *Baugemeinde* became a roof organization for over thirty groups by 1953, fostering new social-capital networks.

Successful integration was achieved not only by planning structural and infra-structural policies "from above" but by creating channels for "growing together from below."[25]

Ethnic repatriates enjoyed another advantage denied to subsequent guest-workers: by investing themselves in a shared commitment to building the set-tlement, Espelkamp residents quickly jettisoned illusions of returning to the homeland embraced by other refugees ("Schlesien remains ours!"). All ener-gies centered on shaping a new life in the West, altering their expectations and behaviors. By 1959, only two-thirds of Espelkamp's residents retained refugee status. The second wave would increase the population from 13,000 to 24,200 by 1980.[26] Its early success notwithstanding, Espelkamp's later experiences with *Aussiedler* shows that strategies appropriate for one era may not prove effective in another, especially when government commitment to integration becomes more rhetorical than real.

Peaceful Coexistence: Eastern Resettlers of the 1970s and 1980s

An easing of East-West tensions in the early 1970s contributed to partial reha-bilitation and some freedom of movement for Germans within Soviet borders. Curiously, only 1,600 ethnic Germans took advantage of the chance to resettle in the GDR from 1965 through 1979. Between 1950 and 1961, 3.6 million East Germans "voted with their feet" by fleeing to the Western state. The GDR lib-eralized its own rules for legal emigration in the early 1980s, resulting in the Westward relocation of thirty-two thousand *Übersiedler* during the first half of 1984. The FRG paid for the release of thirty-four thousand more through the late 1980s, and negotiated 215,000 individual GDR cases.[27] Still not accepting that they had become a land of immigration, Westerners felt increasingly squeezed between "native foreigners" and "foreign Germans."[28] Their sense of national claustrophobia would intensify dramatically with the onset of unification.

As late as 1983, sixteen million West Germans (25 percent) were still clas-sified as "expellees" by the Interior Ministry; 25–30 percent of the Bavarians claim to be of Sudeten-German origin.[29] The Federation of Expellees ada-mantly opposed *Ostpolitik*, fearing it would lead to permanent recognition of the postwar borders. Bavaria was the only Bundesrat member to reject the East-ern Treaties; the BdV challenged their constitutionality in Karlsruhe. Focusing on "good neighborly relations" with the Soviet Union and Warsaw Pact regimes, the accords also secured exit rights for German minorities, though few were able to leave without hardship. From a low of 19,100 in 1970, the numbers increased dramatically to 44,200 in 1976, 58,100 in 1978, 69,300 in 1981, and 78,500 in 1987.[30] Through the late 1980s, Polish *Aussiedler* accounted for 51–73 per-cent of all returns, Romanians 15 percent, and Soviet residents only 8 percent.

Over 550,000 of the former were allowed to depart after "professing their Ger-manness," despite the fact that Poland did not officially recognize this minority within its borders until 1988.[31]

While West Germany experienced demographic decline, Espelkamp contin-ued to grow, thanks to new arrivals; another 3,400 Mennonites from the Soviet Union and Paraguay joined the community from 1971 through 1981.[32] By the late 1980s, Espelkamp boasted of the largest Mennonite congregation in the country; another 3,100 new arrivals moved to town from 1987 to 1989, making it proportionately the largest migration site in the FRG. This wave, unfortu-nately, followed a major communal reorganization. Left to their own devices, local authorities were quickly overwhelmed, as "the snowball turned into an avalanche," bringing new conflicts. Changes in social service rules had hardly been implemented, challenging the identity of the town as a whole. The oppor-tunities for integration "from within" were limited by the physical concentra-tion of new settlers and the self-isolation of the Mennonites.

Over a span of thirty years, the migrants of the first hour had become the natives, forgetting part of their own history. Their self-understanding as the real "deportees and refugees" drew clear boundaries between themselves and new migrants. Fear of competition, rising unemployment, and fights among youth groups made it harder to promote contacts between the first and second waves.[33] Large transfers to the Eastern states impelled the government to shift integration costs to the local level; after unification, the city's Social Assistance expenditures grew to over 8 million DM.[34]

Peter Hilkes analyzed an Osteuropa Institute survey involving 1,281 repa-triates from the Ukraine, where co-ethnics had declined from 400,000 in the 1940s to 40,000 by the late 1980s. Two-thirds were born between 1917 and 1938, a generation ahead of the *Spätaussiedler*. Two-thirds had been employed up to the time of migration, 27 percent retired; 57 percent were female. Few had enjoyed higher schooling, with 41 percent completing only elementary grades. Many families had suffered under anti-Kulak policies and Ukrainian ultranationalism; two-hundred thousand who had fled to German terri-tory during the war were transported back to the Soviet Union with Allied approval. The new hardships they faced reinforced their feelings of "Ger-man identity."[35] Some relocated to other parts of the Soviet Union, hoping to expedite the "return" process; exit rules in Kirgistan, Moldavia, and Estonia were less rigid.

Although their pre-migration experiences were traumatic, 62 percent of this group arrived in the FRG under fortuitous circumstances from 1974 to 1980. Three-fourths relied on help from friends or relatives already there, leading 46 percent to choose residence based on those contacts; 72 percent refused to live in settlements designated for "Russian Germans." All but 2 percent had an eth-nic-German spouse, and preferred to speak German; 37 percent found jobs in their fields, 18 percent in related occupations, and 44 percent started over.[36] They, too, can be counted among the "successfully integrated."

The Bremer Sozialhilfe Study (1983–1989) testified to a weaker economic opportunity structure for new arrivals. First-time recipients in 1989 had to rely on Social Assistance for longer stints than cohorts admitted in 1983; the financial burden fell to local agencies. For *Aussiedler*, the dependency stage rose from 1.6 months in 1983 to 4.2 months in 1989; for migrant laborers, it increased from 2.7 months to 5.8 months due to structural unemployment. By contrast, the dependency interval fell from 11.5 months to 5.7 months among refugees and asylum applicants, probably due to a new policy of repatriating refugees as soon as a crisis was judged to have passed.

Paradoxically, A*ussiedler* who possessed high educational credentials in their countries of origin became the least employable upon arrival. Their lack of Western accreditation and language skills led to professional dequalification and underemployment. Many were hurt by the economic downturn of the 1990s; due to their atypical qualifications, they require significant transfer payments to facilitate labor market re-entry. Indeed, of all foreign groups, the *Aussiedler* comprise one of the heaviest burdens on the welfare state, above and beyond their special benefits (housing, language courses, pensions). Local budgets face the biggest strains, given the policy of delegating whole groups to smaller towns or rural areas—and then requiring them to stay put for three years.

In the Bremer sample, one of every eight *Aussiedler* drew Social Assistance, while one of four received housing subsidies. *Sozialhilfe* only accounted for 40 percent of their household incomes, however, compared to 61 percent for refugees and 53 percent among guestworkers.[37] Inter-group differences declined significantly among longer-term residents (five or more years). Smaller communities have been overwhelmed, contributing to public resentment against newcomers. The problem is not foreigners per se, but the lack of budgetary burden sharing. Cities like Berlin, Frankfurt, and Munich exercise a magnet effect—via migration chains—but receive fewer resources than others. Aliens lose federal benefit entitlements by moving out of their assigned areas, but the jobs they find in self-chosen locations may not be permanent. When they fall through the cracks, urban authorities pay the price in response to homelessness, substance abuse, youth violence, rising crime, and welfare.

Under Gorbachev, the Soviet Union adopted a 1989 law allowing exit for purposes beyond family unification and according an individual right to travel. While 104,000 *Aussiedler* abandoned the USSR from 1955 to 1986, 2.3 million rediscovered *Deutschtum* and "returned home" between 1988 and 2000, though only 2.04 million declared German their official nationality in the 1989 census.[38] The collapse of the command economy and the outbreak of ethnic conflict in newly independent republics induced a "migration psychosis," though

Table 3.2 Ethnic Resettlers by Country of Origin, 1989–1995

Year	Total	Poland	Romania	Ex-USSR	Other
1989	377,036	250,340	23,387	98,134	5,175
1990	397,075	133,872	111,150	147,950	4,103
1991	221,974	40,129	32,178	147,320	2,347
1992	230,565	17,742	16,146	195,576	1,101
1993	218,888	5,431	5,811	207,347	299
1994	222,591	2,440	6,615	213,214	322
1995	217,898	1,667	6,519	209,409	293

Source: Beauftragte für Aussiedler and Bundesverwaltungsamt.

many Germans had assimilated to escape discrimination; even more engaged in mixed marriages.[39] After 1990, 90 percent of the repatriates hailed from the former Soviet Republics. Economic conditions in Poland gradually improved, diminishing the flow from that country (see table 3.2).[40]

Recall that the period between 1989 and 1991 was marked by the simultaneous influx of four types of migrants: *Aussiedler*, East Germans, third-world asylum-seekers, and war refugees from Yugoslavia. The total number of resettling "Germans" suddenly in need of jobs and housing rose from 79,000 to over 792,000 in less than seven years, while the number of asylum seekers likewise in need was five times greater in 1990 than in 1984. Although two-thirds of the newcomers were constitutionally entitled to return to Germany, citizen resentment over the high cost of unification (new taxes, mass unemployment) produced a backlash against asylum seekers and aliens, as witnessed in Hoyerswerda, Rostock, Mölln, and Solingen.

In 1990, the Interior Ministry commissioned a study of 1,200 *Aussiedler* households to evaluate their integration experiences. Researchers found high levels of social segregation, coupled with limited regional and occupational mobility; most spent an average of twenty-three months in provisional group housing before moving into private dwellings, a crucial step in feeling "at home." Three-fourths were still in the same district where they had been placed three years earlier. Analysts found strong evidence of re-ethnicization and occupational dequalification. Nearly 75 percent who had joined local organizations preferred to stick to their own ethnic group.[41] Russians, especially, expressed "deep disappointment," mitigated only by knowing that the next generation would have it better. Women were forced to "resume" housewife roles, and family acquired intensified significance as a source of legitimization and support; Romanians seemed best adapted to the new setting. A Caritas study revealed that a majority lacked jobs in 1991–1992, although four-fifths were of working age. Unlike refugees and asylum seekers, *Aussiedler* are not barred from paid employment for the first two years.

Patrick Stevenson emphasizes that the sociocultural construction and preservation of national identities among German-speaking peoples has always depended on linguistic bonding: "the ideological mobilisation of 'the German language' has been a constant feature of attempts over the last 200 years to establish the nature and extent of 'Germanness.'"[42] Yet country-specific studies of these minorities demonstrate that co-ethnics are a lot more heterogeneous than the politicians who set the conditions for their "return." What limited language skills they possess reflect the dialects they took with them decades or centuries ago, hardly suitable for the locales to which they are assigned. While Ukrainian Germans were largely accepted, co-ethnics in Upper Silesia (Poland) were not recognized as full members of the *Volksgemeinschaft*, even during German rule: "Their Catholicism, Slavic origins, and dialects combined with a certain parochialism served to differentiate them from other members of the *Deutschtum*."[43]

Curiously, there has been no outpouring from Hungary, despite the fact that co-ethnics there had more opportunities to preserve their language and habits than in any other CEE state. Still, "the knowledge of German among the middle generation, especially among the younger members, is mainly passive so that, in view of the domestic and educational encouragement of parts [*sic*] of the young to speak German, a generation break becomes obvious. At best the middle generation uses German at home but it does not play any significant part in their professional lives anymore."[44]

Evaluating school data from the 1980s, Peter Nelde finds that two- to three-hundred kindergartens, primary, and secondary schools offered instruction in Hungarian and German to more than thirty thousand pupils; German is also used as a language of instruction in advanced schools in three cities. In some locales where German is offered as a "first language," classes are sooner full of Hungarians than native speakers; the former recognize the professional advantages a second language will bring. There is moreover an observable gap between diverse local dialects and mainstream German: "The mother tongue is usually not standard German but some local variety of it. As a consequence of this, ethnic Germans do not have an easy time learning German at school, while simultaneously the focus on standard German at school makes it more difficult for members of the Hungarian majority to communicate with members of the German minority in their mother tongue."[45] The number of persons claiming German as their mother tongue (19,072 in 1980, 21,893 in 1990) is out of synch with the number declaring German nationality (5,252 in 1980, 17,421 in 1990). "Clearly it is one thing to acknowledge that your mother tongue (whatever this term is taken to mean) is not the dominant language of state authority," Nelde observes, "but it is quite a different matter to declare allegiance to an extraneous and historically antagonistic nationality. Furthermore, for many people the relationship between language and ethnicity is apparently not only self-evident but also negotiable."[46]

This raises the question as to why people denied the right to preserve their Germanness, oblivious to dramatic changes in postwar culture, are most inclined to "return to the Fatherland." The obvious answer lies in an intense desire to escape economic hardship and political instability, the same desire driving millions of others who have come to Germany since the 1960s. The major difference is that this group, until 2000, held a unique "ticket to ride" under *jus sanguinis*. Privileged in terms of admission and financial assistance, *Spätaussiedler* have been disadvantaged by the false expectation that "feeling German" would assist them in adapting to a new country, one in which few citizens want an emotional attachment to the homeland. That gap has grown larger with each generation.

By 1989, there were four million more "World War II refugees" in Germany than in 1949, given the inheritable status. The *Spätaussiedler* of the 1990s competed directly with "automatic citizens" arriving en masse from the GDR (ten thousand per month by January 1991). Known as "Bible Germans" (a primary language source for many), these Late Repatriates are poorly educated, religiously conservative, and linguistically challenged. But they also bring younger offspring, subject to different identity dilemmas upon arrival.

Post-Soviet "Others": Integration Failures of the 1990s

Pre-1990 *Aussiedler* had been viewed as "especially capable of integration, diligent and willing to work, a model image of Germans the way they used to be."[47] The next wave, after 1991, brought a new type, labelled *Spätaussiedler*, and a further turn for the worse in the socioeconomic opportunity structure. Highly motivated and technically trained, they arrived just in time for the unification boom. Based on earlier experiences, experts predicted "good opportunities on the labor market" given their relative youth, trade skills, and a likely increase in consumer demand. The *Aussiedlerbonus* witnessed from 1983 to 1991 failed to rematerialize, however, leaving late arrivals disproportionately unemployed. New technology-intensive processes and higher productivity demands thwarted even the skilled males among them. Post-unity repatriates exceeded those establishing themselves in Germany by the late 1980s: 2.3 million came with the third wave (1990–2002), although the pace slowed considerably after 1995.

The barriers to effective integration have multiplied both in quantitative and qualitative terms. The Wall's collapse made it possible for millions to flee unstable regions. It also produced a snowball effect insofar as each wave increased the prospect of departure among relatives and neighbors left behind, inducing "a kind of peaceful ethnic cleansing."[48] Other beneficiaries of the Wall's collapse were

Table 3.3 "Late Migrations" by Country of Origin, 1995–2002

Country of Origin	1995	1996	1997	1998	1999	2000	2001	2002
Poland	1.677	1.175	687	488	428	484	623	553
Former USSR	209,409	172,181	131,895	101,550	103,599	94,558	97,434	90,587
From:								
Estonia	363	337	136	69	116	80	77	79
Latvia	360	248	124	147	183	182	115	44
Lithuania	230	302	176	163	161	193	97	178
Kazakhstan	117,148	92,125	73,967	51,132	49,391	45,657	46,178	38,653
Kyrgistan	8,858	7,467	4,010	3,253	2,742	2,317	2,020	2,047
Moldavia	748	447	243	369	413	361	186	449
Russia	71,685	63,311	47,055	41,054	45,951	41,478	43,885	44,493
Ukraine	3,650	3,460	3,153	2,983	2,762	2,773	3,176	3,179
Uzbekistan	3,468	2,797	1,885	1,528	1,193	920	990	844
Bylorussia	227	186	168	161	172	189	331	313
Yugoslavia[1]	178	77	34	14	19	0	17	4
Romania	6,519	4,284	1,777	1,005	855	547	380	256
Czech/ Slovakia	62	14	8	16	11	18	22	13
Hungary	43	14	18	4	4	2	2	3
Other States[2]	10	6	0	3	0	6	6	0
Total	217,898	177,751	134,419	103,080	104,916	95,615	98,484	91,416

Sources: *Bundesverwaltungsamt, Bundesministerium des Innern*
1) includes Croatia, Slovenia, Bosnia-Herzegovina and Macedonia, as independent states since 1992–1993
2) "Other regions," including expellees who arrived over other states.
3) Figures as of 1991 apply to united Germany.

not so happy to see them come. Among 628 East Berliners, 61 percent believed they should have stayed behind, because they "were very different from Germans, caused a lot of problems, and cost too much money"; 18 percent thought they "were better than Turks," but only 5 percent thought it was great "that Germans could finally return to their historical homeland."[49]

Table 3.4 Applications for Entry and Repatriation, 2002

Country of Origin	January 2002	February 2002	March 2002	April 2002	May 2002	June 2002	July 2002	Total 2002
Former Soviet Republics	9.239	5.225	4.879	5.352	4.710	4.126	4.994	38.525
Poland	23	30	25	21	41	7	32	179
Romania	70	35	30	19	53	44	87	338
Other states	16	15	10	16	12	19	29	117
Total 2002	9.348	5.305	4.944	5.408	4.816	4.196	5.142	39.159
Comparison with 2001	10.755	7.586	6.533	5.751	5.946	5.329	6.150	83.812

Source: Federal Ministry of the Interior, August 2002.

New legislation evoked *Torschlusspanik* among would-be migrants, that is, fear that the gates might shut permanently. The 1990 Law on Admitting Ethnic Migrants (*Aussiedleraufnahmegesetz*), followed by the 1993 War Consequences Conciliation Act brought new selection procedures, tests of Germanness, and restricted "return" to persons born before 31 December 1992. The process now begins at FRG embassies and consulates in the country of origin; applicants must answer a fifty-page questionnaire in German. The "asylum compromise" of 1993 set a cap at 225,000, reduced to a permanent quota of 100,000 in 2000. Approved applicants are referred to a central coordination office in Niedersachsen to allow for dispersal.[50] Changes in the Federal Expellees Law (*Bundesvertriebenengesetz*) adopted in 2000 explicitly define persons to be excluded, such as former communist elites. The FRG stopped providing free flights in 2000; émigrés must now arrange and pay for their own transport. Families receive a flat sum of €100 per person upon arrival (with exceptions for hardship cases).

The new requirements have created a substantial backlog in federal offices; "recognition" of ethnic status and family unification has been complicated by the proliferation of binational marriages, leading to assimilation and corresponding loss of language skills. Non-nuclear family members are now subject to regular rules for foreigners. Officials started requiring language tests in 1996; failure allows administrators to withdraw preliminary approval and deny residency permits. There are two types of tests, individual and "qualified" (taken by all family members); if applicants pass the latter, they are entitled to accelerated admission. Despite the ostensible increases in "German-nationals" counted in post-Soviet censuses, the proportion who can prove their commitment to

Table 3.5 Language Tests for Repatriates, 1996–2000

Year	Number of Tests Completed	Tests passed (in percent)
1996 (July-Dec.)	8,196	72.9
1997	57,236	63.9
1998	58,929	57.8
1999	22,862	51.6
2000	35,004	47.7

Source: Rita Süssmuth et al. (ICI) *Structuring Immigration, Fostering Integration, report by the Independent Commission on Migration to Germany* (Zuwanderungsbericht), (Berlin: 4 July 2001), 177.

Deutschtum based on language has declined (see table 3.5). The Federal Administrative Court upheld these tests, ruling that family knowledge of the language is imperative for integration and should be acquired before applicants burn their bridges. Answers need not be grammatically perfect (unlikely even among natives) but must extend beyond single words or simple phrases.[51]

Although the number needing integration assistance has never been so high, public funding prospects have never been so low. The FRG has increased spending for infrastructural projects to enhance living standards for minorities abroad. Two counties in Siberia received DM 46 million in 1995, added to DM 66 million in 1996, in exchange for "self-administration"; Poland was granted DM 20–25 million per year to assist Germans.[52] The FRG has financed over nine thousand language courses in 450 "encounter centers" in Russia and Kazakhstan since 1996.[53] Other measures have included humanitarian aid, start-up help for small businesses, investment loans, and support for one thousand sister-city partnerships in Central/East Europe. The Interior Ministry increased its integration budget from DM 10 million to DM 32 million, then to DM 45 million in 2000, despite the economic crunch.

The transfer of costs to communal governments has been especially tough. Unemployment benefits for repatriates have been replaced with an "integration subsidy," reducing the benefit from fifteen to six months. Thereafter they move on to Social Assistance, further straining local budgets already burdened by cuts in unemployment insurance for other aliens. Living expenses are no longer paid during job-retraining periods; free language instruction has been reduced from twelve to ten to six months, though *Spätaussiedler* skills are well below those of earlier cohorts. Since courses are run through Labor Offices, only those actively seeking employment are eligible; despite €500,000 (2002) in federal financing, spouses and the elderly have little access to instruction. If linguistic competency is the key to national identity as well as to successful integration, then why limit free instruction to six months? Paradoxically, most Turkish residents can speak German and read electoral ballots but, lacking citizenship, are barred from filling them out. Co-ethnics are immediately enfranchised but evince no interest in political participation or civic mobilization.

Inadequate language skills contribute to unemployment, and thus to higher welfare expenditures among a population that would certainly prefer to work. Besides extending instruction to all family members, it would make sense to combine language basics with occupationally specific training; courses along these lines helped to place 60–90 percent of workers completing them in 2002. Federal Commissioner for Ethnic Settlers, Jochen Welt, advocated channeling these through one agency to ensure uniform testing standards, cut competition among providers, and streamline administration.[54]

Many skilled workers face occupational dequalification upon arrival. There are no federal data on co-ethnic welfare recipients, since they "disappear" once they are classified as citizens. Local studies reported a sharp increase when benefits were cut to six months: 15 percent of the repatriate households drew Social Assistance in 1995, compared to 3 percent among indigenous families. One-third of Dietz and Holl's sample lived in subsidized housing (2.8 percent among nationals).[55] *Spätaussiedler* are twice as likely to receive *Sozialhilfe*. In Osnabrück/Emsland, for example, assistance payments rose from DM 700,000 in 1992, to DM 3.1 million in 1993, to DM 14 million in 1994.[56] By 1996, two-thirds of those repatriates lacked occupational certification; they accounted for 50 percent of the jobless in Alfshausen, Neuenkirchen, Ankum, and Fürstenau.[57]

Residential concentration compounds the competition for scarce jobs, although national dispersal is supposed to facilitate local integration. Under the 1989 Residential Distribution Law (*Wohnortzuweisungsgesetz*), extended through 2002, new arrivals must stay in designated areas for three years, unless they supply proof of employment and housing elsewhere. Each *Land* was assigned a specific quota as of 1990, also applied to asylum seekers/refugees. Niedersachsen was allocated 9 percent, North Rhine-Westphalia 21.8 percent; Eastern states receive 20 percent, total.[58] Small towns in big states purportedly have underused capacities, as well as more physical space. Unprepared for the 1989–1990 onslaught, officials first utilized newly vacated American or Russian military barracks and apartments. Population growth in western Niedersachsen, added to the *Aussiedler* influx, placed new pressures on housing markets; real estate speculators quickly bought up whole streets in designated towns, knowing they could impose higher rents (80 percent are renters).[59] The fact that small towns lack an independent resource base enabling them to cope with chain migration was not considered.

Integration requires a nexus between housing, employment, and social interaction. Early resettlers shared critical experiences with the native population,

Table 3.6 Repatriate Distribution, according to State, 2002

Resettled to:	Aussiedler Total	Former Soviet Union	Poland	Romania	Other countries
Baden-Württemberg	11,245	11,075	77	90	3
Bayern	13,191	13,058	35	92	6
Berlin	2,461	2,440	18	2	1
Brandenburg	3,379	3,368	9	2	0
Bremen	768	767	1	0	0
Hamburg	1,942	1,936	5	0	1
Hessen	6,536	6,477	50	6	3
Mecklenburg-Vorp.	2,636	2,632	4	0	0
Niedersachsen	7.872	7.833	31	8	
Nordrhein-Westfalen	20,018	19,709	280	26	3
Rheinland-Pfalz	4,325	4,310	9	5	1
Saarland	1,307	1,300	2	5	0
Sachsen	5,984	5,966	8	8	2
Sachsen-Anhalt	3,544	3,534	8	2	0
Schleswig-Holstein	3,003	2,993	10	0	0
Thüringen	3,205	3,189	6	10	0
Total	91,416	90,587	553	256	20

Source: Federal Ministry of the Interior (BMI), June 2003

viz., widespread social leveling in the face of defeat, miraculous economic recovery, and rapid industrialization. While many had engaged in agriculture before the war, this is no longer the case. Germans in agriculture fell sharply from 2.26 million in 1970 to 888,000 in 1993.[60] Subsequent cohorts have encountered welfare chauvinism, structural unemployment, and the export of jobs to foreign production sites.

The federal "distribution" system denies newcomers the social capital resources they could deploy if allowed to join relatives and friends in other cities. Policymakers assumed that small towns or rural areas would afford more contact with locals. Studies show that communities of five thousand or fewer warrant less contact, since locals tend to be suspicious of outsiders.[61] *Spätaussiedler* are seen as "foreigners with German passports," irritating the permanent residents with their folkish-nationalistic orientations.[62] Real integration occurs via the workplace, yet the settlement areas lack service sectors and new investment. More cosmopolitan, highly educated Russian Jews, by comparison, are not hampered by false expectations that they would be able to live as "Germans in Germany." Evading the dispersal rules, a disproportionate number of post-Soviet Jews have settled in Berlin, where they experience substantially less culture shock.

Life in small towns holds few recreational opportunities for youth who comprise 21–30 percent of the latest wave. Rural areas lack discos, clubs, museums, restaurants, and job-training venues. Rejection by local adolescents leads to re-ethnicization, self-isolation, aggression, and substance abuse. Some districts heavily populated with repatriates are labeled Little Kazakhstan. When small communities can't afford essential integration services, cross-cutting social networks are unlikely to evolve. Berlin took in twenty-seven thousand *Aussiedler* between 1980 and 1996. Officially, the Marzahn-Hellersdorf district has one of the smallest foreign concentrations at 3 percent; in reality, it is home to nearly thirty-five thousand post-Soviet migrants (14 percent), their new German passports notwithstanding. Unemployment hovers around 20 percent, but most feel comfortable in the *Plattenbau* settlement, largely because their neighbors learned some Russian in GDR schools.[63]

Although the eastern *Länder* are stereotyped as hostile to foreigners, Erfurt (Thuringia) adopted a proactive approach to integration worthy of emulation. Recognizing the need for programmatic coordination, city administrators initiated a Round Table in 1999 to address Late-Resettlers' problems. Participants included twenty-nine volunteers, including three representatives from the Youth Office, three from Social Services, two from Labor Offices, one each from Sport and Cultural affairs; others include members of refugee associations, sport organizations, two *Aussiedler* associations, the Red Cross, and multiple private service providers.[64] They developed user-friendly services that foster self-help as well as acceptance among the locals. The Round Table created a task force to survey fifty repatriates, from ages six to sixty (and beyond), to establish baseline figures and program criteria.

The second phase defined the nature/extent of migrant "needs" through open-ended interviews with firms running residency homes, social workers, etc. The city trained staff working with the newcomers, and established a Council for the Elderly, facing social isolation. It added occupational programs for ethnic youth, who share many problems with other "foreigners" in school. Erfurt has linked relevant agencies, projects, and contacts through a clearing house; it proposes quarterly activity plans, supplies program information in two languages, conducts workshops, expert conferences, and forms "Working Groups" as needed (it took a similarly proactive stance regarding women's issues after unification).

City officials have moreover taken concrete steps to bring locals and new compatriots together. They stage an Integration Festival in July, sponsored by the mayor, and publish a bilingual orientation booklet with key agencies' addresses, a city map, even information regarding bankruptcy/debt counselling. The Erfurt Russian Ensemble has fifty members (but no practice hall). Beate Tröster reports some competition among network actors ("part of democratic life"), but the holistic approach saves time and money, supplies early warning systems and accountability mechanisms, and shortcuts the learning process for all linked groups.[65]

Klaus-Dietrich Frank reports on comparable efforts in Erftkreis and Cologne. One group, Cooperation with Eastern Europe (Zusammenarbeit mit Osteuropa e.V., or ZMO) organizes *Spätaussiedler* on a non-territorial basis. Erftkreis, a county of five-hundred thousand residents spread across nine towns, has a Council for Expellees and Late Resettler Questions. Utilizing the Round Table model, local authorities see the neighborhood as the place where integration begins; new arrivals are drawn into community organizations before self-isolation sets in. A further Round Table in Cologne brings together city government reps, youth and cultural offices, social services providers, sports, musical, church associations, police and school representatives, and even members of the fire department.

Erfurt's approach is reminiscent of the Espelkamp experiment in the 1950s; unfortunately, the model is no longer used in Espelkamp itself. Between 1985 and 1996, its population grew by 21 percent due to migration.[66] Instead of revitalizing the community, new Mennonite groups became "rigorously self-isolating." Local parties lost interest in the project once it became divisive at the national level. In 1992, the town imposed a preliminary ban on further entry, triggered by financial burden shifting under the Kohl Government. Ironically, the chancellor most intent on unifying Germans was the one pushing quotas, segregation, and funding cuts for integration benefits. A community that built its reputation by figuring out "what works" seems little inclined to apply those lessons to the present. Oberpenning concludes: "local migration hot spots like Espelkamp have come to feel the consequences of failed social policies in crude ways, caused by short-sighted budgetary cuts at a time of high migration need."[67]

Female "Birds of Passage": Dequalification and Redomestication

Women constitute 52 percent of the nationals and 46 percent of Germany's "foreign-born" residents. Studying migration patterns in 1993, Stephen Castles and Mark Miller cited the *feminization of international migration* as one of the most striking trends of the last two decades—then ignored its significance.[68] Under the traditional model, migration starts with the recruitment of young, single men, followed by older married males; the next stage sees the arrival of wives and children, coupled with vague plans for return. The process ends, well into the next generation, with permanent settlement. If women are counted, it is usually as "dependents" confined to reproductive labor in the private sphere. Family unification becomes a code-word for the primordial unity of women-children-household, separated from politics, economics, and citizenship, still viewed as male prerogatives.

As Eleonore Kofman determined, however, "female birds of passage" often pursue different flight patterns than those specified by malestream scholars; feminist scholars have begun to chart their alternative courses.[69] Representing a complex constellation of dynamic social relations, gender determines "who stays, who moves, where, why, how often."[70] Women accounted for half of all non-Commonwealth entrants to the United Kingdom from 1963 to 1972.[71] The UK was not alone in denying them equal rights to family union from late 1960s onward, until the European Court of Human Rights nullified the practice in the 1980s. Today women born in Britain can bring in men under the "primary purpose rule," liberalized by the Court of Justice in the 1990s for those married five years and/or with children. Women, single and married, entered Germany as independent workers prior to the 1973 hiring freeze, a pattern mirrored among Portuguese, Spanish, and Yugoslav laborers in France. Of the 2.6 million *Spätaussiedler* arriving from 1987 to 1999, 51 percent were women.

Migration moguls rarely write about the global care chains emerging as ever more aliens assume the burdens of child care and household management, enabling indigenous women to pursue lucrative employment.[72] As Rainer Münz notes, few Germans think about their illegal Polish cleaning ladies when they rant and rave over "too many foreigners." Live-in domestics and nannies are denied family unification rights (requiring waged employment and adequate housing), a blind spot in the 1983 European Convention on Migrant Rights. Italy and Spain now issue visas for domestics, largely for the purpose of reducing illegal workers.

In contrast to their western counterparts, eastern women were pulled into the workforce in the 1960s and 1970s as an alternative to foreign recruitment. By the 1980s, 85 percent of the Soviet women held full-time jobs. Occupations like food processing, health, and child-care were feminized; banking, insurance, and trade also became female labor preserves. Even non-traditional domains like chemistry, machine-tooling, printing, painting, and public transit employed 20 percent women. The socialist response to "the women's question" neither ended the unequal division of household labor, nor granted women their share of decision-making power: "In practice, Soviet-type 'emancipation and equality' meant that gender divisions ceased to exist and women were treated by the state as badly as men: doing the same hard work for equally low salaries, similarly abused by state and party bureaucrats, getting equally miserable health care provision insensitive to their needs, and so on."[73]

The collapse of the Soviet Union and the grab-bag privatization schemes that followed eliminated state-financed support structures that had aided women in combining family and career; by 1992, they comprised 80 percent of Moscow's unemployed. Yet the Moscow Institute for Socio-Economic Population Studies found that female émigrés were more skeptical about leaving than men, (correctly) anticipating even less occupational opportunity in Germany.[74]

Women experience a disproportionate decline in their socioeconomic status, coupled with long-term unemployment as a result of resettlement. Inadequate language skills play a role, but the real problem stems from Germany's refusal to recognize their professional credentials and job experience, a process known as *dequalification*. Dequalification is an imposed status, hitting women hardest in fields historically dominated by men, e.g., medicine and engineering. Job training in the country of settlement is extended to men as breadwinners; women receive less information about labor-market mechanisms and are excluded from retraining "since they are unlikely to find work anyway."[75] Unemployment forces women into "traditional" caretaking roles, exacerbating stress on families already under pressure to adapt to a new environment. Paradoxically, women are expected to integrate the family socially and culturally at the same time they are isolated and marginalized. Policymakers fail to grasp migration as a family project.

Two clear examples include Russian Jewish women who have relocated to Israel and the wives of post-1990 *Aussiedler*. Although both groups are privy to reactivated citizenship and special benefits relative to other foreigners, women face greater discrimination in their new homelands than they did under the authoritarian regimes they left behind. The result is "both a 'brain drain' for the country of origin and 'brain waste' for the host country. . . . Besides low wages and poor working conditions, their downward mobility entails negative stereotyping and sexual harassment. Together these byproducts of resettlement seriously compromise the personal identity and psychological well-being of immigrant women."[76]

One female repatriate mused in Germany: "We used to make jokes, saying we could work as cleaning ladies as necessary." In fact, they wind up doing just that. Although the period from 1984 to 1990 saw major increases in work permits issued to health and education workers, female physicians from Russia and Bosnia found themselves wielding brooms and mops rather than stethoscopes and scalpels in German hospitals. Language barriers notwithstanding, she continues, "we're used to working. We cannot imagine the rest of our lives without work. In Russia it was the case that a woman was strong and had her own voice, when she actually had a career. But I don't know, here in Germany lots of women sit at home and think that is normal."[77] None had previously functioned as full-time housewives, characterizing the experience as monotonous, boring, difficult, isolating, and devoid of personal focus—one reason why German fertility rates have plunged, as women choose careers.

A 1991 panel study by the Institute for Labor Market and Occupational Research (IAB) examined the employment status of 3,427 *Aussiedler* and *Aussiedlerinnen* enrolled in language courses; they also interviewed 2,495 participants two years after course completion.[78] Between 1988 and 1996, women exceeded men among the "returnees" (with 1989 as the exception); 95 percent had relatives in Germany. The dominant age groups were under-twenty (29–38 percent) or twenty-five to forty-four (31–35 percent); 11 percent were sixty or older.[79] By 1993, 79 percent of the men and 54 percent of women were employed; 14 percent and 26 percent, respectively, remained jobless (those who stop looking for employment disappear from the statistics). A closer look reveals an even bigger gap: 70.5 percent of men but only 32 percent of the women held full-time jobs; 16 percent of the women (1.6 percent of the men) worked part-time. Given the dearth of childcare facilities and Germany's half-day schools, it's not surprising that only 34 percent of mothers with small children were employed (half full-time); having older or no children raised the figure to 60 percent. Ethnic differences were also notable: 71 percent of the Romanians, 66 percent of the Russians, and 62 percent of the Poles held paid jobs, among women only 59 percent, 54 percent, and 52 percent, respectively.[80]

Less than one-third continued in their previous occupations. Male electricians stood the best chance of building on past skills; other men served as hired hands, security guards, and labored in warehouses or construction. Women worked as domestics, packers, kitchen-help, and as caretakers for the elderly; 15 percent wound up as cleaning ladies, though only ten (of 121) had done so back home. The key variables influencing successful job hunts were sex, age, parental status, and language. For women, language resulted in the strongest positive correlation; 65 percent whose skills were "very good" were employed, in contrast to 33 percent among the "not very good" group. Job prospects were most negatively affected by the presence of small children. Female earnings amounted to 68 percent (for native women, 71 percent) of male wages in production, 74 percent in white-collar domains.[81] Language and children were not factors in men's success.

Aussiedlerinnen are expected to shore up family stability, as unpaid housewives, at the very point when their own identities are radically challenged. Analyzing a survey of 229 families and interviews with 286 families in 1992, Siegfried Greif, Günther Gediga, and Andreas Janikowski report that it took unskilled females 4.5 years and academic women 5.3 years until 80 percent had found jobs[82] Romanians were more likely to succeed than Soviet women. Although they possessed higher qualifications prior to migration, 69 percent of

Table 3.7 Reasons for Unemployment among Repatriates, 2002

Reasons given:	Total	Male	Female
Unpaid housewives and house-husbands	713	12	701
Children not yet in school	8.280	4,160	4,120
Children in *Hauptschule* (ending in 9th grade)	14,936	7,576	7,360
Attending technical or advanced schools	1,388	735	653
Attending technical college or university students	1,496	655	841
Finished school without specific occupation	2,064	954	1,110
Retired, "too old"	9,887	3,780	6,107
Other reasons	303	145	158
Total	39,067	18,017	21,050
Work Status	*Total*	*Male*	*Female*
Gainfully employed	52,349	25,824	26,525
Not employed	39,067	18,017	21,050
Total	91,416	43,841	47,575

Source: Federal Ministry of the Interior (BMI), June 2003.

the women had been occupationally downgraded by the time of the third interview, compared to 45 percent of the males.[83]

Of course, professional men also experience dequalification insofar as "emigration implies the renunciation of much of one's accumulated social capital, which would leave as typical Soviet consumer with a sense of not having much capital at all."[84] *Spätaussiedler* encounter the same problems as Russian Jews in seeking a proper fit between the human/social capital they bring with them, and the cultural capital required by the host country (despite few direct contacts between these groups). Jeroen Doomernik's interviews with the latter highlight the absurd rigidities of the German labor market. A former economic engineer/economist, Leonid (age fifty-seven) learns to speak German quickly, due to his familiarity with Yiddish. Realizing that his age would prevent him from attaining comparable status in the FRG, he reconciled himself to the idea of menial labor: "I applied at a large car-dealer. They wanted someone to wash their cars, polish and park them, that kind of thing. They asked me, Have you cleaned cars in Germany before? So I didn't get the job." Rare is the American teenager who has not displayed these skills at local car washes, raising money for school functions. The employment exchange was no help: "They aren't allowed to offer me a job which is below my qualifications."[85]

Gender roles reversed by male dequalification also strain family life. A former German major at Riga University, Irina (age twenty-seven) admitted, "Most people lose by leaving home because they were already somebody in the Soviet Union. I on the other hand was nothing, and gained by moving. I became someone, and therefore emancipated. For my husband, it is much more difficult. He wanted to make it big in business but didn't manage it." Irina "defines the problem" after she has already voiced her frustration over Boris (forty-one) and his failure to learn German after nearly four years: "And he doesn't do any housework. I have to work all day and when I get home he hasn't done anything. He can't cook and he can't clean." Of the twenty-eight couples Doomernik interviewed, five divorced or separated within a few years, including Irina and Boris.[86]

The dequalification that frustrates many *Spätaussiedlerinnen* stands in stark contrast to the "happily anticipated" dependence of Russian women who arrive as imported brides. Marriage-migration is pursued as a deliberate strategy in response to material instability and legal chaos in the homeland. Although privy to accelerated naturalization proceedings, these women seem intent on upholding "traditional" family roles; ironically many are too young to have witnessed such practices in the former Soviet Union. Women under age thirty tend toward de-emancipation: "All girls try to find a 'good' man, so that they don't have to work. They see their mothers, who at forty already look run down and overworked, and they don't want to end up just like them."[87] Stephan Beetz and Tsypylma Darieva infer that many reconstruct romanticized versions of their personal stories in order to avoid the stigmatizing label of "economic refugees." Wedding formalities take place "without romance, almost half in flight" on the way to Berlin.[88]

German-Russian marriages more than doubled after the Soviet collapse; the number of Slavic women in Berlin rose from 5,676 in 1991 to 12,034 (including Jews). In 1993, post-Soviet Union women and German men accounted for 10 percent of the new binational marriages in Berlin, increasing to 20 percent by 1995.[89] Social status appears to outweigh aesthetic considerations: "it's a question of having a husband, not an especially 'masculine' type." Hoping to find an *Intermann*, women subscribe to Russian language newspapers in Berlin, or have their names placed in card catalogues back in the Ukraine in the hopes of finding an eligible German.[90]

Few are aware of the legal complications that add up to major insecurity after arrival. Abused women married for less than three years may be subject to deportation even before divorce proceedings are final, though hardship exemptions were finally introduced in 1997. Generally less well educated, these women are cut off from the community and the workforce, where social integration is more likely to occur. Absolute material dependence, isolation, and frustration over intrafamilial cultural differences lead to lopsided conflicts; some are forced into prostitution.[91] Brides are not restricted regarding places of residence, since they "follow the man"; they focus on status measured in terms of material consumption rather than professional qualification. Interaction between brides and *Aussiedlerinnen* is rare.

Female resettlers arriving after 1990 encountered disadvantages above and beyond the usual rigidities of the German labor market, where career tracks, like parallel lines, never intersect. First, the Western state lacks child-care facilities and all-day schools. Unification effectively shut down facilities in the East as Western authorities "transferred" old GDR debt to local governments, causing unemployment to rise to levels exceeding those of the Great Depression. Secondly, East German women, 90 percent of whom worked full-time in 1989, were hardest hit. *Aussiedlerinnen* had to compete with jobless "native speakers," as well as with recognized female refugees fleeing Yugoslavia after 1991. Third, West German employers balked at hiring women for male occupational preserves, like insurance, banking, engineering, and medicine. The country has yet to adopt anti-discrimination laws, even under a Red-Green government. Finally, Western women facing the same problems—lack of childcare, blocked access to old-boy networks providing tips on labor vacancies—display little solidarity with post-Soviet compatriots. There is bound to be a lot of gender-role confusion among the children of professional females who have been reduced to *Putzfrauen* in their search for "a better life" in Germany.

Aussiedler Youth: Another Lost Generation?

Conflicts over gender identity are the last thing migrant children need. Many were removed against their will from familiar environments; they miss friends, relatives, and neighborhood hangouts. "That was my home, I was born there. Everyone knew my father," said one. The stress of the move is coupled with language disorientation; most can't even read the alphabet. They spend the first few months in cramped hostels, witnessing family tensions over unemployment. Parents lose their authority, unable to answer questions about the new system. Few youth experienced direct discrimination before departing, but their "German identity" is challenged in new ways once they enter the FRG.

Beate Tröster offers an ironic example of why integration sometimes goes awry, even among those trying to adapt: one mother was told by a teacher in the *Hauptschule* that her fourteen year-old son was "too smart" for the eighth grade. Ending in ninth grade, this school form has become a dumping ground for students judged unfit for highly skilled labor. The mother was surprised to learn her son should be moved up to a *Gymnasium*. Reflecting on words like

Hauptstadt (capital city) and *Hauptstrasse* (main thoroughfare), she thought she had enrolled her son in the top school.[92] Only 7.1 percent of post-Soviet youth are found there. One mother's semantic error does not explain why teachers disproportionately shunt *Aussiedler* into dead-end institutions across the republic. In 1996–1997, 12 percent of all NRW students were enrolled in *Hauptschulen,* but 27.6 percent among *Aussiedler* (22.5 percent among other ethnics). Of the four million families who have "come home to Germany," 60 percent have arrived since 1989; nearly 38 percent (250,000) are under age twenty, up to 54 percent younger than thirty. The time to integrate them is while they are young.

Barbara Dietz and Heike Holl compared the attitudes of 253 *Aussiedler* and 253 native adolescents (age fifteen to twenty-five) concerning ethnic identity, school, living conditions, job prospects, recreation, life goals, and democracy. The former had come to Germany between 1990 and 1994. Many who had already completed school held diplomas not recognized in Germany; 75 percent took language courses divorced from school curriculum. Subsidized instruction was reduced from twelve to ten months, then from eight to six months after 1993.[93] Half cited language as the biggest barrier to integration; German, as one noted, "is something we only spoke with grandma." About 46 percent of their families spoke only Russian, 46 percent a mixture of Russian and German; in the case of binational parents, 61 percent used Russian only.[94] Upon entering school, they are required to begin their "first foreign language," usually English, in the fifth or sixth grade. It would make more sense to allow them to continue in Russian as a "foreign language," in order to concentrate on German; instead they are forced to learn two new languages at once.[95]

Rather than investing in instructors qualified to teach German as a second language, officials are reducing access to courses. As the principal at one elementary school stressed: "The financial cutbacks will not pay out in the long run—these youth will later become unemployed welfare recipients rather than employed taxpayers."[96] Indeed, the jobless rate among young *Spätaussiedler* stands at 35 percent, double the rate of their 1984–1990 counterparts. Dispersal policies have produced ethnically concentrated neighborhoods such as Lahr (Baden-Württemberg) and Osnabrück. Like Turkish children in Kreuzberg, these youngsters have little contact with native speakers until they enter school. The president of Berlin's Free University, Dieter Lenzen, caused a stir in 2005 by declaring in an interview that Turkish children may perform poorly on PISA tests because of naturally lower IQs.[97]

Language problems force teens to hang out with co-ethnics; accustomed to a different leisure culture, they can't afford "normal" recreational activities, due to non-earning parents. Activities that were free in Russia (youth clubs, music, athletics) are commercialized in Germany. Males are particularly vulnerable to the temptations of drugs, alcohol, and vandalism. Among the Dietz and Holl sample, 16 percent had been "rejected" by local youth often, 43 percent occasionally due to ethnic background; only 13 percent felt welcome, 26 percent did not. Over 70 percent desired more contact with local teens. One youngster summarized the thoughts of many: "I thought we were coming to Germany to live among Germans. But wherever we went, we were only Russians." In this case, locals responded: "They should go out and learn how to speak proper German before they start making demands."[98]

Kids can be cruel, especially when their own lives lack excitement and opportunity. Roland Eckert, Christa Reis, and Thomas Wetzstein conducted a microstudy of two youth cliques (age fourteen to eighteen) in a rural town of 2,400, of whom seven hundred were migrants. The town offered few services and little industry; the next city was two hours away. Leisure-time options were limited to the *Hauptschule*, involvement in local clubs, or alcohol. The German clique consisted of eleven boys and two girls. Repatriates included thirteen boys, two girls; half were Mennonites, not all spoke German.

Neither group has a very good grasp of what it means to be German, or why there is a special constitutional connection between ethnic heritage and citizenship in the Federal Republic. The first remark is typical of many I have reviewed: "Yeah, what should I say, for Russians I was a German, for Germans here I'm a Russian. I don't know what I am."[99] Different approaches to human relations are apparent from the start; the new kids on the block claim "they aren't exactly friendly here." For them, solidarity with friends matters, but friendship "comes from the soul"; one objected to the fact that a Bosnian child was accused by the whole class of "burdening the German tax system."[100] Most feel they are stigmatized by the media. They describe their German counterparts as childish and materialistic. The latter consider "the Russians" boring and strange: "The problem is that a third or a half of them have such a funny religion. They have to run to church every three days, aren't allowed to join clubs and such. So it's a little hard to deal with them."[101]

There is also misunderstanding concerning short- versus long-term opportunity structures. For now, Russian-Germans admit, "we don't have problems here, everything is good." Another observes, "the Boss wants to hire *Aussiedler* . . . maybe they work better and don't need as much as Germans, that's clear!" The natives counter, "Russians work for DM 14 [an hour], the rest comes from the Labor Office, fifty-fifty. We can't say the Russians are competition . . . we aren't even in the running."[102] Local teens insist, "they have things pretty easy at the moment." They continue:

> You only have to report that you were born in Moscow, and then you get a five-year, interest-free loan, that naturally isn't bad. Then you get irritated that you aren't from Russia.

> They can't even speak two or three sentences of German. . . . It doesn't matter, when they had a German shepherd dog, then they were Germans. That's the way it is.

Yeah, or when they had an aunt who was from Germany, then they were Germans. . . . Yeah, she had German shepherd blood in her veins. . . . Get bit once and you were a German.[103]

School is the usual conflict site, until the native speakers move on to advanced education. Physical violence is accepted as a normal state of affairs. Locals complain, "One to one is ok. Whoever wins, has won, end-of-story, but they come with three or four to beat you up."[104] In larger cities, émigrés clash "with Gypsies and with Turks. They come and beat us up, and we don't even know where they're coming from."[105]

These exchanges make one wonder just how often politicians insisting on *jus sanguinis* as the foundation for citizenship communicate with their own offspring. But the identity differences don't end here. In their countries of origin, post-Soviet youth associated German identity with ethnic descent (41 percent), "always feeling German" (31.6 percent), and family traditions (21.7 percent); only 13 percent saw the German language as an identity component.[106] The latter seems to acquire new salience once they move to the FRG, but the more

Table 3.8 Co-ethnic and Native Views on "Being German" Question: *What does it mean to you, personally, to be a German?*

Characteristic	Aussiedler	Native-born
Speaking the German language	29.6%	9.5%
Growing up in a German family	26.8	16.6
Living with equal rights among Federal-Republicans	25.6	5.1
Holding German citizenship	15.0	18.2
Cultivating German traditions	9.4	4.0
Having Federal-German friends	6.7	0.4
Embodying German virtues	5.5	2.8
Pursuing German culture	2.3	3.6
Growing up in Germany	0.0	18.2
I don't connect anything special with it	9.9	39.1
Other	8.3	9.5
Don't know	7.5	2.0

Source: Survey conducted by the Osteuropa-Institute, reported by Barbara Dietz and Heike Roll. 1998. *Jugendliche Aussiedler—Porträt einer Zuwanderungsgeneration*. Frankfurt: Campus, 162.

interesting responses regarding Germanness stem from the indigenous group, as table 3.8 illustrates.

Nearly 40 percent of youth born in the FRG see "nothing special" about being German. One-fifth relate it to where they grew up, only 16.6 percent connect it to family life. Neither group puts much stock in German culture, virtues, or traditions. The greatest point of overlap between the two, less than 20 percent, pertains to formal citizenship, although co-ethnics clearly do not feel they enjoy all the rights that go along with it. These results correlate with my own findings regarding younger cohorts' utter disinterest in some deeper German "essence."[107] What, exactly, are national politicians trying to preserve by refusing to pass an immigration and integration law? There are certainly more direct ways to streamline welfare expenditures and to prevent undocumented workers from "taking" German jobs.

Teens are particularly sensitive to marginalization; their feelings of insecurity can lead to withdrawal tendencies, or to open conflicts. Though originally rooted in migration, exclusion becomes permanent when the minority condition is not addressed. Male youths lose contact with locals after elementary school (age thirteen and older), during a critical phase of identity formation; the result is self-ethnicization. Girls do better in school, making it easier to embrace identities based on merit, diligence, and endurance. The Dietz study characterized 15–30 percent as "youth at risk."[108]

Joachim Walter and Günther Grübl studied those who had already fallen between the cracks in Baden-Württemberg. Roughly half of those age fourteen to eighteen and nineteen to twenty-one who have landed in prison since 1993 are foreign born; this is only "the tip of the iceberg," since others have completed sentences or secured probation. Prior to 1993, *Aussiedler* accounted for 3 percent of the new internees; by 1997, the number rose to 15.6 percent (105 of 672), two-thirds born in the former Soviet Union; half wanted to "go home."[109] Comprising only 5 percent of the state's pupils, their internment rate is twice as high; they spend more time in pre-trial detention, face longer sentences, and are granted less probation. They engage in substance abuse at twice the rate of Germans (26 percent vs. 14.5 percent), and commit more sexual assault (8.3 percent vs. 2 percent of the rest).[110] Most have only attended *Hauptschule.*[111] As Heinz Kuhn declared in 1970: "What we don't want to pay for integration today, we will have to pay later in expenditures for police and resocialization."[112]

The state response is simplistic at best; it needs to prosecute violent offenders, but this does not provide a positive basis for identification with the rule of law among teens from "lawless" or mafia-driven regions. Youth work has to take place at the local level, but communal governments are going broke due to other migration costs. The SPD-Green government designated the integration of young resettlers a priority, largely because they have become a visible problem group: "There's a social time-bomb ticking here."[113] In 2000 it adopted an "emergency" plan against youth unemployment; the Riester Program allocated DM 2 billion to create one hundred thousand new jobs. Working with the German Sport Union, it initiated "Action: Sport with Foreigners," involving four thousand individual measures "as a real vaccination" against gang activity, drugs, vandalism, and criminality.

Communal governments are figuring out that they cannot treat integration problems at the margins. The fact that many new entrants since 1990 are young means that most have a realistic chance of integrating by adulthood. But this will require more than abstract professions of Germanness.

"You can't go home again" and Other Identity Conundrums

Since 1945, more than twenty million people have entered the Federal Republic and stayed there. Lawmakers need to bury their mythical assertions regarding the "temporary status" of 7.3 million people who have no intention of going home, and the "innate" abilities of another 4.3 million to embrace the German way of life. *Aussiedler* experiences since the 1990s suggest that Thomas Wolff was right: "You can't go home again." Or, as Gunter Grass told me during a May 1989 conversation about East German identities: "Identity? Homeland? I believe that "home" is something one can only define as something that one has lost."[114]

In July 2004, Germany finally adopted a law allowing permanent migration under special conditions. While still highly restrictive, it largely nullifies the conservative organic approach to citizenship that has dictated complex legal distinctions among would-be settlers for over a century. German migration historians question whether *jus sanguinis* ever functioned as the best mechanism for ensuring the social, political, and economic integration of minorities. Indeed, notions of cultural qua racial purity implicit in this approach lent themselves all too easily to genocidal practices under the Nazis, and legitimized the politics of exclusion even under a democratic state.

Complex legal frameworks often lag far behind political-cultural change. As Dietrich Thränhardt stresses, "Immigration processes are just as much a daily occurrence today in Germany as emigration processes were over a hundred years ago. From eating by the Italians, at the Greek place, or in Chinese restaurants, to the workplace in industry, differences in heritage are taken for granted. In the Ruhr region, the big industrial melting pot, Turkish names are as much a part of daily life as Polish ones. We find new mosques along with new Baptist churches in places of ethnic resettlement from Russia."[115] German politicians remain ironically impervious to parallels between the new identity crises witnessed among "blood relatives" from Kazakhstan, on the one hand, and the culture shock cum language deficiencies confronting early Turkish guestworkers, on the other. They are likewise blind to the problems FRG-born

"Turkish" youth would now face, were they to return abruptly to a country few have known across a span of fifty years. No matter what their legal classification, migrants everywhere search for intangible homes away from home.[116]

The descendants of expellees constitute a paradoxical case. As late as 2000, these "refugees" still received federal subsidies, though the Schröder Government cut funds from DM 52 million (1998) to DM 34 million (2004).[117] Having built new lives in a wealthy, democratic Germany, why would expellee offspring want to go back? Over 200,000 miners have lost their jobs in Schlesien; women are turning to prostitution to compensate for their "bare misery."[118] Do second-generation Sudeten-Germans, age forty to sixty, expect to learn Czech upon returning to their other "homeland"? Do they seek moral retribution for atrocities committed against their parents—or are they more interested in the real estate? All too many *Erbgemeinschaften*—descendants of Westerners who "lost" GDR property, then banned together after 1990 to sue for restitution—immediately sold it to real-estate speculators once they had successfully "reclaimed" it.[119] By contrast, many Czech slave laborers from WWII, dying at the rate of fifteen per day, still have not received their compensation.

Antje Volmer put it bluntly in a summer 2000 Bundestag debate over EU enlargement: "The topic of expulsion belongs in the Museum of German History."[120] Blood may be thicker than water, but it is hardly a basis for promoting democratic tolerance and economic opportunity. It makes little policy sense to draw lines between *Spätaussiedler*, war-refugees, non-deportable asylum seekers, and other foreigners, all facing the same barriers to integration: language deficiencies, limited education, lack of jobs, and arcane labor regulations.

Berlin Commissioner Barbara John reflected in 1999 on the paradigmatic question, *what is an integrated foreigner?* She noted several critical indicators: mastery of the German language (as the only native FRG politician who speaks Turkish!), school certification, labor-market participation, mutual respect, and willingness to embrace common values and institutions. What matters is not the presence of differences but their valuation. An advocate of "best practices," she supports permanent settlement rights for long-term residents, and realizes that denying work permits to spouses for years hinders integration. Society "can only profit from immigration when it undertakes active integration."[121] John even helped to establish a Muslim cemetery in Berlin. Human, cultural, and social capital are what matters—not pseudo-genetic predispositions.

Reacting to CDU-Minister Günter Beckstein's call for a "Christian-German *Leitkultur*," Dieter Oberndörfer, like John, challenges lawmakers' monocultural assumptions. Integration is a German responsibility:

> Whoever demands that foreigners integrate themselves into German culture first has to answer the question: *what is an integrated German?* Are Southern or Northern Germans, Catholics, Protestants, secular or non-denominational citizens Germans, those who have converted to Islam or Buddhism, academics or farmers, SPD

members or CSU voters the right model for integration and integrated Germans? The question . . . has no answer, given the fact that our cultural forms and life-styles are part of an ever more pluralistic society. A definitive answer would contra-dict individual cultural freedom, the freedom to choose a world-view and religious creed, the foundation of a modern, free constitutional state protected by the Basic Law. Citizens are free to decide on their own what German culture means, and how it is to be defined. The culture of Germany is the culture of its citizens. And the culture of its citizens is nothing static, it changes and pluralizes itself. . . . Cultural freedom must be guaranteed to all citizens regardless of their ethnic heritage, reli-gion or worldview. This is also true for migrants of foreign descent. Only then will they be able to integrate themselves into our state and become good patriots.[122]

Persistent efforts to block immigration by way of opaque legal categories, discretionary administrative criteria, arcane bureaucratic processes, and harm-ful historical myths has led to many bizarre cases, such as the Polish family circumstances described by Norbert Cyrus:

A woman who came to Berlin in the 1980s as an *Aussiedlerin* lives here permanently and is employed at a Berlin administrative agency. Her niece has likewise been recognized as an *Aussiedlerin* but lives with her family in Poland. She has rented an apartment in Ber-lin that she sublets to commuting Polish laborers. The apartment is watched over by her mother who, in contradiction to her sister and daughter, has not been recognized as an *Aussiedlerin* because she submitted her application too late. This woman is still trying to secure recognition as an *Aussiedlerin* but meanwhile lives as an unregistered [illegal] Polish citizen in Berlin who takes care of the elderly for a German family. Her son, who has also remained a Polish citizen, commutes between Poland and Berlin, where he occasionally undertakes renovation work without a work-permit.[123]

This chapter demonstrates that neither ethnicity nor blood/descent con-stitute necessary and/or sufficient conditions for effective socioeconomic or political integration in modern Germany. The successful incorporation of millions of migrant-refugees prior to 1990 owed more to the FRG's politi-cal interest in sustaining belief in unification, its moral commitment to the victims of two world wars, its unprecedented economic recovery, and its deep desire for reconciliation with neighboring states than to the binding influ-ences of a unique *Kulturnation*. Dating back to 1949, the privileged legal status enjoyed by three generations of ethnic resettlers—*Vertriebene*, *Auss-iedler*, and *Spätaussiedler*—guaranteed their access to housing, work permits, and social welfare benefits as a function of Article 116 GG. The collapse of the Iron Curtain induced a profound change of heart regarding "blood-ties" and the absorptive capacity of the nation-united. The geopolitical condi-tions giving rise to unlimited exit from former Soviet regions have yielded to restricted entry to the Fatherland under amended asylum qua migration policies since 1993.

Espelkamp's experiences across three (metaphorical) generations of repatriates further shows that the successes of the 1950s and 1960s were a direct result of planned, holistic, and locally orchestrated integration policies. Rather than pitting different groups against each other based on abstract notions of Germanness, authorities promoted self-organization and networking in response to real material needs. Abandoning the myth of return at the outset, these groups quickly developed a shared stake in community building, which then fostered new sources of social capital, transcending territorial origins, dialects, and expulsion experiences. The more the state seeks to shift the burden to communal governments—i.e., when the market failed to deliver additional "miracles" in the 1980s and 1990s—the less socially, economically, and politically integrated subsequent waves of co-ethnics prove to be.

Neither ethnic hierarchies, legal complexities, or shifting admission policies have put a stop to migration since 1989–1990. They have simply forced ever more people into a state of mobile illegality. It is time to end the ethnic masquerade with regard to citizenship, and likewise time to jettison the rhetoric of *Leitkultur* in relation to religion and refugees, the focus of the next chapter.

Notes

1. Although outward migration dates back to the twelfth century, this study focuses only on developments since Germany's founding as a modern nation-state.
2. Klaus J. Bade, "Einführung: Aussiedler. Deutsche Einwanderer aus Osteuropa," in Klaus J. Bade and Jochen Oltmer, Hg., *Aussiedler: deutsche Einwanderer aus Osteuropa*, IMIS, Bd. 8 (Osnabrück: Universitätsverlag Rasch, 1999), 19.
3. Rainer Münz and Rainer Ohliger, "Long Distance Citizens: Ethnic Germans and Their Immigration to Germany," in Peter Schuck and Rainer Münz, eds., *Paths to Inclusion: The Integration of Migrants in the United States and Germany* (Providence/Oxford: Berghahn, 1998), 160ff.
4. Volker Ronge, "German Policies towards Ethnic Minorities," in Rainer Münz and Myron Weiner, eds., *Migrants, Refugees and Foreign Policy: U.S. and German Policies toward Countries of Origin* (Providence/Oxford: Berghahn Books, 1997), 126.
5. H. J. Heintze, "The Status of German Minorities in Bilateral Agreements of the Federal Republic," in Stefan Wolff, ed., *German Minorities in Europe: Ethnic Identity and Cultural Belonging* (New York/Oxford: Berghahn, 2000), 205ff.
6. The debates that did occur were tied to "compensation and apology" affecting Germans expelled from CEE territories after 1945. See Ann L. Phillips, *Power and Influence after the Cold War: Germany in East-Central Europe* (Lanham, MD: Rowman & Littlefield, 2000).
7. Horst Teltschick claims that Kohl never questioned the permanent nature of the borders before the Wall fell but refused to declare this, hoping to "prepare" hardliners and expellees for formal recognition; cited in Emil Nagengast, "The German Expellees and European

Values" (paper presented at the German Studies Association meeting, Houston, TX, October 2000) 14ff.

8. Bade, "Einführung," 32.
9. Gerd Stricker, "Ethnic Germans in Russia and the Former Soviet Union," in Wolff, *German Minorities in Europe*, 165.
10. Ibid.
11. Bade, "Einführung," 18.
12. Ronge, "German Policies towards Ethnic Minorities," 124.
13. Ibid.
14. Barbara Dietz and Klaus Seghers, "Policies towards Russian and Other Successor States," in Münz and Weiner, *Migrants, Refugees and Foreign Policy*, 148.
15. Nagengast, "The German Expellees," 8.
16. Hannelore Oberpenning, "Zuwanderung und Eingliederung von Flüchtlingen, Vertriebenen und Aussiedlern im lokalen Kontext—das Beispiel Espelkamp," in Bade and Oltmer, *Aussiedler*, 289.
17. Ibid., 287.
18. Ibid., 290.
19. Ibid., 287.
20. Ibid., 298.
21. Ibid., 298.
22. Ibid., 302.
23. Ibid., 300.
24. Ibid., 302.
25. Ibid., 299.
26. Ibid., 296.
27. Rainer Münz and Ralf Ulrich, "Changing Patterns of Migration to Germany," in Klaus J. Bade and Myron Weiner, *Migration Past, Migration Future: Germany and the United States* (New York/Oxford: Berghahn Books, 1997), 74.
28. Klaus J. Bade, "From Emigration to Immigration: The German Experiences in the Nineteenth and Twentieth Centuries," in Bade and Weiner, *Migration Past, Migration Future*, 24.
29. Nagengast, "The German Expellees," 8.
30. Hedwig Rudolph, "Die Dynamic der Einwanderung im Nichteinwanderungsland Deutschland," in Heiner Fassmann and Rainer Münz, eds., *Migration in Europa: Historische Entwicklung, aktuelle Trends und politische Reaktionen* (Frankfurt/Main: Campus, 1996), 166.
31. Karl Cordell, "Poland's German Minority," in Wolff, *German Minorities*, 92.
32. Oberpenning, "Zuwanderung und Eingliederung," 303.
33. Ibid., 307.
34. Ibid., 311.
35. Peter Hilkes, "Migrationsverläufe: Aussiedlerzuwanderung aus der Ukraine," in Bade and Oltmer, *Aussiedler*, 62–65, 71.
36. Ibid., 77–78.
37. Ibid., 69.
38. Stricker, "Ethnic Germans in Russia," 170; also, Rita Süssmuth et al. (ICI), *Structuring Immigration, Fostering Integration*, report by the Independent Commission on Migration to Germany (Zuwanderungsbericht), (Berlin: 4 July 2001), 174–175.
39. Stricker, "Ethnic Germans in Russia," 171.
40. Ronge, "German Policies towards Ethnic Minorities," p. 130.
41. Ulrich Mammey, "Segregation, regionale Mobilität und soziale Integration von Aussiedlern," in Bade and Oltmer, *Aussiedler*, 107–126.

42. Patrick Stevenson, "The Ethnolinguistic Vitality of German Speaking Communities in Central Europe," in Wolff, *German Minorities*, 109.
43. Cordell, "Poland's German Minority," 66.
44. Peter Hans Nelde, "Bilingualism among Ethnic Germans in Hungary," in Wolff, *German Minorities*, 127.
45. Ibid., 132.
46. Stevenson, "The Ethnolinguistic Vitality of German Speaking Communities," 110.
47. Dietrich Thränhardt, "Integration und Partizipation von Einwanderungsgruppen im lokalen Kontext," in Bade and Oltmer, *Aussiedler*, 232.
48. Dietz and Holl, *Jugendliche Aussiedler*, 30.
49. Reported by Nelli Chrustaleva Freinkmann, "Die psycho-soziale Situation russischer Emigranten unter besonderer Berücksichtigung der deutschen Spätaussiedler" (conference documentation, *Aussiedler in der Berliner Schule—Chancen und Probleme*, Berlin, 25 October 2001), 30.
50. Different nationalities do congregate in certain regions; in the IAB study, 60 percent of Polish settlers landed in NRW, Romanians in Bavaria and Baden-Württemberg, while post-Soviets gravitated to NRW, Niedersachsen, and Baden-Württemberg. Barbara Koller, "Spätaussiedler auf dem Arbeitsmarkt: In einem anderen Land," *IAB Materialien*, Nr. 2/1999.
51. ICI, *Structuring Immigration, Fostering Integration*, 177.
52. Ronge, "German Policies towards Ethnic Minorities," 136.
53. Reported in ICI, *Structuring Immigration, Fostering Integration*, 180.
54. Jochen Welt, "Die Aussiedlerpolitik der Bundesregierung: Zwischenbilanz und Ausblick," in *Neue Wege der Aussiedlerintegration: vom politischen Konzept zur Praxis* (Bonn: Friedrich Ebert Stiftung, 2000).
55. Barbara Dietz, "Jugendliche Aussiedler in Deutschland: Risiken und Chancen der Integration," in Bade and Oltmer, *Aussiedler*, 167–168.
56. Thränhardt, "Integration und Partizipation," 233.
57. Hans-Joachim Wenzel, "Aussiedlerzuwanderung als Strukturproblem in ländlichen Räumen," in Bade and Oltmer, *Aussiedler*, 276.
58. Ibid., 265.
59. Ibid., 279.
60. Koller, "Spätaussiedler auf dem Arbeitsmarkt," 11.
61. Wenzel, "Aussiedlerzuwanderung," 269.
62. Ibid., 279.
63. Rainer Ohliger and Ulrich Raiser, *Integration and Migration in Berlin: Zahlen—Daten—Fakten* (Berlin: Beauftragte für Integration und Migration, 2005), 49.
64. Beate Tröster, "Das Netzwerk für Integration in Erfurt," in *Neue Wege der Aussiedlerintegration*.
65. Ibid., 102.
66. Oberpenning, "Zuwanderung und Eingliederung," 303.
67. Ibid., 312.
68. Stephen Castles and Mark J. Miller, *The Age of Migration* (London: Macmillan, 1993).
69. See, for example, the special issue on Gender and Migration edited by Katharine M. Donato et al., *International Migration Review* 40, no. 1 (2006): 3–256.
70. Patricia R. Pessar and Sarah J. Mahler, "Gender and Transnational Migration" (paper presented at the Princeton University conference on Transnational Migration: Comparative Perspectives, Princeton, NJ, 30 June–1 July 2001).
71. Eleonore Kofman, "Female 'Birds of Passage' a Decade Later: Gender and Immigration in the European Union," *International Immigration Review* 33, no. 2 (1999): 269–299. Also, Michael Jones-Correa, "Different Path: Gender, Immigration and Political Participation," *International Migration Review* 32, no. 2 (1998): 326–349.

72. See Pierette Hondagneu-Sotelo, *Doméstica: Cleaning and Caring in the Shadows of Affluence* (Berkeley, CA: University of California Press, 2001); also, Grace Change, *Disposable Domestics: Immigrant Women Workers in the Global Economy* (Cambridge, MA: Southend Press, 2000).

73. Larissa I. Remennick, "'Women with a Russian Accent' in Israel: On the Gender Aspects of Immigration," *European Journal of Women's Studies* 6 (1999): 442.

74. Manuela Westphal, "Familäre und berufliche Orientierungen von Aussiedlerinnen," in Bade and Oltmer, *Aussiedler*, 134.

75. Ibid., 139.

76. Remennick, "'Women with a Russian Accent,'" 455. Kofman also addresses "brain waste."

77. Westphal, "Familäre und berufliche Orientierungen," 142.

78. Barbara Koller, "Aussiedler der grossen Zuwanderungswellen—was ist aus ihnen geworden?" *Mitteilungen AB* (Arbeitsmarkt- und Berufsforschung), no. 4 (1997): 772.

79. Ibid., 768–769.

80. Ibid., 776–779.

81. Ibid.; Koller, "Spätaussiedler auf dem Arbeitsmarkt," 11.

82. Siegfried Greif, Günther Gediga, Andreas Janikowski, "Erwerbslosigkeit und beruflicher Absteige von Aussiedlerinnen und Aussiedlern," in Bade and Oltmern, *Aussiedler*, p. 91.

83. Ibid., 102;

84. Jeroen Doomernik, *Going West: Soviet Jewish Immigrants in Berlin since 1990* (Aldershot/Brookfield: Avebury, 1997), 95.

85. Ibid., 130.

86. Ibid., 154–155.

87. Ibid., 397.

88. Stephan Beetz and Tsypylma Darieva, "Ich heirate nicht nur den Mann, sondern auch das Land: Heiratsmigrantinnen aus den ehemaligen Sowjetunion in Berlin," in Hartmut Häusserman and Ingrid Oswald, eds., *Zuwanderung und Stadtentwicklung* (Opladen: Westdeutscher Verlag, 1997), 388.

89. Ibid., 390.

90. Ibid., 392–393. *Intermann* is a play on the term *Intershop*, special stores in the former Eastbloc where citizens could buy Western-imported goods or scarce items from the home market, albeit only with Western currency.

91. Ibid., 389.

92. Tröster, "Das Netzwerk für Integration in Erfurt."

93. Dietz, "Jugendliche Aussiedler," 158.

94. Ibid., 159.

95. Ursula Strahl, "Chancen und Probleme junger Spätaussiedler in der Grundschule" (conference documentation, *Aussiedler in der Berliner Schule—Chancen und Probleme*, Berlin, 25 October 2001), 47.

96. Dietz, "Jugendliche Aussiedler," 166.

97. Christine Richter, "FU-Präsident soll sich entschuldigen," *Berliner Zeitung*, 21 July 2005.

98. Dietz, "Jugendliche Aussiedler," 174; further, Joachim Walter and Günther Grübl, "Junge Aussiedler im Jugendstrafvollzug," in Bade and Oltmer, *Aussiedler*, 187–188.

99. Roland Eckert, Christa Reis, Thomas A. Wetzstein, "Bilder und Begegnungen: Konflikte zwischen einheimischen und Aussiedler Jugendlichen," in Bade and Oltmer, *Aussiedler*, 195.

100. Mareike Wehmann, "Freizeitorientierung jugendlicher Aussiedler und Aussiedlerinnen," in Bade and Oltmer, *Aussiedler*. Wehmann conducted in-depth interviews with eleven co-ethnics, age 16–19, in Belm, a town of 15,000 outside Osnabrück in 1996.

101. Eckert, Reis, and Wetzstein, "Bilder und Begegnungen," 196.

102. Ibid., 200.

103. Ibid., 196–197.

104. Ibid., 200–202.

105. Ibid., 215.

106. Dietz, "Jugendliche Aussiedler," p. 161

107. Joyce Marie Mushaben, *From Post-War to Post-Wall Generations: Changing Attitudes towards the National Question and NATO in the Federal Republic of Germany* (Boulder CO: Westview, 1998).

108. Dietz, "Jugendliche Aussiedler," 175.

109. Walter and Grübl, "Junge Aussiedler," 177–189.

110. Ibid., 181–183.

111. Christian Pfeiffer and Peter Wetzels, "Integrationsprobleme junger Spätaussiedler und die Folgen für ihre Kriminalitätsbelastung," in *Neue Wege der Aussiedlerintegration*.

112. Bade and Oltman, *Aussiedler*, 38.

113. Welt, "Die Aussiedlerpolitik," 13.

114. Joyce Marie Mushaben, "Introduction," in *What Remains? The Dialectical Identity of Eastern Germans* (forthcoming).

115. Thränhardt, "Integration und Partizipation," 229.

116. Helmuth Berking, "'Homes away from Home': Zum Spannungsverhältnis von Diaspora und Nationalstaat," *Berliner Journal der Soziologie*, no. 1 (2000), pp. 49–60.

117. "Naumann: Nein zu Vertriebenen-Stätte," *Die Welt*, 21 September 2000.

118. Jan Puhl, "Prostitution in Polen: Nacktes Elend in Schlesien," *Spiegel* Online, 21 July 2004 (www.spiegel.de/politik/ausland/0,1518,309512,00.html).

119. Daniela Dahn, *Wir bleiben hier oder wem gehört der Osten? Vom Kampf um Häuser und Wohnungen in den neuen Bundesländer* (Berlin: Rowohlt, 1994).

120. Stenographischer Bericht, Deutscher Bundestag, 109. Sitzung (9 June 2002), 10298.

121. Barbara John, "Was ist ein integrierter Ausländer?" *Der Tagesspiegel*, 6 June 1999.

122. Dieter Oberndörfer, "Was ist eigentlich ein integrierter Deutscher?" *Frankfurter Rundschau*, 24 October 2000.

123. Norbert Cyrus, "Mobile Migrationsmuster: Zuwanderung aus Polen in die Bundesrepublik Deutschland," *Berliner Debatte INITIAL* 11 (2000): 95–103.

CHAPTER 4

CHANGING PLACES, TEMPORARY FACES

Religion, Refugees, and Diasporas

Two extremities in a free Europe:
They used to be locked in,
Now they are locked out.
— Markus Schönherr, *One Europe Magazine*

There are three types of migration. The first type is difficult migration. The second type is very difficult migration. The third type consists of extremely difficult migration. . . . I can only hope that my migration will be the first kind.
— Gregory Salomonov, planning to leave Riga[1]

E legant in its simplicity, Article 16 of the Basic Law proclaimed without qualification: "Persons persecuted on political grounds enjoy the right to asylum." Rooted in efforts to atone for its crimes against humanity under National Socialism, Germany's unqualified promise to harbor victims of persecution stood as one of the world's most generous asylum laws for four decades. The practice of asylum was not immune to Cold War influences, however.

Notes for this section begin on page 165.

Definitions of *political persecution* varied significantly from east to west. The Federal Republic opened its doors to persons oppressed for advocating free speech/assembly, the right to organize parties/elections, independent media, and other democratic liberties. Less universal in its formulation, East German law granted safe haven to persons opposing racial/ethnic hatred, anti-fascists, trade unionists, and persons advocating "friendship among peoples" or (paradoxically) national wars of liberation.

Asylum applications filed in the FRG rose from 4,792 in 1973 (covering 5,595 persons) to 41,953 (51,493 persons) in 1979. The figure more than doubled in 1980, peaking at 92,918 (for 107,818 persons), accounting for two-thirds of all applications submitted in Western Europe.[2] The majority sought refuge from East European regimes. The GDR saw a major influx of refugees in response to right-wing coups in Greece, crackdowns in Franco's Spain, and the 1973 overthrow of Allende in Chile. Applications in both cases covered dependents and family members, on the assumption that men were political activists, women and children only indirect victims of oppressive systems.

The 1975 Helsinki Accords, including the "third basket" on human rights, led to a flurry of democratic initiatives, resulting in state crackdowns on intellectuals after the creation of *Solidarity* in Poland and *Charter 77* in Czechoslovakia. The 1970s not only saw a quantitative increase but also a qualitative shift in FRG applications, from Soviet-bloc dissidents to victims of armed conflict and economic deprivation in the Third World. These trends, in turn, precipitated a radical shift in public discourse: Terms like *pseudo-applicants*, *asylum parasites, economic refugees*, and *asylum cheaters* moved from the neighborhood bars into the *Bildzeitung*, and even into the bourgeois press.[3] Court cases filed in the 1970s challenged the motives of asylum applicants. One critical verdict held that "torture as a punishment for the non-violent attempt to claim forbidden democratic basic rights in a persecuting state in which torture was a usual instrument for punishment or interrogations was no longer defined as 'political' persecution and therefore was no longer adequate grounds for asylum."[4] Over the next two decades, Germany would move from restricting the practice of unqualified asylum to almost eliminating the constitutional right.

The treatment of refugees and asylum seekers allows us to test the validity of the radical-democratic approach to migration advocated by Third World and human-rights activists, as well as most Greens. The results are far from encouraging for those hoping to extend universal personhood and local participation rights to long-term residents in any EU country, irrespective of national origin. This chapter addresses five myths that have dominated public discourse as well as asylum practices since the late 1970s with regard to three core groups: Jewish "quota refugees" from the former Soviet Union; Bosnians and Kosovars forced to flee their homeland as a consequence of war in Yugoslavia; and persons victimized by Islamic fundamentalism. I argue that just as ethnic descent has led to overly complex legal categorizations applied to migrants, religion has been used to establish dysfunctionally complex classifications among refugees, with few positive consequences for their successful integration.

We first review the legal standing accorded successive waves of refugees, and the benefits available to each. The chapter then contextualizes the asylum myths and the constitutional changes adopted as part of a larger "compromise package" in 1993. I follow this with profiles of three refugee groups defined in terms of their religious affiliations, describing their experiences in Germany. Next I analyze the male-normed nature of asylum law and Germany's problems in coming to terms with Muslim women, especially since the terrorist attacks of September 11th. The argument here is that post-1990 efforts to block migration by adopting new exclusionary criteria, grounded in cultural differences and/or pseudo-emancipatory goals for women, are just as ineffective as earlier efforts to restrict migration based on ethno-national criteria. As stressed in the *6th Report on the Status of Foreign Families*, illegal migrants of all sorts managed to establish themselves in Germany long before there were such things as legal migrants—if only because there was no law allowing people to enter as "non-exceptions" prior to 2004.[5] Both work against the country's future socioeconomic needs.

Political Persecution, Contingency Refugees, and "Little Asylum"

In the mid-1980s, the Kohl Government negotiated with the GDR to tighten entry restrictions at the Schönefeld Airport in East Berlin to stem the flow of refugees from Third World states. I remember hearing the news in Stuttgart while researching Pershing II missile deployments, wondering why no one objected to Bonn's efforts to add "concrete blocks" to some parts of the Berlin Wall at the same time Ronald Reagan was exhorting Mikhail Gorbachev to tear down the rest of it. The Bundestag approved a five-year ban on paid labor by asylum applicants in 1987; it added visa restrictions for persons entering from nine African and Asian countries. As chapter 3 showed, the Wall's collapse triggered exponential increases not only in refugees flows but also among East Germans and co-ethnics more intent on voting with their feet than with ballots in newly democratizing states.

Real asylum rights, ensuring unlimited residency rights and legal access to jobs, were granted to very few. First-time applicant totals rose from 1,906 in 1953 to 16,284 in 1956 (invasion of Hungary), averaging 4,000 per year in the 1960s. It peaked again in 1969 at 11,664 (Prague Spring), shooting up to 107,818 in 1980 (martial law in Poland). Applications dropped to 19,737 in

1983 but the fall of the Wall and war in Yugoslavia saw further exponential growth, from 193,063 in 1990, to 256,112 in 1991 and to 438,191 in 1992.[6] The formal recognition rate declined from a high of 29 percent in 1985 to 1.8 percent in 2003. Between 1990 and 2004, the rate of positive decisions (Article 16 GG criteria) ranged from 9 percent (1995) to a new low of 1.63 percent in 2004.[7] The 1991 Maastricht Treaty initiated the process of "Europeanizing" migration and asylum policy by way of its intergovernmental "third pillar." Following the Schengen accords, the 1997 Amsterdam Treaty recognized a need to harmonize these policies beyond questions of border control.[8]

Prior to 2000, only persons who could prove they had been persecuted by state actors were eligible to apply for constitutionally-mandated asylum status (§16 GG). That rule was modified by a High Court verdict in August 2000 recognizing "quasi-state" forms of persecution, due to civil war in Afghanistan. Earlier judicial rulings had declared Afghanis, especially women, ineligible insofar as the Taliban regime, recognized by only two other rogue polities, did not comprise a real state. The new criteria hold that "war parties" exercising a form of stable domination and a monopoly of force over a core territory do exercise "state power."[9]

The Federal Republic also accords a status known as *little asylum*, grounded in the 1951 Geneva Refugee Convention (codified as §51 of the Aliens Act). A person whose "life or freedom is threatened because of his [*sic*] race, religion, nationality, his belonging to a specific social group or because of his political convictions" in the home state is protected against deportation, after certification by the Federal Office for Foreign Refugees. So-called *Convention refugees* receive a "passport" and residency permit good for two years; it can be renewed at six-month intervals if recognition is not revoked due to improved homeland conditions. The number of Convention refugees rose from sixteen thousand in 1996 to seventy-five thousand in 2002 (table 4.2).

Persons who face torture, the death sentence, degrading treatment, or other concrete dangers may be "tolerated" (*Duldung*) as temporary refugees under §53 of the Aliens Act (AA). Protection from immediate deportation can be extended under §30 AA; residency is granted for short periods, but access to social assistance is denied. A fourth category consists of "quota refugees," deriving from Germany's historical responsibility toward specific groups. Their number declined from 12,000 in 1996 to 6,800 in 2002, owing to new rules for Jewish migrants from the former Soviet Union, some of whom took advantage of accelerated naturalization processes.

A final designation applies to the "collective victims of war." The breakup of Yugoslavia brought three distinctive waves fleeing "ethnic cleansing" in 1991–1992, 1994–1996, and again in 1999. Arrivals from Bosnia Herzegovina reached a high of 345,000 in 1996, dropping to 28,000 by late 2000; 31,451 more arrived from Kosovo in 1992, followed by 11,121 in 2002. Nearly 85,500 were repatriated by March 2001, including 7,400 against their will. Bavaria was quick to declare that order had been restored and conditions were "safe" in the

Table 4.1 German Refugee/Asylum Classifications

Refugees and asylum-seekers are classified as follows under German law:

* *Persons entitled to asylum* are recognized victims of political persecution under Article 16a (1) of the Basic Law. They have proved that they are victims of persecution directed specifically at their person by state entities in the entire territory of their country of origin. People who have entered or wish to enter the country from a 'safe third country' cannot rely on Article 16a of the Basic Law. Instead, they are turned back at the border or expelled to the transit state if this is known and is prepared to accept them. The safe third countries comprise all EU states, plus Poland, Switzerland, the Czech Republic, and Norway. Germany is thus surrounded by a belt of countries who may re-accept refugees. Persons entitled to asylum have a right to bring their *family members* to Germany.

* The Geneva Convention on the Legal Status of Refugees of 28 July 1951 defines a *Convention refugee* as a displaced person who, because of a membership in a particular political or social group, religion, race or nationality, cannot or will not return to his or her own country for fear of serious persecution. Anyone who comes within the scope of this Convention is recognized by states that have signed it as being in need of protection. Most such countries lack provisions comparable to Article 16a of the Basic Law and equate victims of political persecution with Convention refugees. Exact information on the number of Convention refugees living in Germany has only been available since 1996. Convention refugees have a right to bring their *family members* to Germany under certain conditions.

* *Quota refugees* are ones accepted in the course of humanitarian aid campaigns. They are granted a permanent right to stay in Germany without first having to apply for asylum.

* *Refugees of war or civil war* gained the possibility of provisional acceptance without separate evaluation of each case under s. 32a of the Aliens Act effective since 1 July 1993. It is a political decision whether acceptance under s. 32a of the Aliens Act is granted. The war refugee status is conditional upon no application for asylum having been made or refused, and such refugees cannot demand to live in a specific place or state in Germany. The figures in Table 8 relate solely to civil war refugees from the republics of former Yugoslavia, primarily Croatia and Bosnia-Herzegovina, who were not subject to s. 32a of the Aliens Act but whose deportation had temporarily been suspended in most cases.

* *De facto refugees* form the largest group, comprising those who have not applied for asylum or whose application has been refused. Their deportation is deferred because they face serious, real danger to their lives or freedom in their own country, or because urgent humanitarian or personal grounds dictate that they should be allowed to remain in Germany for the time being.

* *Stateless persons* are also included in the Federal Ministry of the Interior statistics on refugees. These are displaced persons from World War II and their descendants.

Source: Commissioner for Migration, Refugees and Integration (formerly, Commissioner for Foreigners), *Facts and Figures on the Situation of Foreigners in the Federal Republic of Germany* (October 2000), 15–16.

Table 4.2 Refugee Totals according to Legal Classification, 1996–2002

Year	Convention Refugees	Quota Refugees	De-Facto Refugees	Bosnian War Refugees
1996	16,000	12,000	500,000	345,000
1997	25,000	10,000	360,000	245,000
1998	32,000	10,000	370,000	100,000
1999	44,000	9,500	423,000	50,000
2000	54,000	8,000	370,000	30,000
2001	69,000	7,000	361,000	24,000
2002	75,000	6,800	415,000	under 20,000

Source: Data derive from the official websites of the Federal Commissioner for Migration, Refugees and Integration, and the Federal Interior Ministry.

homeland; only twenty thousand were still in Germany by 2002.[10] The last five years have added new departure points for refugees and asylum seekers, e.g., Kurds from Turkey and Iraq.

The refugee influx of from 1990 to 1992 evoked public panic as well as xenophobic attacks, leading politicians to erect a legal *cordon sanitaire* under the Asylum Procedure Laws of July 1993. They codified temporary asylum for war victims, and adopted carrots-and-sticks for other groups.[11] Municipal authorities now extend residency permits only for short periods and have significantly cut benefit levels. Since 1993, financial aid has shrunk 20–30 percent relative to Social Assistance; most now receive in-kind aid (food, clothing, shelter), restricting their physical mobility. Similar constraints were introduced for war-refugee provisions in 1997. Only 124,000 of 370,000 of the de-facto refugees enjoy residency qua work permits. The number of aliens drawing Social Assistance rose from 81,000 in 1980 to 524,000 in 1995; the number of Germans dependent on welfare jumped over the same period, suggesting structural employment is to blame.[12] Carrots take the form of grants (up to DM 9,000) to help families return home, where local authorities receive another DM 8,000 if the family stays at least four months. This purportedly saved Germany DM 5,000 per month, having spent DM 17 billion as a host country by 1999.[13]

The amended law denies refugee status to persons arriving from safe countries of origin or by way of safe third states, vaguely defined as any state surrounding Germany or ones that have also ratified the Geneva Convention.[14] One "innovation" entails abbreviated decision making at airports. Individuals arriving from safe states, or lacking identification papers, are confined to a special "transit area" for processing. Border guards, acting under the Federal Office for Recognizing Foreign Refugees (FORFR), deny entry to those whose immediate-asylum claims seem unfounded. If FORFR is unable to make a determination within two days, or if an administrative court cannot render a judgment within fourteen days, the applicant is to be admitted. Implementation is not as easy as it sounds, however. One of Germany's international hubs, the Frankfurt/Main airport, frequently makes the headlines due to poor conditions, extended detentions (in one case, almost two years), and deaths. An Algerian woman committed suicide there after eight months in the "transit zone"; government officials blamed the victim for her own death, claiming she had hindered processing of her case by destroying her papers.[15] According to Nazare Abell, EU states have been able "to shift duties away and have increased the number of refugees in orbit."[16]

The "compromise" feature of the Asylum Compromise consists of an annual quota for *Aussiedler* (originally set at 225,000, later 100,000) and contract workers (100,000). The Aliens Act was also liberalized with respect to naturalization rules. Families separated by one member's need to flee immediately can no longer expect to be reunified; accelerated deportations for those already in the country have given rise to local sanctuary movements. The Constitutional Court upheld the asylum amendments in 1996. Sitting in another Stuttgart living room, I remember asking Bundestag Member Peter Conradi (SPD) shortly after the vote, "what remained" of the constitutional right to asylum? He responded, "Actually, nothing."

In November 2000, Marieluise Beck, federal commissioner for integration (formerly, commissioner for foreigners), issued a document summarizing five myths that have framed—or more accurately, distorted—the asylum debate since 1989. These myths highlight a key barrier to resolving Germany's demographic deficit: namely, public misperceptions, fueled by politicians seeking partisan advantage. Rather than treat sources of the problem, like the extraordinary fiscal burdens imposed on local authorities by federal policies, the tendency is to add layer after layer of control devices focusing only on the symptoms. The result is a legal morass that provides job security for bureaucrats and lawyers at the same time it compounds hardships for adults and children already traumatized by events they were forced to flee. Though I draw on the Commissioner's descriptions, the refutations flow from my own research.

Myth #1: *Germany leads all other European countries as a Land of Asylum.* Cross-national data show that Germany ranks eighteenth in terms of refugee admissions; topping the per capita list in 2003 were Switzerland, the Netherlands, Austria, and Sweden. The 1990s led to exceptional numbers due to the end of the Cold War, dissolution of the Soviet Union, and war in Yugoslavia. Now that conditions have stabilized, new admissions have dropped to 1987 levels. EU law regarding migration needs to focus on redistribution qua burden sharing, and granting asylum seekers more freedom of choice regarding places of settlement.

Myth #2: *The overwhelming majority of asylum seekers are economic refugees.* A mere 3–7 percent of the applicants receive formal asylum status; the rest are denied permanent residency, precluding access to the legal labor market. They are forced to become "welfare burdens," though most would rather work for pay, live in their own apartments, and learn the language by interacting with native speakers on the job. Many were skilled professionals back home. Persons with temporary permits, renewable for six months at best, are unlikely to be hired by employers paying a living wage. German labor laws, not parasitic tendencies, institutionalize their economic dependency. The welfare problem is not that refugees are leading lives of luxury (four to six people crammed into a single hostel room) but that Germans insist on "cures" and paid church holidays that the state can no longer afford. Nor have the 97 percent "denied" asylum status come to cheat the system, since 22–29 percent are granted some other refugee status; 48 percent cannot be deported because of recognized dangers at home. The Commissioner notes "The protection rate is significantly higher than the recognition rate."[17]

Myth #3: *German asylum law is unique and therefore especially attractive.* The most unique feature of this law, its "unqualified" nature, was eliminated in 1993 or substantially undermined by the Schengen accords. Its rigid, bureaucratic implementation, the stigmatizing nature of aid provision, family-hostile housing conditions, and a lack of cultural sensitivity to specific refugee groups render it anything but attractive to applicants. Individuals from warring regions may be forced to share the same hostel. The most compelling feature for many is Germany's geographic proximity to the countries from which they are fleeing.

Myth #4: *German asylum law is the most liberal in the world.* Only 2 percent of the 120,000 Albanians forced to flee Kosovo were granted formal asylum, though that war played itself out on prime-time television, However, 70 percent of the applicants in Great Britain and Italy, 57 percent in Austria, and 48 percent in Switzerland were granted full asylum in 1999. Of the 97 percent denied Article 16 GG protection, 70 percent submitted formal appeals, implying they had sufficient evidence to get into a German court. Another 35,000 filed suits against their deportation orders. Germany lags behind Canada and the United States in recognizing gender-specific forms of asylum; it also deports children of permanent residents.[18]

Myth #5: *German decision-making processes take forever, allowing more pseudo-refugees to abuse the system.* Commissioner Beck asserts that 75 percent

Table 4.3 Duration of Asylum Proceedings

Months / Years	Under 3 months	3-6 months	6-12 months	1-2 years	2-3 years	3-5 years	More than 5 years
Total cases (=Persons)	12,139	10,678	22,480	31,234	19,934	23,159	14,430
In Percent	9.1	8.0	16.8	23.3	14.9	17.3	10.8

Source: ICI, *Structuring Immigration, Fostering Integration* (Berlin: 2000), 125.

of all cases are decided within six months; courts complete their work, on average, within one year. In "simple cases," the entire procedure takes less than six months; the problem is that few are simple cases. Persons forced to flee at short notice may start out with proper documents but have their papers, valuables, and money stolen by smugglers who dump them at the border. Other federal sources offer a very different picture. The ICI reported that only 17.1 percent of the 134,054 cases heard in various courts were decided in six months or less; 16.8 percent took up to a year, 23.3 percent up to two years, 14.9 percent up to three years, and 17.3 percent three to five years. Nearly 11 percent (14,430) dragged on for over five years. The time required varied from state to state; 39 percent of the Berlin cases and 19 percent in Hesse exceeded five years, compared to 2.1 percent in Saxony.

The average length of proceedings completed by Administrative Courts (first instance) rose from 9.9 months in 1993 to 20.1 months in 1999. Securing a definitive verdict on asylum cases is a lengthy procedure, but the fault lies with the system. In 2001, the Constitutional Court criticized the commissioner for asylum for spending too much time appealing positive decisions, instead of reviewing appeals by rejected applicants.[19] Whole families are traumatized a second time by such proceedings, forced to live for years under the constant threat of "immediate" deportation.[20]

The Asylum Compromise has done little to solve the "refugee problem," despite a decline in new applications. Statutory changes may have stemmed the quantitative flow, but "they have increased the number of illegal or irregular domestic residents, in part through illegal border-crossings, in part by extending stays beyond periods set for residency permits." Moreover, "the sharper and more invincible the walling-off of major European target countries . . . the higher the profits for organized crime," operating through worldwide smuggling networks.[21] A higher concentration of foreigners in western locales and urban areas contributes to the juridical backlog.[22] The system lacks qualified interpreters, along with lawyers and judges familiar with conditions in the countries of origin, while the complicated classification system

Table 4.4 Asylum Decisions according to Legal Status, 1986–2003

Year	Total Applications	Recognized under §116GG^a)	%	Guaranteed Non-Deportation	%	Barriers to Deportation^b)	%	Rejected Cases	%	Formal Decisions	%
1986	55,555	8,853	15.9			31,955	57.5	14,747	26.5		
1987	87,539	8,231	9.4			62,000	70.8	17,308	19.8		
1988	88,530	7,621	8.6			62,983	71.1	17,926	20.3		
1989	120,610	5,991	4.97			89,866	74.5	24,753	20.5		
1990	148,842	6,518	4.38			16,268	78.1	26,056	17.5		
1991	168,023	11,597	6.9			128,820	76.7	27,606	16.4		
1992	216,356	9,189	4.25			163,637	75.6	43,530	20.1		
1993	513,561	16,369	3.19			347,991	67.8	149,174	29.1		
1994	352,572	25,578	7.25			238,386	67.6	78,622	22.3		
1995	200,188	18,100	9.04	5,368	2.68	3,631	1.81	117,939	58.9	58,781	29.4
1996	194,451	14,389	7.4	9,611	4.94	2.082	1.07	126,652	65.1	43,799	22.5
1997	170,801	8,443	4.94	9,779	5.73	2,768	1.62	101,886	59.7	50,693	29.7
1998	147,391	5,883	3.99	5,437	3.69	2,573	1.72	91,700	62.2	44,371	30.1
1999	135,504	4,114	3.04	6,147	4.54	2,100	1.55	80,231	59.2	42,912	31.7
2000	105,502	3,128	2.96	8,138	7.88	1,597	1.52	61,840	58.6	30,619	29.0
2001	107,193	5,716	5.33	17,003	15.86	3,383	3.16	55,402	51.7	25,689	24.0
2002	130,128	2,379	1.83	4,130	3.17	1,598	1.23	78,845	60.6	43,176	33.2
2003	93,885	1,534	1.63	1,602	1.71	1,567	1.67	63,002	67.1	26,180	27.9

Source: MARIS, for the Federal Office for the Recognition of Foreign Refugees, available online at www.bamf.de, 2004.
a) Only persons formally recognized under the Basic Law and their family members enjoy unlimited residency and employment rights, as well as the right to eventual naturalization.
b) These individuals must renew residency permits every six months and are generally excluded from (legal forms of) paid labor.

necessitates different evidentiary rules and appeal processes, fostering agency turf battles.

Reforms advocated by Beck and ICI members include steps to simplify the entire classification system, as well as to outfit the courts with resources and technologies for expediting legal proceedings. Conventional and de-facto refugees "tolerated" for years should be allowed to get on with their lives with real residency rights and work permits. In 2001, the waiting period for asylum applicants and tolerated refugees hoping to enter the legal labor market was reduced to one year; war refugees receive immediate work permits. Language courses and family unification are needed to foster social integration and stable communities. Federal requirements should be enforced by central authorities to guarantee equal protection; federal revenues should be used to secure that protection, rather than making local authorities pay the price for decisions made at the national level. A perennial problem even in well-intentioned democracies is that people who make the laws rarely have real-life contact with the persons whose behavior they seek to regulate. The following sections attempt to put a "human face" on German asylum and refugee policy.

Jewish "Quota" Refugees

The return of Jews to Germany since 1945 can be classified as a case of "difficult migration." More than half a million lived there at the outset of the Nazi reign of terror. In May 1945, two-hundred thousand displaced persons were still within its borders, plunging to twelve thousand by 1948 due to emigration. Holocaust survivors resurrected fifty-one communities in 1945, followed by sixteen more in 1946; by 1952, eighteen thousand Jews held memberships in seventy communities, "a pale shadow of the 600,000 Jews of the Weimar Republic."[23] Refugee waves from Iran, Hungary, Poland, and the Soviet Union expanded their ranks through the 1960s. More than forty synagogues and community centers were erected from 1950 to 1967. The number remained constant through 1980, hovering around thirty thousand (two generations).

By 1998, sixty years after the pogrom known as *Kristallnacht*, another forty-five thousand had moved to Germany, bringing forty thousand non-Jewish family members to the "land of the perpetrators." During the same period, roughly eight-hundred thousand Jews from the former Soviet Union moved to Israel, another four-hundred thousand to the United States.[24] Israel had asked western governments not to take in Jews as refugees, hoping to compel them to resettle there; 68.6 percent went elsewhere between 1975 and 1989. This is one Israeli request Germany will never honor, as a matter of historical responsibility.[25]

The United States radically reduced its quota for post-Soviet Jewish migrants in 1989. Shortly after the onset of the 1990 Currency Union but prior to unification, the GDR's freely elected government granted asylum to foreign Jews threatened by discrimination in Central/Eastern Europe. The *Volkskammer* issued a formal apology, expressing "shame and sorrow" over the old regime's policies toward Israel and its military role in crushing democracy during the 1968 Prague Spring. Applicants had to do little more than register in East Berlin and provide some evidence of Jewishness, e.g., a Soviet passport listing their nationality. Many already in Germany on tourist visas were permitted to stay; those who entered between June 1990 and February 1991 were recognized retroactively under 1980 contingency (quota) refugee rules, established to cover thirty-three thousand Vietnamese "boat people." The deadline was extended twice; the first wave numbered 8,535.

The Federal Republic continued the practice after unification (October 1990) but introduced formal admission proceedings and state-distribution formulas. As of November 1991, candidates had to apply at one of sixteen German consulates or embassies; instructions for the four-page application are in Russian and German. One must document "Jewish nationality" using identity cards, passports, birth certificates, or original papers, or have at least one Jewish parent. Submissions are channeled through a Central Administrative Office in Cologne that compares them with a national foreigner registry to eliminate persons with criminal backgrounds or fake documents. The CAO forwards approvals to the states, seeking placement for individual cases in consultation with local Jewish agencies. Word is sent back to the consulate, which then contacts applicants and sets up a departure date, issues visas, etc. Federal distribution quotas are less strictly enforced for this group than holds true for *Aussiedler*. By late 1991, Berlin had taken in more than three times its official 2.3 percent "contingent," since newcomers can move to places with dependent relatives. North Rhine-Westphalia registered 22.4 percent, Bavaria 13.9 percent, and Baden-Württemberg 12.2 percent.[26] Jewish refugees, like ethnic resettlers, are "able to come in through the 'front door' to Germany," while other asylum seekers and migrants "are forced to use the back door."[27]

Bureaucratic processing can take several months to a few years. Doomernik found serious backlogs at the consular level; in November 1993, officials were issuing numbers at one consulate in the Ukraine for appointments to return completed applications two years down the road.[28] The Foreign Ministry does not divulge application data or processing times. Rejection rates run less than 0.58 percent, compared to 97 percent among regular asylum applicants.[29] As of March 1994, 44,247 applicants had been assigned to a particular *Land*, only 16,597 (37.5 percent) had arrived.[30] A total of 185,600 applications were submitted through 1997 (about 2,000 per month); of the 137,500 Jews accepted from 1991 to 1999, only 112,980 quickly relocated (table 4.5). Visas originally carried no expiration date, leading some to apply for exit, only to hang on to

Table 4.5 Jewish Migration from the Former
Soviet Union, 1993–2002

Year	Arrivals
1993	16,597
1994	811
1995	15,184
1996	15,959
1997	19,437
1998	17,788
1999	18,205
2000	16,538
2001	16,711
2002	19,262

Source: Federal Ministry of the Interior, Federal
Administrative Office, 2003.

their traveling papers as an insurance policy in case conditions worsened in the homeland. They must now organize out-migration within one year, or their permits expire.

Unlike *Aussiedler*, Jews do not automatically become citizens, but their Geneva Convention status renders them eligible for naturalization after seven years. They enjoy unlimited residence rights, work permits, housing, and "absorption assistance" for six months; the Red Cross and the Otto Benecke Foundation help to secure immediate housing. In April 1991, over 1,700 in Berlin were lodged in twenty-eight hostels, usually two to a room with basic furnishings; in contrast to other refugees, Jews are not forced to stay in collective housing. Within a year, they can be certified for "social (subsidized) housing" (SH), provided their earnings do not exceed state-defined limits. The larger problem is a chronic shortage of SH apartments, and fierce competition with other groups "urgently in need." Available units, not surprisingly located in run-down neighborhoods, require major renovations; many refuse second-class dwellings in "uncivilized" eastern Berlin. Russians reject apartments relying on coal as "substandard," since subsidized energy in the USSR made central heating affordable.[31] Certificate holders can register with housing agencies, search classified ads, or hire German real-estate agents who demand high commissions. Knowledge of the latter leads many to resort to the homeland custom of bribing Russian mediators to expedite the process.

New families usually move out of the "barracks" within a few months; they are encouraged by the Central Welfare Board of Jews to pursue cultural and religious instruction.

Jewishness, according to FRG quota-criteria, conflates religion with nationality, in contrast to Nazi policies that reduced it to race divorced from religious practice. Soviet classification schemes rendered it an ethnonational trait, the "fifth point" in one's official passport. Over several decades, many opted for assimilation, hoping to eschew educational and occupational disadvantage. Under Soviet law, one could "inherit nationality" from either parent, attesting to the arbitrary nature of ethnicity as a foundation for personal identity. Few practiced their religion under "godless communism"; one survey in the 1980s found that only 7 percent of the Soviet Jews considered themselves "religious." One-fifth occasionally visited the synagogue, 17 percent declared themselves atheists. Binational marriages were very common.[32] Between 1979 and 1989 the Jewish population in Russia fell from 699,286 to 550,422 (21.3 percent), only partly due to emigration; the Ukraine witnessed a similar decrease, from 632,877 to 484,219 (23.5 percent).[33] Practicing Jews consider emigration "cowardly," but their efforts to re-establish communities in the post-Soviet republics are undercut by the Jewish Agency for Israel, soliciting people who want to leave. Once the city with the highest Jewish concentration, Odessa has seen one of the largest exit waves for Israel.[34]

As a result, most who enter Germany have never been "unequivocally Jewish." Many feel Jewish but attach no religious significance to this identity; 20–30 percent of the newcomers are non-Jewish family members. A few rediscover religion after settlement, others move on to Israel. The overwhelming majority sees itself as European, rejecting Israel as "too oriental" or "too hot." Two-thirds of today's German Jewish youth are expected to wed non-Jewish partners.[35]

Established in 1950, the Central Council of Jews (*Zentralrat der Juden*) functions as a roof organization for diverse religious communities; in 1952 the *Zentralrat* was accorded standing as a "corporation of public law," rendering Judaism one of Germany's five officially recognized religions; communities can rely on tax-payer-supplied subsidies and also offer formal religious instruction in public schools, a status still denied the much larger Islamic community. A small Orthodox community, *Adass Jisroel*, encompasses about ten thousand members nationally, 250 in Berlin. The courts have recognized this group (but not the Islamic community) as a separate "public corporation." A third branch consists of the Jewish Cultural Society, created in East Berlin shortly after the fall of Wall.

By the late 1990s, the largest groups were concentrated in Berlin (10,436), Frankfurt/Main (6,289), Munich (5,726), Düsseldorf (4,227), Hamburg (3,273), Cologne (2,763), and Stuttgart (1,828).[36] The capital city offers a "comprehensive infrastructure," including a large community center, library seminar rooms, restaurants, language classes, a newspaper, a synagogue, a primary school, nursing homes, a museum, one college, a hospital, and a cemetery. The *Jüdische*

Gemeinde stages youth activities, organizes Passover and other high-holy-day meals. New arrivals sometimes have to be advised not to drink the ceremonial wine until prayers are completed. It boosted its membership up to 10,000, but few routinely participate. The Berlin tally stood at 700–900 in the mid 1990s; the community added 1,910, then another 1,815 by late 1991. Three-fourths of all community members in Berlin were born in Eastern Europe.[37]

Tensions exist between local Jews and new arrivals, as well as among ethnic groups.[38] Established German-Jews are the ones forced to adapt to changing community interests, as opposed to the usual process of expecting newcomers to acculturate: "In the perception of the old-timers it appears that next to German, Russian has become the 'official language.' As a result, not only the people working for the community speak Russian but in some places even the organizational newsletter is being published in German and Russian. In a number of communities such as Potsdam or Rostock, Russian has actually become the colloquial language. The old-timers are beginning to complain ever more about this development, which they think is rendering them strangers in their own community."[39] At one 1998 *Gemeinde* meeting in Berlin, the German board members on the podium were pictured wearing headphones, needed for simultaneous translations.[40] Migrants from the "European area" of the Soviet Union (70 percent) are Ashkenazi Jews, those from the southern regions (30 percent) are largely Sephardic.[41] Further tensions are found among the offspring of German Jews, the Eastern Jews, and the Israeli–Jews, Heuberger observes. How "normal" is Jewish life in Germany today? "Normal is plural," Michael Wolffsohn writes.[42] Why should Jews be any less pluralistic or diverse in their cultural, political, and religious orientations than Catholics, Protestants, or Muslims spread around the world?

The Jewish Community relies on *halacha* (born of a Jewish mother) as a criteria for membership. Officially a Ukrainian, Youri felt a sense of "belonging" and tried to join the community in Berlin. He was nonetheless denied membership because his mother was not Jewish. Similarly, "Nella, her husband and father were accorded refugee status but her daughter and son-in law were only tolerated (with a Jewish mother) because the son-in-law is Ukrainian."[43] Another interview partner reported, "In Moscow I went to the synagogue only very rarely. Here I go almost every Sabbath. Not so often to the (West German) Jewish Community . . . where they are very cold and unfriendly to us newcomers, but to the (East German) Jüdische Kultur Verein [*sic*]. I really feel comfortable there, very much accepted. . . . So, to sum it up, I came here and refound my Jewish identity but doing so I lost my position in society. In Moscow I was someone, here I am no one."[44] Assuming a different "nationality" made it easier to assimilate in the Soviet Union, but it backfires as a strategy for rapid acculturation in the host country. Competing definitions of Jewishness trigger identity problems among new arrivals, divide families subject to contradictory legal statuses, and create discrepancies between governmental and community statistics.

As chapter 3 revealed, criteria defining "who is/is not a real *Aussiedler*" have done little to stop divided families from devising extralegal strategies to unify themselves. Similarly, complex rules defining *quota refugees* neither hinders illegal entry nor fosters integration. In his twenties at the time of his arrival, "Vadim" from Odessa has a Jewish mother and a Ukrainian father. He considers himself Jewish but his official nationality was Ukranian. His wife has a Jewish father and a Russian mother yet lived "as a Russian." When the initial deadline for recognition was extended in 1991,

> this news went through the country like wildfire. . . . Anyway, we were in Berlin before the next deadline was proclaimed and could therefore stay. My father-in-law stayed immediately and my mother-in-law soon followed, but I returned home to finish my studies. Final exams were in two months. When I returned it appeared that I had to prove that I had been in Germany uninterruptedly, otherwise I could not be granted refugee status. My relatives vouched for me when we went to a notary, and this made it possible for me to stay. My wife arrived ten days later, after the last deadline had elapsed on 6 November 1991. She has not been granted refugee status and has a temporary residence permit. . . . My brother got himself an application form in 1992, which he may return in April 1994. . . . When he came to the embassy recently he was told that he no longer can come to Germany because his nationality is Ukrainian and not Jewish. My mother will visit us in April and I hope we can arrange for her to stay permanently.[45]

Jewish migrants are little inclined to interact regularly with the Russian-speaking enclaves in cities like Berlin, given their divergent sociocultural backgrounds, professional concentrations, and motives for leaving. The former are disproportionately urban (95 percent) and male, between the ages of twenty-five and forty; 73 percent of one Berlin sample held university or college degrees, concentrated in technical, cultural, and scientific occupations (according high socioeconomic status in the USSR). Their human capital is nonetheless undercut by their lack of German language skills; only 15 percent qualified as "very good."[46] Driving their departures was not fear of anti-Semitism but rather a lack of trust in the homeland economy, characterized as "frightfully expensive," hit by "radioactive pollution," and devoid of technical instruments and medicines.[47]

"Marina" from Odessa entered Germany at the age of twenty-seven. She did not identify herself as Jewish, despite having been denied admission to a Soviet arts academy due to nationality. She did not register as a Jewish Community member. Initially a physics teacher who also did English translations, she had no desire to deal with "impudent pupils, interfering parents," or pedantic pedagogy, based on her impression of the German school system. After a brief retraining course in "management," the only job she could find was at a day-care center run by the company that owned the hostel where she lived. That employer threatened to fire her when he heard she was pregnant. She learned that if she did not reveal the father's identity (pretending "he's back in Russia"), she could preserve her independence by drawing welfare benefits.[48] Given the prevalence of young, unmarried mothers on Social Assistance in Germany, one could say that Marina has successfully "acculturated." Alternatively, one could ask why FRG officials don't prosecute employers who violate pregnancy protection laws, especially when they are under state contracts.

As Doomernik observes, "The rate at which an immigrant learns to understand German society *ipso facto* is related to the extent to which he has managed to penetrate the specified societal fields . . . cognitive orientation towards German society develops slowly and seems to take place as a result of their entry into the labour market instead of the other way around."[49] To achieve this, migrants usually need to jettison their professional aspirations and cultural capital as incompatible with German requisites. Adapting to local culture means more than serving *Kaffee und Kuchen*. The more successful migrants are those willing to start over at the lower end of the food chain, to prove themselves full of energy and motivation. Paradoxically, the adaptability displayed in accepting lower social status helps many to acquire basic language skills and accumulate new cultural capital necessary for do-it-yourself integration.

My profile of jobless *Aussiedler* showed that the German labor market is embedded in a (mind-numbingly) legalistic web of career tracks and residency requirements that even "privileged" migrants find hard to transcend. Although they receive similar benefits, Jewish resettlers differ from *Aussiedler* in one significant respect: they are not entitled to automatic recognition of their professional or occupational qualifications, nor will they receive pensions based on years of service back in the homeland. The recognition of diplomas and occupational certification accorded *Spätaussiedler* based on Article 10 of the Federal Expellee and Refugee Law (BVFG) does not extend to Jewish migrants. The latter must undergo additional tests or secure formal "evidence of competency" from the homeland in order to receive bureaucratic approval to exercise their professions, irrespective of language skills.[50]

Consider Doomernik's interviewee, Vadim, a former theater director who was more than willing to start over. After completing a language course, he took a community service job as a massage therapist for the elderly to improve his German through daily contact with native speakers (a sad commentary on the state of FRG elder care). Thereafter he could only secure a training slot in a "retail program." His internship took him to a Reichelt supermarket where he spent his day arranging goods on the shelves ("they call that product presentation"). His other task consisted of "holding a small computer scanner against a barcode and typing in the number of items left on the shelf, which they call product ordering." He summarized his state-subsidized training thus: "That is silly. You can do that after three years of primary education. I am free labour for them but in return they fail to teach me anything."[51] Then consider another equally plausible scenario, described by Jasper and Vogt: "It is conceivable that a late-resettler and a Jewish migrant, who went through an identical educational and occupational socialization process in the Soviet Union—perhaps even sat next to each other on the school bench and received the same grades and graduation certificates—will be treated completely differently in Germany as regards the recognition of their diplomas and professional credentials. While the resettler, for example, enjoys immediate access to a university with his diploma, the Jewish migrant has to endure supplementary testing and maybe even an extended 'waiting period' of several years."[52]

Entrepreneurial types can succeed, but start-ups are usually unconventional or focus on ethnic-niche products. Business ventures take the form of discount shops, videos stores, hairdressers, or import-export stores; others occupy a grey zone, trading in illegal icons, antiques, homeland consumer items, and real estate. Berlin is home to at least two "mafia contingents" engaging in money laundering and smuggling, controlling up to 80 percent of the city's gambling arcades.[53] As one more successful *biznesman*, "Arkadi," opined: "There are three types of immigrants. The first type is the one who rather would earn one mark today than a hundred later. People like that don't learn the language and depend on others. They are the ones who need a broker to find a flat. Secondly, there are those who want to learn German quickly so they can take up their old professions. They're mainly dentists, doctors and engineers. Thirdly, there are those persons who want to be independent and an equal partner within the German business world." He claimed in his own case, "in another four or five years I will be buying an apartment instead of renting it. You see, when you buy the costs are tax-deductible. Perhaps even sooner than that I will get myself a Mercedes. I won't buy one though. Leasing is much more attractive because you can book it under business expenses."[54]

Some post-Soviet Jews resent their classification as refugees, insisting they were not forced to flee religious or social persecution but rather chose to seek a better life elsewhere. As one music teacher qua composer complained bitterly, "I am not a full-valued member of the European Community. Like a dog who just ran in. I have no hopes of getting a normal passport or securing normal status. . . . I consider the law that exists today concerning *Aussiedler* and refugees a racist one, whether the bureaucrats are conscious of this or not. Our situation is ambivalent. I am not a refugee. I did not flee!"[55] Another lamented that the move to Germany has rendered her economically dependent—a plight she shares with *Aussiedler* women: "I am a nothing here. Everyone respected me at home, as a physician—I have worked, taken care of grandkids, cooked—everything. And now I don't even know which apples are supposed to taste best. Everything is so complicated. I am a nothing. Though I had always worked, survived the war. And now I have to go begging at the Social Welfare Office."[56] No one in Germany would dare to call Jewish newcomers "economic refugees," but neither would politicians admit that these are really "immigrants without an immigration law."

Although Israel objects to the its relocation plan (hoping Jews will opt to strengthen their purported homeland), the Federal Republic will not close its gates to Jewish people. Still, Germany is the last place one would expect Israel to turn for lessons regarding citizenship. Their fates inextricably intertwined by the Holocaust, both countries were forced to shape and legitimize their nation-building policies in direct response to World War II. Both embraced a type of ethnic citizenship warranting a right of return to German resettlers and Jewish diaspora groups, paradoxically invoking the same *jus sanguinis* ideal that had precipitated mass expulsions and genocide in the first place. Both states have employed an ethno-organic concept of citizenship since 1948, as an ideological weapon against other populations making claims on the same territory.

The more I read about the Israeli-Palestinian crisis, the more I am tempted to draw comparisons between the intolerant treatment of non-German Turks and non-Jewish Arabs.[57] I concur with Yfaat Weiss that the self-proclaimed Jewish state has created its own golem, allowing ever more non-Jews (defined by *halacha*) to enter Israel to strengthen a nation-state positing Jewishness as its sole raison d'être. Israel finds it "impossible" to embrace Palestinians as citizens under this definition. Amendments to the Law of Return have rendered it a multiethnic society devoid of equal rights, or any rights at all, if the ethnicity in question is "Arab." Prior to 1999, the Federal Republic used comparable blood-and-culture arguments to declare generations of Turkish residents incapable of Germanness. Zeev Rosenhek's analysis of Israeli migration regimes and social rights accorded (or not) to migrant workers conveys a sense of "déjà vu all over again" vis-à-vis Turkish workers in the FRG.[58] Whether one uses essentialist notions of Germanness or Jewishness to control migration, the net result is the same: the imagined community is no match for humans desperate to secure a better life for their families, officially welcome or not, even if migration proves "difficult."

Bosnians, Kosovars, and "Temporary" Asylum

Our next set of refugees, arriving from the war-torn Balkans, has experienced a "very difficult" migration process, conditioned by Germany's shift to a new emphasis on "temporary protection" (TP). Rooted in the 1951 Geneva Convention, a keystone in the "post-Holocaust human rights system," temporary protection affords time-limited asylum to groups subjected to sudden violence or armed conflict. Employed in the case of African states during the bloody decolonizations of the 1960s, in Southeast Asia during the 1970s, and in Central America during the 1980s, temporary protection was invoked in the 1990s to cover nearly two million persons forced to flee ethnic violence in Europe's backyard. The US agreed to harbor ten thousand Kosovars temporarily but quickly retreated and accorded full refugee status, placing them "on a fast track towards permanent residence."[59]

Given its nearly unqualified asylum law through 1992, it is ironic that Germany has become a major test case for chipping away at permanent sanctuary. The 1993 "compromise" introduced a new legal category for the victims of war and civil strife, allowing for rapid admissions without a complete evaluation of individual cases. However, §32a of the Aliens Act requires federal and state governments to agree on the terms of admission and deliberately excludes permanent residency as a future option. Temporary status allows refugees to pursue paid employment provided they do not apply for regular asylum; thus refugees are compelled to make complicated decisions critical to their future well-being as soon as they arrive, with very little understanding of the long-term consequences of such choices.

Like decisions regarding the Convention status of refugees, TP grants governments broad discretion in defining eligibility: they may raise or lower the threshold for admission "by manipulating concepts of persecution, the persecutor's identity, the grounds for status, the causal link between harm and the persecutor's motive, and the cessation and exclusion of clauses of the 1951 Convention." Consequently, "approval rates tend to be low even for nationals of states notorious for political repression and violence."[60] Joan Fitzpatrick characterizes temporary protection as a "magic gift," extending protection to forced migrants unable to meet criteria set by the 1951 Convention and promising group protection "when the determination of an individual's status proves impossible."[61] The dark side is that discretionary TP may dislodge this protection from the realm of enforceable human rights.

Germany's inability to close the book on history was reflected in its reaction to the Yugoslav breakup. While the negative lessons of appeasement had divided peace activists over the 1991 Gulf War, it united them again, albeit in a state of paralysis, vis-à-vis the outbreak of violence among Serbs, Croatians, and Bosnians, from 1991 to 1999. The initial response to violence in its own backyard was best expressed by my friend Wally Baur in Stuttgart: "No war, no way, no where, no time, and especially no Germans." Politicians and peace activists stressed history in explaining their reluctance to play a direct role in the Balkans. Cognizant of Croatia's complicity with the Third Reich and Serbia's bitter memories of the Nazi occupation (*Serbien muss sterbien*), they feared any German presence on Yugoslav soil would affirm Serbian claims that the new conflict was the same struggle for survival by means of other wars.

Bonn's reluctance to exert strong regional influence right after regaining sovereignty through unification was complicated by sympathy with its Yugoslav guestworkers (755,000 in 1991). Viewed as more "assimilated" than Turkish or

Italian workers, a majority was Croatian.[62] The UN imposed a weapons embargo in September 1991, followed by an EU ban on trade with Serbia in November, neither of which proved effective. The Kohl cabinet recognized Slovenia, Croatia, and Macedonia on 11 December, after thirteen cease-fires produced no break in the fighting. The UN sent two contingents of "blue helmets" in 1992, to no avail. The focus soon shifted from the independence drive in Slovenia, to the Serbian occupation of Croatia, to the rape and slaughter of civilians in Bosnia. Not all of the war's immediate victims headed for Germany; 2.74 million people found themselves displaced in their own country, including 690,000 in Croatia, 110,000 in Serb-controlled Krajina/East Slavonia, and 550,000 in Serbia. Another 700,000 left the homeland altogether.[63] Witnessing brutal attacks against foreigners, coupled with a sea change in public attitudes toward asylum-rights, the FRG nonetheless allocated DM 658 million in humanitarian aid, and granted "temporary protected status" to 350,000 Bosnians during Stage One. An estimated seventy to seventy-five thousand settled in Berlin neighborhoods already heavily populated with "foreigners," e.g., Spandau, Neukölln, Kreuzberg, and Wedding.[64]

Stage Two commenced with the 1995 massacre of an estimated five thousand to seven thousand Bosnian men in the UN "safe-haven" of Srebrenica. The Bundestag voted to deploy German troops and Tornado fighter-planes in response to attacks on UN peacekeepers. In 1996 the Kohl Government signed an agreement bent on returning displaced Bosnians to the homeland; local authorities allowed their residency rights to expire, despite resistance to the "reintegration" of Muslims in Serbian areas.[65] By December, lawmakers had approved the deployment of three thousand Bundeswehr soldiers to Bosnia-Herzegovina. Of the 345,000 Bosnians tolerated in 1996, fewer than twenty thousand still held that status by 2002. In 1997 Serbs and Montenegrans comprised the second largest foreigner group (721,000) in Germany, after the Turks. "Significantly traumatized persons" as well as those who had lived there six or more years or who had secured insurance-obligatory jobs for two years received an *Aufenthaltsbefügnis*, renewable after two years.

In 1998, the Kohl Government refused to stop the return of Kosovo Albanians, declaring they no longer faced direct persecution, though lawmakers approved German forces for the SFOR operation in June.[66] By April 1999, people were again being driven out of Kosovo by the hundreds of thousands. Temporary protection had yet to be accepted as a practice commensurate with the European Charter of Fundamental Rights, but it quickly became the rule rather than the exception. Decisions regarding temporary refuge during the Bosnian and Kosovo crises left the FRG riding the proverbial horns of a dilemma: "Ethnically based armed conflict is largely aimed at driving out disfavored populations. Offering durable asylum to the victims of 'ethnic cleansing' poses a moral and political dilemma to the receiving states, which wish to avoid complicity

Table 4.6 State Distribution of Bosnian War Refugees, 1996–2000

Bundesland	1996 Total	%	1999 Total	%	2000 Total	%
Baden-Württemberg	60,000	17.4	9,713	13	4,487	13.1
Bavaria	71,000	20.6	4,256	5.7	2,500	6.7
Berlin	32,000	9.3	15,000	20.1	9,713	6.7
Brandenburg	2,000	0.6	386	0.5	268	0.7
Bremen	3,000	0.9	689	0.9	485	1.3
Hamburg	12,500	3.6	3,360	4.5	2,158	5.8
Hesse	35,000	10.1	10,013	13.4	5,843	15.8
Mecklenburg-Vorpommern	1,000	0.3	88	0.1	56	0.2
Lower Saxony	23,000	6.7	2,906	3.9	1,900	5.1
North Rhine–Westphalia	75,000	21.7	22,850	30.6	6,000	16.2
Rhineland-Pfalz	17,500	5.1	2,785	3.7	1,425	3.8
Saarland	4,000	1.3	1,047	1.4	890	2.4
Saxony	2,000	0.6	300	0.4	58	0.2
Saxon-Anhalt	2,000	0.6	256	0.3	100	0.3
Schleswig-Holstein	4,000	1.2	1,050	1.4	800	2.2
Thuringia	1,000	0.3	61	0.1	35	0.1
Total	345,000	100	74,760	100	37,078	100

Source: Federal Office for the Recognition of Foreign Refugees, 2001.

in genocide and to resist the persecutor's fait accompli. The Kosovo experience suggests that concerted intervention, accompanied by temporary protection in regional and more distant states, can reverse ethnic cleansing. However, Kosovo also demonstrates that rapid repatriation, even when voluntary, may precipitate new population displacement if conditions are insecure."[67]

Germany's legitimate interest in resisting "ethnic cleansing" in Kosovo does not explain why it subsequently applied TP and compulsory-return policies to victims of non-ethnic oppression after it had already raised the barriers for individuals in 1993. In May 1998, Foreign Minister Klaus Kinkel (FDP) and Interior Minister Manfred Kanther (CSU) threatened Asian and African countries with cuts in development funds, should they refuse to repatriate fifty to seventy thousand persons "unwelcome" in Germany. The development minister rejected the plan as inhumane for Ghana, Nigeria, Togo, Gambia, Sudan, Vietnam, Bangladesh, Sri Lanka, Pakistan, and India. That did not deter Kinkel from obliging Morocco to take back 9,700 persons lacking papers and residency rights.[68]

Further amendments to the Asylum Provisions Act radically cut benefits, evoking pubic outcry from the Protestant and Catholic Churches as well as from Amnesty International. The Catholic Church (with the exception of Bishop Johannes Dyba of Fulda) declared its support for sanctuary or "church asylum."[69] The government tried to send back 20,000 Vietnamese refugees, but only six thousand departed. Meanwhile, violence escalated between the Kosovo Liberation Army (UCK) and Serbian "security forces" in the not-so-autonomous Balkan province amidst a hotly contested German election campaign. By late summer, some two-hundred thousand Kosovo Albanians had fled the area, rising to more than 300,000 in September. At the end of the month, the Kohl Government of sixteen years was displaced by a new coalition under Gerhard Schröder (SPD); Joschka Fischer became the first Green foreign minister. By November 1998, 265,000 of 350,000 Bosnians had returned home or migrated elsewhere; the government claimed it relied on "voluntary return."[70] That year saw the lowest number of asylum applications (eight thousand) since the tightening of conditions in 1993: of those, 4 percent were granted formal asylum, 3.7 percent received "little asylum" (85 percent were Kosovo Albanians).[71]

Inconsistent standards for granting temporary protection became ever more problematic for Germany and other EU states due to the protracted nature of the war. Pro Asyl criticized new rules requiring visas for Kosovars (on the grounds that there was "no group persecution"), soon overturned by the Administrative Court. After only a few months in office, Fischer flew to Belgrade in March, hoping to persuade Serb Slobodan Milosevic to accept NATO peacekeepers. NATO assaults on Belgrade and Kosovo commenced on 24 March 1999, aided by Bundeswehr troops. Although federal and state officials had failed to reach consensus over financing protection for Bosnians, they did agree to cover Kosovo refugees evacuated from Macedonia.[72] The bombing triggered a new outpouring of refugees, many Kosovo Albanians landing in the border states; ten thousand entering the FRG were granted three-month, renewable stays. Another 14,726 arrived by May, having been evacuated from camps in Macedonia; CDU/CSU-governed states refused to accept them, arguing that other EU states were not admitting their share.[73]

The Italian government, for example, was blamed for allowing new refugees to cross its territory to seek protection in Germany. The UN, in turn, criticized Germany's treatment of ten thousand children, after it declared victims age sixteen and older capable of defending themselves in asylum proceedings.[74] By the end of the Kosovo campaign, the FRG was hosting 180,000 refugees who were "obliged to leave" but could not be deported due to unacceptable homeland conditions. Nearly 96,000 did go back by late 2001, many benefiting from free airfare and emergency money (DM 450); roughly 11,000 were returned against their wills. By the end of 2002, 93,256 persons of Yugoslav origin were still "tolerated": 33,000 were minors, 45,506 held restricted residency permits. Facing a backlog, the state granted two-year residency permits to 20,000 parents and children who had entered by July 1993, along with childless couples admitted after January 1990. Less than 10,000 new asylum applications were submitted in 1999, stemming largely from Yugoslavia, Turkey, Iraq, and Afghanistan; 3–4 percent were accorded official recognition.[75]

Conflagrations of the last decade have inflicted major costs on local governments, owing to housing shortages, school violence and rising crime. They have also reversed years of effective community integration. Berlin's guestworkers offer one example of groups torn apart by civil war:

> The war was and is in every head. Even worse is the poison of nationalism. . . . All of this affected and continues to affect the long-term Yugoslav residents in Germany, who now fall apart into Croatians, Serbs, Slovenians, Bosnians, etc. Cultural associations offering support in the diaspora disintegrated, and they exist today only in new ethnically separated forms. Restaurants have "nationalized" themselves. Yes, even language and newspapers frequently have a stigmatizing effect these days. Variations of Serbo-Croatian, the pronunciation of vowels, verbal constructions or a somewhat different terminology can reveal the regional origin of the speakers and with that his probable membership in an ethnic group.[76]

The breakdown of ethnic organizations in Germany denies refugees access to the very support structures that could facilitate their integration.

Some refugee experiences are more horrifying than others, but one thing they have in common is the physically demeaning and psychologically degrading reception many encounter as a result of temporary protection. The US internment of refugees, adults, and children, in hard-core prisons while they wait out their hearings is no less inhumane. The 2003 Migration Report shows that a majority have lived in Germany since 1998, 78,487 for more than nine years, 12,531 over twelve years. If the strategy is to make life so unbearable for persons already subjected to major trauma that few will want to stay, it is clearly not working. Treacherous homeland conditions, not the hostile host-state environment, determine their decision to remain or return to the homeland.

Enacted during Stage Three of the Yugoslav conflict, the Amsterdam Treaty obliged the EU to adopt "minimum standards for giving temporary asylum protection to displaced persons from third countries" who cannot return to their homelands or otherwise require "international protection" by 2004. The EU has yet to address the lack of effective burden sharing, a leading cause of popular resentment in places that do provide physical shelter. As a result, "states weary of their obligations under refugee law may look upon a TP regime as a strategy to shift refugee protection from the realm of law to that of politics and voluntary humanitarian assistance."[77]

One also observes a proclivity for shifting the burden to neighboring states, though the latter, also underdeveloped, find it hard to treat the fundamental needs of their own citizens. They face a delicate ethnic balance, easily tipped by a sudden influx of one group. Shortly after thousands of Kosovars sought refuge in Macedonia, NATO was forced to restore political stability. Germany is still directing peacekeeping processes there, having freed the United States for a subsequent assault on the Taliban in Afghanistan. In June 2004, Interior Minister Otto Schily proposed the establishment of new asylum camps in Africa, ostensibly having learned very little via the flight of Tutsis from Rwanda that upset the ethnopolitical balance and triggered further violent outbreaks in Zaire and Burundi.[78] I concur with Fitzpatrick that asylum is increasingly viewed "as an act of grace rather than as an international legal obligation."[79]

Fundamentalism and Islamic Diaspora Communities

According to a Bundestag inquiry conducted in 2000, the number of Muslims in Germany lies between 2.8 and 3.2 million.[80] Though religion was not a factor in regulating guestworker or refugee status prior to 1990, fundamentalism has strengthened its salience in the immigration debate. Religion increasingly serves as an identity marker within groups lumped together in German consciousness, e.g., "Turks" who define themselves as Alevis, Sunnis, Shi'ites, or Suffis. Muslims are further divided along ethnonational lines, ranging from Turks, Iranians, Saudis, and Somalians, to Indonesians, Bosnians, and Afghanis. Since September 11th, political officials have nonetheless conflated religion with other cultural traits used to classify groups as "worthy" or "incapable" of integration.

The Alevis acquired a deeper sense of ethnoreligious identity living in the diaspora. Originating in Anatolia, this heterogeneous group, composed of Turks, Kurmanci-Kurds, Zazaki, and Syrians broke with Sunni Islam, preferring ritual life grounded in local community. Although they revere Ali and the Twelve Imams, Alevis reject Sharia and most Islamic "pillars." In theory, men and women participate as equals in religious assemblies; there is no veiling requirement, no prescriptions on ritual impurity regarding menses or childbirth.[81] My Alevi friends feel no qualms about consuming alcohol. Their most important ritual is the *cem*, called together by a traveling religious leader; certain beliefs are held secret by way of "holy families" and *takiya* (obscuring one's identity to avoid persecution). This mystically oriented group formed holy linkages with persons of the same lineage, including wandering dervishes. They wrote their own verses, played special musical instruments, and created a separate justice system to avoid contacts with state. Alevi youth of the 1960s favored extreme-left causes and militant parties, due to mounting oppression by the secular Turkish regime.

Many relocated as guestworkers in the 1960s but displayed little interest in ethnic organizations or religious activities prior to the 1980s. An estimated twelve to twenty-five million Alevis remain in Turkey; the community encompasses 300–400,000 members in Germany, 40–50,000 of whom live in Berlin.[82] Hamburg and Berlin witnessed an initial mobilization with the founding of the Union of Patriots and the Union Party in 1979 at a time when most "Turkish" associations were focused on homeland politics. A 1978 assault by state military forces against the community in Maras, Turkey, later acquired legendary status as a "massacre" among laborers abroad; thirty-three persons were killed, but violent incidents in Maras, Sivas (1993), and Gazi Mahallesi (1995) perhaps had more to do with right-left battles than with "re-imagined" Sunni versus Alevi conflicts.[83]

Membership in some ninety organizations, loosely united under the Federation of Alevi Communities in Germany (AABF), ebbed and flowed following the 1980 military coup in Turkey. Breaking with *takiya*, the Union resurfaced as a political organ dominated by radical leftists and Marxists. One homeland organization, *Dev Yol*, was shut down and its leaders detained in 1986. Leftist ideologies lost their potency, but a new push for Kurdish autonomy, and a state crackdown qua Sunni-driven assimilation campaign, led the Alevis to reconsider their own status. Religious consciousness emerged as political Islam took hold in neighboring states. Club life assumed a transnational quality; activism was tied to Turkish developments that, in turn, triggered new debates on Alevism in the Turkish press. Two AABF functionaries campaigned for seats in the homeland parliament in 1999; German Alevis sent a delegation to protest deliberation of a subsequent law against non-orthodox religious orders.

Authorities in Hamburg and Berlin began to support cultural activities and identity discourses through the mid 1980s to counter repression in Turkey. In 1988, twelve Alevis broke with the dissimulation principle (founding communities on the basis of local origin) to form the Alevi Culture Group and sponsor Project Alevism.[84] Affording new opportunities for self-definition, the first Alevi Culture Week in October 1988 featured musical events (*saz* playing), religious ceremonies, panels on religious instruction and citizenship rights, plays commemorating the "massacres," and youth dance classes. The Hamburg Alevi Kültür Merkezi became a registered organization in May 1990. The movement spread to other cities like Düsseldorf, resulting in an umbrella organization, the Federation of Alevi Communities, and a chain of organizational fissures to match. Another Turkish attack at Sivas in 1993 provoked a demonstration attracting sixty thousand Alevis to Cologne.

By the early 1990s, Alevis could choose among more than one-hundred organizations, divided into national wings, the AABF with 89 member associations

(12,000 Alevis), and the Federation of Kurdistan Alevis (FEK) with 22 organizations encompassing 2,000 people. The Republican Education and Culture Center Vakfi (CEM Vakfi) boasts of another 21 associations covering 2,400 members; about 20,000 Alevis belong to formal organizations in Germany.[85] Most local leaders and sympathizers "abhor competition and conflict"; some Kurdish groups are Kurdistan Worker's Party (PKK) sympathizers, others are not. A small albeit engaged group of functionaries and artists offers a homogenized image of a community actually subject to fissures along class, educational, and ideological lines. Despite theological equality, Alevi associational life is "clearly gendered at every level": women prepare food for festivals, men conduct the organizational business. Shortly after a Berlin court granted the conservative Islamic Federation the right to offer religious instruction in public schools in 1998, the Alevis demanded a comparable right, opening up new discursive space in four schools to replace the "victim rhetoric" of the 1980s.[86] Though many travel to Turkey with their children, Alevi lives are clearly anchored in Germany.

Kurds are another group subsumed (and ignored) under the label "Turkish" until they began protesting human-rights violations in the homeland. In the 1920s, Mustafa Kemal campaigned to eliminate all "non-Turkish" elements in the country, excising references to Kurdistan from government documents and renaming Kurdish settlements. Kurds were brutally repressed after the 1980 coup, leading to an outpouring of asylum seekers. Numbering twenty to twenty-five million, Kurds comprise the world's largest stateless people. Of an estimated five-hundred thousand in Germany today, 85 percent are migrant workers, 15 percent refugees.[87] Kurds accounted for 60–80 percent of all asylum seekers from Turkey between 1979 and 1999.[88] The Federal Office for Migration and Refugees reported that of the 9,570 "Turkish" applications submitted in 2002, 7,822 involved Kurds (5,091 of 6,301 in 2003). They accounted for 3,664 of 10,242 Iraqi asylum seekers in 2002, 1,678 of 3,850 in 2003.[89]

Equivalent to 25 percent of the Turkish guestworkers from 1961 through 1974, Kurds mobilized sporadically during the 1980s, but their ranks swelled considerably following a 1993 PKK ban.[90] Created in 1978 by Abdullah Öcalan, the PKK focused almost exclusively on homeland developments, leading to "the transnationalization of domestic conflict." Turkey felt compelled to respond to events on German soil, thus "galvanizing support for the most extreme Kurdish groups."[91] As a cadre organization (estimated at ten thousand members, with up to fifty thousand sympathizers), the PKK established its hold in specific neighborhoods, and was suspected of running drug and smuggling rings. The charge that the PKK constituted a terrorist organization engaging in violent attacks on Turkish establishments ironically coincided with increasing German attacks against foreigners, e.g., in Mölln and Solingen.

Interior Minister Kanther (CDU) banned the organization and confiscated its properties in November 1993. By 1995, Kurds were charged with 230 arson attacks against Turkish travel agencies, stores, and banks. In July, 250–300 Kurds initiated a "hunger strike for human rights" in Frankfurt/Main, emulating a similar action in Ankara. They were rushed by columns of police and water cannons less than a week later, triggering a flash of violence. Demonstrators shouted "First the Jews, then the Kurds," matched by anti-PKK calls "Get lost, terrorists!" The altercation dragged on for three days, leading to vandalism and a blockade for Kurds trying to enter the city; 180 were taken into custody. Berlin's Interior Minister Heinrich Lummer (CDU) accused sympathizers of instigating a "multi-conflict society."[92]

1999 brought demands for the accelerated deportation of Kurdish protestors who turned to violence following the kidnapping and arrest of PKK leader Öcalan. It is curious that Germany would deport persons back to Turkey who had fled their homeland, in part, because of state persecution. Their refugee status "had a catalytic function" for identity formation among Kurds, analogous to that witnessed among the Alevis. Because Germany does not allow extradition to countries with the death penalty, Öcalan's arrest in January 1999 led to the elimination of capital punishment as Turkey accelerated its push for EU admission.[93] Another paradoxical feature of FRG policy is its embrace of the Turkish position refusing to recognize Kurds as a distinctive, oppressed minority.

Despite the special family protection (Article 6) embedded in the Basic Law, parents can only select state-approved names for children clearly identifying their sex. This silly regulation applies to Kurds but not to other persecuted ethnicities: "Kurds with Turkish nationality could not give their children Kurdish names; German authorities accepted only names found on lists provided by Turkish consulates. Second, there were programs of mother-tongue education for Turkish labor migrants' children; Kurdish children with Turkish nationality had to attend these classes given in Turkish even if their mother-tongue was Kurdish."[94] FRG arms sales to its NATO ally are purportedly used to combat Kurdish uprisings, leading many to believe that Turkish-German relations flourish at the expense of minority rights.

Had officials not propagated the myth of return over a stretch of thirty years, the seeds of extremist movements embodied by the PKK and the Grey Wolves might have fallen on less fertile ground. Some Turks became Kurds after their arrival "because the Turkish state denies them cultural recognition and the German state denies them political recognition."[95] The PKK now abjures armed struggle against the Turkish state, but the status of Kurds in the homeland, Iraq and elsewhere has hardly improved.[96]

Iranians have had an easier time securing asylum status, dating back to the 1979 Islamic Revolution. Roughly 107,000 Iranians reside in the FRG. Born in the 1930s and 1940s, many came to study (55,545 in 1966–1967) and decided to stay. Long-term residents evince high degrees of professionalism: more Iranians are doctors (1,051 in 1992) than is true for any other nationality.[97] A

Table 4.7 Recognition Quotas for Asylum Seekers by Nationality

| Country of Origin | Recognized Asylum Status | | | | | "Little Asylum" | | | | |
| | 1997 | | 1998 | | | 1997 | | 1998 | | |
		%	First Applications	%	Follow-up Appeal %		%	First Applications	%	Follow-up Appeal %
Yugoslavia	552	1.92	464	1.20	42	0.10	157	0.55	558	1.34	70	0.17
Turkey	3086	11.07	2193	9.59	466	2.04	663	2.38	455	1.99	119	0.52
Iraq	2034	16.98	808	8.31	17	0.17	7436	62.07	2807	28.88	2	
Afghanistan	558	9.62	142	2.48	27	0.47	431	7.05	23	0.40	26	
Vietnam	9	0.03	13	0.29	1	0.02	61	2.23	6	0.14	20	
Iran	821	18.91	483	12.36	19	0.49	345	7.95	227	5.81	95	2.43
Sri Lanka	273	4.61	186	4.23	5	0.11	67	1.16	34	0.77	5	
Georgia	29	1.00	11	0.39	2	0.07	4	0.14	5	0.18	0	
Syria	202	10.44	174	6.91	17	0.67	106	5.48	237	9.41	9	
Armenia	24	0.61	16	0.59	1	0.04	5	0.13	11	0.41	4	
Algeria	30	1.24	15	0.61	1	0.04	19	0.79	9	0.37	2	
Azerbaijan	46	4.76	44	2.95	1	0.07	111	11.48	201	13.47	0	
Bosnia-Herzegovina	23	0.09	25	0.56	0	0.00	9	0.04	11	0.25	0	
Pakistan	120	3.33	115	3.69	14	0.45	1	0.03	6	0.19	6	
India	2	0.06	1	0.04	1	0.04	7	0.18	3	0.12	1	
Sierra Leone	4	0.72	3	0.18	2	0.12	2	0.36%	1	0.06%	0	

Source: Data supplied by the Bundesamt für Migration und Flüchtlinge (www.bamf.de).

second wave entered after the Revolution. A third group "spontaneously" sought asylum between 1992 and 1994; 30 percent of nearly 18,000 applications were filed in the Netherlands, but a majority went to Germany, making Iranians the sixth largest non-EU nationality (164,200).[98]

Iranians are described as socially successful but still homesick. Sigrid Bafekr and Johan Leman studied (mostly male) intellectuals who pursued "an unchanging urge to be with people of their own kind."[99] They construe their cultivation of homeland culture as a matter of personal identity but do not mobilize further as an "ethnicity bearing" collective: they commonly admit, "I think European and I feel Persian." Meeting every two to three months on Saturdays over a three-year interval, they took no stance on the 1979 revolution but rather performed music, exchanged poetry, celebrated Persian holidays, and lectured on culture "in perfect German," although one interviewee insisted: "I shall never make peace with myself as long as I do not, with every word, look for the other word in my language."[100]

The late 1960s saw intense New Left protests against Shah Pahlavi of Iran, charging him with major human-rights violations. Leftist dissidents would have been the first to flee, but some who came to Germany after the Khomeini takeover probably sought to escape retribution for their roles in sustaining the Shah. Striking here is that cosmopolitan Muslims who enjoyed elite status under the old regime are more welcome as asylum seekers because they sought to escape religious fundamentalism. Germany accepted political refugees who left Turkey after the 1980 coup, only to project its worst fears of religious extremism onto German-Turkish residents hoping to offer Islamic instruction in schools. Obviously not all Muslims are "created equal." Nor are women and men, when it comes to finding refuge from new forms of political-cultural persecution.

The Taliban Effect: Addressing Gender-Specific Persecution

According to UN Refugee Agency (UNHCR) reports, women and children make up 85–90 percent of the world's refugees, yet states rely on male-normed definitions of *persecution*. "Acceptable reasons" for asylum have historically focused on persecution centering on conventional political activities, e.g., creating parties or labor unions, agitating for freedom of speech. The last decade has seen a dramatic rise in unaccompanied minors seeking physical security but often subjected to unlimited detention or rapid re-deportation to conflict zones, without legal counsel. Women and children may be excluded from conventional types of participation by law or custom, but this doesn't render them safe. Degrading projections of their exotic sexuality promoted by sex tourism and "mail-order bride" catalogues render them vulnerable to forced prostitution and trafficking. As Bridget Anderson muses, there is still "lots of money to be made out of girls and women."[101] Kidnapped sex workers have been routinely deported for immigration violations before they get a chance to testify against the mafia types who smuggled them in and stole their paltry earnings. There has been a sharp increase in female asylum seekers in recent years, now that Canada (1993), the US (1995), Australia (1996), and other states recognize gender-specific claims.

Men are usually the first to flee in the face of direct threats, leaving women and children behind. Their experiences in refugee camps can be just as traumatic as those in conflict zones, as seen among Sudanese, Rwandan, and Albanian women; Kosovars were abducted by sex traffickers. Mass rape in war has its own "tradition of impunity"; it is depoliticized, deemed "sexual or personal in nature," labeled a crime against honor, a "regrettable excess," or subsumed under "crimes against humanity."[102] In 1996, the International War Crimes Tribunal finally defined rape as a crime of war *sui generis* following the heinous sexual violation of Bosnian Muslims.[103] Loss of a male breadwinner means a lack of income, but wife status renders one dependent on a husband's successful asylum application, even if she suffered brutality. Post-traumatic stress, cramped hostel conditions, and degrading economic conditions contribute to domestic violence upon arrival, yet the woman is unable to leave if the man's asylum status has yet to be decided.

Let us now consider women who faced "extremely difficult migration," not only owing to personal abuse as tools of war but also because asylum law subjects them to forms of dependency and double jeopardy unknown to men. The first case relates to the early stages of war in Yugoslavia. "Drinka," a forty-year-old woman, had been a successful, career-driven banker who managed credit accounts for Yugoslavia's largest industries, then shifted to investments. A Croatian, she was forced to flee Sarajevo already under siege in 1992; she took the last train out of the city, accompanied by her two daughters. Her husband, a psychologist and social worker dealing with troubled youth, moved in with friends when their street became a battleground. Once in Germany, she spent three months squeezed into a four-room apartment with twenty people, owned by a friend's father. After one year, Drinka was granted "tolerated status" but had to apply for an extension every six months.

She taught herself some German by listening to radio, television, and music tapes but hated her state-imposed dependency—allegedly "ruining" the welfare state. "My job is my freedom, and I did not let anyone take that freedom from me, not even my husband. . . . I hate it, accepting welfare benefits, I don't want to be dependent. I spent my whole life giving, giving away, because I had enough. I was always the helper, never the recipient, I can't stand exchanging roles. I was willing to do anything to get back on my feet. And I couldn't stand being unoccupied any more. . . . I went to work house-cleaning, applied for all kinds of jobs that I could not get because my German was bad."[104] By the time she was interviewed, Drinka had moved up to managing a hotel breakfast buffet; her employer paid for her German classes. Starting to forget their native language, her daughters were doing well in school. After more than a year, this hard-working refugee (up every morning at 4:00 AM), finally heard from her husband; she urged him to come to Germany but concluded her conversation declaring, "I miss my city. The homesickness keeps getting stronger. I would like to go back. At some point I want to go back."[105]

Also a victim of the Yugoslav war, "Azra" hails from a small Bosnian village where her neighbors were Muslims, Croats, and Serbs. When interviewed, she lived in a Malteser hostel, a kind of Salvation-Army dormitory outside Hamburg with other mothers and children from Bosnia, Afghanistan, and Poland. Her husband had worked as a radio/television technician; they built a home, and had two children, age four and nine, when they were forced to flee. Azra's spouse has been missing since 1992, after he went into the woods with other men to hide from the Serbian militia. Her father (age sixty-two) and father-in-law (eighty-four) were executed in the village the same day. A young niece was kidnapped and gang raped; an aunt who had survived Auschwitz saw parallels in the bestiality that followed. It took Azra and her family a month to reach Germany by trekking through Hungary. They were housed with their children in a containership in the Hamburg harbor, sharing four to five cubic meters of space. Scared by the presence of unattached African men on the ship, they were further terrorized by constant rumors of neo-Nazi attacks.

Azra summarizes her experience as "Hell for everyone. Criminality was preprogrammed." She continues: "I thought [Germany] was a great, beautiful, rich and secure country . . . but now Germany is completely alien to me. We are so isolated and have seen nothing of Hamburg. Because we have no money to go into the city. Because we do not speak the language. . . . With my husband I would have lived anywhere in the world. Without him, I want to go back. And to rebuild something with other women left alone."[106]

These women are among the lucky ones: they avoided rape and were admitted to Germany; one found a niche for herself and her children, the other remained herded together with many desperate people for over three years—without counseling, language training, or positive social contacts. Because the war in their own backyards came as a shock to affluent, peace-oriented Europeans, many rushed to provide humanitarian assistance to the first wave. By the time of violence broke out again in Bosnia (1995), Germans already overwhelmed by unemployed Easterners, nearly two million *Spätaussiedler*, post-Soviet Jews, and Third-World migrants; politicians insisted "the boat was full." Though it declared outright war victims temporary refugees, Germany's war history prevents it from deporting many it has judged unacceptable. Those who stay are denied a meaningful existence, however, to deter others from coming. The net result is a tremendous waste of human capital, not to mention, hopelessly shattered lives unbecoming a democratic state.

Born in 1963, "Im Ratha" spent her formative years undergoing "ideological cleansing" at a forced labor camp in Cambodia, starting in 1975. Her family in Phnom Penh was exterminated by Pol Pot. She endured "three years, eight months and twenty days," sometimes marching twenty kilometers to the fields, on the verge of starvation, until the camp was liberated by Vietnamese troops. Altering documents to make her old enough to apply, she was one of six girls awarded a scholarship to Czechoslovakia (a "fraternal socialist state") in 1985. She had secretly learned English, helping her to master Czech, but was made to study economics rather than journalism. In 1989, just as the Wall fell, she helped to organize a demonstration in front of the Cambodian Embassy in Prague. The students were immediately stripped of their scholarships, but Vaclev Havel personally intervened to finance her studies. A Czech employee at the Cambodian Embassy warned her not to return home due to civil war. When her extended residency permit ran out, she sought a three-month visa for Germany in March 1991, and filed an asylum claim after it expired.

Living with friends in Berlin at the time, she was required to move into ex-military barracks in Eisenhüttenstadt (East Germany):

> There were gigantic problems. So many nationalities, so many cultures. Too many. Every day there were fights, lots of drinking and also theft. The police had to come frequently. Then the Neo-Nazis came with Molotov cocktails. They even beat up foreigners in telephone cells. After fourteen days I thought I was going crazy. I talked to the manager for so long until he helped me to get away. From Eisenhüttenstadt I went on to Strausberg. A camp in the middle of the woods. There was no street in the vicinity, no bus, no place to shop. The worst was, however—I was the only girl among a hundred men. Day and night I had to lock my door, barricade myself in. In order to eat, though, I had to go into the mess hall. I can't tell you how horrible that was.[107]

Moved again, back to the outskirts of Berlin, Im Ratha finally had her court hearing but there were no interpreters who spoke Khmer. She tried to tell her story in broken German and English but was rejected immediately, because she had studied and "had not arrived directly from Cambodia"—though the Khmer Rouge were at war, and Czechoslovakia was not a "safe third state" when she entered. Her appeal could take years: "And I wait and wait and wait. The waiting is the worst part here."[108] By age thirty she had given up hope of having a family.

The stories are heartbreaking, the conditions in the asylum hostels anything but family friendly or conducive to youth integration. The legal uncertainty is psychologically debilitating, and compulsory unemployment defies any economic logic one could imagine in a cash-strapped, demographically challenged country like Germany. Add a big cup of gender bias and stir. It still took several years of extreme, misogynist oppression under the Taliban to bring gender-specific absurdities inherent in national asylum laws to light.

A Constitutional Court verdict in August 2000 forced bureaucrats judging the merits of asylum applications from Afghanistan to reset their legal compasses. The Federal Republic had refused to recognize claims filed by women, especially, on the grounds that they were not subject to persecution by "state actors": the Taliban regime that seized power in 1995 had only been recognized by two other governments. The plaintiffs had come to Germany "facing physical danger and death" for collaborating with the Soviets prior to 1992 (another ironic twist—offering protection to foreign communists while denouncing them at home). Recall that the FRG had extended full asylum to men fleeing Khomeini's Islamic government in Iran.

The justices addressed the question "Under what conditions does a structure of domination exercise state or state-like power for the purposes of political persecution, entitling individuals to asylum protection under Art. 16GG?" Authorities were admonished for applying an abstract definition of *statehood* that did not consider the victims' subordination to a concrete system of violence and command in a core territory. Germany participated in massive NATO assaults against the Taliban despite their "non-state" status, from November 2001 through May 2003, after the terrorist attacks on New York and Washington, DC.

In 2001, the federal agency responsible for refugee decisions (BAFl) had granted asylum to 23.7 percent of the Afghan applicants (only 1 percent in 2002), yet 38.7 percent enjoyed protection against deportation; in 23 percent of the other cases there were still "impediments to deportation." Afghan women brutalized by warlords or subject to female genital mutilation proved no exception. The reason for cutting off recognition was the purported end of Taliban domination in 2001, though warlords are still fighting everywhere but Kabul. In 2003, state interior ministers decided to permit forced returns for war victims as soon as it was warranted by home-state conditions; persons found guilty of criminal offenses or posing a security threat were supposed to leave first. The Permanent Conference of Ministers simultaneously admitted that "an orderly and non-dangerous return" for many was not yet possible.

Serving as head nurse in the Kabul hospital at the age of twenty (after international-aid workers fled), UM-St. Louis student Belquis Ahmadi told me in 2000: "I was to undress an injured woman to find out where the bleeding came from. I was trying to pull off her boots, when the woman screamed as loud as she could. I didn't realize that I was trying to pull off the remaining part of her leg which had been half amputated. . . . I had witnessed cases of women's breasts or other parts of their bodies had been cut off (for belonging to some other ethnic group), as well as men who had nails hammered into their heads."[109] Genocide has morphed into new forms of gendercide, stretching from Bosnia to Rwanda, from Kosovo to China.[110] Although it did not rule on gender-specific persecution, the Constitutional Court verdict held direct implications for such cases, e.g., for female refugees from Algeria, Jordan, Pakistan and the Ivory Coast.[111]

Germany was among the first to assist Afghanistan after the Taliban were driven out or at least underground. Enjoying good relations with the country prior to 1979, it reopened schools for girls, committing €15 million.[112] Ursula Müller, former gender-mainstreaming officer in the Foreign Ministry, was sent to assist with reconstruction. The minister for development and economic assistance, Heidi Wieczorek-Zeul, declared women "the heart of a peaceful Afghanistan," essential for the creation of a democratic civil society. Wieczorek-Zeul hosted a parallel peace summit for Afghan women during the 2002 Petersburg negotiations after the fall of the Taliban; official talks included only two females among more than sixty delegates. The Red-Green Government provided support for the fifteen hundred delegates who assembled in June 2002 to elect an interim government. The Friedrich Ebert Foundation staged a Women's Congress in Kabul shortly before, hoping to establish a minimum quota of 160 female "pioneers" as participants in the Loya Jirga. Belquis Ahmadi was one of them.

A September 2004 study on "EU-Enlargement, Migration and Trafficking in Women" stressed the growing need for gender protection against human trafficking, victimizing up to 4 million adults and 1.2 million children per year. An estimated 90 percent of all southeast European sex workers are forced into prostitution through abduction; 10–15 percent are under age eighteen; among those rescued in Kosovo between December 2000 and May 2003, 49 percent were between the ages of fifteen and eighteen, 32 percent only eleven to fourteen. A majority arrived from Albania, Rumania, Bulgaria, and Moldavia. The International Organization for Migration reports that nearly half a million Central/East European (CEE) women are sold to West European handlers each year. They suffer double exploitation, made to work at low paying jobs during the day and forced into service as prostitutes at night.[113]

In July 2004 the Bundestag and Bundesrat finally agreed on an Immigration and Integration Law, enacted in January 2005. It recognizes non-state and gender-specific grounds for asylum, and extends limited residency permits to reduce the hardships involved in "chain-toleration" (*Kettenduldungen*, §60a), i.e., the need to reapply for extensions every three months. The elimination of the *Aufenthaltsbefügnis* for those who cannot be deported to active war zones, replaced by temporary status, means less security for others.

The Integration of Permanently "Provisional" Refugees

The real-life experiences of refugee groups portrayed in this chapter go a long way in refuting the five myths commonly associated with postwar asylum policies in the Federal Republic. Article 16GG was never as elegantly simple as it sounded. Germany no longer leads the EU states in the number of persecuted aliens it accepts each year, nor in terms of the "especially attractive" conditions they encounter once they get in. The "overwhelming majority" are not economic refugees but rather persons trapped by political decisions that deliberately reinforced blood lineage as a foundation for citizenship. While its decision processes are, in truth, heavy handed, contradictory, and "never ending," the root cause of so-called asylum abuse has been Germany's own failure to adopt effective integration policies across four decades.

The groups presented here moreover highlight three kinds of migration experiences—difficult, very difficult, and extremely difficult—grounded in legally constructed but culturally suspect "religious" differences. Applied to Jewish refugees, Bosnians, Kosovars, and persons fleeing Islamic states, the extent to which a religion can be (re)aligned with European traditions defines any one group's chances of "recognition," and thus access to integration services. As one Berlin official noted, "There are strong differences between the Jewish and Turkish Communities: in the Jewish Community there is a group of people who, as Germans, in Germany with a specific religious alignment, pose no problems either for security or religious tolerance."[114] The Jewish Community, however, plays a contradictory role in the social integration of quota refugees insofar as its sole organizing principle, religion, is one to which only a minority ascribe. Only a small segment help in revitalizing Berlin's Jewish community; ethnic differences restrict communication and identification across subcultures. Still, many who have distanced themselves from Judaism send their children to Jewish day schools and *Gemeinde*-financed youth activities; this owes partly to a dearth of other family-friendly facilities for migrant children. The average per capita subsidy for Berlin's 10,000 Jews is DM 3,000 compared to DM 10 for its 180,000 Turkish residents.[115]

The first Turkish Islamic groups to establish themselves in Germany were outlawed in the secularized homeland; the mix included Sunni-oriented *Sueleymanli*, right-wing *Milli Görüs*, and Alevi-related *Nurcu*. Religious instructors financed by the Turkish Ministry for Religious Affairs continued to agitate against the Kemalist government at home. Some took a more radical right turn in the host country because of homeland persecution, matched by a radicalization among leftist groups in Germany. Turkish Muslims first applied for recognition as a religious "corporation" in 1977 (see chapter 7). Three decades later, German authorities still insist that Islam lacks appropriate organizational structures, theological consistency, and a guarantee that it is an "enduring" faith—as one of the three world religions.[116] Berlin's Muslim population rose from 140,000 to 200,000 in the 1990s, due to the influx of Bosnians forced to seek asylum for ethnoreligious reasons. The latter receive few of the integration benefits accorded Jewish "quota refugees."

Religion proves just as ineffective as ethnic heritage in assessing a group's real prospects for adaptation to German life. Even when it succeeds, it fails, as one man's predicament shows: "Here in Germany everything is a bit strange. Sometimes I have problems knowing who I am. At home we speak Russian and Polish. I think about whether I am Polish, Jewish or Russian. I have come to the conclusion that I am Jewish and remain Jewish and that I will never become a German. I have very little to do with Germans. My friends are mostly from Russia or Israel."[117]

Another paradoxical feature of German refugee/asylum policy is that the conflation of religion and identity in the case of Jews leads to a double victimization of the people it is intended to compensate. Shortly after unification, Peter Glotz (SPD) affirmed the decision to accept Jewish migrants for historical reasons: "The Germans brought guilt upon themselves . . . it is the least we can do, now that there are Jews again who wish to come back or to come for the first time to the land of the Holocaust not to calculate in petty terms but to solve ensuing problems as non-bureaucratically and with as little noise as possible."[118]

Micha Brumlik cautions, however, that "Jews run the risk of being turned into something resembling a museum of Judaism, a people to be visited as if out of antiquarian interest." New forms of anti-Semitism arise "not only despite Auschwitz but rather because of Auschwitz." A country that has failed many times to reach consensus on how to memorialize its dead Jews embraces a new generation of Jews as "a living memorial for the greatest disgrace of German history."[119] Michael Bodeman observes that Jews are often used to "certify" German mastery of the past: "Even today the Jewish minority as an incorporated group must carry out ideological labor for Germans . . . instrumentalized by the German state for both internal and external political ends."[120]

While Glotz saw Jews "coming back" in a metaphorical sense, Jörg Schönbohm (CDU) attributes a quasi-ethnic right of return to Jews, analogous to that enjoyed by *Aussiedler*: "Turks come here to participate in the German economy, to earn money. . . . Jews come here because it was their home, or the home of their parents, and they want to live here."[121] This is the stuff of which new myths are made. Russian Jews have been declared "honorary Germans" to persuade skeptical citizens that they possess a special capacity for integration denied second and third generation Turks. Ex-Commissioner and ICI member Cornelia Schmalz-Jacobsen provides a reality check: "When I go to an *Aussiedler* settlement—and in my former electoral district there are such things—it doesn't feel like one is in Germany anymore, because everyone is speaking Russian. . . . But we put a template over them and say 'these are Germans!' And we put the same template over the Jews. 'God knows where these people were born, but somewhere there were German roots, and they must all be taken care of and financed.'"[122]

Secular Germany is "cutting the foot to fit the shoe," promoting one religious community at the expense of others, despite the fact that its own citizens distrust any "true believers," accounting, in part, for their aversion to George W. Bush. People who insist on "being German among Germans" are just as suspect as Muslim women in headscarves. Lawmakers declare some groups "capable of integration," then render this a self-fulfilling prophecy by extending special assistance to the chosen few to make it possible. Yet even with special benefits, these groups are less willing to participate in mainstream society than others denied the extra help.

Aussiedler "reactivate" their citizenship upon arrival, irrespective of language skills; post-Soviet Jews can apply for accelerated naturalization (seven years) without renouncing their original citizenship. First- and second-generation Turks must wait at least ten years, meet specific housing criteria, demonstrate economic independence, and renounce homeland citizenship. Their applications may be put on hold for two years; if their economic circumstances change (through unemployment), they can lose eligibility. A readiness to integrate "has little to do with the Jewish or Turkish communities, it seems, but rather with the German state." Its chief advice to the latter is to insist that the best way for them to integrate is to "stop being Turkish."[123]

What matters in all of these cases is the opportunity to develop new combinations of human, cultural, and social capital suitable for the new environment. Doomernik's observations regarding Jewish quota refugees can be extended to other groups: human capital may or may not retain its original value. As we saw with *Aussiedler*, migrants with limited professional skills but personal determination are the quickest to find new (albeit low-paid) jobs, while certified experts are the least employable. Social capital accompanies chain migration, but German distributional policies and employment bans ghetto-ize specific groups, nullifying their networking value. Homeland forms of "Vitamin C" (Connections) re-emerge, despite a lack of German "Vitamin B" (*Beziehungen*), negating the need to interact with or establish trust in local institutions. Survival skills valued back home may be seen as deviant or illegal in Germany.

Successful integration requires not only transparent rules of eligibility but also a uniform interpretation of the requirements pertaining to entry. It further depends on efforts to match individual skills or group attributes with non-stigmatizing channels of assistance. For victims of persecution, the decision to emigrate is far from voluntary; this makes it even harder to renounce one's accumulated social and cultural capital. "The compatibility of an immigrant's cultural capital is first and foremost relevant when he [*sic*] is eligible to participate in the receiving state's central institutions. This generally means he needs to have a legal status which goes beyond that of a temporary resident."[124] Doomernik continues, "When the immigrant arrives at the point where he has managed to find a job, he will in most cases be among German-speaking colleagues and will be expected to use that language actively. This again enhances his cognitive adaptation to German society and he will learn to understand 'how things are done'. In this way his dependence on compatriots and institutions for immigrant aid rapidly decreases."[125] The reverse is also true: the longer one is denied secure legal status and kept out of a job, the more dependent and less able one is to accumulate new forms of "capital."

Conservative politicians insist that children over age twelve are incapable of effective integration; in reality, adults over thirty are the ones "too old to start at the beginning and too young to give up."[126] Doomernik's findings concerning Russian Jews are confirmed by both East German and *Aussiedler* experiences:

> One could say that every step in a person's life is registered and sanctioned. An individual's choice almost always relates to some part of the state bureaucracy. Schooling involves fees, grants, exams, work implies qualifications, taxation, minimum wages and insurances, unemployment involves social security and other benefits, birth and death require registration. . . . This principle works best for people who have lived with it all their lives. Every major step in a person's public development follows a previously documented and sanctioned one. . . . Not only does society structure a person's development over time, step by step, but it also limits the width of his [*sic*] operational scope.[127]

This is especially true with regard to the German labor market. An unemployed English major can not easily work as a waiter (*Zumutbarkeit*), nor can a physicist with a PhD randomly drive a cab—s/he has to undergo training and testing as a certified taxi driver. The longer the training and the higher the level of education, the smaller the number of occupational choices permitted, even for citizens. All systems have a funny habit of ignoring their own rules, however, when it comes to exploiting the cheap labor of persons rendered vulnerable by migration.[128] Urban communities, meanwhile, have a curious habit of ignoring national prejudices in adapting to their own multicultural populations, as the next chapter demonstrates.

Notes

1. Cited in Jeroen Doomernik, *Going West: Soviet Jewish Immigrants in Berlin since 1990* (Aldershot/Brookfield: Avebury, 1997), 43.
2. Klaus Bade, "Migration und Asyl im geteilten und vereinigten Deutschland," *Blätter für deutsche und internationale Politik* 1 (2001): 235–236.

3. Beate Winkler, ed., *Was heisst denn hier fremd? Thema Ausländerfeindlichkeit: Macht und Verantwortung der Medien* (Munich: Humboldt, 1994); Frank Esser and Hans Bernd Brosius, "Television as Arsonist? The Spread of Right-wing Violence in Germany," *European Journal of Communication* 11, no. 2 (1996): 235–260.

4. Bade, "Migration und Asyl," 236.

5. Bade, writing for the *Sixth Family Report* (Drucksache 14/4347, 2000), 51.

6. Data stem from the Bundesamt für die Anerkennung ausländischer Flüchtlinge.

7. Ibid.

8. Steffen Angenendt, ed., *Asylum and Migration Policies in the European Union* (Bonn: Europa Union Verlag, 1999); Bernd Marschang, "Mißtrauen, Abschottung, Eigensinn—Entwicklung der europäischen Asylrechts—Harmonisierung bis zum Amsterdamer Vertrag," *Kritische Justiz* 31, no. 1 (1998): 69–83.

9. *Migrationsbericht der Ausländerbeauftragten im Auftrag der Bundesregierung 2003* (Berlin), 37ff.

10. *Migrationsbericht der Ausländerbeauftragten 2001* (Berlin), 50.

11. Joan Fitzpatrick, "Temporary Protection of Refugees: Elements of a Formalized Regime," *American Journal of International Law* 94, no. 2 (April 2000).

12. Steffen Angenendt, "Germany," in Angenendt, *Asylum and Migration Policies*, 181.

13. Ibid., 189.

14. See Nazare Albuquerque Abell, "Safe Country Provisions in Canada and in the European Union: A Critical Assessment," *International Migration Review* 31, no. 3 (Fall 1997): 570–59. Canada was the first to recognize gender-specific grounds for asylum though it has bowed to EU pressures to recognize "safe country, exclusion, and first host country" concepts á la Schengen.

15. "Bundesgrenzschutz handelte unrechtmässig: Schutzsuchender Algerier ohne Asylprüfung nach Dubai zuruckgewiesen," *Pro ASYL* press release, 18 December 2003; "Neue Asylunterkunft auf dem Rhein-Main Flughafen still und leise in Betrieb gegangen," *Pro ASYL* press release, 30 May 2002.

16. Abell, "Safe Country Provisions," 588.

17. "Mythen im deutschen Asylrecht" (www.integrationsbeauftagte.de/mythen.htm).

18. One sensationalized case involves "Mehmet," who had a heavy criminal record by age 14. Matthias Gebauer, "Keine Entscheidung über Mehmet," *Spiegel* Online, 23 April 2001.

19. Veronika Vitt and Friedrich Heckmann, "Migration in Deutschland: Chronologie der Ereignisse und Debatten," in Klaus J. Bade and Rainer Münz, *Migrationsreport 2002: Fakten—Analysen—Perspektiven* (Frankfurt/Main: Campus, 2002), 251.

20. Anne Rademacher, ed., *"Ich bete jeden Tag, bitte lass uns bleiben!"* (Munich: Goldmann, 1993); also, Klaus-Henning Rosen, ed., *Die zweite Vertreibung: Fremde in Deutschland* (Bonn: Dietz, 1992).

21. Bade, "Migration und Asyl," 239.

22. ICI, *Structuring Immigration, Fostering Integration* (Berlin: 2002), 125.

23. Michael Brenner, "Epilog oder Neuanfang? Fünf Jahrzehnte jüdischen Lebens in Nachkriegsdeutschland," in Otto R. Romberg and Susanne Urban-Fahr, eds., *Juden in Detuschland nach 1945: Bürger oder "Mit"-Bürger?* (Bonn: Bundeszentrale für politische Bildung, 1999), 37.

24. Romberg and Urban-Fahr, *Juden in Detuschland*, 11.

25. Barbara Dietz, "German and Jewish Migration from the former Soviet Union to Germany: Background, Trends and Implications," *Journal of Ethnic and Migration Studies* 26, no. 4 (October 2000), 639.

26. Doomernik, *Going West*, 54.

27. Paul A. Harris, "Russische Juden und Aussiedler: Integrationspolitik und locale Verantwortung," in Klaus J. Bade and Jochen Oltmer, *Aussiedler: deutsche Einwanderer aus Osteuropa* (Osnabrück: Universitätsverlag Rasch, 1999), 249.

28. Doomernik, *Going West*, 56. Foreign Minister Fischer became the focus of vehement Bundestag hearings in 2005 after liberalizing visa procedures "too much" for Ukrainians.

29. Harris, "Russische Juden und Aussiedler," 248.

30. Doomernik, *Going West*, 59.

31. Ibid., 147.

32. Willi Jasper and Bernhard Vogt, "Integration und Selbstbehauptung: Russische Juden in Deutschland," in Romberg and Urban-Fahr, *Juden in Deutschland*, 215.

33. Doomernik, *Going West*, 15.

34. Ibid., 17–18.

35. Rachel Heuberger, "Jüdische Jugend in Deutschland: Zwischen Isolation und Integration," in Romberg and Urban-Fahr, *Juden in Deutschland*, 206.

36. Ibid., 200.

37. Judith Kessler, *Von Aizenberg bis Zaidelman: Jüdische Zuwanderer aus Osteuropa in Berlin und die Jüdische Gemeinde heute* (Berlin: Ausländerbeauftragte des Senats, 1997).

38. Micha Brumlik, *The Situation of the Jews in Today's Germany* (Bloomington, IN: Jewish Studies Program, 1991).

39. Jasper and Vogt, "Integration und Selbstbehauptung," 214.

40. Ibid., 212.

41. Elena Slominski, "Akzeptanz oder Emanzipation? Judinnen aus den GUS-Staaten in Deutschland," in Romberg and Urban-Fahr, *Juden in Deutschland*, 222.

42. Michael Wolffsohn, *Meine Juden, eure Juden* (Munich: Piper, 1997), 229.

43. Doomernik, *Going West*, 145–146.

44. Ibid., 101.

45. Ibid., 117.

46. Ibid., 82–84.

47. Ibid., 75, 81.

48. Ibid., 102.

49. Ibid., 140.

50. Jasper and Vogt, "Integration und Selbstbehauptung," 219.

51. Doomernik, *Going West*, 109.

52. Jasper and Vogt, "Integration und Selbstbehauptung," 219.

53. Doomernik, *Going West*, 65.

54. Ibid., 132.

55. Jasper and Vogt, "Integration und Selbstbehauptung," 218.

56. "Chaja," cited in Kessler, *Von Aizenberg bis Zaidelman*, 21.

57. Daniel Levy and Yfaat Weis, eds., *Challenging Ethnic Citizenship: German and Israeli Perspectives on Immigration* (New York/Oxford: Berghahn Books, 2002).

58. Zeev Rosenhek, "Migration Regimes and Social Rights: Migrant Workers in the Israeli Welfare State," in Levy and Weiss, *Challenging Ethnic Citizenship*, 137–153.

59. Fitzpatrick, "Temporary Protection of Refugees," 9.

60. Ibid., 9.

61. Ibid., 1.

62. Heinz-Jürgen Axt, "The Impact of Refugee Flows from Former Yugoslavia," in Münz und Weiner, *Migrants, Refugees and Foreign Policy*, 6.

63. Angenendt, *Asylum and Migration Policies*, 5.

64. Christian Schölzel, *Vom Balkan nach Berlin: Ein Streifzug durch die Beziehungen zu Jugoslawien und seinen Nachfolgestaaten* (Berlin: Ausländerbeauftragte des Senats, 1999), 94.

65. Münz and Weiner, "Migration, Flucht und Aussenpolitik," in Steffen Angenendt, ed., *Migration und Flucht* (Bonn: Bundeszentrale für politische Bildung, 1997), 205.

66. Vitt and Heckmann, "Migration in Deutschland," 229.

67. Fitzpatrick, "Temporary Protection of Refugees," 5; Boris Kanzleiter, "Kosovo-Roma haben Angst vor der Abschiebung," *Berliner Zeitung*, 2 June 2002.
68. Vitt and Heckmann,"Migration in Deutschland," 230.
69. Ibid., 247.
70. Ibid., 234.
71. Ibid., 235.
72. Ibid., 255.
73. For a broader picture, see Axt, "The Impact of Refugee Flows."
74. Vitt and Heckmann, "Migration in Deutschland," 263.
75. Ibid., 261.
76. Schölzel, *Vom Balkan nach Berlin*, 92.
77. Fitzpatrick, "Temporary Protection of Refugees," p. 6.
78. "Deutschland: Schily schlägt Asyllager in Afrika vor," *Migration und Bevölkerung* 6 (August 2004): 1.
79. Fitzpatrick, "Temporary Protection of Refugees," 15.
80. Deutscher Bundestag, *Islam in Deutschland*, Bundesdrucksache 14/4530; Marieluise Beck, ed., *Bericht zur Lage der Ausländer*, 23 August 2002 (Berlin), 247ff.
81. Krisztina Kehl-Bodrogi, *"Was du auch suchts, such' es in dir selbst." Aleviten (nicht nur) in Berlin* (Berlin: Concept Verlag, 2002), 20ff.
82. Ibid., 40.
83. Martin Sökefeld and Susanne Schwalgin, "Institutions and their Agents in Diaspora: A Comparison of Armenians in Athens and Alevis in Germany" (WPTC-2K-11 Universität Hamburg, paper presented at the sixth European Association of Social Anthropologists Conference, Krakau, 26–29 July 2000).
84. Ibid., 15.
85. Ibid., 19. The directory and analysis of ethnic organizations published by North Rhine-Westphalia does not list Alevi organizations separately. Ministerium für Arbeit, Soziales und Stadtentwicklung, ed., *Selbstorganisationen von Migrantinnen und Migranten in NRW*, Wissenschaftliche Bestandsaufnahme (Düsseldorf, 1999).
86. Marlies Emmerich, "Aleviten wollen an vier Schulen unterrichten," *Berliner Zeitung*, 5 February 2002; Kehl-Bodrogi, *Was du auch suchst*, 63–65.
87. Ministerium für Arbeit, *Selbstorganisationen*, 82.
88. Birgit Ammann, *Kurden in Europa: Ethnizität und Diaspora* (Hamburg: Lit, 2001), 135.
89. Bundesamt für Migration und Flüchtlinge, ed., *Migration und Asyl in Zahlen: Tabellen, Diagramme, Erläuterungen* (2004), 26–27.
90. Ammann, *Kurden in Europa*, 121.
91. Brett Klopp, "The Transnationalization of Domestic Conflict: Kurdish Politics and the PKK in Germany" (paper presented at the Georgetown University Graduate Student Conference, 23–25 October 1999), 2.
92. Ibid., 24
93. "Türkei masslos im Triumph über PKK," *die tageszeitung*, 19 February 1999.
94. Andreas Blätte, "The Kurdish Movement: Ethnic Mobilization and Europeanization" (paper presented at the EUSA conference, Nashville, TN, 27–29 March 2003), 6.
95. Claus Leggewie, "How Turks became Kurds, not Germans," *Dissent* (Summer 1996): 79.
96. Günther Seufert, "Die Türkische Regierung will an einen Strategiewechsel der PKK nicht glauben," *Berliner Zeitung*, 27 March 2002.
97. Sigrid Bafekr and Johan Leman, "Highly-qualified Iranian immigrants in Germany: The role of ethnicity and culture," *Journal of Ethnic and Migration Studies* 25, no. 1 (January 1999).

98. Khalid Koser, "Social Networks and the Asylum Cycle: The Case of Iranians in the Netherlands," *International Migration Review* 31, no. 3 (Fall 1997): 592–611.

99. This is also true of Iranian-Americans; see Azadeh Moaveni, *Lipstick Jihad: A Memoir of Growing Up Iranian in America and American in Iran* (New York: Perseus Books, 2005).

100. Bafekr and Leman, "Highly-qualified Iranian immigrants," 107–108.

101. *Bridget Anderson, "Reproductive Labour and Migration" (WPTC-02.01, paper presented at sixth Metropolis Conference, Rotterdam, 26–30 November 2001).*

102. Dorothy Q. Thomas and Regan E. Ralph, "Rape in War: Challenging the Tradition of Impunity," *SAIS Review* (Winter/Spring 1994): 81–99.

103. Marlise Simons, "For First Time, Court Defines Rape as War Crime," *New York Times*, 28 June 1996.

104. Rademacher, *"Ich bete jeden Tag,"* 13, 16.

105. Ibid., 23.

106. Ibid., 150–151.

107. Ibid., 38.

108. Ibid.

109. Transferred to St. Louis as part of the Federal Refugee Redistribution Program, Belquis revealed her story to me bit by bit in personal e-mails.

110. Adam Jones, "Gendercide and Genocide," *Journal of Genocide Research* 2, no. 2 (June 2000): 185–211.

111. Bundesamt für Migration, *Migration und Asyl*, 136.

112. In 1977, women held 15 percent of the seats in the Afghan parliament; they comprised 70 percent of the teachers, 50 percent of the civil servants, and 40 percent of all physicians. Some 10,560 girls entered grades one through six in special winter schools in Kabul on 15 January 2001.

113. Tanja El-Cherkeh, "Neue Studie: Migration und Frauenhandel," *Migration und Bevölkerung* 7/04 (October 2004).

114. Jonathan Laurence, "Reconstructing Community in Berlin: Of Jews, Turks and German Responsibility" (paper presented at the Conference of Europeanists, Chicago, March 2004), 17.

115. Ibid., 9.

116. Gerdien Jonker, "Die Islamische Gemeinden in Berlin zwischen Integration und Segregation," in Hartmut Häusermann and Ingrid Oswald, eds., *Leviathan*, 17 (1997), 347–364. Also, Ahmet Akgündüz, "Migrations to and from Turkey, 1783–1960: types, numbers and ethno-religious dimensions," *Journal of Ethnic and Migration Studies* 24, no. 1 (1998): 97–120.

117. "Artur," cited in Doomernik, *Going West*, 20.

118. Harris, "Russische Juden und Aussiedler," 250.

119. Laurence, "Reconstructing Community in Berlin," 14.

120. Bodeman, cited in ibid., 4.

121. Cited in ibid., 14.

122. Ibid., 19.

123. Ibid., 18.

124. Ibid., 163.

125. Doomernik, *Going West*, 161.

126. Ibid., 92.

127. Ibid., 91.

128. Oliver Tolmein, ed., *Besonderes Kennzeichen D. Wahre Deutsche, Staatsbürger zweiter Klasse und die unsichtbaren Dritten* (Hamburg: Konkret, 2001).

CHAPTER 5

LEARNING-BY-DOING

Ethnic Enclaves and Economic Integration in Berlin

> Döner consumption is like visiting a brothel; hundreds of thousands do it every day, but they deny social recognition to the ones who provide the service.
> —Eberhard Seidel-Pielen, *Aufgespiesst!* (1996)

> One seldom finds so much philosophizing about returning to the homeland as among migrants who will never return.
> —F. Boverkerk (1974)

> You are what you eat.
>
> —Anonymous

The ubiquitous presence of pizza, döner kebab, and Asian-noodle stands throughout Germany makes it very clear that guestworkers have redefined the culinary tastes of most citizens since the 1960s. By 2001 there were more than fifteen hundred Italian, seven hundred Chinese, fifty-six Indian, and fifty Thai restaurants, not to mention fifty McDonald's franchises in Berlin alone. Less

Notes for this section begin on page 216.

apparent is the extent to which ethnic foods have generated a plethora of spin-off industries, leaving an even bigger mark on the German economy. Indeed, the country's fiscal well-being relies heavily on the continuing economic activities of ethnic entrepreneurs, despite myths portraying them as a disposable industrial reserve army. Thriving ethnic enclaves in Schöneberg, Wedding, and Kreuzberg have come to signify long-term commitment to the larger community. They have also become money-generating tourist attractions.

Over 58 percent of Germany's minorities live in cities with populations of 500,000 or more, another 22 percent in towns up to that level. Thus the place to look for social and political integration is not at the abstract national community level but rather at the real-existing metropolitan level. New forms of urban citizenship have emerged, allowing an ethnic middle class to extend into new neighborhoods. Recognizing that ownership brings collective responsibility, successful entrepreneurs exercise local leadership and foster social capital, linking dominant and minority cultures. Ethnic enclaves in Berlin have begun to function as do-it-yourself democratic communities. Economic self-mobilization has created new civil society venues, motivating otherwise apolitical ethnics to acquire citizenship—and then to participate more actively than many who are automatically entitled to such rights, e.g., EU nationals.

By the late 1980s, ethnic entrepreneurs were reporting DM 25 billion ($15.4 billion) in taxable sales, and investing over DM 6 billion locally, adding 9 percent to the gross domestic product. Self-employed migrants contributed DM 12.8 billion to the national pension insurance fund, only DM 3.7 billion of which was paid out to foreign retirees prior to unification. Another two million guestworkers poured DM 16 million into the general tax fund, along with DM 8 billion in value-added taxes for daily consumption. The purchasing power of 1.7 million Turkish consumers amounted to DM 50 billion ($30.8 billion), based on average monthly earnings of DM 3,650 ($2,253).[1] Comprising 8.5 percent of the paid labor force when unification occurred, migrant businesses had become a self-sustaining segment of the economy.

Reacting to sensational xenophobic attacks, the Federation of German Industries testified in 1991 that "some areas of public life, such as garbage collection, janitorial services, and gastronomy would collapse" without migrant workers.[2] The low-status nature of these jobs—situated, in Gunter Wallraff's terms, *ganz unten*—has long shrouded the indispensability of foreign laborers (over 14 percent) in nine of fifty-two key industrial sectors, including mining, construction, and automobile production.[3] In stark contrast to industrial orientations of the 1930s, corporations like Daimler-Benz recognize that their market interests "are much too internationalized and Europeanized to engage in a right-radical direction."[4]

The Institute of German Business predicts that the "demographic deficit" will require the FRG to import 12.5 million workers by 2020. However, the foreigners once recruited to fill Germany's low-status jobs have jettisoned their willingness to work under "3-D" conditions—dirty, dangerous, and difficult. Locally educated minorities are increasingly drawn to white-collar occupations, up from 12 percent in 1970 to 19 percent in 1990. The number of self-employed rose from fifty-one thousand in 1970, to two-hundred thousand by 1990. Nearly thirty-three thousand Turkish-owned shops, travel agencies, and restaurants generated more than seven-hundred thousand jobs in 1991, refuting the claim that migrants "steal German jobs."[5] Ethnics are creating their own businesses to escape long-term discrimination, disadvantage, and dependence.

This chapter examines changing patterns of socioeconomic opportunity and political identification, based on a dramatic expansion of the ethnic economy since 1990. I show that Germany's refusal to pursue active integration policies across a span of thirty years has unleashed surprising do-it-yourself integration processes among minorities. A closer look at ethnic mobilization in Berlin reveals important linkages between education, entrepreneurship, and sociopolitical integration. I argue further that ethnic associations have fostered participatory consciousness in ways that contradict long-standing assumptions about what it takes to prove "worthy" of German citizenship.

Long excluded from integration benefits accorded other minorities, Germany's well-established Turkish community has developed strategies for inclusion that build on a practical-communitarian framework for citizenship. The result mirrors scholarly emphasis on civil society and social capital in fostering the trust, reciprocity, and connectedness needed to "make democracy work." This approach recognizes migrants' socioeconomic contributions to the local environment, enhances collective identity, and adds new salience to participation grounded in constitutional patriotism. Participatory rights make more sense when they derive from having a stake in day-to-day community outcomes, as opposed to relying on imagined communities rooted solely in ethnic descent.

The experiences of Italians and other EU nationals, together with Poles and Green-Card workers, are suggestive of a mobile-transnational approach to citizenship. Appearances can be deceiving, however. Post-national and transnational theories focus primarily on welfare rights tied to market operations; political "claims-making" is a second-order concern. At the higher end of the food chain, jet-setting technicians, managers, and professionals find their benefits warranted by the multinational corporations employing them; pension schemes, profit sharing, and even tax status no longer depend on nationality. Voting rights are less important than their power to shape policies through corporate lobbying.

My analysis builds on two constructs rarely connected in the literature, namely, economic enclaves and urban citizenship. I describe the scope of ethnic enterprises, incorporating personal success stories among Turkish entrepreneurs as well as gender dynamics. We then consider other economically active minorities, juxtaposing the experiences of Italians, privy to work/residency rights due to their EU-national status, and border-hopping Poles, EU nationals since 2004 but not yet eligible for full freedom of movement. Shifting to urban citizenship, I reflect on the relative merits of practical-communitarian versus mobile-transnational approaches to migrant labor. I conclude with reflections on the ways in which Turkish "co-citizens" are reshaping the political opportunity structure in the Berlin Republic, now that they have jettisoned the myth of return.

Cultivating the Ethnic Economy in *Modell Deutschland*

Immigrant entrepreneurship has become a growth industry, both in relation to the new businesses established by "persons of migration background" (formerly "foreigners"), as well as in regard to scholars writing about this phenomenon. Most authors cite the positive influence of family networks, access to cheap labor, alternative credit sources, pre-existing social capital, community trust, and specialized tastes as factors assisting ethnic businesses.[6] Others use the negative role of host-country discrimination, "rigged markets," and high unemployment to explain the rise of entrepreneurial niches among ethnic minorities. A third school addresses the institutional qua regulatory context (mixed embeddedness) that may foster or inhibit the rise of an ethnic economy.[7] Few, if any, link processes of economic self-insertion with new modes of political participation, especially in Germany, where the "expendability" of foreign workers has long been used as an excuse for denying them formal citizenship.

Ethnic resources comprise a set of mixed blessings, supplying cultural supports and societal restraints. As Ivan Light and Steven Gold observe,

> Ethnic connections reduce the costs of doing business and provide investment capital, advice, raw materials, training, and access to customers. Networks render job referrals and training, and ethnic-based trust reduces conflict between workers and owners. Ethnic-based feelings of shared fate provide a basis for political action that can permit groups to win concessions from government agencies and establish a common standpoint for addressing conflicts within opposing groups and interests. These resources provide group members with financial, human cultural and social capital, which yields a path to economic progress that would have been unavailable in their absences.[8]

The ethnocultural dividends of one era can morph into the competitive disadvantages of another, and vice versa. Among the first generation, "ethnic-based cooperation delivers resources to persons without the financial or educational means otherwise required for their acquisition."[9] Denied the benefits of sociopolitical integration, successor cohorts fall prey to an insidious mobility trap: semi-skilled jobs in established ethnic enterprises appear inviting at first glance;

when coupled with a rigidly regulated labor market, however, they ultimately limit workers to the ethnic track, reducing career options and social mobility.

Mainstream scholars view ethnic-enterprise formation as a rational response to high unemployment among disadvantaged minorities. Focusing on US patterns, Light and Gold note: "In all probability, the general labor market will never provide enough good jobs for all. . . . Although the inadequacy affects everyone to some extent, even the native-born white majority, the burden of scarcity falls most heavily on the less assimilated or acceptable white groups, visible minorities, non-Christians, refugees and immigrants. For affected individuals, who are numerous, the inadequacy of the general labor market leaves scant alternative to utilizing their own resources to improve their economic chances."[10]

While some countries extend welfare benefits to migrants rendered jobless by structural change, Germany is taking a leaner and meaner stance toward its long-term unemployed. Its complex system of residency permits, naturalization requirements, and refugee classification denies some groups *any* access to the labor market, though judicial processes regarding their status may take up to ten years to complete.[11]

My research shows that ethnic enterprises in Berlin are sooner rooted in active than in reactive motives. As Light and Gold argue, the "self-employed amass and own more wealth than do wage and salary owners," rendering "ethnicity lucrative for at least some of the people all of the time."[12] Turkish-German entrepreneurs establish businesses to secure their own livelihood, yet they generate new jobs at a faster pace than traditional employers. This refutes claims that foreigners deprive Germans of jobs or shamelessly exploit the welfare state.

Entrepreneurial success depends on resources, but the critical question "is no longer whether class and ethnic resources combine [but rather] how they combine and in what proportions."[13] This raises a further question: What does Germany do, or not do, to allow for effective resource coupling, given its pressing need for job-creation? Subsequent generations face qualitatively different start-up conditions: while they may internalize parental values and business practices, their interaction with the host society will be significantly transformed as a result of enhanced language skills and intercultural competence. Alternatively, ethnic self-employment may decline with successive cohorts, as naturalized offspring find more desirable positions in the formal labor market. Having tracked the progress of ethnic entrepreneurs in North Rhine-Westphalia for more than a decade, the Center for Turkish Studies (ZTS) outlines four sets of variables facilitating the successful establishment of ethnic businesses, summarized in table 5.1.

Given the lack of formal occupational training in the USA, a migrant's cultural capital, by default, includes vocational capital as well as social capital, especially in the event of chain migration. Germany's highly regulated housing and labor markets undercut the cumulative value of human, cultural, and social capital. While ethnicity may offer distinctive advantages over impersonal

Table 5.1 Parameters of Ethnic Entrepreneurship

Migration-Related Factors Affecting Market Entry
a) shift in focus to host country
b) size of available ethnic market
a) differentiation/heterogeneity of population structure
b) rise in educational qualifications
c) improvement in legal framework conditions
d) increasing acceptance among German clientele
e) founder's boom creates its own dynamic

Group & Cultural Factors Supplying a Positive Framework for Entrepreneurship
a) higher income expectations
b) providing better future for children
c) openness to risk
d) enjoy family and social support in own community
e) emotionality, spontaneity, and flexibility
f) offers more social mobility
g) capital accumulation
h) possess intercultural competence

Labor Market Factors Lowering Opportunity Costs for Self-Employment
a) Subjectively perceived or objectively experienced migration-specific discrimination
b) greater prestige associated with self-employment as opposed to labor dependence
c) threat of unemployment
d) acceptance /modest expectations for success
e) willingness to invest more of own labor

Institutional Factors Offering a Favorable Climate for Start-Ups
a) greater acceptance as a social/economic/political policy measure
b) wide acceptance of independent entrepreneurship in Turkish media
c) establishment of own business associations
d) "consciousness raising" among German policy makers
e) targeted promotion of entrepreneurial starts
f) special projects promoting migrant businesses (e.g., Regional Transfers in NRW)

Source: Zentrum für Türkeistudien, Hg., *Die ökonomische Dimension der türkischen Selbständigen in Deutschland und in der Europäische Union* (Essen: June 2001), 8.

market relations, migrants expecting to build on community interactions are sometimes stopped cold by legalistic, contractual obligations in the FRG, beginning with the need for "unlimited" residency and formal accreditation. In most migration cases, human capital cannot be reduced to education since it also needs to be embedded in a larger "learning" environment, replete with opportunity costs; families may restrict educational advances by daughters, or bar wives from paid labor while utilizing their cognitive skills in an unpaid capacity.[14]

Although labor-market discrimination can serve as a motive for self-employment, it does not provide the means necessary for community-rooted entrepreneurship. Among Turkish workers, money that might have covered start-up costs or assets that could be used as loan collateral were sent "home" as remittances through the 1980s, based on the myth of return. Purportedly neutral mechanisms for capital accumulation are "skewed from the start insofar as bank loans 'have historically ignored the capital needs of small business owners of every ethno-racial background'."[15] Banks insist on forms of collateral hinging on legal requirements like residency status. Some ethnic communities may have strong traditions of family lending, but gender biases are likely to operate here as well.

The Center for Turkish Studies cooperates with the state in tracking ethnic business formation. Despite legal barriers to self-employment, researchers registered a veritable "founders' boom" since 1985, tapping into enormous consumer potential and extending into the mainstream economy. The ZTS surveyed 1,187 Turkish businesses in 1994, concentrating on the Ruhr region, Cologne, and Düsseldorf. Though gastronomy and groceries headed the list, Turkish employers were active in ninety-five other branches. The heaviest concentration of ventures with "limited liability" or *GmbH* status (19.6 percent) were in construction (46.7 percent) and the service sector (25.9 percent). *GmbH* standing reduces personal risk and improves access to capital; insofar as 80 percent of the self-employed surveyed were sole proprietors, attempts to expand or diversify carry significant personal costs.[16]

The average entrepreneur had been independent for 6.3 years. The younger the owner, the lower the capital base; over half of the eighteen to twenty-nine year olds started with less than DM 30,000, often in the service sector. Owners drew on investments of DM 500,000 or more for single stores or skilled-trade establishments (60 percent). A majority (58.3 percent) initially relied on family funding (71.8 percent of the larger retailers). Banks tended to finance restaurants (41.9 percent), one reason why so many start-ups occur in this sector. Job creation extended well beyond the needs of unemployed *Existenzgründer:* 1,187 ethnic businesses supplied jobs for 4,947 people, averaging 4.2 per business. Nationally, 13,800 Turkish firms had supplied jobs for 58,000, including 467 Germans. One-fourth provided apprentice places (56 percent in skilled trades, 53 percent in construction). Younger owners are eager to create jobs: 38 percent hoped to expand, and 31 percent had seen a 30 percent increase in sales volume over two years.[17]

Andreas Goldberg and Faruk Sen attribute their success to a dramatic growth in the flow of German tourists to Turkey (over seven-hundred thousand in 1995) leading to an "increasing acceptance of garlic" and exotic foods.

It owes further to better access to foreign goods, generational dynamics, and "willing workers," including family females. A majority had lived in Germany over fifteen years, 48 percent over twenty years. More than half had attended German schools; three-fourths described their language skills as "very good." While 59 percent had been workers before the start-up, only 10.5 percent were forced to find new jobs, despite the thesis that self-employment is "a coping strategy for foreigners in times of unemployment." One-fifth were motivated by desires for higher income, 12 percent sought independence, and 10.5 percent social mobility. Women comprised 13 percent of the self-employed ethnics; 78 percent were age eighteen to twenty-nine (72 percent among men). Female businesses operate with only half as much capital as male ventures but are more likely to receive bank loans (63 percent to 42 percent) insofar as women are perceived as more risk averse and trustworthy.[18]

Beyond language or discrimination, the problems Turkish proprietors faced in consolidating their businesses did not differ substantially from those of German self-starters: e.g., a lack of accounting expertise (17.5 percent), marketing difficulties (15.8 percent), and inadequate knowledge of the branch (17.8 percent). Fewer migrants took advantage of advisory services, however. Four-fifths were unaware that they could draw on public financial resources: only eight of 1,187 firms had done so.[19] North Rhine-Westphalia has two programs, GO Gründungsnetzwerk NRW and MOVE Mittelstandsoffensive NRW, to support ethnic business formation, along with Regional Transfer Points to address migrant-specific problems. Their concerns include "provisional" residency and legal status, the fact that higher education is not matched by changing employer perceptions, and a dearth of successful ethnic role models. The state is actively cultivating ethnic start-up potential by offering personal consultation, fostering networks, and improving owners' managerial skills. In 1999, the Transferstellen organized 450 activities, reaching out to 19,000 entrepreneurs, stressing the need for apprenticeships for 500,000 ethnic youth. New jobs rose from 186,000 in 1996 to 265,000 in 1998, bringing DM 46.1 billion in sales, and DM 11.1 billion in investments.[20]

By the late 1990s, 2.4 million Turks accounted for 27 percent of the migrant population; 1,998,534 are non-citizens, added to 470,000 naturalized residents. Representing 61 percent of all workers recruited, 53 percent have lived in Germany for over fifteen years.[21] In 2001, the Center for Turkish Studies interviewed 1,142 self-employed workers, later combined with survey responses from another 2,035 Turkish adults. From 1985 to 2000, the number of Turkish-owned businesses rose from 22,000 to 59,500, a growth rate of 170 percent and double the ethnic population growth (73 percent) during this period. The self-employed account for 7.2 percent of 830,000 Turkish wage earners, up from 5.2 percent in 1996. The average entrepreneur is 37.6 years old, and has lived in Germany 22.3 years; one in five is female.[22]

Many have moved beyond ethnic niches. The synergy effect is obvious in neighborhood markets: 77 percent share ties with German companies, including delivery and distribution networks. These merchants are shaping the macroeconomic picture as well. Their trade volume topped DM 55.7 billion in 2000, a 10.7 percent increase (DM 5.4 billion) over the previous year. Self-investment increased from DM 12.4 billion to DM 13.6 billion (9.7 percent), averaging DM 228,000 per producer. The number of paid workers grew from 293,000 to 327,000. Nearly 17 percent had hired German employees, 8.7 percent had workers of other nationalities.[23]

The majority fell within the small- to medium-business range: 46.5 percent had three coworkers, 43.7 percent had four to nine; only 9.8 percent boasted more than ten laborers. Nearly 41 percent had been in business for less than five years, 12 percent for less than two years; 26 percent had "adequate experience" after six to ten years of operation. Among the well consolidated, 33.4 percent had existed for ten years, 16 percent for eleven to fifteen years, and 17.4 percent for sixteen years or more.[24] Most rely on targeted distribution and Turkish advertising. Outside of funeral parlors and wedding halls (e.g., *Nostalgie Festsäle)*, few focus solely on the Turkish community; 89 percent have German customers. National food chains now cater to ethnic tastes even in terms of packaging.

Turkish Delight: From Guest to Gourmet in the *Döner-Capital*

Major cities have long served as laboratories for integration. Berlin is no exception. While the total population declined from 3.47 million to 3.38 million between 1993 and 2004, the number of foreigners rose from 393,000 to 448,200. Deaths outnumbered births; average Berliners (age 43) are aging faster than their federal counterparts (40.5). Turks comprise the largest minority, accounting for 85 percent of non-citizens in Western districts; less than 5 percent live in the East.[25] Concentrations range from 3 percent in Marzahn-Hellersdorf and Treptow-Köpenick, to 27 percent in Mitte. Russians prefer Charlottenburg, Marzahn, and Lichtenberg; Turkish-Berliners congregate in Kreuzberg, Neukölln, Tiergarten, and Wedding. In 2003, 3,389 persons enjoyed full asylum rights, 5,287 applications were pending, and 17,408 were "tolerated," accounting for 1.2 percent, 0.8 percent, and 3.8 percent of the aliens, respectively.[26]

Berlin experienced economic shock therapy in 1990, when its national subsidies of forty years suddenly disappeared, despite the fact that it has borne costs of "growing together" witnessed nowhere else, like the need to reconnect its subway and sewer systems. Western districts faced a jobless rate of 16.4 percent among nationals in 1996, compounded by higher levels among Easterners. Unemployment among ethnic laborers rose to 24 percent, but their problems were ignored in the shuffle of capital functions from Bonn to Berlin—though their once peripheral neighborhoods along the Wall are now prime real estate in *Stadtmitte*.[27] Structural unemployment in the late 1970s to early 1980s coincided with increasing social differentiation and niche marketing in the post-Fordist economy. Younger residents with allowance money to burn developed a taste for new cuisines coinciding with the "McDonaldization" of food processing. Traditional German fast foods like *Currywürste* and *pommes frites* were overtaken by döner kebab and pizza-by-the-slice. Self-employment among aliens more than doubled after 1985, while German start-ups declined by 3 percent. Nationally, Turkish businesses (38,700) lagged slightly behind Italian enterprises (45,000).

Turkish unemployment more than doubled between 1990 and 1996, from 6,230 to 17,464; among foreigners, jobless figures rose from 19,000 in 1991, to 46,000 in 1998, nearly double the rate of Germans in Berlin-Brandenburg, 34.4 percent versus 18.9 percent.[28] Youth are especially disadvantaged in a city with three major universities and several technical colleges, already churning out surplus academics. By late 2004, joblessness among German Berliners stood at 17.4 percent, compared to 37.9 percent among non-citizens.[29]

Table 5.2 Turkish Self-Employment and Asset Growth, 1985–2000 (in Deutschmarks)

Year	1985	1990	1995	1998	1999	2000
Total	22,000	33,000	40,500	51,000	55,200	59,500
Average Investment per Business	173,000	173,000	204,900	218,000	224,000	228,000
Total Investment per Volume	3.8 bil	5.7 bil	8.3 bil	11.1 bil	12.4 bil	13.6 bil
Average Sales Volume per Business	782,000	758,000	840,000	904,000	912,000	936,000
Total Annual Sales (in Billions)	17.2	25.0	34.0	46.1	50.3	55.7
Employees per Business	3.5	3.3	4.1	5.2	5.3	5.5
Total Number of Employees	77,000	100,000	168,000	265,000	293,000	327,000

Source: Zentrum für Türkeistudien (ZfT). *Die ökonomische Dimension der türkischen Selbständigen in Deutschland und in der Europäische Union.* Essen: June 2001, 12.

Table 5.3 Minority Unemployment (percent), 1980–2000

Ethnicity	1980	1985	1990	1995	1998	2000
Greeks	3.8	11.5	10.0	15.7	18.2	16.1
Italians	4.8	14.3	11.0	15.9	18.0	15.2
Portuguese	2.0	7.4	5.8	11.9	13.0	11.5
Spanish	3.0	8.8	7.2	10.7	12.6	11.7
Yugoslavs	2.6	10.0	6.3	9.2	11.6	11.2
Turks	5.9	14.6	10.3	18.9	23.2	21.2

Source: Amtliche Nachrichten der Bundesanstalt für Arbeit (ANBA).

Table 5.4 Self-Employment in Berlin (1991, 1994, 1997)

Self-employed among Berlin residents: Absolute numbers		
	1991	*1994*	*1997*
Female	38,400	48,400	54,900
Male	92,600	111,300	125,100
Total	131,000	159,700	180,000
Self-employed of German nationality		
Female	36,000	43,400	49,000
Male	85,600	95,400	109,200
Total	121,600	138,800	158,200
Self-employed among those of foreign nationality		
Female	2,400	5,000	5,900
Male	7,000	15,900	15,900
Total	9,400	20,000	21,800

Source: Statistisches Landesamt Berlin, and Felicitas Hillmann, *Türkische Unternehmerinnen und Beschäftigte in Berliner ethnischen Gewerbe*, WZB discussion paper FS 1 98–107 (1998), 12

An active commissioner for foreigners, Barbara John, contributed to the city's decision to establish advisory offices and starter-capital funds to assist would-be entrepreneurs after unification. Locally, the number of self-employed foreigners rose exponentially, from 9,400 in 1991 to 13,300 in 1993, to 21,800 in 1997 (table 5.4).[30] According to the "Urban Renaissance Study," Berlin evinces the highest ethnic entrepreneurial rate in the FRG. Among Germans, 11.7 were self-employed in 2003, among non-citizens, 13.7 percent.[31]

By 2005 the number of self-employed non-nationals in Berlin reached 23,600 (5,400 businesses), equivalent to 9 percent of all ethnic entrepreneurs in Germany. Neighborhood enclaves have paved the way for major marketing. The gastronomy sector (restaurants, bakeries, specialty foods) was the first to undergo multicultualization. Nowadays 36 percent of all ethnic eateries in Berlin are owned by Turks, including some "Italian" restaurants; 26 percent of the ethnic *Selbständige* concentrate on meal service, compared to 9 percent among Germans. One reason is structural: While non-EU citizens must possess an unlimited residency permit to start *any* business, those in skilled trades also need to possess a *Meisterbrief* (master certification); homeland accreditation is usually not recognized. The Chamber of Industry and Trade admits that minorities face sectoral exclusion with regard to apprenticeships. Persons of migrant background thus gravitate to openings that are more labor- than human-capital intensive, even in cases of "skill-mismatch."[32]

Nearly 28 percent of Berlin's non-Germans work in the processing sector, in contrast to 19 percent of the natives; 11 percent of all non-citizens work in the restaurant/hotel business. In 1992, some fifty-five thousand restaurants across Germany provided one-hundred thousand paid jobs and employed twenty-seven thousand family members; aliens fill 90 percent of the hotel/restaurant jobs not covered by social security/health benefits.[33] The exponential increase in ethnic restaurants has been accompanied by a proliferation of "ingredients" and "equipment" suppliers (only six of thirty-five survive). The 1996 edition of Berlin's *Turkish Yellow Pages* listed 2,500 companies, half of which were tied to the food sector; the 2003 edition ran over 280 color-glossy pages. Rudolph and Hillman undertook a pilot study of forty-three food-sector firms concentrated in Kreuzberg in 1996: the sample covered fourteen *Imbisses*, fourteen grocery stores, ten bakeries, three restaurants, and two cafés. Four dated back to the 1970s, a third were founded in the 1980s, twenty-four were established in the 1990s. Sixteen had been motivated by the desire "to be their own boss," many were intent on escaping factory work. One-third responded to a perceived *Marktlücke*, but only two mentioned unemployment as grounds for their start-ups.[34]

Most had two to four employees; four of five relied on family members but hired Turks to fill other vacancies. The food sector evinces clear gender differences. Family members contribute to "flexibility," but there are no data on women working behind kitchen doors. Rudolph and Hillman suggest that the ratio is three men to one woman. In June 2004 I ate dinner at a pricy Thai restaurant in the Kantstrasse, the second opened by its proprietress.

Although a large ethnic community serves as a positive resource, food-sector concentration among Turkish entrepreneurs leads to fierce price competition, coupled with low profit margins. The same conditions that render this branch easy to enter—low capitalization, no educational requirements, built-in reliance on local customers—also foster self-exploitation. Nowhere is this more apparent than in the world of döner producers, the fast-food item that "conquered the republic." The humble döner kebab, a made-in-Germany "Turkish specialty," not only symbolizes the triumphs and failures of many a migrant entrepreneur; it also links the socio-political integration of producers to the resocialization of consumers initially averse to immigration. As Eberhard Seidel-Pielen observes, "The *döner*-sellers . . . and not the state-subsidized and bureaucratized integration specialists built the load-bearing bridges of understanding in the glowing heat of the *döner* grills."[35]

Labeled "sharply seasoned" in 1956, the first Yugoslav and Turkish dishes to make it into Germany contrasted starkly with the heavy, overcooked preferences of the natives, ranging from *Eisbein*/sauerkraut, *Eintopf* and cabagge rolls, to *Bouletten* and boiled potatoes (differentiated as to their *halb-fest* or *kochfest* quality). The presence of forty thousand Turks in Berlin gave birth to the first import-export stores in Kreuzberg in the early 1970s. Although the origin of döner kebab is still disputed, access to a few basic ingredients led to the rapid proliferation of *Imbiss* stands.[36]

Chef Rennan Yaman reports that the first döner, consisting of marinated lamb, grilled and served on bread, was sold on the street sometime between 1965 and 1970. An entrée version served at the upscale restaurant Istanbul in the Knesebeckstrasse took hold at "the end of the 60s," but the general consensus is that the döner did not enter mainstream culture until it assumed fast-food form. The first Turkish butcher shop opened its doors in Berlin in 1968; five grocery stores were up and running by 1970.[37] The High Court did not accord "constitutional" standing to *halal* slaughter methods (freedom of religion) until 2001, however.[38] Claiming to be the first *Imbiss*, located at the intersection of Adalbertstrasse and Oranienstrasse only a few blocks from the Wall, Asma Alti (Under the Grapevines) belonged to the family Kör-Bilal. The owners of Hasir, also in the Adalbertstrasse, likewise claim to have been among the first to have perfected the döner; they now manage six different restaurants.

The fact that foreigners were forced to absorb 44 percent of the job losses following the first OPEC oil crisis may account for the mushrooming of döner stands once the 1973 recruitment freeze forced Turks to choose between going home or pursuing family unification. The first barrier to success, Seidel-Pielen stresses, was overcoming a German resistance to strong, spicy flavors (lamb, garlic), an aversion that dissipated as affluent natives began spending weeks of paid vacation in ever more exotic places. The second barrier was securing unlimited residency permits, attainable after eight years; by the mid 1970s most first-generation guestworkers had lived in the host state for at least a decade. The third impediment proved even more challenging: overcoming bureaucratic discretion. Non-nationals were granted business licenses only on the condition that "the intended activity does not harm the comprehensive economic interests of Berlin" and "when there is an overarching economic interest or a special local need."[39] In 1980, the Chamber of Industry and Trade approved 57 percent of the applications submitted, by which point three-fourths of the Imbiss customers were Germans.

The final barrier to success continues to haunt would-be entrepreneurs to this day: cut-throat competition. Small business owners only secure an adequate income "when no one works less than thirteen hours a day, and all of the family and relatives help out"; the result is usually "exploitation and self-exploitation ... without boundaries."[40] Berlin is famous for its döner wars, depending on the neighborhood. The production costs of a standard döner in the mid 1990s amounted to DM 3.74, at a time when *Imbisses* along the Kottbusser Damm and the Adalbertstrasse were charging customers a mere DM 2.90.[41] Now costing €4–5 in more affluent districts, döner prices in Neukölln and Kreuzberg may run about €2.50—"with sauce." Attempts to unify pita producers to raise their prices commensurate with inflation in Hamburg caused the rest to gang up against one baker seeking a fair day's return for a labor-intensive process.[42]

These impediments notwithstanding, the number of döner-related businesses increased from 500 to 11,000 between 1970 and 1980, followed by another great leap forward, ahead of the *Currywürste*, 1981 to 1983. Berlin's health minister identified 217 stands in 1983, topping 1,300 by 1994.[43] By the mid 1990s, consumption levels had reached 720 million kebabs-to-go per annum, sold at more than 10,000 *Imbisses* nationwide.[44] The döner proved to be a popular export product, spreading to the Netherlands and even back to "the motherland." Franchises like Döner King have taken root in Cologne and Bonn.

The ethnicization of national tastes became a topic of concern at the highest levels after unification. Gottfried Haschke (CDU) who had served as GDR

Table 5.5 Fast-Food Consumption in Germany in the 1990s

Enterprise	Sales Volume	Franchises
Döner sales (total)	DM 3.6 billion	1,300 (est.)
McDonalds	DM 2.6 billion	570
Mitropa AG/DS	DM 5.29 million	597
Mövenpick Gesellschaften	DM 3.59 million	45
Nordsee Deutsche Hochseefischerei	DM 3.56 million	292
Burger King	DM 3.4 million	94
Wienerwald	DM 2.33 million	170

Source: Eberhard Seidel-Pielen, *AUFGESPIESST!*, 1996, 13.

agricultural minister under Lothar de Maizière, declared in 1994: "I am, God knows, not xenophobic, but in many German cities foreign cuisines are dominating the market. We have to do something for German cuisine." He proposed that a special consumption tax be levied on exotic foodstuffs, until it was revealed that Turkey was importing ten thousand tons of beef from the Eastern state of Saxony for döner production.[45] In 1995, Hannelore Kohl wrote in a cookbook featuring the portly chancellor's favorite foods (stuffed pork bellies) that the Germans' growing taste for ethnic cuisine was undermining their sense of national community![46]

Entrepreneurial success not only stimulates emulation and thus competition; it can also provoke deep resentments among less-enterprising segments of the population who feel cut out of the system. "Mom-and-pop" kiosks have gone where corporate outlets fear to tread, including places in "the wild East" where high unemployment has been accompanied by xenophobic violence. One such town is Hoyerswerda, declared a "foreigner-free" zone after neo-Nazis attacked an asylum hostel in 1991. Despite arson assaults against *Imbiss* owners, Hoyerswerda is home to over fifteen döner stands serving 60,000 residents.[47]

Competition has also triggered market tensions between "purists" and "mass producers." Mehmet Altindag is a Munich Kebapci producer who opened his own restaurant, Sultan, in 1970. He insists: "Not everyone can produce a kebap. For that you need four things: a heart, a head, eyes and, above all, feeling."[48] The Berlin Administrative Court had other concerns regarding the final product, invoking the *Hackfleischordnung* of 1976 in an effort to differentiate between unwholesome, ground-meat versions of the *Döner-Spiess* (costing DM 6 per kilo) and specified lamb/mutton cuts (DM 10–12 per kilo). The result was the "Berliner Purity Law" (*Festschreibung der Berliner Verkehrsauffassung für das Fleischerzeugnis Kebap*) sponsored in 1989 by the Union of Turkish Merchants.[49] The first conviction was handed down in December 1991, following a jury trial against a 27-year-old producer. The latter was fined DM 6,000 for manufacturing *Spiesse* consisting of 21.4 percent "real meat," and 78.6 percent ground meat, of which 22.8 percent was fat (20 percent is the legal limit) and 6.2 percent starch (absolutely *verboten*).[50] What could possibly be more integrated into German society than an ethnic food product that has its own administrative court ruling and *Reinheitsgebot*?

Representing the other camp is Enfil Tütüncübasi, who studied business economics in Marburg and entered the family meat-delivery business in 1983. Together with his brother, an engineer, he developed a supplemental product line, shifting to full time döner production in 1989. He developed an automatic assembly-line for *Spiess* production—the "best technology, made in Germany"—now used in Turkey as well. By the mid 1990s, the Kardesler Döner Fabrik dominated markets in Frankfurt/Main, Bavaria, and Baden-Württemberg, generating five tons of meat product daily with forty-eight employees.[51]

Berlin's FinalTa hired thirty-seven "specialists" to turn out five tons of rotisserie meat per day, ranging from 15–150 kilos each. It faces thirty-five established competitors. Of course, no döner is complete without its specially designed pita bread. Having transcended bakery start-up costs of DM 500,000–600,000 since 1995, Bereket Brot produces up to 100,000 breads per day; it is pursuing do-it-yourself integration with a product innovation of its own: "Multigrain-Flatbreads for the Nutritionally Conscious."[52]

Turkish entrepreneurs have accomplished what politicians failed to do for three decades, busy as the latter have been weeping crocodile tears over a lack of guestworker integration: They have created new jobs, introduced technological inventions and networked non-traditional supplier and distributor networks in ways that benefit even indigenous grocery chains like Reichelt and Edeka. The humble döner kebab has fostered innovation with regard to rotisseries, safety mechanisms for grills, and automated bakery processes. As Tütüncübasi declares, "The negative image that the *döner* enjoys among intellectuals from Turkey doesn't disturb me. It has fostered the integration of Turks in Germany. The best contacts and opportunities for conversation usually take place over food. That breaks down barriers. We *döner* producers brought the Germans a new taste experience. The *döner* was the means by which we showed Germans: We have something to offer. We hadn't really succeeded with either textiles or vegetable stores."[53]

Self-Made Men: Success Stories among Berlin's "One-and-a-Half" Generation

Under revised ownership regulations of 1998, Turkish Berliners can start their own businesses after five years of legal employment or ten years of legal residence. They still receive less preferential treatment than EU nationals, since Turkey has not signed a reciprocal agreement permitting Germans to establish independent businesses. No *Meisterbrief* is required to open businesses involving textiles, food services, boutiques, dry cleaning, alterations, or housecleaning. Berlin's *Turkish Yellow Pages* reflects a corresponding expansion of these sectors: entries increased from 2,467 in 1996, to 3,596 in 1998. According to a Senate study, 67.5 percent of Turkish men and 53.7 percent of women consider self-ownership a "desirable state of affairs."[54]

We now consider the creation of two very successful enterprises in Berlin, based on interviews I conducted in summer 2004. The first, represented by Saim Aygun, co-owner of the Hasir restaurant chain, is more or less typical of the gastronomy branch. The second, with Sabahattin Sari, founder and CEO of Manolya, and Medianess, focuses on entertainment and media electronics; his success story is matched by very few national IT specialists.

My interview with Mr. Aygun took place in German and Turkish; his assistant translated at various points but since the latter had arrived only a year earlier, the answers to my questions were very short. Aygun entered Germany thirty years ago, with three of his six brothers, to study political science at the Free University. Originally from Anatolia, he had acquired some restaurant experience in Turkey, and worked with an uncle in Berlin until 1971. One reason why no one can pinpoint the origin of the döner is that few restauranteurs had time to record their own stories, working fourteen to sixteen hours each day. Aygun and his brother established their first restaurant "about 25 years ago" (an article hanging in one of the franchises specified March 1971). A Turkish-German parliamentarian later advised me that some entrepreneurs are reluctant to provide details if their initial financing came through "irregular" sources. This owner also refused to estimate the restaurant's annual sales volume.

Before I could begin, Aygun pointed to a number of framed newspaper articles featuring the restaurant and food reviews in the *Tagesspiegel* and the *New York Times*. The restaurant has seen visitors ranging from President Johannes Rau to actors and actresses. My first night back I saw Birol Ünel (the male lead in *Gegen die Wand*, winner of the Golden Bear Award at the 2004 Berlin International Film Festival) sitting at a table outside. *Hasir* refers to a form of rattan that is supposed to evoke "a good atmosphere, a feeling of being on vacation." The menu features a girlish Anatolian belly dancer resembling Betty Boop; the co-owner indicated that they had no qualms about serving beer and wine to customers, even though he is a Muslim. His mother wore a *Kopftuch*, "but it was a modern scarf."

The first restaurant that I visited in the Adalbertstrasse in the late 1970s was destroyed by a gas explosion linked to the grill, lacking a safety mechanism or shut-off valve. Fifty persons were on the premises, but no one was injured. Relocating to a building fifty meters away, it reopened a month later. That restaurant, located along the U-Bahn's (in)famous *Linie 1*, was a male domain, filled with smokers and tea drinkers during the day but attracting younger Kreuzberg fans at night; the main dishes are displayed in a glass counter taking up a third of the ground floor. Shortly after the Wall fell, they opened a second establishment in Wilmersdorf, close to *KaDeWe*; it offers an extended menu, "ambience" (white tablecloths), and wall hangings. Others followed at two-to-three-year intervals, the third appearing in Schöneberg near Winterfelder-platz, the site of violent anti-Reagan and squatter demonstrations in the 1980s. Then came Spandau (*jot-we-de* or *janz weit draussen*), and later Stadtmitte near Hackescher Markt, spacious, elegant and dark. They have since added a family-friendly area with an open charcoal grill to the initial site in Kreuzberg, while retaining the *Imbiss* character of the old section. One brother returned to Turkey to open two hotels, the Titanic Resort and Hotel De Luxe in Lara / Antalya, with Hasir restaurants.

Saim Aygun insists he entered the restaurant business out of *Menschenliebe* and because "it's fun." Like two other entrepreneurs in my sample, Aygun sees himself as a member of the "One and a Half Generation," that is, as someone who came not as a guestworker-recruit, willing to work any time, any where under any conditions á la Wallraff, but as someone seeking higher education who then pursued a different course. One of the factors compelling Germany to import skilled technicians by way of the Green Card has been its long-standing principle of "prohibition subject to possible granting of permission." It refuses to accord permanent residency to foreign students who graduate from its *own* universities, fluent in the language and familiar with "the German way of life."[55] Manual and service-sector labor affords an easier path to permanent residency status, even without fluency.

"Lots of bureaucracy, not citizenship," Aygun noted, was the biggest barrier to successful entrepreneurship. A second problem was the dramatic increase in prices that had accompanied the introduction of the Euro in 2002, accounting for "50 percent of the lost profits": a crate of tomatoes doubled in price, from DM 9 to €9, while lamb rose from DM 8 to €6 per kilo. Because he lacks the three years of schooling needed to qualify as a *Diplom Gastronom*—versus his thirty years of real-world experience—he cannot legally train apprentices, although he could enlist three to four Turkish-German youth per year.[56] He complained about the high cost of employer social-insurance contributions, suggesting there should be a trade-off or tax deduction for training apprentices. He admitted, when pushed, that all restaurant personnel are male (at least eighty employees), though he hastened to add that there are "four or five women in the office."

His brother, a *Diplom Chemiker*, is a founding member of the Turkish-German Employers' Association Berlin-Brandenburg (TDU), established in 1996 (referring to their dual identities, not to cooperating Turkish and German firms). It provides "advice and support internally, interest representation externally" for its more than eighty members. He no longer needs to pursue such contacts, having already built his network. Saim Aygun has not taken on German citizenship, nor has his wife, "brought over" from Turkey about fourteen years ago. His three children were born in Germany after 1993; under the 1999 Citizenship Law they qualify for *jus soli* citizenship but will have to decide at age twenty-three which nationality they intend to keep. Having denied its Turkish residents formal citizenship for so long, Germany is about to discover that many who are now eligible have decided it is not "an honor and a privilege," and that they can get along just as well without it.

Sabahattin Sari named his enterprise *Elektronikkette Manolya* after his daughter "Magnolia." Born in 1956 in Ankara, he was impeccably dressed in a black suit, wore a Rolex watch and had me served cappuccino in a spacious office shared with his wife; one wall consisted of an extraordinary, six-foot long aquarium. The waiting room was lined with motivational posters. One featured two guys about to go over the edge of a major waterfall, wondering if it were "time to call the boss and ask him what to do." The caption underneath read: "It all depends on your vision!"

Stemming from a well-to-do family, his parents sent him to study in Germany in 1976, one of three children sent abroad for higher education. Sari was the first to label himself a member of the One-and-a-Half Generation, having come to Germany neither as a guestworker nor as the child of one; he sought skilled-labor opportunities from the start. He chose the Technical University of Berlin, assuming that having relatives in town would ease his transition. Initially speaking no German, he passed the language proficiency test after nine months, allowing him to study economics. His father's position as a labor-union executive accounts for his self-identification as a Social Democrat.

Working his way through school, Herr Sari quit in 1980 short of completing his degree, and in 1981 married "Dilek," who had come to Berlin at age seven. Deciding to "go independent," he and his new wife rented "40 square meters" in Kreuzberg, aided by a DM 10,000 bank loan in 1982. It "seemed like a lot of money back then," but he "earned it all back from the German government, or had [his] daughter and son pay for the loan," insofar as the parents received DM 5,000 for each child (*Kindergeld*) from the state.

His was a one-man business in Kreuzberg. He sold radios, TVs, hi-fis, and gadgets, based on an early affinity for electronics as a "continuously developing, futuristic field, leading the way in other domains." They had so little inventory during the early days that he displayed the TV/radio/hi-fi system they had received as a wedding present to make the shop look full. He profited from the fact that first-generation guestworkers, speaking little German, preferred to purchase goods in a store where they received personal service. "Since bargaining is in our blood," many may have also believed that by coming to a fellow Turk, they could talk down the prices, etc. Cultural ties clearly fostered customer relations built on trust; he often turned over products based on personal credit. Many remain *Stammkunden* who like to seek his advice—although his managerial responsibilities (and demeanor) now put him in a completely different league. Regulars afforded a kind of extended family, an ethnic resource, although capital accumulation was always a concern.

Sari closed his first shop within six months to move to a bigger space in Moabit; he kept that store but "took the plunge" and opened a second outlet when the Wall fell in 1990, anticipating pent up consumer demand on the part of Eastern Germans. It sits, ironically, on Karl Marx Street. They added a third store in the Kant Strasse near Bahnhof Zoo in 1994, reacting to a dramatic influx of Russian-*Aussiedler*, Poles, and Russian-Jewish refugees (who have turned Charlottenburg into their own ethnic enclave). Traveling more and accumulating capital, he opened another franchise in the Prinzenallee (Wedding) in 1998, and moved the executive offices to a generously renovated space there in 1999.

A very amiable interview partner, Sari is clearly a man of vision and strategy. He outlined three stages of business development, involving, first, a focus on *Fachgeschäfte* (specialty retail), building on face-to-face customer relations. Here typical variables cited in the ethnic economy literature apply: the ability to build on ethnic ties, personal trust, reliance on a neighborhood clientele, language and cultural competence. He then shifted toward wholesale, becoming a key provider to companies like Saturn ("Circuit City"), while pursuing suppliers in other countries. The arrival of the Euro—"fortuitous" for global players—reduced transaction costs, enabling him to supply goods more cheaply to Russia, Poland, Austria, Cyprus, Egypt, and Iran. His current distribution network reaches as far as Singapore.

The third stage centered on the Internet domain, reaching out to non-local clientele. The company developed computer software that allows it to set a slightly lower price than other competitors in the nanosecond it takes for offers to appear on the screen in response to a product search. The software automatically calculates and displays a cheaper price. Without a trace of conceit, Sari noted: "We are doing what the global economy requires—we are permanently growing, despite the very negative economic picture in Germany right now. . . . Electronics is an area that cannot stop growing, changing. Social and economic progress depends on it." Modernization has helped to cut costs and reduce personnel, but this has not meant eliminating workplaces, since he faces an ongoing need for employees with higher qualifications. When hiring a truck driver, for example, Herr Sari expects the applicant to be fluent in Turkish and German, as well as to demonstrate a familiarity with computer technology. Any worker may start as driver, "but the ones with ambition will move onwards and upwards."

Now the CEO of two firms, Manolya (retail stores) and Medianess (Internet division), Sari employs about fifty people, but expects to add ten to twenty more to accommodate his new Internet capabilities. Having crossed the fifty employee threshold, his company is entitled to train apprentices; it has done so for seven years, hiring about four per annum (no *Meisterbrief* exists in this domain). He receives "hundreds of applications" each year that he cannot honor because of limited, field-related capacities, although he recognizes the extraordinary unemployment problems facing Turkish-German youth. Out of a pool of mostly male applicants with engineering diplomas, he recently chose two— one male, one female; he admits to hiring mostly males because they need to haul equipment through the store ("I couldn't impose that on a woman"). One male executive with whom I spoke briefly was German. There are three female accountants among the office staff; he trusts women absolutely in this capacity "because of their attention to detail." The front office is run by a bilingual woman, able to respond to Internet inquiries.

Sari is already planning his next stage of development: not building more customer-service stores but expanding into other countries, starting with an

Aegean concentration. "Going global," he stresses, "is the only way to survive. The Internet does away with a need for certain personnel: the customer can print out his own order, the computer software calculates the best deal, figures out the transport costs, finds a direct link to delivery system, sets up an appointment, etc." Sari expected to gross €70 million in sales in 2004 but added that he is aiming for €700 million in five years: "You have to have a goal . . . to keep on growing, to keep pace with globalization." Small- and medium-sized businesses can't keep up, they will go under without growth.

As a self-starter, Sari faced the usual irritation with bureaucracy, complex application forms, and *Gewerbesteuer* (taxes), but encountered nothing worse than what a "regular business person" might expect. Their small-credit loan rendered them independent at the outset, but he had to arrange multiple appointments with Sony representatives to set up a supply chain. The reps stood him up several times at the beginning; when they finally met to work out a contract, he lacked sufficient capital/collateral to cover his up-front costs. He laughed at the irony that he is now one of Sony's biggest distributors. He jets off to Italy for face-to-face CEO meetings and can sometimes set his own terms; he may sell at prices 1-percent lower than his competitors but can over-compensate in volume, since prices in Germany are significantly higher than those in other EU sites like Belgium and the Netherlands.[57] Sari complained repeatedly that high "benefit" costs (*Lohnnebenkosten*) are driving Germany out of the market; it can't compete with lower labor costs in Eastern Europe and Southeast Asia.

He characterized the existing economic structures as "a mess." Germany may be stuck with Euro requirements placing strict limits on deficits and debts, but the real problem is the lack of investment. He attributed "countless bankruptcies, nearly 6,000 this year" to banks' refusal to grant loans to small- and medium-sized businesses facing very rigid criteria. He found the BASIS II Program conditions (dictating levels of "know how" and insisting on 10 percent in personal capital) "almost as bad as the Copenhagen Criteria," deadly for future start-ups. Pulling in close to 48 percent in top rates, the Federal Republic needs a simplified tax structure, a lower general rate, and fewer withholdings. Employer's benefit costs run about 25 percent of wages, compared to 15 percent in Belgium and the Netherlands.

"As a businessman," he views the German system as "just not competitive." Siemens and Bosch have transferred the manufacturing of their "starter models" (e.g., no-frill washing machines) to Turkey, where lower production costs still allow for profit—instead of selling cheap models at a loss as they increasingly do in Germany. In the grand scheme of three economic blocks (US, Europe, Asia), the FRG is disadvantaged in terms of logistics, conditions, and costs: "it doesn't matter anymore where the goods come from as long as they can be delivered and you can keep wage costs low." He rejects low-wage jobs but is frustrated by Germans who willingly settle for "a bit less social-aid in exchange for not having to work." Every country needs a welfare system, says the son of a union official; the state should provide as much help as possible for persons in need but not for those who don't want to work.

Though not an SPD member, he shares the party's principles "as a social being," yet sees Germany driving itself out of the market. A founding member of the TDU in Berlin, Sari served as its spokesperson and executive board member but has since withdrawn from several networking organizations. The meetings are too time-consuming: "The larger the organization, the less they can accomplish without complicated procedures." He still contributes by sponsoring specific events or partnering in local activities. He remains active in co-op organizations linking suppliers and others in the electronics field.

The Saris' children are in their early twenties. No one in the family has pursued German citizenship. Herr Sari objects to the lack of dual citizenship, since he has accumulated assets in Turkey and stands to inherit others (no longer a legal problem). He sees no need to jettison his personal/emotional identity. Like many others, he never intended to stay more than twenty years, claiming his mother still hasn't digested the fact that he did not return home. His son has yet to complete military duty—one month in Turkey versus the twelve months required in Germany. Once that obligation is behind him, "the family as a whole will probably apply." Citizenship would allow them to vote, but he can already "articulate and aggregate political interests" by interacting regularly with politicians; he mentioned sitting with SPD Executive Müntefering at various dinners.

By this point, Dilek Sari had entered the office, and shared a few strong thoughts on the citizenship question: "Excuse, me but that [topic] really makes me mad." She objected to "the haughty attitude and condescension" Germans display when it comes to "granting" citizenship. She has received a national award from Federal President Johannes Rau and the German Industrial Chamber of Commerce (DIHK) for creating meaningful apprenticeships for Turkish-German youth; award-ceremony photos line another wall of the office they share. "I work here, pay substantial taxes, and have a major business that contributes to the German economy." No wonder she believes that rather than having her "submit" to arcane conditions, Germany should simply grant her citizenship as thanks for her civic contributions and social engagement in the *Haupstadt* community.

Self-Made Women: Building Rooms of their Own in Berlin

By the mid 1990s, Berlin was home to more than five thousand Turkish businesses extending jobs to twenty thousand workers. The ethnic-economy literature assumes that stigmatization and discrimination are driving forces of self-employment. It weighs the significance of split labor markets, internal solidarity, mutual support, and physical separation from the dominant culture. Drawing on the American experience, it also stresses the myth of the "self-made man." Women are rarely mentioned as entrepreneurs in their own right; instead they are subsumed under "family enterprises" as unpaid labor reserves. Ivan Light and Edna Bonacich reported in the late 1988s, for example, that 60 percent of Korean businesses could only sustain themselves due to the contributions of unpaid family workers.[58]

Prior to the 1990s, the ethnic economy rarely offered women a path for self-advancement. Despite some reconfiguration of gender roles after the 1960s, women are still expected to "transmit" homeland culture and ensure family well-being. Often confined to part-time or temporary labor, they remain unemployed longer, earn less, and hold the least desirable jobs in the service sector. As migrants, they face additional constraints regarding public roles, their status still defined by ethnocultural norms. Turkish women evinced the lowest rates of paid employment among ethnic females in the 1990s, under 30 percent (41 percent among Germans), especially above minimum wage.

No matter how they define themselves, migrant women are assumed to lag behind "modern" natives. *Bildungsinländerinnen* have clearly been affected by changing cultural roles, generational dynamics, and higher unemployment rates (despite higher educational levels). Regional studies reveal a higher de facto rate (13 percent) of self-employment in this group. In 1998, Felicitas Hillmann interviewed fifty female entrepreneurs and employees, analyzing the gender-specific dynamics of the city's ethnic economy.[59] Turks accounted for 31 percent of the city's non-natives, 90 percent of whom toiled in the West. Hit hard by structural adjustments, persons holding jobs covered by social insurance fell from 11.6 percent to 7.2 percent between 1991 and 1997; among women, the rate declined from 10.3 percent (40,286) to 6 percent (31,349). Two-thirds of Turkish females were concentrated in the service sector; 29.8 percent participated in manufacturing, only 6.6 percent in construction. Migrant women comprised 78 percent of the healthcare workers, 76 percent in cleaning services, and 62 percent of the private household workers.[60] A 131 percent increase among foreigners compares to a mere 30 percent increase in native start-ups since unification.

The figure for women-owned businesses rose from 2,400 in 1991, to 5,000 and 5,900 by 1997, accounting for 27 percent of the city's "foreign" entrepreneurs. In domains most attractive to women of entrepreneurial spirit, Hillmann counted 56 new textile sites, 273 food-sector additions, 25 more focusing on cosmetics/body products, another 31 travel agencies, 18 more kiosks, and 3 cleaning services among 1,129 newly registered businesses by 1998. The key question is whether these women see the economic independence that accompanies self-employment as constituting the beginning or the end of an emancipatory process.[61]

Three-fourths of Hillmann's interviewees had established businesses in the 1990s, 21 percent prior to unification; this option proved most attractive to second- or third-generation members. Six of fifty had come to Berlin as workers between 1968 and 1972; five had been born in Berlin. Others entered as children, spouses, or tourists; most were twenty to forty years old. The majority claimed Turkish or Kurdish as their native tongue; 40 percent had attended school in both countries, 36 percent were educated entirely in Germany. Over half (52 percent) were married, 27.5 percent single; one-fifth were divorced. Nearly 79 percent had children, three-fourths of whom were minors; 38 percent lived in Neukölln, 23 percent in Kreuzberg, and 10 percent in the East.[62]

Two-thirds were self-employed, but all were familiar with "the double burden": 43 percent remained completely responsible for household work, 20 percent "shared" it (in two cases, with jobless house-husbands); only one had hired help. Half said that little had changed in terms of family roles beyond "more independence" and "too little sleep"; many worked ten hours per day, seven days a week (e.g., food and kiosks).[63] At the same time, 85 percent of the owners were "satisfied," earning DM 2000–3000 (net) per month; dependent workers averaged DM 1,420 per month. In 40 percent of the cases, revenues only covered running costs (due to a slow economy); 28 percent reported gradually increasing sales.

Although the sample is not random, women's motives for self-ownership parallel those of men in ZTS studies: more were motivated by "choice of career" than by unemployment. Older women described themselves as typical of the first generation, seeking an escape from factory work. Nine younger women "wanted to be [their] own boss." Born or raised in Germany, they wanted to break with "unacceptable occupational perspectives. . . . we needed a long time to get our qualifications but entry into the labor market just didn't happen. What remains is either unemployment or self-employment."[64] Three were dissatisfied with very low pay, five decided with their partners to open shops; 41 percent named female role models as a source of inspiration.[65]

Women-owned businesses are heavily concentrated in the food, cosmetics, beauty-parlor, clothing/alterations, and cleaning sectors. Travel agencies and hair salons/cosmetics attract younger women (age twenty-three to thirty-one), counting on two to four employees; women age forty or older were found in textiles, alterations, or cleaning businesses. Start-up investments ranged from DM 12,000 to DM 165,000; most fell between DM 15,000–40,000 (less than male investments). Like their male counterparts, these women cited financial issues as their biggest problem; only 41 percent relied on family loans, 39 percent secured bank funding, and 31 percent used their own savings. Generating steady customers and acquiring management skills came next, added to tough competition among Turkish businesses per se. The latter were seen to "make their own markets kaput" through price cutting; one "just has to hang in there."[66] Hair and cosmetic salons were usually one-woman operations; travel agencies employed two or three workers, food service providers hired four or more. Most admittedly created "DM 620 jobs" (not socially insured), and recruited other women by way of personal networks.

Few rely primarily on ethnic suppliers and distributors. For businesswomen, price is ostensibly more important than nationality: twenty-four of these owners contract, above all, with German firms; only 16 percent relied on "mostly Turkish" producers; another six had no Turkish customers. One young woman insisted, "I don't want to be typically 'Turkish' because I want to offer something special and of quality." Another stressed, "I hardly have any contact to Turks, and I don't ring a big bell announcing I am Turkish." Only one sent money back to Turkey.[67]

The ethnic economy literature values the traditional sex hierarchy as an economic advantage for "typical" entrepreneurs. Gold and Sen posit that "they can naturally expect woman [*sic*] in their own family to work without pay at all . . . being considered as an extension of a woman's domestic duties."[68] Turkish women are reluctant to "get entangled in hierarchical family relations" by hiring men, however: 60 percent said that family support had been "very important in the initial stage," but few regularly employed relatives. If unable to count on supportive family males, they recruit other nationalities, "as long as they are qualified."

Many claimed they could not find relatives with appropriate credentials. One twenty-two year old indicated she "would rather avoid the troubled atmosphere with family." Employing relatives would "undermine the distance between boss and workers—and I place great value on qualification."[69] If a family member shows up late for work, for example, it is supposedly "not a problem"; flexibility for a cousin means lost productivity for the businesswoman, however. These women do not consider themselves embodiments of the ethnic economy; instead they live by systemic rules: competition and quality. Many located businesses outside their neighborhoods (in Friedenau or along the Ku-damm) to cultivate non-ethnic clientele: "I like the district," said one. "The customers have money. I would rather have German customers." While some enjoyed interacting with the community in Neukölln, 38 percent "just happened to wind up" there, challenging another (malestream) hypothesis regarding ethnic social capital as a key resource for women.

While Hillmann asserts that "entrepreneurial activity among migrant women is a pro-active response to job discrimination," I argue further that informalization generates new market openings for women.[70] Few pursue self-employment at the outset, but holding less-secure jobs leads them to take the plunge; the opportunity structure is far from static. US studies likewise suggest that women-owned businesses are growing at a faster pace in recent years.[71] Starting their own business has become a "first choice" for younger persons of migrant background.[72]

Employer prejudices vis-à-vis Muslim job applicants have intensified since September 11th, disproportionately disadvantaging women as headscarf wearers. Having finally attained formal citizenship, women of migrant descent stand poised to assume a variety of civil service careers—long the bastion of university-educated male elites. Excluding headscarf wearers from these domains, affording the best-paid, most-secure jobs in Europe, guarantees their continuing relegation to low-paid, insecure, service-sector jobs. Yet one woman in Berlin has turned even this form of discrimination into a lucrative business: selling "designer headscarves" for fashion-conscious Muslims![73]

Over half of Hillmann's sample held German citizenship, or had at least applied for it.[74] Older employees often did not, even after ten to fourteen years of residency. One declared that she lived "with my heart in Turkey, my head rather in Germany." Women under age thirty "don't really know what life is like in Turkey"; females from twenty to twenty-five account for 57 percent of the naturalizations in Berlin. Possessing language skills and intercultural competence, they expect their children to "integrate": 70 percent of those with small children relied on day-care facilities instead of family members who may only speak Turkish or Kurdish. Blurring the boundaries between Turkish-German groups, these women are turning gender mainstreaming into ethnic mainstreaming.

My conversations with Berlin entrepreneurs indicate that even though women and men follow different paths to economic independence, they share an understanding that their contributions, big and small, should entitle them to political equality. Paradoxically, others who do possess participatory rights in Germany, like *Aussiedler*, are the least inclined to use them. We now turn to one allegedly mobile-transnational group whose ability to integrate is not questioned by politicians, though it should be: Italian laborers.

Leaving *La Dolce Vita*: Italian Workers and Their Discontents

The literature on *transnationalism* suggests the image of happy traveling merchants who not only deliver a steady supply of exotic goods to globally conscious consumers, but who also feel at home in two cultures, according them a crucial mediating role. The Italian experience in Germany gave rise to an "imagined community" of border-crossing guestworkers enjoying the best of both worlds that simultaneously upheld the myth of return. In reality, the freedom of movement enjoyed by these aliens resulted in far from satisfying "transnational" lifestyles, with negative consequences for their offspring.

Italian labor migration in the 1960s and 1970s rested on a touchy precedent, starting with a 1937 German call for 30,000 foreign agricultural workers. By

1941, 270,000 Italians were working in the agricultural, mining, construction, and brick-making sectors. Mussolini's defeat saw them transformed into forced laborers, subject to mishandling. A 1953 study of 5,334 Italians indicated that most had lived in Germany for over ten years. Rather than process Nazi exploitation directly, the Italian government pushed for a 30-percent wage increase for land workers in 1957 and protested barrack-housing conditions (triple deckers with straw mattresses). This led to counter-complaints by German officials: "We didn't want to have the newly built dwellings for refugees and persons bombed out of their homes, with bedrooms for less than six persons and at least 10 cubic meters of 'breathing space' for each renter, being claimed by Italians while the German victims just stood by."[75]

A 1955 recruitment pact foresaw residency and work permits as mechanisms for labor-market steering; a joint commission was formed in January to specify working conditions and strict criteria for "strong bodies." Negotiations were especially tough over equal wages and child payments for those left behind. The German Commission in Verona would select recruits, then verify their occupational and medical certification. In 1956, a third of the three thousand contract workers for agriculture were paid less than official rates, with illegal employment already taking root in mining and construction. So many entered without "legitimation cards" that the Commission issued warnings to Bavarian border guards in 1958; the Saarland presented itself as an easy daytime-crossing point.[76] Major waves headed for Baden-Württemberg, North Rhine-Westphalia, Bavaria, and Hessen; urban concentrations were seen in Wolfsburg, Offenbach, Solingen, Ludwigshafen, and Pforzheim.

Unions and politicians opposed labor imports in the face of 7-percent unemployment among refugees, but employers argued that foreigners had to cover "the primitive work in Germany" to permit skilled training for natives. Mocked as *Spaghetti-Fresser*, Italians were relegated to the bottom of the ladder but moved up once Yugoslavs and Turks followed in the mid 1960s. Their numbers rose from 18,597 in 1956 to 48,806 in 1959, jumping to 121,685 a year later.[77] Early waves hailed from underdeveloped regions, especially the south, where thousands were kept landless by an oppressive *padroni* system. Child labor was common; unmarried daughters were deemed "a serious financial burden" for poor families.[78] Lacking formal education, southerners spoke rural dialects that even compatriots could not understand. They perceived German accents as heavy and imperious ("Man, why are they always cursing?").[79] Many without papers wound up at the Munich train station with no money, no food, and no idea where to go next. Catholic groups assisted, but costs became an issue between *Caritas* and the state.

Dissatisfaction was mutual: by German standards, southern Italians were not very productive. They came north with high expectations but took an immediate dislike to the dirty, dangerous, and difficult conditions in industry, low wages, and arduous fieldwork, in contrast to the leisurely style known back home. Many reneged on labor contracts within weeks, without enough money for a return trip. Ruhr mining companies wanted residency permits made contingent on contract compliance, but Italian officials protested. Employers accused Italy of misusing "sickness" certification, and demanded a second opinion in 1962, fearing the importation of tuberculosis and sexually transmitted diseases.[80]

At least they couldn't blame women for the latter! Most female migration took the form of marriage recruitment. Italian authorities refused to allow contracting for single females or women under the age of twenty-one. "Madonna worship" and the stress on family honor played a role but so did higher salaries in Switzerland. Only 5,800 female workers arrived between 1956 and 1961 (many more from Spain, Greece, Yugoslavia, and Turkey).[81] Women shared the regional backgrounds of their husbands; marriages were often arranged, but family unification took four to ten years to complete. Initially, 72 percent of the men, 99 percent of the women brought spouses; 58 percent lived with partners in 1968, 62 percent in 1972, 80 percent in 1980, and 90 percent by 1986. The number of women increased by 75 percent between 1973 and 1980; 33–37 percent engaged in paid labor.[82] Although employers utilized Italian and Turkish wives to foster company loyalty and to save on housing costs, most worked part-time in the informal sector, later helping out in family businesses. The social climate they encountered was devoid of "openness" and communal life. Productivity demands were higher but personal autonomy was also appreciated, relative to the oppressive conformity of the village.

Poverty was a necessary but not sufficient condition for migration. Mehrländer's 1974 study found 38 percent motivated by unemployment, 29 percent by a desire to earn more money, and 29 percent on other economic grounds.[83] Men found work with the German Railway, and in mining, construction, and metallurgical industries. Reconstruction heightened a need for brick makers, quarry workers, and strong bodies for the health-impairing zinc works. Comprising a sub-proletariat of unskilled laborers, few Italians managed to add to their qualifications; skilled workers accounted for 19.6 percent of the recruits in 1962, 19.4 percent in 1973.[84] A 1967 survey showed that only 20 percent had completed vocational education, compared to 37.5 percent among Spaniards, 25.5 percent for Turks, and 24 percent among Greeks.[85]

Their numbers grew from 48,000 to nearly 500,000 in ten years. Their share of jobs in the metallurgy sector rose from 25 percent in 1961 to 35 percent in 1970 but fell from 35 percent to 20 percent in construction. Union membership rose from 25.6 percent to 31.3 percent among Italians who acquired passive voting rights after 1974; union activities followed Catholic/socialist/communist cleavage lines, however. A wave of mining strikes saw a shift to (cheaper) Turkish workers. Even high-class hotels and restaurants in Bavaria developed a penchant for Yugoslavs and Turks, "preferably illegal ones."[86]

Another turning point was the adoption of European Community Regulation #15 in September 1961, mandating freedom of movement for all EC citizens with valid personal identity cards. They could take up residence in any EC state, rendering legitimation stamps and residency requirements moot. The EC rule, FRG officials complained, meant that border police could not prevent "criminals and persons with contagious diseases" from entering. The Economic Ministry had to admonish the Federal Labor Agency as late as 1966 that demanding "good-character" attests from local mayors was no longer permissible, nor could they shut out communists since the PCI (Italian Communist party) remained a legal party in Italy.[87] The proportion of those officially recruited fluctuated from 51.9 percent in 1957, to 66 percent in 1960, plunging to 6.8 percent by 1967. EC migrants still had to secure an *Aufenthaltserlaubnis* at local registration offices, but these could only be denied for endangering the public order, security, or health.[88]

From Bakers to Breadwinners: Italian Women

The Germans hoped to recruit Italian women "for jobs too unattractive for men," for domestic work, restaurants, or ice cafés, and textile production. Yvonne Rieker's interviews with thirty couples from southern Italy reveal that women faced problems of acculturation different from those of men. Born 1934 in Puglia, Carmina Matecchichia, recounted hard but pleasant village work: "Every day I went to the fields in the early morning. In the evening I went home to prepare dinner, afterwards I had to clean the dishes and prepare everything for the next day, because in the morning I had to leave early for the fieldwork. Only on Sundays all of us stayed at home. Around ten we went to Mass, afterwards we had lunch together. In the afternoon I went out of the house sometimes and met other women at the street, but often I stayed at home. For there had always been work to do. There had been no entertainment, no pleasure at that time."[89] In the village, separation of work and leisure occurred along highly gendered lines. Men met at the piazza or in cafes to play cards or discuss politics; women remained house bound beyond church and market. In Germany, families had ovens and washing machines, confining women to their apartments, although men exhausted by industrial jobs spent more time at home, once televisions became affordable.

Couples planning to start their own businesses back home viewed wifely earnings as a way to expedite the process. The need to juggle homemaker duties and paid work came as a shock to many, but life was physically less demanding and personal income shifted the balance of household power. The fact that Germans viewed work outside the home differently helped many to overcome their ambivalent desire for personal earnings and a chance to contribute to the family income. Worried about their wives' safety and "honor" (as in Turkish culture), men also feared a loss of power within the family, sometimes leading to new restrictions on female mobility. One noted resentfully that her husband expected her home after she finished work, preventing her from making friends, or improving her language skills with colleagues.

Many abandoned traditional roles over the years. Born in 1947 near Reggio di Calabria, Tilda Comperatore quickly found a job:

> I worked in a dry-cleaner, at the wringer in a laundry, where I also had to mend some clothes, then I started to work in a big textile factory. . . . But afterwards, when I already had two children I stayed at home for fourteen months. Then I started piece rate work at *Blaupunkt* in the electrical industry. I worked there for four years. I was so proud, because I really did earn some money there. I bought myself a coat, a fur coat, it was really beautiful. I worked in changing shifts. We produced such small things, small coils, a very difficult work. Two women had to work together there, I was at the machine producing the coil and the other woman had to finish it with a small tweezers. We worked well together, we produced approximately twenty coils more than others a day and so we always had some pieces in reserve. I liked my colleagues very much, we still meet sometimes today, we are still friends.
>
> My husband helped me. When I had the early shift he arranged everything for the children. I had some difficulties about this with my brother. But my husband and me, we helped each other a lot. But after four years my son was born and I had to quit work. At former times [*sic*] I had a neighbor who helped a little to take care of the children when my husband and me both had to work. With three children to take care of this was no longer possible. After a while I started to work at a smaller factory, three hours a day in the late afternoons when my husband had the early shifts. After ten years I had a permanent pain in my elbow, it was hard to bear and then I quit work altogether.[90]

A couple willing to share domestic chores testifies to acculturation and "reconstructed masculinity." Another couple, "Nunzia" (1935) and "Giuseppe," tended to clash head-on. Nunzia engaged in hard, unskilled labor, for low pay, as a way to improve their standard of living. Her husband (a coal miner) and children railed against her desire to work, but now that she enjoys a small pension of her own, Giuseppe respects his wife's "stamina."[91]

Second-generation women, born or raised in Germany, are better educated than males, but even women born in the 1980s face labor-market disadvantages. More have taken on white-collar jobs, yet many remain concentrated in dead-end sectors as hairdressers, clerical workers, or saleswomen. They also experience longer stints of unemployment. These women do not see their employment as a transitional stage, nor would they consider remigration. Sonya Haug shows that the more education and the higher the income one receives in Germany, the lower the return tendency; the larger the family left behind and the lower the language skills, the more likely their departure.

The yo-yo nature of Italian labor migration posed special problems for the second generation. The Joint Commission expressed concern as early as 1962 that many Italian children were not attending school.[92] Although most learned "high" Italian (not local dialects) by way of special schools, second-generation offspring could not pursue their own educational goals, nor did parental promises prepare them for village life. A 1972 study found that 10 percent of all foreign workers interrupted their workstays for over half a year, 20 percent among Italians. The real costs of "pendulum-migration" fell to the children: the very young were sent back to be cared for by grandparents, then brought to Germany to enter school, or returned to Italy when they reached school age, or they first entered the FRG after completing homeland educations. Haug observes:

> If the decision to return or to stay is not made in the early stage of life but rather put off as long as possible, then it is often the case that children are shunted back and forth between Germany and Italy in inconsistent ways. . . . The cross-border commuting of children shows up in sharp relief when they reach school age and the family is still undecided. In some families with several children, they would even be treated differently. This leads to a situation in which some children have grown up in Italy, the others in Germany . . . it may be a rational strategy *for the family* to keep all of its options open as long as possible. This is usually considered a transitional stage that will end relatively soon, one way or another, but in every case it means a longer school period *for the children*, followed by a reversal of the decision that brings heavy consequences . . . after they have completed their schooling in Italy, one sees that they have worse chances of achieving structural integration, compared with their own siblings (emphasis added).[93]

Haug's 1997 study of Herten (South Baden) attests to the successful integration of Italians in a small town with a relatively concentrated population: 5.7 percent in 1983, down to 4.8 percent in 1996. Women and men were evenly matched, but the cohort distribution was bimodal, the largest groups consisting of eighteen to twenty-three and forty-one to fifty year olds. The average length of stay was thirty-two years. Half of the couples had met/married in Italy; women followed up to eight years later. Most first-generation migrants built homes in Italy but had meanwhile purchased local dwellings; two second-generation residents had started businesses (cleaning service, beauty parlor). Only 20 percent had been born in Germany, but most offspring were educated locally; they learned the "mother tongue" by attending special schools once a week. Travel to Italy was limited to annual vacations. Haug admits that the stable lives and widespread "satisfaction with Germany" depicted in her sample are at odds with nationally representative studies.[94]

For children, migration became a project without a direction or endpoint, undercutting their opportunities for educational integration, an experience shared with Turkish offspring. Half left school without certification in 1979,

Table 5.6 Educational and Occupational Status among Minorities

School Type	Germans	Turks	Italians	Yugoslavs
Hauptschule	35.6	75.3	81.7	59.4
Realschule	30.0	16.2	10.6	19.8
Gymnasium	34.4	8.6	7.8	20.8
n =	1907	396	180	106

Educational Level	Germans	Turks	Italians	Spaniards
No certification	0.7	17.9	12.6	10.7
Hauptschule				
Drop out	8.6	38.2	37.7	22.9
with certification	42.8	28.7	32.2	30.4
Realschule				
Drop-out	1.7	2.9	2.1	4.3
With certification	26.0	6.9	9.5	17.0
Tertiary Level				
without degree	1.2	1.3	1.0	2.8
with degree	7.3	2.0	1.4	4.7
University degree	11.8	2.0	3.5	7.1

Labor Market Position				
Manual Worker	37.4	87.5	75.4	65.2
White Collar	62.6	12.5	24.6	34.8
n =	11,704	2,853	1,073	253

Work Status				
Unskilled	31.3	54.8	54.2	46.4
Skilled	38.1	31.2	25.2	28.6
managerial	30.6	13.9	20.6	25.0
n =	66,241	330	238	84

Source: Compiled from data provided by Hartmut Esser and Wolfgang Seifert for the Independent Commission on Immigration.

though girls fared better than boys. The probability that Turkish and Yugoslav youth would lack vocational training was 1.5 to 1.6 times greater than for Germans, 2.2 times higher for Italians. A majority, concentrated in Bavaria and Baden-Württemberg, faced systemic discrimination: foreign children were relegated to separate classes to "prepare" them for the homeland. Italian youth hoping to complete the *Abitur* first had to jump from the "national" school (with limited language skills) into a regular *Realschule*, then into the *Gymnasium*.[95] More Italians were enrolled in special schools for the learning impaired than in college-prep courses. High drop-out rates and delinquency among Italians are ignored by politicians but stressed in relation to Yugoslav and Turkish youth. By 1982, 55 percent of the Italians had lived in Germany for over ten years; 45 percent expressed a desire to "go home" in 1979, versus only 8 percent in 1989.[96]

Like Turkish guestworkers, first-wave Italians transferred earnings to the homeland in anticipation of retirement, but many were irritated by the inefficiency and corruption they encountered upon return. Some grew bitter, realizing that their departures had opened up jobs for those who stayed behind; only three of fifty-one families who remigrated could sustain themselves with small businesses.[97] Close family ties declined through the 1980s, as offspring turned to intermarriage (Italian men and German women); births resulting from mixed marriages rose from 27.9 percent in 1980 to 41.1 percent in 1990, but lagged behind Spaniards (80 percent).[98] Italians spend less recreational time with one another than with other ethnic groups: by 1995, 69 percent met with Germans at least once a week.

An ostensibly transnational lifestyle allowed Italians to maintain contacts with the homeland, as well as to exchange carloads of goods across boundaries, but one shouldn't confuse personal movement with global mobility. They "*pendled*" back and forth due to "the limited attractiveness and the insecure nature of the jobs . . . usually handed down to the unskilled Italian workers."[99] They fared no better in a homeland experiencing "modernization without development." Transnationalism, in theory, posits a degree of individual autonomy and rational choice that real-existing migrants lack. Subjected to "new delocalized social realities and fields," unskilled laborers wind up psychologically homeless in two states, in contrast to high-tech cosmopolitans, who consort with like-minded, affluent types and thus feel at home everywhere they go.[100] Rieker's work is replete with persons who have lost their Italian identities in a practical sense but feel no emotional ties to Germany beyond their children and grandchildren. Recall the comment by Barbara John's secretary: "Ach, the Italians? . . . We hardly notice them!" Benign neglect hardly counts as integration.

How Transnational Italians Tamed the Toscana Faction

Protected against the 1973 recruitment stop by EC membership, Italians, like Turkish workers, projected a return to the homeland so far into the future that it never happened. The return quotient stood at 46 percent in 1966, dropping to 21 percent in 1967, and less than 10 percent in 1987. By 1997, 70 percent had resided in Germany for ten years, 50 percent for twenty years or more. A rough total of 600,000 has remained stable for three decades, not counting those who disappear from the statistics through naturalization.[101]

Italians who came to Berlin differed from those heading for industrial zones in *Restdeutschland*. As forced laborers or interned WWII soldiers, some had learned German and started family businesses during the first wave. Others came to take advantage of special subsidies; cut off from the regular labor supply, the walled city sought its own unskilled workers for construction. Chain migration ensured temporary accommodations and first jobs, including street musicians with accordions and monkeys. Despite claims that there was "no real national cuisine in Italy," ten to twenty restaurants opened their doors in the 1960s. Initially relying on *Plockwurst* and local cheese, they created *pizza alla tedesca*, later switching to pepperoni and mozzarella. Ethnic food was cheap, prior to the use of imported ingredients. Filling their cars during recession-related trips home, these entrepreneurs focused on supplying an ersatz-vacation "atmosphere," with checkered tablecloths, candles in Chianti bottles, and fishing nets suspended from the ceilings.[102] The Berlin mystique and a boisterous student movement attracted leftists after 1968, leading to more ice cafés and restaurants around Kreuzberg (with no mandatory closing time). Males predominated (68 percent) as the numbers rose from 1,364 in 1960 to 11, 000 in 1995; 10,300 live in Charlottenburg, Schöneberg, and Neukölln, albeit not in an identifiable "enclave." Today fifteen hundred restaurants and three hundred Italian groceries are dispersed throughout the city.[103]

Berlin was hard hit by deindustrialization, even before the Wall fell. Nearly half held socially-insured jobs in 1977, 26 percent in 1983, and 14 percent in 1995; manufacturers pulled out once subsidies ended. The proportion of Italians in service jobs grew from 48 percent in 1983 to 58 percent in 1994. Compared to Turks, the Italians saw no founder's boom outside the food sector, but the latter was transformed by way of niche marketing. Pizza joints were bought up by Turks or Arabs whose compatriots were willing to work for less, while Italians shifted to regional cuisines. New entrepreneurs settled in Prenzlauer Berg after squatters were forced out. Thanks to unification, Berlin experienced a building boom as government construction projects filled the former "death zone." The chief architect behind the Debis Building (costing DM 8 billion), close to Potsdamer Platz, was Renzo Piano, at home in Genoa and Paris. Easterners commissioned household renovations even before their property claims were settled. Construction became a round-the-clock job, despite the fact that *die Baustelle der Nation* relied on sub-sub-sub-contracting that not only denied East Germans jobs but also produced scandals and law suits. Undocumented Italian and East European workers were often exploited, then deported without pay after completing *state* projects!

A new middle class consisting of academics, professionals, and aging leftists, privy to generous vacation benefits, gave rise to a new breed of consumers that "knows exactly what 'real Italian' is."[104] Italo-Berliners quickly adapted to the evolving tastes of the so-called Toscana Faction, whose unofficial member list reads like a *Who's Who* of once-radical SPD and Green Party protesters (see www. toskanafraktion.de).[105] By the late 1980s, elites including Gerhard Schröder and

Joshka Fischer began to frequent vacation spots in Tuscany; many even bought summer homes. Their taste for imported *prosciutto* has given new meaning to the term *antipasto*. "The Scene" began learning Italian, creating a niche for language teachers; restaurant owners introduced post-modern interiors with marble, chrome, and white walls, allowing them to rename former pizza joints *Trattoria* and *Osteria* while doubling their prices. Second-generation Italians rediscovered cultural capital, courtesy of expedited shipping/import channels. Just as spaghetti and Chianti gave way to upscale wines and *vitello saltimbocca*, textile activity yielded to shoes and fashion design (Russian Jews took over the alteration shops). Merchants specializing in fresh pasta, cheeses, and pastries at Winterfelder Markt inspired sales of exclusive cappuccino machines and culinary "musts" like custom-made ovens. Traditional building skills were marketed to eco-affluent homeowners willing to pay for "all-natural" materials like *Terrazo*, stucco, and marble inlays. Nationally, the number of self-employed Italians rose from 12,000 (1974) to 36,000 or 5.7 percent (1992), motivated by the same factors leading to Turkish entrepreneurship.

Not everyone has risen to the top: 34,300 Italians (of about 150,000 laborers) were jobless in 1993.[106] Those who still cater to fast-food lovers and US tourists have to compete with the döner and hamburger trade. "Italian" textiles and leather goods, available through chains like Benetton and Steffanel, are produced by Chinese migrants in sweatshops back home.[107] *Pendel-migration* continues: During two days in Venice and Florence in 2004, I encountered three young waiters who had already worked in Germany and then returned. Successor cohorts still score poorly in schools, like so many Turkish youth. Despite persisting educational and occupational deficits, the Italians have fared better than other groups in terms of social integration. Germans appreciate their "open and vivacious patterns of communication," leading them to posit strong cultural affinities, though the Italians they recruited never saw the inside of their favorite museums in Florence or Venice. Italian foodmeisters claim the same degree of success in resocializing Germans as the Turkish döner kings: "The Germans and the Italians somehow understand each other, and now through the bars, the restaurants, the ice-cream parlors—we have Italianized the Germans. . . . Back then there were all of these food items we couldn't get; nowadays we can get everything. Eggplants, artichokes, no one here knew what they were. Those were exotic fruits here. But now you can get everything. That's why I say that you can't feel bad about being here anymore, because we also have a piece of Italy here, in the shops, and there are so many restaurants, a little piece of home you can find everywhere."[108]

If Germany is becoming more "Italian," it is easier for migrants to stay without betraying the land of origin: "In practical terms I have made myself at home with my life in Germany." Like Turkish youth, Italian teens are more religious than the natives: 30 percent of the males and 50 percent of the females pray every day, compared to 18 percent and 31 percent among German adolescents.[109] They evince blended identities. The major social distinction is that Germans *want* to believe that Italians are about the same, but Turks are too different. Turkish and Italian attitudes toward a lack of political rights overlap as well. Asked about a desire to participate in federal elections, one Italian resident of many years responded:

> Yes, why not? If they would make it possible for me. After all, I live here and therefore have an interest in voting for a party that says something to me. . . . But soon there will be European citizenship and then we'll be able to take on that one. . . . Yes, it would please me to be able to vote in Germany, then I'd have the same rights others have. I work here, I also pay my taxes here, and so that would only be just. After the thirty years I have lived here, that would be right. I don't have a temporary residency permit any more, I have a permanent one, that means that I have just as many rights as the Germans. Except that's not true, I don't have equal rights because then I would be able to vote. And not only for European Parliament elections. Somebody should really fix that.[110]

Neither Haug nor Rieker find evidence of the satisfying "transnational" existence described in the literature. The stories they tell are usually the result of tough, personal compromises between an inability to meet the formal criteria required for permanent immigration, and pressures to reconcile migration-related lifecycle choices: "We have the grandkids here but we may have to go back anyway," unable to sustain the same quality of life based on irregular pensions. Like Haug, I contend "that this form of transnationalism definitely does not give rise to a romantic, multicultural niche, but rather serves as an emergency-response to many otherwise irreconcilable life goals, and to a life-style marked by a kind of stress that cannot be withstood in the long run."[111]

Mobility without Migration:
Polish *Grenzgänger* as the New Guestworkers

Polish migration to Germany has an even longer history, but its character has changed dramatically since 1990. Departures were provoked by multiple partitions in the 1700s, as well as by labor surpluses in agriculture through the 1800s. Intellectuals, dramatists, and musicians cultivated their own newspapers, cultural centers, and churches in Berlin prior to the disruption of war. Nearly 3.5 million abandoned the homeland, followed by another two million (1918–1939), then five million during WWII; a majority landed in the United States or Canada. The Nazis exploited thousands as slave laborers and expelled 1.2 million Poles to free lands for resettlement by *Volksdeutschen* in 1940–1941; as payback, the Polish state drove out 4.1 million ethnic Germans in the late 1940s. Poland expelled 60,000 Jews by 1948; 15,000 were forced into exiled by a Communist purge of "Zionist elements" in 1968.[112]

The period from 1950 to 1990 saw a steady outpouring of fifteen to thirty thousand Poles per year, once the socialist regime allowed citizens to keep their passports at home.[113] Escaping economic hardship was the main motive. Highly educated individuals sought political or religious refuge during the Cold War era. The 1980s saw the flight of young inhabitants from urban areas (Warsaw, Gdansk, Katowice). The number of long-term migrants fell by more than half, as did the flow of ethnic "resettlers," from 250,000 in 1989 to 1,175 by 1996.[114] Poland only began registering *Aussiedler* and tracking its returnees after 1990.

The share of temporary laborers doubled after unification; since then Poland has run a negative migration balance (more leaving than returning), although figures for the 1990s fall 40 percent short of the annual average (28,000) for the 1980s. With all due respect to Peter Schneider, one could view these workers as the original *Mauer-Springer* (Wall Jumpers). They are now labeled *Grenzgänger* (border crossers), reflecting changes in their legal status over the last decade.[115] For Germans, *Grenzgänger* is almost synonymous with *smuggler* or *thief*, as summarized in the adage: "Today stolen, tomorrow already in Poland." For Poles, the word still carries the 1980s connotation of *European traveler*; many view themselves not as smugglers but as "small entrepreneurs." [116]

WWII-related expulsions remain a highly controversial issue in German-Polish relations.[117] Both countries claim to value their otherwise "good neighborly relations"; generational change has been accompanied by active reconciliation efforts. Border-hopping migrant workers have unintentionally fostered *change through rapprochement*: economic opportunity leads temporary workers to display fewer hang-ups toward Germans than persons who rarely leave home. Ulrike H. Meinhof and Darius Gallasinski confirm this, having analyzed citizen identities in towns divided by redrawn national boundaries and disruptive population exchanges after WWII.[118] One such town is Guben/Gubin, as it is known to its respective German and Polish residents; both groups have cultivated "boundaries in the head" across four generations. Despite its designation as a EuroCity privy to ECU [European Currency Unit] 115 million in subsidies to "improve transport" in Spree-Neisse-Bober), the peoples of this city continue to evince "stubborn segregation and separateness in full sight of their neighbors."[119]

George Schoepflin recognizes that national groups living in close proximity try to guard against assimilation by defining "markers" in times of major socioeconomic transformation:

> While the socioeconomic change is taking place, members of ethnic groups (ethnonational, ethnoreligious) evidently need the sense of security associated with group membership, because so many of the codes of morality and behavior will be under threat from the transformation. . . . Members of a group have to know who they are ethnically while the social adjustment is taking place. . . . When, however, two groups, each with a separate consciousness but possessing few markers, find themselves in proximity and are undergoing socioeconomic transformation, there is bound to be trouble. . . . Under these conditions, the assimilation of one group by the other

will appear feasible, so that both parties will define their perspectives by the other and inevitably resent the appearance of advantages enjoyed by the other.[120]

Poles in border towns stress the "absolute boundaries" that separate them from the other side in terms of language and culture. Mindful that they "are going into this Europe barefoot" relative to powerful Western neighbors, these Poles fear that Germans will demand a return of "lost properties" or buy up land at prices they cannot afford, as happened in East Germany after unification. "True Gubeners . . . are sick of hearing about" their status as a model European Town.[121] They see the EU as Germanized, threatening real nationalism, the heart of Polishness. German locals construe European identity more positively, albeit with stress on the organized crime and illegal migration they expect enlargement to bring. Recent history has reinforced regional identities ("We Brandenburgers"); economic erosion in the Eastern *Länder* has done little to foster positive national feelings since 1990.

Polish "separateness" finds legitimation in the 1997 constitution that reifies "the Polish nation, all citizens of the Republic, and also the ones who believe in God as the source of truth, justice, the good and the beautiful."[122] Catholic Poland hopes to root "individual freedoms" in an ethnoreligious construct that parts of Europe, including Germany, have used to exclude Turkish "others" from membership. Placing limits on property restitution is one way that Poles are attempting to preserve the homeland, and perhaps avoid an irreversible brain drain, by explicitly linking restoration rights to permanent residence in Poland. Property rights as well as compensation for violated rights are tied to collective nationality. The paradox here is that transient workers in Germany place their ethnonational identities on hold, realizing that the money they earn will allow them to enjoy life as "real Poles" upon their return. Like Italians, they enjoy a degree of social integration without structural integration. The question for future researchers is whether or not they will still be dreaming of a permanent return to the homeland, once they have worked in Germany for ten to twenty years.

For now, Polish laborers in Germany have become the equivalent of Mexican workers in the US, documented and undocumented.[123] Migration laws follow clear territorial lines that rarely coincide with the functional space of economic demand, e.g., the need for IT workers. German lawmakers want to block permanent settlement, but employers are addicted to a continuous flow of cheap, flexible workers. The latter are then "criminalized" as an excuse to prevent integration. Even family unification depends on a confluence of legal and illegal pathways. According to Frauka Miera, "While belonging to Germany was always assumed and institutionally constructed on the part of *(Spät)aussiedler* and German-Ethnics, it is constantly challenged and tested among family members and marriage migrants who follow. When loyalty to the state and conformity to the existing family model cannot be made sufficiently credible, then membership in the host society is contested through the loss of residency rights."[124]

"Non-membership" is an institutional given: bilateral agreements signed in 1991 created four legal categories for East European laborers. Foreign guestworkers, age eighteen to forty, with good command of German, may qualify for on-the-job vocational training limited to eighteen months. Au pairs are included in the "in-plant training" group, exonerating employers from minimum wage requirements. In 2000, 23,000 applications were approved. Next come the seasonal workers, found predominantly in agriculture, fruit/vegetable processing, and the hotel and catering sectors. Stays are restricted to three months; this classification accounted for 219,000 of 342,050 "temps" in 2000. The ostensible purpose of contract workers is to "enhance cooperation" with foreign companies, based on annually specified quotas; 65,000 entered in 2000. Finally, there were 2,500 daily cross-border commuters granted permits in 2000. In addition, Green Cards (equivalent to an American H-1B visa) are issued to information-technology workers possessing university degrees or earning over €51,000 per year. Permits are good for five years, and families can relocate, but spouses have to wait a year before engaging in paid labor. Aiming to recruit 20,000, the GC program only brought 7,000 approved takers by 2001, 12,500 by 2003, though employers say they lack 250,000 IT experts. Official statistics do not provide national or gender breakdowns, making it impossible to determine how many Poles hold such permits.[125]

Polish laborers can be called in for "very short" assignments, provided no suitable Germans or EU nationals are available, e.g., for the back-breaking asparagus harvest. Work contracts are issued for two years, three in exceptional cases. In guestworker domains, the term is one year with a maximum extension of six months; one then has to complete an equivalent work stint in Poland before reapplying, to preclude a right to established residency as well as to prevent family relocation. "Temps" lose their residency rights if the employer uses them at sites not specified in the original permit.[126] Polish companies granted contracts in Germany are responsible for social insurance and taxes. There is no official explanation as to why companies, not workers, should enjoy long-term relationships with the host society. Nor does it say much about the commitment of Polish-Catholic officials or German-CDU businessmen to "family values."

Legal status is only one dimension of transnational migration, however. Krystyna Iglicka studied two urban and two rural communities (populations under twenty thousand) known for a high migration propensity since 1990. She discovered that a break in the traditional migration chain (first illegal males, then legal females) has led to two forms of shuttle migration that emulate Italian patterns. One group of shuttlers consists of irregular petty traders, short and long term; the other group, labeled *settled migrants*, embark on money-earning trips lasting three to five years. The proportion of shuttle migrants remains steady (35 percent), while settled migrants have increased slightly (3 percent). Shuttlers often register as unemployed at home, expecting to find temporary or consecutive foreign contracts. There is little differentiation between the two groups in terms of education or marital status; men prevail among the short-term border hoppers, women among the settled migrants. The commuters include persons under the age of twenty-five.[127]

Denied the freedom of movement guaranteed EU nationals after 1961, Poles realized that "the easiest and fastest way to get to Germany was illegal and people simply took this opportunity."[128] Illegality assumes many forms: working without permits, overstaying tourist visas to work, utilizing counterfeit documents, tax avoidance, etc. Malgorzata Irek has observed three distinct migration waves since the mid 1980s. Characterized as *El Dorado*, the first was dominated by Polish proto-capitalists (also known as *Conquistadores*) prior to the fall of the Wall. Berlin's Four-Power status allowed Poles to secure "personal invitations" and to enter the Western sectors without visas; controls were weak, largely because the Jaruzelski regime tolerated private-sector activities to compensate for chronic shortages under the planned economy.[129] The state was moreover willing to send cheap labor(ers) abroad, providing the first conduit for undocumented trade relations. So-called Workers' Trains were packed on Monday mornings and Friday nights; returnees boarded the *Berolina* and the *Hoek van Holland* at the Ostbahnhof or Lichtenberg stations, crossing at Frankfurt/Oder.

As I learned during a 1987 trip to Gdansk, black-market currency rates were pegged against the dollar (equal to one bottle of vodka), at a time when Polish wages averaged $10–15 per month. Cigarettes and alcohol could be purchased very cheaply at state PEWEX stores, and sold for enormous profits (150 percent gain for a carton of Marlboros) during weekly trips to the West, no matter how small the stash.[130] As cigarettes became big business and controls tightened, itinerant merchants immediately shifted to new products (textiles, sweets, medications, cosmetics) and new "hiding techniques" among fellow travelers. Teachers, single women, even doctors found that a few trips yielded more than their monthly salaries, allowing them to pay off loans, build homes, and supply whole neighborhoods with videos and satellite disks.

The second phase, labeled *Mecca*, saw the rise of trade bazaars, the "wild Polish markets" starting at Potsdamer Platz that moved into shops along the Kantstrasse, close to the Zoo train station. Berlin's status as a transit zone entitled foreigners to rebates on value-added taxes until a new German-Polish treaty was signed in April 1991; the short stretch between Aldi stores and Bahnhof Zoo triggered limits on quantities (shampoo, deodorant, margarine, candy) sold to Poles. Connections and bribes evolved along with complex supply-and-demand networks. Irek reports that enterprising traders regularly moved from Poland to Czechoslovakia, then on to Romania where they sold Czech goods, second-hand clothing, medications, jewelry, and condoms. At the next stop they traded currency for dollars, Bulgarian *lewa*, and Deutschmarks, while selling Polish cosmetics to Western tourists or Arabic students along the Black Sea. Heading to Turkey, they picked up luxury goods, leather products, and exotic foods, after selling silver, crystal, fox coats, cameras, and appliances. Returning north, they used accumulated capital to buy West German wares, slipped into Poland, where border-crossing GDR residents bought "guaranteed west German products for exorbitant east German prices." On the last workday before unification, one-hundred thousand GDR citizens crossed the Oder/Neisse bridge into Słubice to shop.[131]

Poles built their own networks to ensure easy transit between Berlin and the homeland. The third stage commenced after the fall of the Wall, as more successful traders switched to legal import-export businesses, having already proved their ability to energize suppliers, make quick investments, and take risks. They were joined after 1990 by growing numbers of unemployed, for whom illegal work and trade became a crucial survival strategy.[132] Those operating outside legal channels professionalized their supply chains by using "ants" (students, elderly, children), who were paid a daily sum plus travel costs. Occasional losses (confiscations) were calculated into the sales price. Asked if he were ashamed of exploiting children, one man responded: "Not at all. It's shameful when the man can't feed his family or when they live in dirt or have to steal. I'm proud of the fact that I'm able to live so well under the new conditions, and besides it is always a patriotic deed to cheat the Germans."[133]

Although "the era of quick earnings in the west" ended with the onset of a market economy at home, Polish citizens continue to see Germany as a land of temporary opportunity. The number of registered Poles stood at 291,673 in 1999, but as many as a million might be working in the FRG without permits.[134] Stefan Alscher and colleagues report that 4,847 persons were taken into custody at the German-Polish border in 1998.[135] Control actions include car checks for luggage, raids on construction sites, and capricious treatment by bureaucrats. The number of prosecutions in Berlin rose from 4,131 in 1992 to 11,484 in 1997; 6,199 producers and construction sites, and 8,058 workers, were investigated in 1998.[136] Polish women comprise the largest group among the estimated seven thousand illegal prostitutes in Berlin. The "private" nature of women's work renders it nearly impossible to control. They are proving to be shrewd business managers in other sectors as well.

Female Entrepreneurs: The Polish *Putzfrau* Brigade

There have been no reported raids on affluent homes to snare undocumented Polish housekeepers or nannies working at black-market rates. Few Germans see their own willingness to consume "privately imported" goods and services as contributing to the growing problem of undocumented labor, especially now that established professionals from the '68 Generation have overcome their hang-ups about exploiting cheap domestics. I know several Berliners who utilize Polish services ranging from house cleaning to floor laying, adding credence to the local saying: "Kommst du aus Poland immerzu, das Gesetz drückt beide Augen zu" (If you come from Poland on the sly, the law is sure to close both eyes). The *Tageszeitung (Taz)* ran one investigative report on Polish domestic helpers as early as 1990.

Irek offers a fascinating account of one thousand interviews with regular border crossers riding the German-Polish rails between 1987 and 1994. Her sample included 300 cleaning ladies, 64 of whom she later visited in Berlin or Poland. The Polish *Putzfrau* brigade has likewise seen three evolutionary stages. The first wave of the 1980s consisted of young, single women, often semiprofessionals (like nurses) who spoke some German, came to finance educations or accumulate capital for businesses back home. Certain they "would bring no shame to the Polish state," they earned up to DM 1,600 monthly, forty times more than their normal salaries. They found reasonable accommodations and regular jobs including vacation time and occasional gifts. Several worked for bachelors, who paid more but provided no extras. Female professionals were allegedly the worst employers, "cheap, condescending, and demanding." Within a few years, some married, moved up the ladder, or returned to Poland. Those who assimilated mirror German attitudes toward the East: "Desire to return? Never had it. Poland is a lost country and has no future prospects. There is only theft."

The capital city commissioned its first survey of 1,203 Polish residents in 1994 (Italians only appear in multiethnic polls). According to Barbara John, one of the more "amazing" findings was that, "despite the relatively short nature of their stay, Poles have put down economic and social roots in Berlin. Not even the difficult living conditions Poles faced in the 1980s—insecure residency status, the denial of work permits, the inaccessibility of welfare benefits—appear to have negatively influenced this rooting. Of course, the survey does not capture the words of those broken by these conditions who returned to Poland, only those who succeeded by gritting their teeth and moving on."[137] John's positive summary is at odds with the data: 56 percent had seen no improvements in their lives, based on the dramatic changes of 1989–1990. Most cited rising prices, unemployment, and higher taxes. Their access to German residency permits was downgraded, from a regular *Aufenthaltserlaubnis* to a functionally limited *Aufenthaltsbefugnis* in 1991. Only a third enjoyed unlimited residency; 68 percent knew nothing about a new German-Polish Treaty on Neighborly Relations and Friendly Cooperation. About half had experienced discrimination or unequal treatment: 44 percent at the hands of bureaucrats, 24 percent at the workplace, and 24 percent at the local Foreigners' Offices! They felt less threatened by post-unity xenophobia in 1994, but 42 percent had witnessed or experienced verbal or physical assaults. Roughly 70 percent thought their situation would improve with an anti-discrimination law.[138]

Community relations have stabilized, and Poles are once again welcome additions to the labor pool, especially during the harvest season. The city derives many benefits from their presence for "obvious" reasons, described by

Frankfurter Allgemeine Zeitung publisher Gerhard Gauck: "The Poles do not wear headscarves, nor can they be recognized on the basis of skin color. They do not build their own houses of worship, they don't demonstrate, or organize themselves, at least not in visible form. They don't live in concentrated urban quarters. They leave the communal representation of foreigners up to the Turks, Serbs and the Greeks. One could almost say they don't exist, given the fact that they are out of sight. They don't want to be seen. Hardly any group of aliens has integrated itself without a sound like the Poles."[139] "Invisibility" is not an effective indicator of successful integration—similar things are said about Italians. Shuttlers rely on ethno-community ties for jobs, dwellings, and social life, having constructed a parallel society they hope to leave behind sooner rather than later. Polish "culture" takes place above ground; gainful employment takes place underground or at the margins of the economy insofar as primary sector jobs have been rationalized or outsourced out of existence. What remains is low-paid service work, devoid of benefits, making it easier to leave.

For decades, Turks and Italians were treated more or less uniformly as an industrial reserve army, despite the substantial religious, cultural, and linguistic differences found within each group. After Maastricht, Italians were legally upgraded as EU nationals. Ethnically homogeneous and religiously cohesive Poles, by contrast, have been subject to diverse legal classifications and opportunity structures. Some have been accorded automatic citizenship as *Aussiedler,* others claimed undisputed political asylum for opposing "communism," while a third group has been expected to function as temporary workers with no claims on the welfare state. Like their Russian counterparts, legal Poles often pave the way for chains of undocumented migrants who move back and forth across the border at will, no matter what complex legal barriers Germans use to stop them.

In the Polish case, transnationalism becomes a way of life for specific groups; it is a combination of higher living costs and restrictive skilled labor regulations in the West that conditions frequent returns to the homeland. Polish laborers are to the post-Wall period what Italians were to the postwar era: persons forced by economic necessity to take on Germany's dirty and difficult jobs, at wages no permanent resident would accept. Polish cleaning ladies are displacing Turkish domestics, though Germany has yet to experience a political "Nannygate." Highly educated Poles take on unskilled jobs they would refuse at home, in order to earn the quick cash that goes a long way upon return. They suffer few identity problems, seeing their work sojourns in purely instrumental terms, preserving their social status and enhancing consumption in the homeland.

On 1 May 2004, Poland was officially admitted to the European Union. One major concern in the enlargement negotiations was the state's lack of an effective border control system vis-à-vis eastern countries. While conditions have been met for the "free movement" of most goods, Polish workers will not enjoy the full complement of EU rights for several years to come, in contrast to Italians. Although Poland is part of *Schengenland*, the "free movement" of its workers remains limited, subject to compliance with new EU rules. This, along with the nation's physical proximity, may keep Poles true to their dream of "living" in the homeland. It is also likely to ensure Germany a steady stream of cheap, border-savvy, yet illegal Polish laborers for another ten years.

The irony is that Poles, like GDR citizens, developed an extraordinary capacity for entrepreneurial and improvisational activity in response to chronic scarcities under the old regime. Unlike Italians, they possess a cohesive national identity, a deep respect for culture and education, a talent for transferring social capital, and a go-getter mentality that could easily turn Poland into a booming economy—if only they had the investment capital to match. For Poland, transnational migration leads to brain drain. In contrast to the United States, where foreign mathematicians, engineers, and natural scientists are used for the purposes of brain gain, the German approach results in brain waste.[140] Polish migrant labor is used to spare Germans the need to overhaul their arcane occupational and educational structures sooner rather than later.

Why do Germans have a special fondness for Italians but not for Poles? When it comes to immigration policy, lawmakers have done an about-face regarding Robert Frost's claim, "Something there is that doesn't love a wall." The fall of the Wall transformed Berlin's status from the last Cold War bastion on the Western front, to the biggest frontier town in an expanded Central Europe. As long as the West/East border remained impenetrable to all but a few daredevils risking death, people clamoring for freedom of movement on the other side were entitled to sympathy as dissidents or as victims of oppressive regimes. Nowadays, Uwe Rada notes, "Hungarians in Berlin are perceived as enrichment, Hungarians in Austria are a threat." Italians are more welcome than Poles because they do not stem from a border state. For the record, neither do Turks, but Germans then switch discourses, arguing that "religion matters."[141] Since 1990, FRG politicians, like their Texas and Arizona counterparts, insist that "good fences make good neighbors."

Mixed Embeddedness:
Urban Citizenship through Economic Integration

This chapter reveals the ways in which the myth of return, applied to three groups of long-term guestworkers since the 1950s, has gradually evolved into a myth of transnationalism, implicit in new legal categories of seasonal workers, contract workers, and Green Card workers. Turkish merchants, Italian *pendlers*, and Polish shuttlers have all pursued do-it-yourself integration strategies, producing different outcomes with regard to their identification with and contributions to the local communities in which they reside. Though the cases considered here do not add up to a representative sample, they illustrate three types of emerging transnational actors. The first is the upwardly mobile *transnational entrepreneur* (Turks) who is reshaping the global economy, as projected in the theoretical literature. The second group consists of semi-skilled *transitional-transnational laborers* (Italians) whose border-crossing activities are limited to a single country or ethnic niche. The third group consists of unskilled (or mismatched) *temporary-transnational workers* (Poles) who display little interest in "belonging" or identifying with the local environs.

Rainer Bauböck draws on the increasing "transnational connectivity" between cities to argue for a practical brand of urban citizenship that would guarantee equal participatory rights at the local level regardless of national status.[143] The proliferation of Sister City partnerships over the last decade is but one symbolic manifestation of the cultural connectedness of once-distant urban communities. The mushrooming of corporate headquarters in urban cores like Potsdamer Platz is another. In real life, cities have become the contested territory upon which ethnic groups are compelled to "define their identities, stake their claims, wage their battles and articulate citizenship rights and obligations."[143] Providing *diversity of access* as well as *access to diversity,* cities direct the flow of educational opportunity through neighborhood schools and cultural exchanges. Besides managing (deficit-prone) housing and transportation systems, urban centers bear the social costs—substance abuse, domestic violence, crime, and gang activity—for those whose welfare eligibility has run out at other levels. Migrants are disproportionately drawn to the legal and illegal job opportunities, ethnic enclaves, and integration prospects afforded by metropolitan areas. Vulnerable to "open admission and easy exit," cities are the place where social integration succeeds or fails.

Practicing urban citizenship, Bauböck stresses, is usually not a formal process requiring passports or other local documents. As my study shows, however, cities *are* part of the legal machinery allocating citizenship rights. Guaranteed autonomy under the Basic Law, local governments have the power to grant residency permits, work permits, housing subsidies, and social assistance, thus granting them the power to "exclude." It is no coincidence that naturalization rates are higher in Berlin and Hamburg than in Munich. Nor is it surprising that proportionately more applications are approved by district officials in Kreuzberg and Neukölln than in the affluent neighborhoods of Steglitz and Zehlendorf. The Berlin government finally moved to remedy the unequal opportunity inherent in "administrative discretion" by mandating uniform naturalization criteria as of spring 2004.[144]

Migrants not only develop local identities but also local needs. As disadvantaged denizens, they are often more dependent on public services for health care, housing, and even legal counsel. Turks comprise 33 percent of the Kreuzberg population, 27.7 percent in Wedding, and 25 percent in Tiergarten. Despite the Constitutional Court's 1991 rejection of communal voter rights, I concur with Bauböck that it is time to promote urban citizenship as a home base for democracy. Whether imposed by way of local ordinances or national constitutions, rules denying *some* foreigners quintessential rights of political participation in the places they reside are unjustifiable, insofar as "cities are political communities of a different kind and they can assert this by granting full local citizenship to all residents within their jurisdiction. This could be achieved through a simple non-discrimination clause that would prevent any nationality-based exclusion from local rights and benefits. Such a clause could still allow for a reasonable grading of rights according to length of residence."[145]

Metropolitan citizenship neither mandates onerous national duties (like conscription) nor renunciation of personal identities. As practical communitarians, Turkish entrepreneurs are emerging as urban leaders, engaging in bounded solidarity, and political action, through economic mobilization. When it comes to political integration, one can usually rely on US President Bill Clinton's campaign motto: "It's the economy, stupid!" The Turkish community has been forced to rely on economic enclaves to build a participatory base otherwise denied it by virtue of German citizenship laws. A comparison with Turkish patterns of participation in the Netherlands (chapter 7) moreover indicates "it's the legal structure, stupid"—not innate cultural traits—that restricts identification with the new homeland.

Acting through roof organizations like the Association of Turkish-German Entrepreneurs and the Turkish Union Berlin-Brandenburg (TBB), ethnic businesses enjoy access to federal and state ministries, political parties, social agencies, and welfare organizations. Although individuals lack the passports needed to participate in conventional politics, they are "making claims" on local and state governments to improve life conditions for minority residents. They have also democratized their own structures: four of the twelve TBB executive board members are female. The director's wife is moreover an elected member of the Berlin Assembly. I agree with Gerdien Jonkers that "the Turks are the avant garde. . . . They have organized themselves in the Turkish Bund, an organization that evinces the whole pallet of integrational capabilities: language competence, internal differentiation, professionalization, conviction. . . . The integrative resources among this immigrant group derives from education, union experience and active political participation. This is the reason why their integration has made the greatest progress."[146]

As non-nationals, Turkish entrepreneurs in Germany are denied EU citizenship, placing them at a competitive disadvantage vis-à-vis Turks in other member states. This explains increasing naturalization rates among would-be entrepreneurs.[147] Ethnic businesswomen and men have benefited from relatively liberal rules in Berlin, where 42 percent of all naturalizations involve dual citizenship.[148] Given the Amsterdam Treaty's explicit protection against discrimination based on race, sex, religion, national origin, and sexual orientation, I believe that an extension of EU equal treatment policies will force the Constitutional Court to revisit its rejection of voting rights for alien residents by 2015. Non-citizens are essential to the well-being of major cities, and they are just as likely to rely on its services: "As workers, taxpayers, consumers, neighbors, they are persons who constitute part of the life of the (nationally bounded) political community—the very community that citizenship in its internal mode considers the proper domain of concern."[149]

At least two very significant lessons emerge from this study as regards German economic stagnation and decline. First, *Weltoffenheit schafft Jobs*—"openness to the world creates jobs"—as politicians in the Berlin-Brandenburg region have discovered since the late 1990s.[150] Multiculturalization entails a variety of economic *and* social processes benefiting minority and majority cultures. Secondly, it is not their ostensible "failure to integrate" that results in high unemployment among migrants but rather high unemployment that hinders their effective integration. The cause of that unemployment lies in the rigidities of the German labor market, not in immutable cultural traits ascribed to a given ethnicity. Italians and Poles are presumed to be culturally related to Germans, yet both groups evince less progress toward structural integration. Seidel-Pielen clearly rejects the use of static cultural markers in relation to ethnic entrepreneurs: "Don't even start to research what position your dealer holds with regard to the PKK, the Grey Wolves, towards the Islamicist Erbakan, what stand he takes vis-à-vis democraticization processes in Turkey, or how he feels about the universal values of the Enlightenment. . . . As regards the quality of the *döner*, it is totally uninteresting whether the producer is an Alevi, Arameic, a Greek-Turk, a socialist, a fundamentalist, an Armenian, a Jew, a Sunni."[151] Much more important for the future of Germany are his/her contributions as a successful business manager and job generator.

Purportedly the least "assimilatable" but also the most active mobilizers in Germany, Turkish residents have made substantial progress toward integration, albeit not in ways anticipated by national policymakers. Against all odds, Turkish entrepreneurs have established broad community ties that will foster political incorporation in the face of generational change. Compared to alienated repatriates, their experiences demonstrate that it is not "blood" but day-to-day social interaction that shapes citizenship and fosters integration. We now turn to comparative urban experiences with regard to interest associations and political enfranchisement.

Notes

1. Joyce Marie Mushaben, *From Post-War to Post-Wall Generations: Changing Attitudes towards the National Question and NATO in the Federal Republic of Germany* (Boulder, CO: Westview, 1998), 326ff.
2. German Information Center, *Foreigners in Germany. Guest Workers Asylum-Seekers, Refugees and Ethnic Germans* (New York: 1991), 2–3.
3. Gunter Wallraff, *Ganz Unten* (Cologne: Kiepenheuer & Witsch, 1985).
4. Mushaben, *From Post-War to Post-Wall Generations*, 327.

5. Ibid, 326–327.
6. Ivan Light and Steven J. Gold, *Ethnic Economies* (San Diego: Academic Press, 2000).
7. Robert Kloosterman, Joanne van der Leun, and Jan Rath, "Mixed Embeddedness: (In)formal Economic Activities and Immigrant Businesses in the Netherlands," *International Journal of Urban and Regional Research* 23, no. 2 (June 1999): 253–267.
8. Light and Gold, *Ethnic Economies*, 128–129.
9. Ibid., 108.
10. Ibid., 52–53.
11. Rita Süssmuth et al. (ICI), *Structuring Immigration, Fostering Integration*, report by the Independent Commission on Migration to Germany (Zuwanderungsbericht), (Berlin: 4 July 2001).
12. The self-employed enjoy two to fourteen times more net worth than their salaried counterparts, as noted in Light and Gold, *Ethnic Economies*, 57–58.
13. Ibid., 104.
14. Felicitas Hillmann, *Türkische Unternehmerinnen und Beschäftigte in Berliner Ethnischen Gewerbe*, WZ-Berlin, FS I 98–107 (December 1998).
15. Light and Gold, *Ethnic Economies*, 86.
16. Andreas Goldberg and Faruk Sen, "Türkische Unternehmer in Deutschland. Wirtschaftliche Aktivitäten einer Einwanderungsgesellschaft in einem komplexen Wirtschaftssystem," in *Leviathan*, no. 17 (1997), *Zuwanderung und Stadtentwicklung*, 73.
17. Ibid., 73–74.
18. Ibid., 63ff.
19. Ibid., 74–75, 80.
20. Zentrum für Türkeistudien, *Die Regionalen Transferstellen für ausländischer Existenzgründer und Unternehmer in NRW* (Essen: ZTS, October 1999); Goldberg and Sen,"Türkische Unternehmer in Deutschland," 80–81.
21. Zentrum für Türkeistudien, *Die ökonomische Dimension der türkischen Selbständigen in Deutschland und in der Europäische Union* (Essen: June 2001); Gerhard Hatz, "Die Märkte als Chance für Ausländer—Ausländer als Chance für die Märkte," in *Leviathan*, no. 17 (1997): 170–191.
22. Ibid., 7–8.
23. Ibid.
24. Ibid., 11.
25. Rainer Ohlinger and Ulrich Raiser, *Integration und Migration in Berlin: Zahlen—Daten—Fakten* (Berlin: Beauftragte für Integration und Migration, 2005), 10, 15.
26. Ibid., 20.
27. Marc Fischer, "Realities Continue to Divide a Rejoined Block in Berlin: Aldalbertstrasse East Must Run to Catch West," *Washington Post*, 8 October 1990.
28. Ohlinger and Raiser, *Integration und Migration in Berlin*, 13.
29. Ibid., 27.
30. Hedwig Rudolph and Felicitas Hillmann, "Döner contra Boulette—Döner und Boulette: Berliner türkischer Herkunft als Arbeitskräfte und Unternehmer im Nahrungsgütersektor" in *Leviathan*, no. 17 (1997), *Zuwanderung und Stadtentwicklung*, 95.
31. Ohliger and Raiser, *Integration und Migration in Berlin*, 24, 26.
32. Rudolph and Hillmann; "Döner contra Boulette," 89.
33. Ibid., 90–92.
34. Felicitas Hillmann and Hedwig Rudolph, "Redistributing the Cake? Ethnicisation Process in the Berlin Food Sector," WZ-Berlin, FS1 97–101 (Berlin: 1997).
35. Eberhard Seidel-Pielen, *AUFGESPIESST: Wie der Döner über die Deutschen kam* (Berlin: Rotbuch, 1996), 9.

36. Helmuth von Moltke reportedly ate *Kiebabtschi* during his 1836 trip to Constantinople, described as "Hammelfleisch, grilled, laid in bread." Ibid., 21.
37. Skilled laborers must register in the *Handwerksrolle*. See Czarina Wilpert, "Germany: From Workers to Entrepreneurs," in Robert Kloosterman and Jan Rath, eds., *Immigrant Entrepreneurs: Venturing Abroad in the Age of Globalization*, (Oxford/New York: Berg, 2003), 233ff.
38. Joyce Marie Mushaben, "More than Just a Bad Hair Day: The Muslim Head-Scarf Debate as a Challenge to European Identities," in Holger Henke, ed., *Crossing Over: Comparing Recent Immigration in Europe and the United States* (Lexington Books, 2005): 182–220.
39. Seidel-Pielen, *AUFGESPIESST*, 51.
40. Ibid., 59–60.
41. Ibid., 133–134.
42. Ibid., 107–108.
43. Ibid., 12, 58.
44. Ibid., 11.
45. Ibid., 148.
46. A rare but painful allergy to sunlight forced Frau Kohl to miss her son's wedding to a Turkish woman in Istanbul shortly before her self-inflicted death in spring 2002.
47. Seidel-Pielen, *AUFGESPIESST*, 127–131.
48. Ibid., 88.
49. Ibid., 80.
50. Ibid., 84.
51. Ibid., 91–94.
52. Ibid., 112.
53. Ibid., 92.
54. Cited in ibid., 17.
55. The Independent Commission recommended that time spent in Germany be rewarded, and that spouse qualifications also be included in the assessment. This would eliminate the need for assessing "equivalency" as well as "the so-called individual priority examination" for temporary labor that "is bureaucratic, time-consuming and, in many cases, not an efficient means of filling vacancies." ICI, *Structuring Immigration, Fostering Integration*, 58–62, 91ff., 101.
56. Zentrum für Türkeistudien, *Ausbildung in türkischen Betrieben*, ZFT-aktuell Nr. 75 (Essen: 1999).
57. While I waited for Sari I overheard a German colleague negotiate with an unknown telephone partner over five thousand cameras in the Netherlands.
58. Ivan Light and Edna Bonacich, *Immigrant Entrepreneurs: Koreans in Los Angeles, 1965–1982* (Berkeley: University of California Press, 1988), 4.
59. Felicitas Hillmann, *Türkische Unternehmerinnen*; Hillmann, "Rotation *light*? Oder: wie die ausländische Bevölkerung in den bundesdeutschen Arbeitsmarkt integriert ist," *Sozialer Fortschritt* 5–6 (2003): 140–151.
60. Ibid., 10.
61. Reported by Zentrum für Türkeistudien in 1995.
62. Hillmann, *Türkische Unternehmerinnen*, 22.
63. Ibid., 37.
64. Ibid., 40–41.
65. Ibid., 27.
66. Ibid., 29.
67. All citations appear in ibid., 41.
68. Ibid., 70.
69. Ibid., 36.

70. Hillman, *Türkische Unternehmerinnen*, 44; Hillmann, "Ethnische Ökonomien: eine Chance für die Städte *und* ihre Migrant(inn)en?" in Norbert Gestrin and Herbert Glasauer, eds., *Jahrbuch StadtRegion 2001: Einwanderungsstadt* (Opladen: Leske + Budrich, 2001), 35–56.

71. "St. Louis among metros with fastest growth in women-owned firms," *St. Louis Business Report*, 21 September 2004; the number of women-owned firms grew 18 percent between 1997 and 2004.

72. Parminder Kaur Bakshi, "Small Business Intervention Strategies and Ethnic Minority Migrant Women," V/332/94-EN (Brussels: European Commission, 1992).

73. "Ich wollte nicht so befremdlich auf anderen Menschen wirken mit meinem Kopftuch," *Das Parlament* 54, no. 12/13 (15–22 March 2004): 15.

74. *Integrationsbeauftragte* in both districts confirmed the bureaucratic backlog in personal interviews, June 2003 and June 2004.

75. Yvonne Rieker, *Ein Stuck Heimat findet man immer: Die italienische Einwanderung in die Bundesrepublik* (Essen: Klartext, 2003), 25, 67.

76. Ibid., 45.

77. Ibid., 26.

78. Ibid., 39.

79. Ibid., 89.

80. Ibid., 47ff.

81. Sonja Haug, *Soziales Kapital und Kettenmigration: Italienische Migranten in Deutschland* (Opladen: Leske + Budrich, 2000), 102.

82. Ibid., 171, 196.

83. Ibid., 170.

84. Ibid., 101.

85. Ibid., 114.

86. Rieker, *Ein Stuck Heimat*, 102.

87. Ibid., 55.

88. Ibid., 46.

89. Yvonne Rieker, "Gender Structures of Work and Leisure in the Course of Post-War Italian Migration to Germany" (paper presented at the University of Leiden conference on The History of International Migration: Niches, Gender and Ethnicity, 17–18 June 2004), 3.

90. Ibid., 7.

91. Ibid., 9–10.

92. Ibid., 109.

93. Ibid., 288.

94. Ibid., 268–269, 277–282.

95. Haug, *Soziales Kapital und Kettenmigration*, 116.

96. Ibid., 119.

97. Ibid., 127.

98. Ibid., 116.

99. Ibid., 118.

100. Ibid., 36.

101. Ibid., 178–179, 184.

102. Edith Pichler, "Migration und ethnische Ökonomie: das italienische Gewerbe in Berlin," in *Leviathan*, no. 17 (1997), *Zuwanderung und Stadtentwicklung*, 111.

103. Ibid., 108.

104. Ibid., 113. Mario Tamponi, *Italien in Berlin* (Berlin: Ausländerbeauftragte des Senats, 2000).

105. The list included: Gerhard Schröder, Bjorn Engholm, Oskar Lafontaine, Joschka Fischer, Peter Glotz, Heide Simonis, Jan Ulrich, Klaus Wagenbach, Konstantin Wecker, Otto Schily, Claudia Roth, Jürgen Trittin, Heiner Bremer, and Werner Kilz, as well as European notaries Tony Blair, Sting, Neil Kinnock, and Leon Jospin.

106. Rieker, *Ein Stuck Heimat*, 115; Haug, *Soziales Kapital und Kettenmigration*, 192.

107. Antonella Ceccagno, "Chinese in Italy at a Crossroad" (derived from *CINESI D'ITALIA Storie in Bilico tra due culture*, 1998).

108. Rieker, *Ein Stuck Heimat*, 131–132.

109. Ibid., 117.

110. Ibid., 140–141.

111. Haug, *Soziales Kapital und Kettenmigration*, 290.

112. Krystyna Iglicka, "Mechanisms of migration from Poland before and during the transition period," *Journal of Ethnic and Migration Studies* 26, no. 1 (January 2000): 61–74.

113. Ibid., 62.

114. Ibid., 69–70; further, Klaus J. Bade and Jochen Oltmer, eds., *Aussiedler: deutsche Einwanderer aus Osteuropa IMIS, Bd. 8* (Osnabrück: Universitätsverlag Rasch, 1999), 22.

115. Peter Schneider, *Der Mauer-Springer* (Berlin: Rotbuch, 1982). This pre-unity novel explores Berliners' ambivalence toward division, imagining how life would be different if someone could simply jump over the Wall to experience life on the other side.

116. Malgorzata Irek, *Der Schmugglerzug: Warschau—Berlin—Warschau* (Berlin: das Arabische Buch, 1998); Norbert Cyrus, *Grenzkultur und Stigma-Management*, Schriften des Polnischen Sozialrates (Berlin: April 1997); Uwe Rada, *Berliner Barbaren: Wie der Osten in den Westen kommt* (Berlin: Basis Druck, 2001); Raymond Bonner, "Poland Becomes Big Conduit For Trafficking in Narcotics," *New York Times*, 30 December 1993.

117. Deutsch-Polnische Gesellschaft Bundesverband, eds., *Polen und Juden: Geschichte, die trennt und verbindet* (Berlin: 2002); Thorsten Klute,"Entscheidungsklagen ohen Erfolgsaussichten," *Dialog* 66–67 (2004): 6–8; Angelica Schwall-Dueren,"Zentrum gegen Vertreibung: Offener Brief an Erika Steinbach," *Dialog* 65 (2003–2004): 54–61.

118. Ulrike H. Meinhof, and Dariusz Galasinski, "Reconfiguring East-West identities: Crossgenerational discourses in German and Polish border communities," *Journal of Ethnic and Migration Studies* 28, no. 1, (January 2002): 63–-82.

119. Ibid., 64–67. Also, Christoph Dieckmann, "Die unsichtbare Stadt," *Die Zeit*, 27 November 2000.

120. George Schoepflin, "Nationalism and Ethnic Minorities in Post-Communist Europe," in Richard Caplan and John Feffer, eds., *Europe's New Nationalism: States and Minorities in Conflict* (New York/Oxford: Oxford University Press, 1996), 163–164.

121. Marlies Menge, "Wir lassen uns nicht bertreiben! Wie ostdeutsche Familien um ihre Häuser kämpfen," *Die Zeit*, 4 October 1991; "East Germans Fear Loss of Homes to 'Westies,'" *Washington Post*, 25 July 1990. Further, Teresa Tavares, *EU Programmes Operating in Selected Border Communities*, N.SERD-199–00023 (January 2001).

122. Grazyna Skapska, "Zwischen Kollektivismus und Individualismus: Staatsbürgerschaft in der polnischen Verfassungsgeschichte," in Christop Conrad and Jürgen Kocka, eds., *Staatsbürgerschaft in Europa: historische Erfahrungen und aktuelle Debatten* (Hamburg: Körber-Stiftung, 2001).

123. Frauka Miera, "Migration aus Polen: Zwischen nationaler Migrationspolitik und transnationalen sozialen Lebensräumen," *Leviathan*, no. 17 (1997), *Zuwanderung und Stadtentwicklung*, 232–254.

124. Ibid., 239.

125. ICI, *Structuring Immigration, Fostering Integration*, 59–61, 63.

126. Miera, "Migration aus Polen," 241.

127. Iglicka, "Mechanisms of migration from Poland," 70–71.

128. Ibid., 62.

129. Irek, *Der Schmugglerzug*, 12ff.

130. Ibid, 29.

131. Ibid., 49.

132. Barry Newman, "West Pledged Billions Of Aid to Poland—Where Did It All Go?" *New York Times*, 23 February 1994.

133. Ibid., 42.

134. Federal Commissioner's Office, *Facts and Figures on the Situation of Foreigners in the Federal Republic* (October 2000), 5.

135. Stefan Alscher, Rainer Münz, and Veysel Oezcan, "Illegal anwesende und illegal beschäftigte Ausländerinnen und Ausländer in Berlin," *Demographie Aktuell*, no. 17 (2001): 20; also, Klaus J. Bade and Dieter Oberndoerfer, eds., *Integration und Illegalität in Deutschland* (Osnabrück: IMIS, 2001).

136. Alscher, Münz, and Oezcan, "Illegal anwesende," 8.

137. Andrzej Stach, *Das polnische Berlin* (Berlin: Verwaltungsdrückerei, 1999), 104.

138. Survey commissioned by Barbara John, *Polen in Berlin* (Berlin: January 1995), 11–12.

139. Stach, *Das polnische Berlin*, 104.

140. Felicitas Hillmann and Hedwig Rudolph, "Jenseits des brain drain: Zur Mobilität westlicher Fach- und Führungskräfte nach Polen," WZ-Berlin, FS 1–96–103 (Berlin, 1996); J. Hryniewicz, B. Janlowiecki, and A. Mync, *The Brain Drain in Poland*, European Institute for Regional and Local Development (September 1992); and M. Morokvasic, "Pendeln statt Auswandern: Das Beispiel der Polen," in M. Morokvasic and H. Rudolph, eds., *Wanderungsraum Europa: Menschen und Grenzen in Bewegung* (Berlin: edition sigma, 1994): 166–187.

141. Ted Perlmutter, "The Politics of Proximity: The Italian Response to the Albanian Crisis," *International Migration Review* 32, no. 1 (1998): 203–222.

142. Rainer Bauböck, "Reinventing Urban Citizenship," *Citizenship Studies* 7, no. 2 (2003): 139–160.

143. Engin Isin cited in ibid., 139.

144. Dr. Robin Schneider in the Office of the Commissioner of the Berlin Senate for Integration and Migration supplied the Senate *Vorlage* (27 April 2004).

145. Bauböck, "Reinventing Urban Citizenship," 139, 150.

146. Gerdien Jonker, "Probleme der Kommunikation zwischen Muslimen und der Mehrheitsgesellschaft," in *Vom Dialog zur Kooperation: Die Integration von Muslimen in der Kommune* (Berlin/Bonn: May 2002), 9.

147. Zentrum für Türkeistudien, *Die ökonomische Dimension der türkischen Selbständigen*, 9; there are 3.5 million ethnic entrepreneurs within EU territory (6.7 percent), generating sales worth DM 68.1 billion; their investment volume grew from DM 11 billion to DM 17.4 billion by 2001. New jobs doubled, from 232,000 to 419,000 during same period, 14.

148. Rudolph and Hillman, "Döner contra Boulete," 103; "Wichtiger Schritt zur Steigerung der Einbürgerungszahlen in Berlin," TBB Presseerklärung, Berlin, 23 June 2003.

149. Kim Rubinstein, "The Centrality of Migration to Citizenship," *Citizenship Studies* 2, no. 2 (2003): 262.

150. Antoine Pecoud, "*Weltoffenheit schafft Jobs*: Turkish Entrepreneurship and Multiculturalism in Berlin," WPTC-01-19 (Berlin: 2001).

151. Ibid., 142.

CHAPTER 6

CHICKEN OR EGG?

Citizenship, Social Integration, and Political Participation

When there are three eggs to be divided up among three men at a table, you can give one to each. You could also give the yolks to one, the whites to the other and the shells to the third. The latter is the usual mode of distribution.

—Ernst Jünger

Enlightenment is man's emergence from his self-imposed tutelage. Tutelage is the inability to use one's understanding without guidance from another. This tutelage is self-imposed when its cause lies not in lack of understanding, but in lack of resolve and courage to use it without guidance from another. *Sapere Aude!* [Dare to know]. "Have courage to use your own understanding!"—that is the motto of Enlightenment.

—Immanuel Kant (1784)

The new millennium saw the enactment of a 1999 law entitling children born on German soil to automatic citizenship. The first person to benefit was Seyma Kurt, the daughter of Turkish parents Mesut and Saliha Kurt, born on 1 January 2000 in Berlin. Seyma's father was likewise born and raised in Berlin, making her directly eligible and allowing her parents to naturalize under less restrictive conditions.

Notes for this section begin on page 266.

Acquiring formal citizenship does not guarantee active political participation, however, as demonstrated by the *Spätaussiedler*. Participation has its own prerequisites: a sense of national identification, political loyalty, social commitment, and a belief in one's ability to make a difference. The question now becomes: How does a motley assortment of foreigners acquire "the right political stuff" in a landscape that has deliberately excluded them for forty years? How has the country's dependence on their economic contributions indirectly enabled second- and third-generation denizens to internalize the values and skills necessary for effective participation?

Democratic institutions are not only representative in a territorial or functional sense; they must also address deeper identity issues, summarized by Abraham Maslow as the need for physiological sustenance, safety, self-esteem, belonging, and self-actualization. Under the centrifugal forces of globalization, democracies require a special kind of "adhesive" to hold them together, one strong enough to ensure internal coherence no matter how heterogeneous the population, yet also porous enough to open spaces for new interests and communities over time. Two key ingredients that hold mature democracies together are collective identity and social capital. Rooted in participatory norms, social interaction, and trust, social capital is the magnet that draws disparate and even conflicting groups into the larger political process. Social capital inheres in "the structure of relations between actors and among actors."[1] Hard to measure, it combines with other resources—human, cultural, and financial capital—to foster engagement at different levels and to produce shared outcomes among individuals with divergent interests.

In the migration context, identity formation entails a process of taking pieces of one's old life—familiar cultural norms, behaviors, and tastes ("habitus," in Bourdieu's words)—and reconfiguring them into new self-perceptions and interactions. It invokes a search for mixed modes of social capital that will lend themselves to effective use under new institutional conditions. Integration, I have learned, requires mutual adaptation, which can only take place in "groups" if it is to be sustained from one generation to the next. Social integration and political incorporation, in other words, can not be achieved by individuals; thus the formula "integration first, citizenship later" puts the proverbial cart before the horse. As late as 1996, 60 percent of the Germans insisted in surveys that "foreigners should strongly adapt to our life style."[2] The truth is, they already have.

The period from 1985 to 2000 witnessed the rise of more than three thousand ethnic associations in the Federal Republic. Foreigners have responded to legal exclusion by building a "civil society within civil society," demonstrating not only their willingness but also their ability to integrate, despite German resistance. Ironically, the exponential increase in migrant "self-help" organizations coincided with lawmakers' mounting concern over the erosion of voluntary associations among FRG natives.[3] Robert Putnam noted an analogous trend across the Atlantic, admonishing that too many Americans were "bowling alone," rather than cultivating the "organized reciprocity and civic solidarity" that renders a democracy responsive to citizen needs.[4] Social capital, in theory, leads citizens to undertake rational and purposive action on behalf of others. It strengthens social trust, facilitating the communication necessary for collective action transcending self-interest. Putnam sees these qualities emerging out of the act of participation; "causation flows mainly from joining to trusting," he claims. Pinpointing the onset of engagement, reciprocity, and trust, however, is like trying to determine the historical precedence of the chicken versus the egg.[5] The question is purely academic.

Marieluise Beck observes, "Integration needs citizen engagement. And the reverse: Citizen engagement requires—and promotes—integration."[6] In earlier chapters I showed that Germany's adherence to an imagined community rooted in *jus sanguinis* has done little to ensure the economic integration of migrants legally defined as members of its extended family. We now consider the extent to which associations formed by groups historically excluded from citizenship are nonetheless moving toward political integration at the communal level. I begin with migration-theoretical perspectives on the relationship between social capital, interest representation, and political socialization. Next we view the political incorporation of migrants through a comparative lens, based on empirical studies from the Netherlands and elsewhere. We then explore the integrative potential of ethnic organizations across Germany, as well as in Berlin. Finally I examine national and local trends with respect to naturalization, participation, and democratic values among youth of migrant background.

Local involvement in ethnic organizations does not preclude participation in German associational life. Political outsiders often volunteer in different ways, reflecting their own migration history; still, ethnic organizations exercise an important "bridge function." If civic participation in local communities promotes social capital and trust on the part of the natives, then it seems logical that strong ethnic organizations and expanding subcultural networks would also promote integration and participation among migrants in the host country. Cross-national research shows that "the political integration of ethnic minorities and the role ethnic communities play can definitely not be described as a zero-sum game. . . . Migrants 'win' when they engage themselves in German civil society, but do not 'lose' when they are active in ethnic organisations."[7] Field studies further confirm that foreigners active in ethnic associations usually possess larger circles of host-country acquaintances; they are more apt to participate in mainstream organizations, and to follow domestic politics than persons who avoid or ignore clubs of ethnic origin.

Social Capital and (Self-)Interest
Organizations: Comparative Perspectives

A grandson of the Enlightenment, Alexis de Toqueville clearly understood the importance of intermediary organizations and self-mobilization for promoting democracy. So did Gabriel Almond and Syndey Verba, known for their pathbreaking comparative studies of civic culture. All three testify to a positive correlation between active participation in voluntary associations, citizen competence, and political accountability: "If the citizen is a member of some voluntary organization, he [*sic*] is involved in the broader social world but is less dependent upon and less controlled by his political system. The association of which he is a member can represent his needs and demands before the government. It would make the government more chary of engaging in activities that would harm the individual."[8]

Gender bias aside, these theorists realized that it takes more than "a vote" to make the state function as an effective arbiter on behalf of competing groups. The more citizens participate, the more confidence they develop in their capacity for collective action, and the less likely they are to leave government to its own devices. "What is true for the Italian regions (á la Putnam), may also be true for a multicultural society. The civic culture of ethnic groups, that is their degree of civic community, will most likely contribute to the working of democracy."[9] Voluntary organizations "are a hotbed for civic competence"; they foster good governance, enhance political legitimacy, and build social trust.[10] Ulrike Schöneberg takes the argument one step further, linking migrant self-organization to deeper integration processes: "Participation in ethnic organizations cannot simply be seen as an indicator of social segregation and cultural distance among immigrants. The connections between organizational participation, direct contacts to majority group members, and cultural assimilation are more complex and depend in part on the goals and activities of ethnic organization. The majority of ethnic organizations can be safely assumed to have positive effects on the social integration of their members within the host society."[11]

Ethnic organizations, at the outset, rarely specialize with regard to function. As a point of first contact for new arrivals, or any who lack language skills, they supply material services as well as abstract opportunities for social bonding. Religiously motivated associations, for example, offer everything from counseling, child care, and elder care, to language courses, worship services, cultural festivals, and monetary transfers to the homeland. They foster collective identity among members, develop adaptation skills, forge informal networks, afford psychological cushions against discrimination, close gaps in welfare coverage, and channel critical information tied to public health, legal rights, and educational options. The more established an institution, the greater the specialization (and regulation) one will encounter. Many copy corresponding structures in the host society, others draw on homeland models—for a while. Sometimes they have no choice but to copy host-country organizational modes: consider the German rule that Muslims cannot offer Islamic instruction in public schools until they qualify for "corporate status."

Organizational evolution follows a trajectory inherent in the three stages of migration: arrival, settlement, and securing a place in the host-country culture. Throughout the first stage (1955–1973), migrants created a limited number of associations with a homeland orientation, assuming that their stay in Germany was temporary. The belief that they would return was reinforced by the financial support first-wave organizations received from home governments. First generation migrants relied on these entities to escape their social isolation, channel remittances, as well as to collect for charitable causes back home (earthquake relief, supplying libraries or clinics). Stage-two organizations (1973–1982) reflect the permanent settlement orientations of the second generation. Initially marked by left-right polarization, ethnic groups shifted to a host-country focus, seeking access to resources for migrant needs in Germany. They served as important discussion partners for local authorities, especially when conflicts arose. Although their function was largely advisory, they did offer a voice to foreigners otherwise excluded from citizenship. This period saw competition qua internal conflict rooted in generational differences and changing gender roles.

The third stage, incorporation (1983–1998), mirrors a new sociopolitical identification with the host state. Second- and third-generation activists have sought recognition as interest representatives and intercultural mediators, claiming the right to involve themselves in mainstream concerns like the environment (e.g., *ImmiGrün*). Responding to globalization, new organizations have assumed external representation functions, i.e., as contact points for homeland entrepreneurs who want to establish trade links. Many employ new forms of human capital, including intercultural competence, to provide educational opportunities for the Germans. Their mobilizational efficacy, access to resources, and policy influence has increased dramatically with the formation of roof organizations like the Turkish Union of Berlin Brandenburg (TBB) and the Turkish Community (Türkische Gemeinde).

Though socialized in Germany, these ethnic organizers do not have to jettison their cultural identities to work their way into host institutions. Their intermediary associations set low thresholds for joining, yet provide significant networking opportunities. They may, however, face a Tocquevillean paradox, as noted by Fennema and Tillie: The more resources ethnic associations can accrue to "solve their own problems," the sooner the state will respond to their articulated needs. The more systemic support a group requires to consolidate itself, the greater the danger that it will become a tool of government policy (or at least be perceived as such), weakening civic ties. Network studies suggest that it is a weak civic community, rather than ethnic-specific factors, that foster dependent or unsustainable organizations.[12] The reverse may also be true: States experiencing serious integration problems need strong ethnic partner organizations. Case studies show that integration policies "cannot implement themselves. They cannot succeed without the cooperation of all agencies, institutions and organizations, especially ethnic organizations per se. The communal arenas are not only the first level for the configuration of human interactions but also the level upon which efforts and support mechanisms have to build for societal integration processes to work. Government policy is thus complementary and subsidiary."[13] The following comparisons underscore the importance of state actions in fostering or impeding integration.

Cross-Border Comparisons and "Best Practices"

The Netherlands

In 1980, Dutch officials issued a report by the Scientific Council for Government Policy, concluding, albeit reluctantly, that the Netherlands had become a "land of immigration." It appeared about the same time as a study by Heinz Kühn on the "Situation of Foreign Residents in Germany." Unlike FRG politicians who refused to accept that aliens were there to stay, the Dutch state pushed for strict limitations on entry, coupled with active measures to ensure integrative opportunities for foreign residents, approved by parliament in 1983. The term *Ausländer* was deemed inappropriate, insofar as many from the former colonies were citizens; 30–40 percent of its Turks and Moroccans pursued naturalization. Since other aliens were not "moving," the term migrant was also confusing. Lawmakers thus opted for ethnic minorities, suggesting that the latter deserved protection as constituent parts of the national territory.

Given a history of deep socio-religious cleavages, the Netherlands developed its own democratic framework known as consociationalism (alternatively, pillarization). The political opportunity structure is rooted in elite collaboration and institutionalized consultation among Catholics, Protestants, and other corporatist groups. First intended to eliminate religious strife, consociational groups "can take almost any content," allowing for rapid formal incorporation and new discursive space.[14] In 1884, nationality legislation granted citizenship "by declaration" to all 18–25 year olds born in the Netherlands. Residents from the former Dutch colonies began arriving in the 1950s. As early as 1960, the State Advisory Committee on the Constitution and Electoral Law mulled over whether to allow Dutch citizens abroad to retain their voting rights. Turkish guestworker migration occurred largely between 1968 and 1974.[15] A 1971 embrace of "residency" as a condition for voting led to the question of whether all municipal residents should enjoy the same right. Avoiding talk of entitlement, the Home Office rejected voting rights for foreigners in 1976 but opened itself to future amendments. The foreign population grew exponentially from 117,000 (1960), to 235,000 (1970), to 430,000 (1980), eventually reaching 757,000 in 1995.[16]

Moluccan terrorists brought the center-right to power in the late 1970s, willing to consider enfranchisement to "repay an historical debt." After colonialism ended, 12,500 Moluccans had been "temporarily" relocated to the Netherlands from Indonesia in 1951. As their number grew to 37,500, the state decided to "do something" to counter mounting social problems. A 1979 report on ethnic minorities urged the state to open the social security system to all residents, simplify naturalization procedures, and pursue active integration. Rotterdam and Amsterdam had already extended voting rights to foreigners in 1979 and 1981.

The Dutch were not the first Europeans to extend local voting rights to aliens. Ireland had done so in 1963, followed by Sweden (1976), Denmark (1981), and Norway (1982). Constitutional changes introduced in 1983 granted local suffrage rights to aliens in 1985, based on five years of legal residency. Third-generation children received automatic citizenship as of 1985, and the ban on dual citizenship ended. The aim was to "increase [foreigners'] bond with society," inducing them to learn the language and familiarize themselves with the political system. Officials launched an information campaign in time for the municipal elections of 1986.[17] A few years later, parliament voted to allow non-citizens to become civil servants. The paradigm shifted from assimilation to integration to multiculturalism. By 1998, 152 minority delegates had been elected to municipal councils.[18]

Current policy rests on three legs. The 1998 Law on the Integration of New Arrivals requires them to complete a one-year language course, six hundred hours of which are state subsidized. Participants must take a language test, unless they apply for citizenship. Non-participation in prescribed integration courses is coupled with negative sanctions, e.g., a loss of welfare benefits. Secondly, the state funds special projects aimed at preventing marginalization and criminality, especially among Moroccans and Antilleans with significant school drop-out rates. Finally, the Law on Consultation with Minority Representative Organizations allows seven roof organizations evincing diverse ideational, religious, and political orientations to coordinate activities with responsible ministers. Dutch welfare organizations are not part of this structure; minorities have been mainstreamed into essential services, with an emphasis on "access and equity."

As in Germany, Dutch integration policy is essentially Big City policy: 60 percent of Turks and Moroccans, 70 percent of the Surinamese and Antillean residents are concentrated in the four largest cities: Amsterdam, Rotterdam, The Hague, and Utrecht. By 1997, there was even a minister for metropolitan and integration policy to assist over 287,000 Surinamese, 280,000 Turks, 233,000 Moroccans, and diverse refugees living among 15 million Dutch citizens;

17 percent of the population is foreign in origin.[19] Accounting for 22–25 percent of the urban residents, they constitute majorities in some districts, but housing policies ensure that no neighborhood consists of only "disadvantaged" groups.[20] There has been a trend in recent years toward the emergence of "black" versus "white" schools in certain neighborhoods, however.

Xenophobic violence is rare in the Netherlands, although the country was rocked by two sensational assassinations, anti-immigration candidate Pim Fortuyn (2002), and anti-Islamic filmmaker Theo van Gogh (2004). Dutch society is known for its extraordinary social tolerance, demonstrated by its "death-with-dignity" policies and drug legalization. In contrast to Germans, Dutch politicians have supported training programs for Imams in the Netherlands as a means of preventing zealous homeland imports. A similar type of tolerance nonetheless applies to organizations of a fundamentalist bent: "To have undemocratic ethnic organisations is better for the democratic process than to have no organisations at all," Fennema and Tillie contend. Even in organizations disposed toward fundamentalism, "people learn to solve the dilemmas inherent in collective action. Authoritarian organisations also create social capital at the individual as well as at the group level and this enables people to attain social goals that would be unattainable without a collective effort."[21] If they fail to do so, they either collapse, or split into new groups.

While Calvinist tradition suggests that work "keeps the moral and material differences among individuals to a minimum," labor-market participation neither guarantees social cohesion nor grants migrants their due, concentrated as they are in low-wage, unskilled sectors. The labor pool grew from 8.1 million to 10.5 million between 1970 and 1996; unemployment rose and part-time positions increased from 600,000 to 1.8 million from 1979 to 1983. Seventy-seven percent of those who lost jobs had below-average educations, 24 percent were of ethnic descent, and 32 percent were under age twenty-five.[22] An emergent stratum of ethnic working poor, added to resentment against "moochers," has triggered privatization of social services for the long-term unemployed (419,000 in 1996), added to cuts in disability benefits. Yet only 350,000 of 700,000 job openings went to the unemployed. One study concluded that employer/coworker discrimination is greatest among groups facing the worst unemployment: Moluccans and Surinamese possess the best language skills but occupy the bottom of the socioeconomic ladder, even with state subsidies, while Spaniards and Turks move to the top.[23] State "arrangements" like the Youth-Work Guarantee Jobs explained only 13 percent of job growth between 1990 and 1995. A mere eight thousand (2 percent) rose above the poverty line, of whom 20 percent saw improvements thanks to household changes. Ruben Gowricharn reports that "two out of five job-holders rise above the poverty line, one out of ten is still below the poverty line years later, and after some time, five out of ten are out of a job again."[24]

Even proactive integration policies can fall short, as Anja van Heelsum and Rinus Pennix show in the case of Amsterdam-Oost. Most dwellings were constructed between 1880 and 1900 just outside the city limits; renovated in the 1970s, they are now occupied by minorities, 21 percent of whom lacked work in 1997. Of forty-three thousand inhabitants, 46 percent belong to groups targeted by integration policies: Surinamese, Moroccans, Turks, and Southern Europeans.[25] In 1996, the District Administration set up an ambitious plan to create one thousand new jobs in three years, to increase minority presence in local administration, stimulate minority hiring and entrepreneurship, support migrant parents with extracurricular programs for youth, and to foster "active citizenship" and "loyalty to the local community" through consultation between ethnic organizations and district administrators. The outcomes differed significantly, as a function of the policy instruments available. Job creation was weak, insofar as authorities had to rely on actors required to cover all job seekers in an area extending beyond the district. Raising the share of administrators and public service workers "failed completely," lacking a legal basis for affirmative action. Contract compliance "remained a paper target," though twenty adolescents received police-supervised training as "neighborhood-watchers," leading to jobs as security workers. The department for economic affairs did not accord entrepreneurial initiatives priority status, with poor results.

Efforts to foster political participation produced mixed results, too. Oost formed a council of ethnic associations that met bimonthly, including four mosque groups. Public subsidies fostered mutual dependence between these organizations and district administrators, but the power balance was unequal, pitting less-educated volunteers against local professionals. Ethnic representatives learned to approach city officials, yet consultations were non-binding; they broadened their networks and roof organizations but criticized the way issues were prioritized. Many distrusted the "Dutch approach" to youth issues: Turkish and Moroccan leaders found toleration of marijuana use in one youth center "absurd," seeing the availability of drugs as a source of trouble. Still, Turks and Moroccans have been more willing to mobilize than Dutch-speaking Antilleans and Surinamese.

Drawing on a larger sample of ethnic associations, Fennema and Tillie register more social capital, greater direct participation, and higher levels of trust among Turkish residents, despite the deeper cultural/linguistic ties ascribed to post-colonials. Their research thus far suggests two indicators of effective political integration among diverse ethnic groups. The first centers on the nature/density of ties between ethnic associations and Dutch institutions; ethnic elites can only foster minority trust in host-country institutions by cooperating regularly with them, and communicating positive experiences back to their constituency. The second critical indicator is actual voter participation: "If they don't trust the institutions, they won't vote, and low trust is more harmful to democracy per se than low participation."[26]

Social capital is not a sufficient condition for collective integration; individuals may find acceptance ("pass") in the dominant culture without effecting a sustainable improvement in the conditions of those left behind. As a group resource, social capital derives from interorganizational ties "that come into being when one person serves simultaneously on the governing board of two or more ethnic organisations," resulting in interlocking directorates.[27] Although it is harder to sustain personal trust as the association grows larger, it becomes easier to institutionalize and transfer collective trust. Overlaps at the elite level enhance communication, allowing denser networks to serve as a proxy for trust invested in individuals: "the more links among organisations of a specific ethnic community, the higher the social trust in that community and the more likely that civic culture will develop." This civic-culture-within-the civic-culture leads to new channels of communication, more opportunities for joint action, and even an "early warning system against potential defectors."[28] Correspondingly, the broader the circle of actors engaged in extracting or returning favors, the more social capital is invested in the group. The community's social capital depends on the "connectivity" among leaders; several overlapping contacts among ethnic elites imply high integration: limited or linear (as opposed to webbed) contacts mean that an ethnic group is neither socially or politically integrated.[29]

Fennema and Tillie examined the interactions of eighty-nine ethnic associations registered with the Amsterdam Chamber of Commerce (signifying stability and professionalization); these entities focused on diverse purposes, e.g., religion, sports, business, academics, and youth activities. They developed a "civic community index" based on the principle of *connectivity* (i.e., the number of organizations plus the number in each "network" plus external contacts or relative isolation of specific organizations). Of the total, forty-one were not linked outside the community. The other forty-eight formed eight "nodes," the largest of which had twenty-nine components, the smallest only three. Neither the absolute number of associations nor their "financial strength" accurately capture the quantity or the quality of social capital available to the group. Antilleans, for example, had the most organizations per person (1:247, Surinam 1:770), but they operated in relative isolation; organizational density was high, but connectivity was quite weak. Moroccans were well organized, the biggest cluster consisting of eighteen associations, but their "string" networks do not lead to efficient communication.

The Turkish community was the ostensible "winner." Despite the fact that many of their associations were religious in nature, including two with extreme nationalist orientations, Turks display the highest levels of civic engagement. All associations cooperate regularly with at least one Dutch organization. Their connectivity is all the more striking insofar as the ex-colonials possess significantly higher educational levels, normally associated with political participation.[30] Turks are also more likely to be self-employed (12.2 percent in 1997), compared to Surinamese (5.4 percent), Antilleans (6.3 percent), and "other Mediterraneans" (7.9 percent).[31] Unlike most EU states, the Netherlands actively promotes entrepreneurship and contract compliance, based on its Law on the Stimulation of Labor Market Participation of Minorities. This raises the question as to whether Turkish networking stems from personal initiatives, deliberate mobilization strategies, or both. The authors conclude: "The network of interlocking directorates is the result of (conscious) organizational strategies. Turkish organizations not only reflect (Turkish) civic community they also build it by creating permanent institutionalized communication channels among organizations."[32]

Another query relates to the "flow of trust" from elites through the organizational network, particularly in the case of religious organizations emphasizing their "differences" from the host society. These researchers find that political trust can substitute for a lack of value consensus or "thin" systemic commitment: "If there are no shared values the role of communication networks becomes more important. And since these communication networks in a multicultural society tend to be fragmented, the role of interlocking directorates that form bridges between the different subnetworks become crucial for the building of social trust."[33]

Political trust increases from the bottom up when members can rely on leaders to represent their collective memories as well as their material interests. Leaders are then able to channel trust and commitment accumulated through associational networks "upward" to political institutions. The Dutch case shows that ethnic engagement and host-country integration are complementary, not competing modes of political incorporation. Ethnic groups need not give up their cultural identities in order to find their space within and among host institutions. A majority in the Netherlands (51 percent) utilize Turkish-language media, but they also read Dutch newspapers more often than other minorities, and are only slightly less interested in local issues (84 percent) than the natives (90 percent)—to a degree not explained by age, education, or other variables. In short, "The more an ethnic group is engaged in its own community's affairs, the more it participates in local politics and the more it trusts the political *institutions*. . . . Civic (ethnic) community creates political participation and political trust."[34]

Turkish residents also register higher voter turn-out, as a comparison of municipal elections shows. The 1994 and 1998 elections triggered significant variations in voter participation among ethnic groups (for reasons not understood): still, Turks had the highest turnout, 67 percent in 1994 and 39 percent in 1998, ahead of Moroccans (49 percent, later 23 percent), followed by Surinamese and Antilleans (30 percent, then 21 percent).[35] Turkish voters (64 percent) exhibited greater trust in parties and institutions than the Dutch themselves (59 percent), while Surinamese (39 percent) and Antilleans (25 percent) who share the language and some history, like German *Aussiedler*, were least trusting.[36] Participation and trust correlate with the "degree of civic community" reflected in the structure of interlocking directorates and associational nodes.

This only partly answers another chicken/egg question: Do democratic structures in Amsterdam work better for Turks, or do Turks work harder to take advantage of formal democratic opportunities? Migration-related variables like language skills or years in residence do not explain different rates of participation, nor does ethnicity explain differences in trust or participation among Turks in the Netherlands, Sweden, Germany, and Denmark. State and local governments clearly have the power to build civic community by opening up the political opportunity structure at the urban level. The key to integration lies in multicultural democracy, "where ethnic minorities participate in the democratic process, thus providing the political elite with reliable information about the political preferences of the migrant population and the democratic institutions with popular legitimacy among the minority groups."[37]

Britain, Sweden, and Denmark

Although neo-liberal Britain relies on less restrictive naturalization requirements than Germany, it still has a long way to go in securing a parliamentary profile reflecting its multicultural makeup. The United Kingdom defines minorities in terms of race rather than ethnicity/nationality, leading to other representational dilemmas. Persons from former colonial territories may vote as British or Commonwealth citizens. The 2001 census reported that 4.6 million (7.9 percent) of its 60 million residents are foreign born. Heavily concentrated in certain regions, they enjoy a degree of political significance not seen in the Netherlands. Nearly half (45 percent) are concentrated in London: 78 percent of its Black Africans, 61 percent of Black Caribbeans, and 56 percent of the Bangladeshis (2001 UK census figures). Together they comprise 29 percent of its population, exceeding Turkish or minority concentrations in German cities.[38] Another 13 percent dwell in the Midlands. Neighborhood density compounds problems of economic disadvantage and social exclusion. In this case, ethnic enclaves are more likely to turn into ghettos than into thriving enterprise zones, since existing social capital does not transcend community boundaries. As Giles Barrett, Trevor Jones and, David McEnvoy show, British cities housing large migrant populations are subject to "severely constrained entrepreneurialism," blocking the economic route to social integration.[39] The British Nationality Act of 1981 cut off an automatic right to citizenship for nationals from former territories.

Three delegates of Indian descent entered the House of Commons in 1892, 1895, and 1922, respectively, as did one woman of Southeast-Asian descent in 1910; another became mayor in 1934. By 1991, 78 constituencies were more than 15-percent ethnic, 25 of which had concentrations of over 30 percent. One hundred of 10,500 local election wards were home to 43 percent of all minority groups.[40] Despite their potential ability to determine ward outcomes, voter registration has been quite low dating back to the 1970s; nearly 25 percent do not take the first step, although the share claiming to vote is higher. Two advocacy groups initiated a campaign, "Operation Black Vote," in 1996, but results were negligible as of 1998; two-thirds of the Asians in six concentrated wards cast a ballot in the 1997 general elections.[41] Insecure residency status, racial harassment, language deficits, fear of identification for other purposes, and general alienation are the common reasons given. Authorities switched to a "rolling register," adding throughout the year, still not reaching targeted groups. Asian turnout exceeds African or Caribbean figures, but there are also substantial differences among Indians, Pakistanis, and Bangladeshis.

UK residents (98 percent ethnics, 91 percent whites) feel that minorities should be encouraged to vote, that equal opportunity is good for integration, and that minorities deserve representation at all levels. The major parties seem committed to diversity but integration is just not happening. The Liberal Party established a now defunct Community Relations Panel in the 1970s, followed by an association of Asian Liberal Democrats, then Ethnic Minority Liberal Democrats. The Labour Party established a Race and Action Group in 1975, but a proposal for Black Sections was rejected in the 1980s. The Anglo-Asian Conservative Society initiated thirty local branches, later replaced by a One Nation Forum. There is even an association serving Asians for Scottish Independence![42] Still, eighteen to thirty-four year olds were less likely to vote than older cohorts in the 1990s. The number of minority candidates in the 1997 elections ranged from nine to eighteen for the three main parties (forty total), seventeen more than in 1992; only nine were elected, all representing Labour. The share of minority councillors in London boroughs rose from 4.1 percent to 11.3 percent from 1982 to 1998.[43]

One explanation lies in British race classifications.[44] Individuals are protected against discrimination in terms of education, employment, etc., but few channels exist for autonomous group mobilization. Political trust is assumed rather than cultivated with regard to all other identity dimensions. The major parties agreed not to "play the race card," drawing on the Commission for Racial Equality's Compact on Free Speech and Race Relations in a Democratic Society (1997). Claims-making is nonetheless forced into a race framework, at the expense of other needs that might be more critical for groups whose identities fall outside the mainstream, e.g., religion. As Ruud Koopmans et al. show, "race relations policies seem to have served the middle class elites from ethnic minorities, whereas the costs appear to have been disproportionately borne by one set of minorities, Pakistani and Bangladeshi Muslims."[45] It is strange to expect Hindus of Indian origin and Muslims of Pakistani descent to coalesce politically in the UK, given their histories of armed struggle in the homeland. France's insistence on laicism/secularity likewise denies all Muslims the "right to difference." Citizenship regimes matter, but so do the particular participatory structures open to disparate groups. The universalist, one-size-fits-all approach does not work for human beings who obviously come in lots of different colors, shapes, and weights.

The Swedish government welcomed foreigners with the promise of "multi-cultural group rights" coupled with political rights in the 1970s but changed its position by the late 1980s. Between 1970 and 1995, its foreign population swelled by four-hundred thousand (5 percent).[46] It adopted more restrictive international practices, required by its EU entry in 1995. Sweden's generosity, embedded in a cradle-to-grave welfare model, provided equal opportunities for ethnic minorities but only by way of corporatist channels.[47] The state formulated its immigrant and minority policy goals in 1975: It was "prepared to receive and educate" newcomers based on the principles of equality, freedom of choice and partnership. This meant ensuring comparable living standards, allowing them to preserve their own language, cultural identity and homeland contacts, even if Swedes, at the time, viewed their foreign-ness "as some sort of congenital indiscretion—a kind of psychic social disease that by rights should embarrass anyone afflicted with it into lying low until the symptoms have disappeared."[48] Immigrant organizations would serve as the primary vehicle for well-defined, non-stigmatized minority-state relations, affording interest representation and participation in advisory and decision-making bodies: there are explicit policies for treating "collective interests." Liberal naturalization rules (five years in residence) were also deemed crucial to successful integration. Denizens who keep their citizenship still enjoy access to welfare benefits and local suffrage.

Initially similar to the Netherlands, Sweden recognized group rights through corporatist structures but now questions its own faith in central planning and public responsibility. Parliament "clarified and reassessed" its position in 1986, deciding that (largely Third World) migrants would not share a constitutional entitlement to group rights granted to one national minority, the Saami (Lapps). The number of asylum seekers increased tenfold, from three to thirty thousand during the 1980s, rising to eighty-four thousand in 1992 during the Yugoslav crisis. Sweden took the symbolic step of turning its minister for immigration into a minister for integration in the 1990s, as thirty to fifty thousand sought entry each year. In 1995, migration ceased to be a purely domestic affair due to EU membership, as refugees came to outnumber labor migrants. Naturalization remains a relatively "quick and easy" process, and rates are high for Europe. Over half (54 percent) of its 940,000 foreign-born residents were Swedish citizens as of 1997; they now make up 11 percent of the population.[49]

New guidelines restricted opportunities for cultural preservation to customs that did not "clash" with Swedish law. Current policy insists that new arrivals be willing to adapt. Those who lack education and language skills challenge fundamental premises of its active labor-market policy, focusing on training and quick reinsertion into the workforce. The state has jettisoned the "cultural rights" framework, recognizing that a socially segregated labor market generates serious wage differentials, and an underclass divided along ethnocultural lines. Accentuating divergent (deviant?) values purportedly makes integration harder to achieve.[50] The emphasis has shifted from "freedom of choice" to personal responsibility: newcomers must acquire all of the tools that enable them to manage on their own. The dramatic rise in joblessness poses the greatest threat to active citizenship, since individualization has weakened state protections for stratified minorities.

Sweden has seen deterioration in the link between economic and social integration, however; by 1996, over 30 percent of its non-Nordic inhabitants were unemployed, compared to 7.3 percent among the natives. Second generation migrants face greater risks, due to structural changes and workplace discrimination. Despite their privileged access to participatory rights, migrant electoral turnout fell from 60 percent in 1976, to 40 percent in 1994 (84 percent among Swedes).[51] Comprising a tenth of the population, foreign-born residents account for 4–5 percent of the local/county council representatives; voting districts do not benefit from neighborhood concentrations, in contrast to Denmark. Sweden introduced some preference voting in 1998 but retained its 5 percent clause. Existing ethnic associations focus more on sports and culture than on interest representation for linguistic or educational demands. Maritta Soininen holds that a system specifically designed to regulate conflicts between capital and labor provides little space for mediating conflicts among "special" (read: cultural) interests.[52] While recognizing that they live in "an unavoidably multicultural society," politicians stress the need to "express basic views of Swedish society on a number of issues of principle" and to "preserve the Swedish cultural heritage," sounding like Germans who insist on the *Leitkultur*.[53]

Lise Togeby shows that local structures also matter in fostering political incorporation among ethnic minorities in Denmark.[54] Although Sweden tries harder to channel information to potential voters in their native tongue, electoral participation has declined, while migrant turnout in Denmark ranks highest in Europe because the rules offer positive incentives. The trick is to persuade incoming groups that they can "contribute" irrespective of personal resources. Denmark's foreign population more than doubled between 1975 and 1997, from 93,931 to 237,695, representing 4.5 percent of all residents. Of its 382,230 naturalized residents, over 77,000 were born in the host country; 40 percent of all non-nationals are under age twenty-five.[55] Naturalization requires seven years of legal residence; dual nationality is not accepted. Over half live in Copenhagen, accounting for more than 15 percent in certain districts. A few local councils have tried to restrict their access to "non-profit" housing.

The 1997 elections attest to active participation among Turkish and Lebanese groups in Arhus and Copenhagen. Togeby attributes the surprisingly high turn-out to the fact that "certain groups in certain cities" engage in local mobiliza-tion: the political opportunity structure in Denmark nurtures collective action. Data from the Danish Board for Ethnic Equality reveal differences between the two cities (61 percent for all ethnicities in Copenhagen, 71 percent in Arhus), as well as among ethnic groups (61 percent for Pakistanis, 25 percent for Leba-nese, a low 20 percent for Tunesians in the former; 73 percent among Turks and Pakistanis, 44 percent for Lebanese, 43 percent for Vietnamese and Iraqis in the latter).[56] Multivariate analysis of Turkish and Lebanese voting yielded mod-est gender differences: Female participation is shaped by cultural integration, individual emancipation, and collective mobilization, while male turnout only correlates with collective mobilization.[57] The lowest rates are found among non-naturalized Lebanese in Copenhagen, the highest among Arhus Lebanese living in the ethnically concentrated district of Gellerup.

Young Turkish women vote at higher rates than young men, while older women evince low rates of participation. The smallest turnout among Turks is found in Copenhagen in areas with little ethnic density; residential concentra-tion enhances Turkish voting in both cities, while a lack of citizenship only matters in Copenhagen. Togeby notes the salience of local elections (more issues are decided at this level) and certain features of the electoral system, e.g., pref-erential voting, proportional representation, and "personal votes." The last seat secured by Social Democrats in Arhus in 1993, for example, required only 426 votes, out of 67,021 cast for the party. Ethnics understand that the odds are in their favor: collective action can propel lower-ranked candidates to the top of the ballot.[58] Turks were elected on SD lists in both cities in 1997.[59] Active politi-cal participation thus derives from double integration. Here, too, migrants and refugees "integrate more easily in their new country if they are well integrated in their own ethnic group." Indicators of double integration include membership in ethnic associations, ethnic neighborhood density, and length of residence: "Living in an ethnic community over a long time . . . will increase chances of double integration and, consequently, also the chances of collective mobiliza-tion in relation to local elections. A weak relation between individual resources and voter turnout will also be interpreted as a sign of strong collective mobiliza-tion, if it is combined with a high voter turn-out."[60]

Despite these indicators of effective incorporation, Denmark has more recently adopted one of the toughest immigration laws in the EU. The anti-migration Danish People's Party secured 22 of 179 seats in Parliament in 2001. Allegedly 98 percent of the Turkish residents have imported spouses from the old country, leading Denmark to refuse residency rights even to indigenous Danes who marry non-nationals! Many binational couples are commuting between Copenhagen and Malmo.[61] The 2005–2006 cartoon scandal (depicting ostensibly blasphemous images of Muhammed) suggests that the populist state is again out of touch with its Muslim residents.

Chapter 5 highlighted the role of mixed embeddedness in shaping day-to-day strategies for ethnic economic integration; it is just as crucial in fostering political integration. Members of the same ethnic group organize, mobilize, and participate in divergent ways across national boundaries, due to formal-institutional *and* informal-discursive differences in the opportunity structure marking each state. In 2001, minority representation in national parliaments ranged from zero in France, to 1.8 percent in Britain, 6 percent in Belgium, and 7.3 percent in the Netherlands. Different degrees of systemic openness not only determine whether or not minorities' material needs will be met but also preordain their chances for political identification with the host state. Further cross-national studies confirm that "extensions of individual [citizenship] rights to immigrants indeed seem to have a positive and linear effect on the presence of immigrants in the public debate. On the group rights dimension, however, we seem to be dealing with a curvilinear effect, in which up to a certain level the acceptance of cultural difference and the granting of group rights strengthens the involvement of immigrants in the political process of their countries of residence. When cultural differences are emphasized too strongly . . . the effect may be that migrant communities turn inward and that their identities and activities are channeled away from the public sphere."[62]

Migrant cultures undergo as much evolution and adaptation as the host cultures in which they are embedded. Even well-intentioned efforts to integrate them by reducing their identities to a core variable like race or religion forces individuals to over-identify themselves with one trait, at the expense of many others, in order to access rights. This neither allows for blended identities nor personal choice, much less social cohesion. I disagree with Yasemin Nuhoglu Soysal's assertion that persons of migrant background enjoy substantial post-national rights nearly equivalent to real citizenship.[63] Many of the welfare/economic rights she stresses have been cut or eliminated since 1990. I do agree that foreigners organize themselves in accordance with the institutional models they encounter in the host country. The Sinti, for example, have been much more successful than Roma in securing Holocaust compensation in Germany: the former copied the Jewish Claims model, the latter did not.[64] Koopmans and Paul Statham show that "while it is true that obtaining the formal nationality does not directly confer many social, cultural or anti-discrimination rights, our data strongly suggest that the symbolic inclusion of immigrants through conferring citizenship creates important opportunities for claims-making on such rights."[65] Germany and Switzerland have proved especially resistant to such claims yet persist in blaming the victims for not integrating themselves.

Do-It-Yourself Political Mobilization

A lack of formal participatory rights can lead to alienation, distrust, withdrawal, and even re-ethnicization directed against the host society. Germans are not alone in realizing since 2001 that what they don't know about alienated aliens—that Al-Qaeda cells operated out of Hamburg—can literally kill them. I do not argue that disenfranchised foreigners automatically turn to terrorism, but governments do need to communicate effectively with ethnic leaders who can monitor trouble spots in their own communities. Opportunity denied over a long period evokes more political apathy than active engagement among ethnic residents. To put it bluntly: Why should successful entrepreneurs like the Saris want to vote as Germans, once they have made it on their own?

Tired of waiting for politicians to "get it," Barbara John initiated her own public-education campaign with publications on nationalities that call Berlin home.[66] John reported that only 6 of 188 UN member states are not represented among the capital's regular residents (excluding diplomats): Belize and five Pacific island nations.[67] Residents have access to "multiculti" educational materials, seminars, and legal guidelines in many languages. The city's annual Carnival of Cultures attracts prominent politicians, hundreds of participants, and thousands of viewers along a five-hour parade route each Spring.

Enfranchisement of foreigners does not mean that conflicts won't arise, only that problems won't be defined in immutable cultural terms but recognized for what they really are: occasionally clashing material needs and interests. Ethnic associations enhance democracy by allowing communities to escape the tutelage status ascribed to them by the majority society. Surveys from Berlin and North Rhine-Westphalia show that a little encouragement goes a long way in fostering ethnic mobilization *and* self-incorporation, especially among German Turks: only 15 percent turn to ethnic organizations to solve local problems, most appeal to public agencies.[68] Ethnic elites are converting weaknesses into strengths through "dialectical thinking."

Jürgen Fijalkowski and Helmut Gillmeister examined the role of self-organization in fostering the integration of heterogeneous groups in Berlin in the mid 1990s. Integration profiles differ among migrant groups; back then problems were mounting in relation to Poles, Turks, Vietnamese, and Russian-Germans, less so among Italians, Yugoslavs, and Spaniards. Rather than attribute this to cultural traits, the authors see differences in legal-qua-residency status shaping the degree of acceptance each finds in German society. All associations stressed ethno-solidarity but were only "generally appreciated" for their ability to resolve migration-related problems.

The researchers discovered big differences regarding a willingness to join associations, as well as in their functions. Turkish organizations were most likely to pursue political interests. Membership had an instrumental function for

Poles: once the latter master personal problems of "settling in," they lose interest in associational life. Ethnic organization held little meaning for Italians.[69] Yugoslavs looked mostly for cultural enrichment. Engaging in ethnocultural activities allows migrants to redirect cultural capital that remains undervalued and underutilized in the dominant culture. Activists take advantage of external chances for interaction without giving up their group-internal orientations. Multiple anchoring points allow these organizations to serve as a conduit for host-society engagement.

What gives these associations their political character is a combination of goals, viz., affirming ethnocultural commonalities *and* attempting to solve individual problems, while recognizing that the latter are linked to structural problems in society.[70] The higher the schooling, the greater the political interest found among migrants: 76 percent of the better educated follow German politics, versus 3 percent of those with low certification. Gender differences also emerge: politically organized men tend toward the SPD; favoring Alternative List/Greens, women care more about host-country than homeland politics.[71] Italians are the least political, aside from *Aussiedler*, though their EU citizenship means they *could* vote in some elections. While Italians face no "pressing problems" with xenophobia, Turks were deeply shaken by arson deaths in Mölln and Solingen; 44 percent felt these events required an official German response, but 72 percent held that ethnic organizations also needed to mobilize, ranging from 12 percent among Italians, to 76 percent among Vietnamese.[72] Yugoslavs were most interested in homeland affairs; many have since returned.

Turkish associations evince above-average activism, even if regular members display below-average degrees of mobilization. This may owe to the fact that Turkish elites are seen as "very representative," capable of realistically portraying member problems to local authorities. There is no substitution effect between internal affinities and external engagement; the relationship is cumulative, insofar as ethnic traditions and host-society ties build on one another in intercultural and ethnopolitical ways. I attribute this to John's active outreach efforts vis-à-vis the Turkish community across two decades. One Turkish leader declared: "Under integration we naturally understand that this society accepts us as we are, instead of demanding from us that we become Germanized."[73] Ethnic and religious differences *within* the community complicate the picture however, polarizing Turks while, at the same time, politicizing their differences. Homogeneous Poles, by contrast, appear to be "active assimilationists." Despite comparable forms of internal fragmentation (Catholic/communist, northern/southern), Italian organizations hold tightly to traditional family ties; rarely interested in mixing, they are less likely to engage politically, and thus, are less effective.

Ethnic groups seemed evenly divided in terms of participatory venues; 38 percent preferred to ally themselves with political parties, 39 percent with

Foreigners' Councils, and 38 percent sought alliances with other foreigners; 60 percent are active in their own associations.[74] Commissioner John indicated to me that Berlin's Ausländer Beiräte were not influential, in contrast to Frankfurt/Main. Filiakowski and Gillmeister conclude that ethnic organizations succeed better than all of the rest in working out problems that impede equal opportunity in Berlin. German associations see their engagement with foreigners as a secondary activity, usually linked to "social work." Ethnic elites criticize systemic constraints, as well as the limited acceptance their activities garner, despite perceived self-exploitation: "For doing what we have to accomplish here with three full-time employees and volunteer activity, a German organization would have at least twenty employees."[75]

Thus the primary function of ethnic self-organization among Berliners of migrant origin is not to minimize or intensify conflicts in relation to the host society, but rather to channel compatriots into the problem-processing institutions of the surrounding society. Fijalkowski and Gillmeister show that rather than acting as "segregation-traps," ethno-specific organizations become "positioning instruments," like a compass, that aid foreigners in maneuvering through complex national institutions: "There is no recognizable connection between resonance in ethnic associational life and ethnic segregation. On the contrary: proximity to these associations goes hand in hand with better social networking, higher capacity for problem solving, improved access to public-political life in the host society, developing away from associations fixated on the homeland, intent on preserving ethnic identities into innovative and cooperative agents of a multicultural civil society."[76] Ethnic associations are at the greatest risk of transforming themselves from feeder channels into segregation traps in cases where official policies block their incorporation into the larger system of interest representation. Blocked mobility induces ethnic elites to use their rejected cultural capital to mobilize their own clienteles, leading to greater distrust of the system.

Activist Faces in Intercultural Spaces

One participant-observer of new intercultural activist trends in Berlin is Ertekin Özcan (born 1946), interviewed in June 2002. Dr. Özcan understands the theoretical linkages between ethnic associations and societal integration. He also values the practical aspects of bridge building, as the executive director of the Federation of Turkish Parent Organizations. A part-time poet and practicing lawyer, Özcan arrived in Berlin in 1973. From 1977 to 1985, he taught at various *Fachhochschulen*, then pursued doctoral studies in political science at the Free University. His 1988 dissertation under Fijalkowski focused on the changing character of immigrant organizations.

From the first Turkish Student Federation and Turkish Workers' Association of the early 1960s through the rise of partisan and religious groups, he documented increasing organizational specialization and professionalization, as well as the emerging host-country orientation through the 1980s. By 1987, 4.5 million foreigners were aligning themselves with more than 3,000 party-political, cultural, and social-service associations; sports clubs; youth and recreational groups; and parental, women's, business, and professional organizations—evincing higher levels of group engagement than found among Germans at the time.[77]

Rather than examine his macro findings, let us consider Özcan's participant observations with respect to the Federation of Turkish Parent Organizations. Its organizational history embodies a critical shift in focus from homeland politics to the host-country needs of settlers. Structural changes of the early 1980s eliminated half a million migrant jobs and placed new restrictions on family admissions from non-EC states. Authorities sought to enroll foreign children in schools and training programs without alienating them from homeland cultures. Nothing was done to create an adequate supply of preschools, however, much less to counter residential segregation or help teachers cope with classroom language gaps. Over half dropped out of school without certification, although 90 percent of one million children had been born/raised in Germany.

The Turkish Parents Organization in West Berlin (TEV-Berlin) grew out of six months of discussion regarding problems with local schools and officials in November 1985. Twenty non-partisan parent groups formed a national federation in 1995, rising to sixty branches in eight states (four thousand members) by 1998–1999.[78] A registered *Land*-level association committed to "advancing the common good," the TEV is open to all, but only parents of school-age children enjoy voting rights; they pay dues of €2.50 per month. The Executive Committee consists of five to seven full and three substitute members, chosen for one year by the member assembly; most EC members stem from the second generation. Each district has its own "initiative," speaker, and delegate council. Separate working groups focus on nursery, pre-, and elementary schools; special-ed, college-prep, and vocational schools; and native-tongue and religious instruction. Its leaders cultivate ties with German parents, German and Turkish Teachers Unions, the TBB, the Turkish Community (TG), and state officials. The TEV does not aim to build its own institutions, in contrast to separate schools under the Greek community. Like its forerunner, the Spanish Parents Association (1973), its main charge is to aid Turkish parents in mastering day-to-day educational challenges.

Children in ethnically concentrated neighborhoods (Kreuzberg, Neukölln, Schöneberg, Beussel Kiez, Hamburg-Veddel) lack German skills. The TEV received its first subsidy in 1987, to focus on the educational role of mothers. It now manages a bilingual daycare center (*Kleiner Frosch*) for thirty-five children age 2–6, but the demand is greater than the supply. It offers regular counseling sessions for seven hundred parents per year, as well as literacy classes for women. Teachers evincing intercultural competence are a scarce commodity in kindergartens, schools, psychological services, and juvenile centers; older pupils from working-class families need homework help and after-school tutoring. After a ten-year pilot project, TEV helped to open eight schools (grades first through sixth) in four districts, offering bilingual education. Its biggest problem remains a lack of formal training places for bilingual teachers.

The challenges facing Turkish pupils are "unfortunately still the same ones," after twenty years of TEV mobilization. In 1999, fifty-four thousand non-German children were enrolled in Berlin schools. The city no longer organizes special classes for Turkish youth. Neighborhood concentration rates of up to 90 percent produce the same effect; 38 percent of the special-ed pupils in Neukölln are Turkish. In 1999, 28 percent quit school without certification, 11 percent with only a *Hauptschulabschluss*; merely 8 percent were eligible for tertiary education (34 percent among German pupils). The Mete Eksi Prize (DM 5000), awarded to youth groups fostering tolerance, reflects experiences with xenophobic violence: it honors a nineteen-year-old youth volunteer, born and naturalized in Berlin, who died comatose after being attacked by bat-wielding neo-Nazis in 1991.

Turkish has yet to be recognized as an alternative foreign language requirement for advancing to the next grade, though nine schools offered it as an elective by 2001. When the CDU government tried to eliminate bilingual education in Schöneberg, the TEV mobilized five thousand signatures in 1992. Studies show that command of the mother-tongue facilitates second-language learning. Parents want German-language Islamic instruction put on par with Judeo-Christian lessons and modules on the home culture brought into social science curriculum, "from kindergarten to the onset of college." Özcan feels that the presence of two men and three women of migrant origin in the Berlin Assembly has made a difference. Özcan Mutlu, a TEV member and Green delegate elected in 1999, worked for several years to establish the Europa Schools that offer bilingual/immersion education to Germans and minorities in nine partner languages: English, Turkish, French, Russian, Spanish, Italian, Portuguese, Greek, and Polish.

As one neighborhood integration commissioner observes: "It's the Turkish Parents Organization that I perceive above all as a highly competent supporter. It undertakes tasks that no one in the district would otherwise take on, not one other association."[79] Many adults who first joined the TEV have moved on to head other interest groups, such as the TBB and the TG. Its non-partisan roof organization, the FOETED, sponsors practitioner conferences, builds professional bridges across state lines, and supports educational initiatives that benefit other children of non-German background. In short, the Turkish Parent's Organization affords the same kind of mobilizational training and social-capital formation that Putnam attributes to PTOs across the United States.

Another TEV activist is Kenan Kolat, director of the TBB. Born in Istanbul in 1959, Kolat moved to Germany in 1981 to study marine technology at the Technical University of Berlin, after four years of study at the TU-Istanbul. Between 1986 and 1990, he worked as a professional social counselor dealing with immigration assistance and the needs of Turkish parents. His volunteer services included board-member positions in the sports club Turkspor (he is partial to volleyball), the Turkish Cultural Association (though he hates folk music), the Turkish Science and Technology Center (BTBTM), and Project Gangway (street workers aiding troubled teens). He helped to establish the TBB, becoming its executive director in 1991. A naturalized citizen since 1994, Kolat further served as federal director of the Turkish Student Association from 1996 to 2000, and as a board member of another national roof organization, the Turkish Community, since 1996. Our interview took place on 12 July 2002.

Emerging out of the Turkish Union in Berlin-West (1983), the TBB was established as a self-help organization in 1991; officially non-partisan, it did absorb a number of SPD organizations. Its delegate assembly, drawn from twenty-one member organizations representing 5,000 members, installed a new executive board in 2001, comprised of four men and three women. It has twenty-eight paid employees on limited contracts, drawing on state funds. The organization "engages in German politics, not Turkish politics." The latter would prove too divisive, given differences between Turks and Kurds in Berlin.

The TBB sees itself as an interest representative for all Berlin-Turks who seek communication with public officials; "peaceful coexistence" among minorities; inclusive immigration, citizenship, and integration policies; and improved labor-market opportunities. It calls for communal voting rights, unrestricted work/residency permits, family protection, and labor-market reform. It has lobbied for an anti-discrimination law, finally introduced in December 2004, and supports EU membership for Turkey. Receiving about €50,000 in city/state and federal subsidies, it sponsors mini-integration courses and directs projects on youth training and labor-market reinsertion. The share of service workers rose from 59 percent to 69.7 percent over the last decade, combined with 44.7 percent unemployment among Turks: "They belong, by a long shot, to the losers of structural change."[80]

Kolat believes in building associational ties in three domains: with Turkish groups, with other ethnic minorities, and within the SPD. The TBB cultivates relations with the TG (two hundred member organizations), the Turkish-German Entrepreneurs (TDU), and the Friedrich Ebert, Rosa Luxemburg and Heinrich Böll Foundations, along with local labor offices. The TBB objected to many passages in the Citizenship Law as too restrictive, e.g., shifting from "simple" language comprehension to "sufficient language competence" tests; these changes "deformed rather than reformed" conditions for older guest-workers. He welcomes Berlin's efforts to harmonize naturalization criteria across district boundaries. Recognizing that 65 percent among millions of non-nationals within EU boundaries are denied §8 Maastricht Treaty rights, the TBB urges minorities to put more effort into language acquisition and ensure that their religious observances are commensurate with constitutional law.

This association advocates an "equal treatment/equal access" approach to integration. This extends to gender relations, though its attempt to engage women from within (Women's Political Forum), together with the Turkish Women's Association (TFB), have fallen flat.[81] The executive director's wife, Dilek Kolat (another TEV member), was elected to the Berlin Assembly (SPD) in 2001, after serving in Schöneberg's city council for four years; Baba Evrim and Sayan Gyasettin are Assembly members for the PDS. The TBB's equality demands include gay and lesbian rights, having cooperated in the last few years with Gays & Lesbians from Turkey: Berlin-Brandenburg (Gladt-BB e.V.).

The TBB has clashed head-on in court with the Islamic Federation of Berlin (IFB); the former supports classroom instruction about Islam, focusing on ethics and shared values in a multicultural society. The ultra-conservative IFB won the right to "instruct" in public schools, spearheaded by its 3,000-member strong Milli Görüs group that expressly advocates government by Sharia. In 1998, the Superior Administrative Court yielded to the fundamentalist community, a byproduct of political resistance to *any* regular (thus regulated) Islamic instruction in schools across two decades. The TBB accuses the IFB of pursuing anti-democratic goals in Germany, in hopes of toppling the "secularist" regime in Turkey.

The Association of Turkish-German Entrepreneurs (TDU) also provides a springboard for community activism, reinforcing the crucial role of interlocking directorates. I interviewed Executive Director Bahattin Kaya in June 2002. Born in 1958, he also came to study industrial economics in Berlin but decided in 1985 to create a major travel agency, followed by his own insurance company. He established the Union of Turkish Travel Agencies (BETÜSAB), having previously served as a TBB speaker. TDU member biographies show that Berlin's most successful ethnic elites stem from the One-and-a-Half Generation. They came for university training in the 1970s, equipped with human and social capital now being channeled into formal networks. Founded by twenty-eight business owners in 1996, the TDU had 150 members in 2004; 10 percent are German—less than a tenth are women. Its purpose is to link and assist 5,800 small- and medium-size businesses that have supplied 24,000 jobs and generated €3.5 billion in sales.[82]

An NRW study of migrant organizations further confirms the presence of the interorganizational linkages Fennema and Tillie deem necessary for internalizing democracy and building civil society. Only 26 (7.8 percent) of 335 Turkish and Kurdish organizations surveyed in 1999 cited contacts with political parties in their country of origin; 112 (33 percent) maintained relations with German political parties.[83] Most are clientele-focused or issue-specific groups;

50 percent were formed between 1989 and 1992. Nearly all (97 percent) open themselves to public scrutiny as officially registered entities; 84 percent enjoy non–profit status, 66 percent have joined roof organizations. Many are connected to large German federations, e.g., the Parity Welfare Association and Worker's Welfare. Over half (55 percent) claim 100 members, 42 percent fall between 101 and 250, nearly 10 percent report from 251 to 500 members; 97 percent support themselves with dues, 88 percent with contributions, only 18 percent by "other means." Most cooperate with other migrant organizations, while 71 percent pursue ties with communal administrative offices or city governments. A surprising 85 percent have no contact with Foreigners' Councils; they prefer to vest their scarce resources interacting with bodies enjoying real decision-making power.[84]

The Polish case evinces a curious disconnect between organizational connectivity and individual engagement. There are over twenty-five cultural and professional organizations in Berlin alone, including the Association of Polish Parachuters, the Club of Catholic Intelligentsia, the German-Polish Lawyers Guild, the Club of Polish Trades and Industrialists, and even a Union of Polish Flops and Refusniks. Like ex-colonial groups in the Netherlands, these organizations lack effective networking by way of multi-tasking elites.

One Polish community mobilizer is Jan Cyankiewicz, interviewed on 23 July 2002. His family was forcefully expelled from Lemberg after World War II, but most of its negative experiences came at the hands of Russians, not Germans. Originally trained as a mechanical engineer, Cyankiewicz was coincidentally visiting Germany as a journalist when martial law was imposed in Poland in 1980; he decided to stay, and was accorded "tolerated" status as a refugee. He was required to live off welfare benefits for three years, despite three formal job offers, until "a Berlin bureaucrat made a mistake," allowing him as the only one of twelve thousand Polish applicants to start his own company. After more than twenty years in Germany, he remains a Polish citizen; his son has undergone naturalization, his daughter has not.

"Socially motivated," Cyankiewicz was a founding member of the Polish Social Council (PSR) that grew out of an initiative by the Committee to Defend Solidarity in 1982. Focusing on the day-to-day problems of new arrivals, the *Sozialrat* draws four thousand visitors per year, including *Aussiedler*, asylum seekers, seasonal/contract workers, tourists, and undocumented laborers. It sees itself as working against persistent stereotypes of Poles as cigarette smugglers and auto thieves, at the same time it tries to defend the interests of Eastern workers. Cyankiewicz engaged in volunteer work early on, playing "pacifier and sheriff" with regard to local conflicts. When he turned fifty-five in 1997, his firm went bankrupt; jobless, he signed on with an Austrian employer who fraudulently withheld the wages of all Polish workers. He initiated a lawsuit against the company, but the fact that he was broke led him to accept an ABM (subsidized job creation) post at the Council after volunteering for six months. For three years he directed one of its major offshoot projects, ZAPO (Central Integrated Contact-point for Commuting Migrants from Eastern Europe).

According to Cyankiewicz, temporary migrants cheated out of their pay by subcontractors are sooner the rule than the exception; human trafficking has also assumed epidemic proportions. ZAPO was created in 1997 to assist those "who cannot get regular residency status in Berlin or perhaps don't want any," who nevertheless need help with housing or work. Its pilot project "to legalize the illegals . . . who don't understand anything about this country" has thus far been rejected by local authorities. His own position expired in 2004; he is now a "business consultant."

The parent organization pursues broader social-work and cross-cultural agendas. Supported by the commissioner for foreigners inter alia, it received DM 1 million in 2002 to cover operating costs and a staff of ten; it also relies on a formal internship program. The PSR organizes youth exchanges, the largest encompassing a joint excursion of three hundred Berlin and Polish teens to Riesengebirge/Jelenia Gora in summer 1996. It raised DM 161 million following the catastrophic flood along the Oder River in 1997. Publishing a settlers' handbook, *Good Advice for Poles in Berlin*, in 1995, it has developed projects for the elderly, young girls, and a women's group (A Polonia). The PSR sponsored open-air festivals featuring alternative culture, e.g., the Warsaw-Berlin-2-Step (1992, 1993); it also runs non-commercial group tours to Poland.

The Polish Social Council is a member of the national roof organization for Parity Welfare Organizations, the Union of Polish Councils, and holds a seat in the Council of Ethnic Minorities in Berlin-Brandenburg. Its staff interacts regularly with officials from the Federal Agency for Labor, the Berlin Ministry for Social Affairs, the Commissioner for Integration, the Berlin Ministries for Youth and Family, Cultural Affairs, the Foreign Ministry, representatives of the European Commission and the European Social Fund, and with non-governmental organs like the Network Self-Help, the Foundation for German Polish Cooperation, and the Goethe Institute. Despite this formal networking, Cyankiewicz expressed frustration (interrupted by at least twenty phone calls over a two-hour period) over the PSR's precarious financial standing and the lack of workers' commitment to Polish organizations. He seemed genuinely impressed when I suggested that his "base," by definition, has little to gain by volunteering for a community it intends to leave, in turn, denying the PSR the "social capital, reciprocity and trust" it needs to compete with local Turkish entities as a regular interest organization.

Active at a very different level, Basil Kerski was born in Danzig in 1969. He grew up in Poland and Iraq, moving to Berlin in 1980 where he studied political science and Slavic literature at the Free University. He worked for a time at the Aspen Institute, the German Council on Foreign Affairs, and the Science Center

(WZB). In 1998, he joined the editorial staff of the German-Polish magazine *Dialog.* Kerski sooner represents the needs of Polish intellectuals and artists, concerned about the state of German-Polish relations. Kerski believes that many issues were subsumed during the EU application process, when Poles should have demanded the same rights as other nationally recognized minorities in Germany, like the Danes, Friesen, Sorbs, Sinti, and Roma (recognized during the Weimar era).[85] The last twenty-five years have seen the arrival of *Aussiedler,* intellectuals, asylum seekers, seasonal laborers, and undocumented workers; the total population may be as high as 1.5 million, yet only 300,000 are registered.

As strong as Polish national identity purportedly is, Kerski finds little evidence of ethnic solidarity, much less effective interest representation outside Berlin: "Neither effective Polish organizations nor interest representatives have established themselves over the last few years, there is no number of Polish restaurants or grocery stores worth mentioning in Germany. Only rarely does one find a strong concentration of Polish migrants in one location or in residential areas . . . at the same time one hears a lot of Polish being spoken in public. Migrants from Poland really only become visible in the numerous and well attended Polish language church services, that take place at many Catholic parishes."[86]

The Poles' failure to establish a typical ethnic community stems from the geographic proximity of the homeland, added to open borders and new opportunities to maintain direct contacts since the fall of the Iron Curtain, e.g., cell phones, the Internet, and satellite TV. Just as importantly, Poles can assimilate (or not) at will, insofar as common religious and cultural traditions facilitate their integration. Kerski (echoing an earlier author) recognizes that Turks do not enjoy this obvious advantage: "In contrast to devout Muslim women, Polish women do not cover their heads with scarves, the men don't differentiate themselves from the Germans, the Poles do not build any of their own places of worship, they don't settle in crowds in certain sectors of the city, and Polish speaking groups do not make appearances in German political life. . . . Does that mean that the integration of Poles in Germany has proceeded without major problems? Why is this group so invisible?"[87]

Poles who came to Germany as *Aussiedler* did so because they wanted to be German—yet repatriates of the 1980s have fewer contacts with the locals than those without citizenship. Most prefer pragmatic adaptation over the abstract cultural preservation. Polish intelligentsia, on the other hand, compete more than they cooperate. Kazimierz Woycicki characterizes the elite milieu as "the little hell of expatriate-Polish organizations":

> As experience shows, they are still dominated by the same neurotic and conflict-addicted activists. Definitive proof of this rests in the fate of the Polish Council in Germany, the Polish Congress and finally the unholy Convention of Polish Organizations. . . . They are constantly breaking apart by way of new fights among themselves. . . . It is the fault of a small pack of "activists" with exaggerated political

ambitions (always the same ones). . . . Those who have attained better social standing and are steadily anchored in their German surroundings refuse to participate in
the life of Polish-speaking associations.[88]

One could argue that Turkish activists depend more on ethnic associations to
preserve cultural identity and to socialize community members for the very reason that they are not accepted as Europeans. At the same time, the deep ethnic
and religious divisions among Turkish, Kurdish, and Muslim groups compel a
deliberate search for common ground, while Polish national unity—and perhaps
four decades of one-party government—narrows the range of real differences
but leads to hair-splitting competition over the rest. My spouse, an engineering manager, has long maintained that academics fight so vociferously among
themselves because they have so little to fight over.

Although all ethnic groups build associations to carry out cross-cutting functions, delivering advice or social services that the host country cannot or will not
provide, those deliberately fostering community socialization while responding
to individual needs emerge as more effective interest representatives. Locally
rooted communities branch out to systematize their contacts with host-country
agencies and institutions, commensurate with the intercultural skills of the second generation. By contrast, migrants reluctant to stick around for community
building, like the rolling stone that gathers no moss, ultimately lack the social
capital they need to promote self-interest. Democratic self-socialization has its
limits, however. If the host country takes no steps, or imposes socioeconomic
policies devoid of real ethnic input, minorities may resort to self-segregation, as
self-defeating as it seems; Antilleans in the Netherlands and Black Caribbeans
in Britain are concrete examples of the latter.

Integration through Participation: Citizenship at Last!

The real significance of urban citizenship is not that it allows outsiders to cir-
cumvent historically determined territorial limits but that it "provides an alternative model of membership that could eventually help to overcome some of
the exclusionary features of national citizenship," while enhancing the quality
of city life from below.[89] One would think in an era of rapidly declining voter
turnout and youth cynicism toward politics that models attracting dynamic,
grassroots activists would be in hot demand. Locally based Citizen Initiatives of
the 1970s, created by student movement veterans, triggered a great leap forward
in German democracy. The '68ers, now in their sixties, should spend less time
in Tuscany and more time in ethnic restaurants recruiting young voters!

The first way to increase integration through participation is to permit local
voting rights based on residency. Claudia Diehl and Michael Blohm hold that

"the combination of restrictive participation opportunities in Germany and a well-developed self-organisation with a strong focus on the homeland" should supply fertile ground for ethnic mobilization.[90] This does not automatically give rise to migrant parties. The Constitutional Court has rejected local voting rights for non-nationals granted in the Netherlands and other EU states. The Foreigners' Councils are token bodies with no power. Fijalkowski and Gillmeister described the limits on Councils in Kreuzberg and Wedding during the 1990s. The mayor of Kreuzberg engaged primarily in "information exchanges" with individual organizations and Council members (twenty-one of twenty-seven naturalized). The Wedding Council consisted of sixteen Germans and sixteen non-nationals (half Turkish); members were appointed by their associations, e.g., parties and religious groups. They could present proposals to City Council members, but there was no direct access to relevant committees or agencies.[91] Berlin subsequently restructured most districts, weakening migrant influence by combining multi- with monocultural districts, e.g., Kreuzberg-Friedrickshain, Templehof-Schöneberg, and Wedding-Reinickendorf. Neukölln was reconfiguring its Migration Council when I interviewed Commissioner for Integration Karin Korte (10 June 2003).

Community alternatives have arisen in many urban contexts, e.g., Contact Groups, Working Groups, parliaments for minorities, non-binding Advisory Councils and Committees on Migrant or Ethnic Minority Affairs. Mannheim's migrant activists "were exceptionally well integrated into German society, *as well as* their own ethnic community with regard to education, language skills, and social ties with majority and minority members" (emphasis in original).[92] Even small, financially strapped Eastern towns like Erfurt recognize the need to develop concrete integration criteria and baseline figures, using a Round Table to address the holistic needs of families.[93]

The second way to foster integration through participation is to make it easier for long-term residents to attain citizenship. The (pre-1999) Mannheim Study found that political diffidence does not result from low social status. Rather, formal legal exclusion renders ethnics "less interested because they cannot influence," much less identify with German parties.[94] In short, "neither immigrants' political attitudes nor their behaviour is a matter of fate."[95] Turks are less active than Germans in civic groups, yet over a third participate in some organization. Both German Socio-Economic Panel (GSOEP) and Mannheim data show that if dual citizenship were allowed, the segment of Turks willing to naturalize would rise from 35 percent to 60 percent nationally, from 57 percent to 73 percent locally.[96] Diehl and Blohm conclude that political apathy among aliens "is not a pure effect of their socio-economic background as measured by education, and it is not counterbalanced by participation in ethnic associations, which neither weaken nor further migrants' political interest in Germany except under very special circumstances."[97]

Thus formal political exclusion explains the gap between majority and minority involvement, preconditioned by differences in their social-structural positioning—not by innate, immutable cultural traits used to justify their exclusion. Citizens of Turkish origin in Sweden, Denmark, and the Netherlands trust municipal institutions, follow local news, and vote at higher rates than other minorities. High turnout is shaped by internal integration, as reflected in networks of ethnic associations. Russian and Polish *Aussiedler* enjoy full suffrage, Italians have limited voting rights in Germany—but neither group uses them. Turkish residents between the ages of twenty and thirty possess no such rights.

That situation changed dramatically following revisions to the Alien Act in 1990. In theory, there are two categories of citizenship rules, one based on entitlement (*Anspruch*), the other on administrative discretion (*Ermessen*). In practice, there are multiple categories (see table 6.1). These "fine distinctions with major consequences" derive from legislative amendments stretching from 1913 to 1990, followed by the paradigm shift of 2000. Entitlement covers eleven categories of persons who meet formal requirements regarding length of residency or constitutional provisions reflecting disenfranchisements due to war, changing boundaries, or statelessness. These persons have a "right" to citizenship, but secondary criteria regarding living conditions, ability to support dependents, employment status, and even grammatical prowess can delay the process for years. Nine discretionary categories apply to foreign spouses, family unification, German descendants in foreign states, and offspring of civil servants or diplomats living abroad.

The vehement debate over national requirements has long obscured major discrepancies in access to citizenship at state and local levels, due to the vagaries of German federalism and communal autonomy. Historically accustomed to diplomats, foreign occupiers, and international organizations, Berlin follows liberal integration policies (by FRG standards), while Bavaria adds barriers of its own. Officials citing an ostensible decline in applications since 1999 need to look at bureaucratic resistance; federal comparisons enable us to discern the real impact of state and local policies on integration.

Multiple factors account for the rush to citizenship after 1990 beyond changes in the law itself. Unification and xenophobic violence rendered older migrants less secure but moved younger residents to seek greater legal protection as citizens. Automatic extension of citizenship to *Spätaussiedler*, unfamiliar with the German way of life, intensified awareness of the second-class status accorded aliens in residence for twenty to thirty years. A bigger force, I argue, is the third generation's coming of age: at age eighteen, persons who have lived in Germany for eight years, attending school for six years, now have an independent right to citizenship, irrespective of parental choices. Over 90 percent were born there, so school attendance is a given. Changes enacted in 2000 apply retroactively to children born after 1990. Some parents acted immediately; others may allow

Table 6.1 Citizenship Acquisition by Entitlement or Discretion

Legal Entitlement (Anspruch)	*Administrative Discretion (Ermessen)*
§85 Abs. 1 AuslG (aliens in residence → for at least 8 years)	*§85 Abs. 2 AuslG* (applies to family members)
§ 4Abs. 3StAG (children under 10 as of January 2000) *§40b StAG*	*§8 StAG* ("regular" foreigners)
§Art. 116 Abs. 2 Satz 1, Basic Law (co-ethnics outside FRG who lost citizenship 1933-1945 for political, racist, religious reasons	*§16 Abs. 2 StAG* (children under 18 whose parents become citizens)
§8 StAngRegG. (co-ethnic residents not qualifying under §Art. 116 who live in FRG)	*§9 StAngRegG* (co-ethnic residents not qualifying under §Art. 116 living outside FRG)
§11 StAngRegG (collectively disenfranchised 1938-1945 on racial grounds)	*§13 StAG* (former Germans and offspring living abroad)
§9 Abs. 2 StAG (co-ethnics outside → FRG not qualified under §Art. 116 who served in Wehrmacht during WWII)	*§9 StAG §9 Abs. 1 StAngRegG* (applies to citizen spouses)
§12 Abs. 1 StAngRegG (persons forced by political/race/religious persecution to acquire foreign citizenship 1933-1945)	*§14 StAngRegG* (aliens living abroad)
§21 HAG (stateless persons in residence for 7+ years) Art 2. of the Law to Reduce Statelessness (persons born stateless in Germany, in residence 5 years, who apply before reaching 21)	*§15 StAngRegG* (federal officials, civil servants living abroad)
§85 AuslG, old version, with *§102a AuslG* (persons 16-23 in residence 8 years with 6 years of school attendance) →	§86 Abs. 2 AuslG, old version (applies to spouses, children)
§86 Abs. 1 AuslG, old version (aliens in residence 15+ years)	a) *StAngG* = State Law on Citizenship 1999 b) *StAngRegG* = Law Regulating State Nationality c) *AuslG* = Aliens Act 1965 (old version), 1990 d) *HAG* = Law Regulating Homeless Foreigners

Source: Compiled from the internal report, "Einburgerungen in Berlin, 2002," A I 9- j02, issued by the Statistisches Landesamt, 5.

Table 6.2 Naturalization Totals according to Bundesland, 1998–2003

Bundesland	1998	1999	2000*	2001	2002	2003	Rate (2003)
Baden-Württemberg	17,670	25,670	29,057	28,112	22,868	19,454	1.51
Bayern	10,616	15,201	20,610	19,922	17,090	14,641	1.24
Berlin	6,794	9,508	6,730	6,270	6,700	6,626	1.48
Brandenburg	232	221	424	434	411	314	0.46
Bremen	1,568	1,817	2,083	1,857	1,936	1,656	1.97
Hamburg	5,221	5,586	8,640	9,832	7,731	6,732	2.67
Hessen	12,555	16,827	20,441	18,924	17,421	17,246	2.46
Mecklenburg-Vorpom.	123	116	295	287	301	289	0.73
Niedersachsen	8,628	10,409	15,427	14,693	12,838	11,655	2.16
Nordrhein-Westfalen	35,611	47,472	65,744	60,566	49,837	44,318	2.36
Rheinland-Pfalz	3,683	5,015	7,338	7,714	7,445	6,898	2.21
Saarland	975	998	1,833	1,235	1,287	1,473	1.63
Sachsen	343	283	455	547	498	492	0.41
Sachsen-Anhalt	202	197	461	447	482	447	0.88
Schleswig-Holstein	2,434	3,734	5,639	5,123	5,128	4,310	2.82
Thüringen	135	213	312	357	354	300	0.63
Total	291,331	248,206	186,688	178,098	154,547	140,731	1.92

* Citizenship Reform Law in effect.
Source: Destatis/GENESIS (Statistisches Bundesamt)

adolescents to decide for themselves, since they must declare either German *or* Turkish citizenship by age twenty-three. Should Turkey join the EU by 2013, that choice may become moot.

Between 1993 and 2004, Berlin's entire population declined from 3.47 million to 3.38 million, while the non-citizen total grew from 393,000 to 448,200 (14 percent).[98] Naturalizations increased by 23.5 percent, from 9,903 (1994) to 12,228 (1995); German passports accorded on an entitlement basis rose 73 percent, while discretionary cases fell to 27 percent; almost half were Turkish (table 6.3).[99] The number granted fluctuated between 10,200 and 12,300 between 1996 and 1999, falling to 6,867 in 2000; these figures lag behind the applications filed, due to processing backlogs in districts like Neukölln and Kreuzberg (table 6.4). Applicants in non-integrated neighborhoods like Steglitz and Zehlendorf face delays of a different sort (a Steglitz administrator refused to be interviewed on the subject). If a resident becomes unemployed or dependent on Social Assistance while her application gathers dust on a bureaucrat's desk, she must secure new documentation, and may become retroactively "ineligible" in that district.

In April 2004, Berlin's State Interior Minister Ehrhart Körting standardized the discretionary criteria applied in each district, in order to expedite processing which takes up to three years. He initiated a city-wide advertising campaign advocating naturalization via native-tongue media outlets, working with ethnic associations to provide effective counseling. Uniform software now calculates whether joblessness and welfare dependence owe to personal responsibility or

Table 6.3 Berlin Naturalizations by Sex and Legal Modus, 1991–2004

Year	Total	Male	Female	Entitlement	Discretionary
1991	7 515	4 149	3 366	1 844	5 671
1992	9 743	5 214	4 529	976	8 767
1993	9 458	4 766	4 692	1 482	7 976
1994	9 903	4 828	5 075	7 029	2 874
1995	12 228	5 677	6 551	8 904	3 324
1996	10 268	4 824	5 444	7 308	2 960
1997	10 485	5 057	5 428	7 698	2 787
1998	12 045	5 831	6 214	9 162	2 883
1999[1)]	12 278	5 910	6 368	8 162	4 116
2000	6 867	3 562	3 305	4 838	2 029
2001	6 273	3 260	3 013	5 103	1 170
2002	6 700	3 453	3 247	5 307	1 393
2003	6 626	3 440	3 186	5 279	1 347
2004	6 507	3 350	3 157	5 133	1 374

Source: Statistisches Landesamt Berlin On-Line.

Table 6.4 Berlin Naturalizations by District, 2002**

District	Total	District	Total
Mitte-Wedding	1,294	Templehof-Schöneberg	978
Friederichshain-Kreuzberg	561	Steglitz-Zehlendorf	354
Pankow	177	Spandau	524
Charlottenburg-Wilmersdorf	662	Treptow-Köpenick	77
Neukölln	1,483	Marzahn-Hellersdorf	70
Lichtenberg	113	Reinickendorf	407
City Total	= 6,700		

** excludes *Aussiedler*
Source: Statistisches Landesamt Berlin, Statistischer Bericht, AI9-j02, 2002, 9.

structural factors. Additional personnel are assisting overloaded caseworkers for one year to eliminate backlogs. Naturalizations reached a new high of 8,168 in 2005. City officials are also pursuing a "multicultural opening of administrative services." Bureaucrats at all levels are to undergo diversity training, and efforts will be made to diversify hiring as well.[100]

Democracies can neither tolerate nor afford the political exclusion of substantial, permanent segments of the population, ranging from 9 percent nationally to 30 percent locally. Not all voluntary associations are healthy for democracy, but it is ideology, not ethnicity, that determines their threat potential, e.g., neo-Nazi groups. Oklahoma City resident Timothy McVeigh did not "bowl alone"—he belonged to a local league before blowing up the Federal Building and being sentenced to death.

A 2001 survey revealed that some residents of non-German heritage display greater support for democratic values than average Germans.[101] Interviewing Germans, Turks, Italians, and Russians, Maria Berger, Christian Galonska, and Ruud Koopmans discovered that most aliens feel closer to Berlin than to their purported homelands. Their political activities focus on German and Berlin developments; few saw intercultural coexistence endangered by September 11th. Anti-immigration hardliners claim that loyalty and local identification exists only in a few cities and states—but that is exactly where ethnics are concentrated!

Voting poses a special problem in Berlin, Hamburg, and Bremen, due to their city-state status; not even EU nationals can participate in elections beyond district levels. The share of Berliners interested in voting was much higher than turnout rates in Amsterdam, registering 87 percent (Germans),

Table 6.5 Naturalizations by Local District

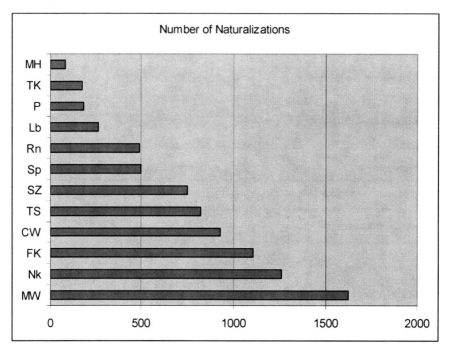

District	District Abbreviation
Marzhan-Hellersdorf	MH
Treptow-Köpenick	TK
Pankow	P
Lichtenberg	Lb
Reinickendorf	Rn
Spandau	Sp
Steglitz-Zehlendorf	SZ
Tempelhof-Schöneberg	TS
Charlottenburg-Wilmersdorf	CW
Friedrichshain-Kreuzberg	FK
Neukölln	Nk
Mitte-Wedding	MW

Source: Compiled from the internal report, *Einbürgerungen in Berlin*, 2002, A I 9- J 06, issued by the Statistisches Landesamt. 2006

83 percent (Turks), 79 percent (Italians), and 63 percent (Russians). By comparison, 67 percent of the Dutch-Turks voted in 1994, 39 percent in 1998, 28 percent in 2000 (declining turnout, perversely, mirrors native behavior). Turkish-Berliners lean toward the SPD or Greens, Russian-Germans favor the CDU.[102] Germans and Italians appear most active in a conventional sense (attending meetings, collecting signatures or donations), while Russians are least engaged. Turks donated more to homeland causes (after earthquakes) but were also more likely than Italians and Russians to participate at both levels. Rather than being mutually exclusive, ethnic-oriented and local activities ostensibly reinforce each other. Turks discuss German, Berlin, *and* homeland affairs daily/often, to a greater degree than other minorities.

Despite observed differences in organizational participation, migrants who follow events in their country of origin develop political orientations toward Berlin and Germany. There is no evidence that they must renounce emotional ties or immerse themselves solely in host-country processes in order to integrate. Germans fear that ethnic activism and dual citizenship will evoke split loyalties and "parallel societies." In the minds of bureaucrats, "it surely isn't beneficial for the chances that they will see their application granted."[103] Berger, Galonska, and Koopmans conclude: "The assumption that ethnic political participation of migrants is a threat to their political integration in the Berlin and German society is something that is unambiguous [*sic*] rejected by the data. Migrants who participate in political activities regarding their country of origin are likely to participate also in German political activities and this correlation is most strong for the Turks. . . . The fears of the assimilationists lack clearly [*sic*] an empirical basis as the two orientations are reinforcing each other instead of being mutually exclusive."[104] Activism on behalf of ethnic associations does *not* rule out commitment to German organizations. Indeed, participatory activities focusing on the former homeland are decisive in explaining political engagement in relation to Berlin and Germany.

While many professions still require German or EU citizenship as a condition for self-employment (testifying further to obsolete labor regulations), migrant interest in political-legal integration extends well beyond a desire to practice medicine, dentistry, or psychotherapy. Independent of educational attainment, Turks are more unhappy with their lack of political rights than other minorities, suggesting greater identification with the FRG. Citizenship would not protect them from unemployment, but it could eliminate the abstract threat of deportation. Convicted criminals are not eligible for naturalization in any case! Nor is citizenship the only factor determining belonging and participation. Urban citizenship can help to reconfigure "the ways in which the system deals with the political expectations of minorities regarding the ability to shape their own social lives and/or the realization of equal rights to organize around the cultural and social needs of different population groups."[105]

To Be, or Not to Be German? Youth Identification

For children of migrant background, the question is no longer whether to stay or return but how to secure permanent spaces for their intercultural skills and identities. Younger cohorts see naturalization as a way to claim Germany as their homeland, not as a concession by authorities that they are fit to stay. Like adults, youth who evince strong skills in two languages, who are active in German *and* ethnic organizations, are more politically engaged than those who only participate in host-country clubs. Rather than yield to forced acculturation, they expand their behavioral options in order to derive benefits from both cultures.

Comparing 1,200 youth of Turkish and Italian heritage (age eighteen to thirty), Claudia Diehl found that the usual human/financial/social capital variables don't make a difference in shaping decisions to embrace German citizenship. Researchers focused on individuals who had lived in Germany for at least eight years, drew no welfare benefits, and displayed language competence, making them technically eligible for naturalization; 92 percent qualified in both groups.[106] Not surprisingly, FRG-born individuals who spoke German with their friends were more intent on attaining citizenship. About 13 percent of the Italians had acquired citizenship at birth through binational marriages; more striking was that only 2 percent of the rest wanted to naturalize; half had no desire to do so. Among Turkish youth, a third planned to naturalize, merely 17 percent rejected the idea. As confirmed in other studies, Turkish residents, supposedly more homeland-oriented and loathe to renounce their nationality, are more intent on naturalizing than Greeks, Italians, Spaniards, and Yugoslavs. They stress a craving for political rights (23 percent Turks, 35 percent Italians) over a desire for occupational opportunity (19 percent Turks, 15 percent Italians).[107] In 2002, Italy adopted a very restrictive immigration law of its own, named after the right-wing populists Gianfranco Fini and Umberto Bossi.

A German Youth Institute study (1996–1997) also explored political orientations among third generation ethnics. The sample encompassed 848 Italians, 826 Greeks, and 830 Turkish youth, added to 2,243 West Germans and 1,257 East Germans; 12 percent of those under age twenty-one held a foreign passport in 1995.[108] Although 70 percent of the Italian, Greek, and Turkish youth born in Germany expected to stay, only 50 percent desired citizenship; 15 percent did not. Meanwhile 7,000 Turks (age eighteen to twenty-five) applied in 1995, 9,130 in 1996, 7,433 in 1997, and 10,205 in 1998; rates among twenty-five to thirty-five year olds were likewise higher than among Italians and Greeks.[109] Greek (67 percent), Italian (64 percent), and Turkish youth (65 percent) all rejected the idea that "religion is a private matter." Religion is never used to explain a demonstrated lack of integration among Greeks or Italians.

Gender differences are also significant. Italian girls were only half as willing as their Turkish counterparts to join ethnic organizations, although males

Table 6.6 Residency Status of Turkish-Berliners, 1999 and 1993

	1999			*1993*		
Have lived in Berlin:	*Total*	*Men*	*Women*	*Total*	*Men*	*Women*
Since birth	19.5	19.4	19.7	7	7.5	6.5
25–30 or more	16.5	18.4	14.1	11.	14.5	7.2
Over 20 years	42.2	42.6	41.8	35.8	35.5	36.2
Over 15 years	8.2	8.5	7.6	15.2	15.9	14.3
More than 10 years	7.1	4.8	9.8	15.4	16.9	13.8
More than 5 years	5.7	5.9	5.6	8.1	4.8	11.6
Less than 5years	0.8	0.4	1.3	7.3	4.6	10.4
Resident Status	*Total*	*Men*	*Women*	*Total*	*Men*	*Women*
Permanent residency	45.8	54.4	35.3	29.8	28.1	31.5
Unlimited residency	46.7	40.3	54.5	60.1	65.8	53.9
Limited permit	4.6	3.1	6.5	9.1	5.3	13.2
Restricted residency	1.2	1.0	1.4	0.3	0.3	0.4
Functionally restricted	0.6	0.3	0.2	0.1	0.3	—

Source: Compilations based on data provided by the office of the Commissioner for Foreigners in Berlin and the Zentrum für Türkeistudien, Essen.

outnumber females in both cases. Still, differences in role perceptions were greater between the sexes than between nationalities. Boys label themselves traditional (42–49 percent), girls are egalitarian (36–48 percent)—up to 44 percent of the latter "completely agreed" that more women should exercise public leadership roles, compared to 13 percent among boys.[110]

Turkish women out-naturalized men by 14 percent from 1994 to 1999, both nationally and in Berlin; among eighteen to twenty-five year olds, twice as many became citizens. Diehl's explanation is contradictory: She assumes that married women with children are more "traditional," thus less "integration-oriented," although men with children are also less likely to apply. She further posits that young women naturalize in order to import husbands from Turkey more easily, enabling the latter to acquire work permits. Spouses of employed migrants must wait a year to resume paid labor, a provision biased against women since importing grooms are more likely to hold jobs than brides, given higher female unemployment. However, all partners of citizens can naturalize more quickly. About half of the entering brides but only 10 percent of the grooms did so, implying that men are less integration-oriented.[111] Local studies moreover show that fewer women import spouses. Commissioner John noted that Berlin men are recruiting brides from Turkey, due to a "woman shortage." Those born in Germany want to study, start careers, and marry later; men want the comforts of home as soon as possible. Females also displayed higher naturalization rates after 2000, claiming 58.3 percent of the new passports issued to eighteen to twenty-three year-olds in 2003. Diehl thus underestimates young women's desire for self-determination, constitutionally warranted equality, and protection against forced marriage under German law.

Similar identification patterns are found among younger cohorts. Bruce Cohen surveyed 698 pupils (age fifteen to sixteen) of working class background at thirty-one Berlin schools in 2001. He drew on eight classes each in

Table 6.7 Naturalizations in Berlin according to Age and Sex, 2002

Years of Age	Total	%	Male	%	Female	%
Under 5	327	4.9	180	2.7	147	2.2
5–9	842	12.6	462	6.9	380	5.7
10–14	656	9.8	327	4.9	329	4.9
15–19	571	8.5	266	4.0	305	4.6
20–24	949	14.2	380	5.7	569	8.5
25–29	554	8.3	250	3.7	304	4.5
30–34	632	9.4	342	5.1	290	4.3
35–39	712	10.6	411	6.1	301	4.5
40–44	553	8.3	337	5.0	216	3.2
45–49	360	5.4	197	2.9	163	2.4
50–54	231	3.4	110	1.6	121	1.8
55–59	161	2.4	97	1.4	64	1.0
60–64	77	1.1	52	0.8	25	0.4
65–69	40	0.6	26	0.4	14	0.2
70 and older	35	0.5	16	0.2	19	0.3
Total	6,700	100	3,453	51.5	3,247	48.5

Source: Statistisches Landesamt Berlin, Statistischer Bericht A I9-j 02, *Einbürgerung in Berlin* 2002, 10–11.

Table 6.8 Youth Orientations in Berlin/Kreuzberg, 2001

Orientations	German Citizens	East Europeans	Turkish Males	Turkish Females
Future Expectations	%	%	%	%
Would like to attend university:	37	41	59	53
Want education to improve job chances	84	79	85	73
Expect to face discrimination at work:	24	30	63	46
Anticipate gender discrimination at work	31	14	15	46
Anticipate religious discrimination	7	7	55	23
See "big problems" where they live (Kreuzberg only)				
Grafitti	42	46	46	44
Alcoholics	39	8	40	28
Drugs being sold	44	17	40	38
Heroine use	30	8	44	41
Crime	32	17	28	30
No jobs	21	17	20	27
No recreational options	21	17	29	31
Litter	39	17	29	38
Noise	8	28	33	31
Worry very much about.... (Kreuzberg only)				
Not doing well in school	30	50	42	61
Finding a job	14	18	41	46
Getting in trouble with police	8	17	27	29
Being attacked by a stranger	16	8	15	49
Being attacked by someone you know	16	8	23	39
I don't go out alone	6	25	15	37

(continued)

Table 6.8 Youth Orientations in Berlin/Kreuzberg, 2001 *(continued)*

Orientations	German Citizens	East Europeans	Turkish Males	Turkish Females
Experience with criminal activities over last 12 months (Kreuzberg only)				
Witnessed Illegal drug use	46	33	48	26
Personally experienced verbal harassment (from youth)	54	42	30	31
personally experienced physical attack by an adult	16	0	22	9
Have personally been drunk	57	42	30	11
Like living in Berlin	93	94	91	94
Feel like a Berliner:	81	45	60	56

N=698 total (87 Turkish); 124 from Kreuzberg (62 Turkish)

Source: Bruce MZ Cohen, "Young People with Turkish backgrounds: a Comparative survey of current lives and future chances in Berlin," presented at the Humboldt Universität, 6–7 June 2003, 15–21.

Marzahn, Prenzlauer Berg, Kreuzberg, and Charlottenburg (87 percent Turkish). The Kreuzberg analysis (124 surveyed) revealed that Turkish pupils were most enthusiastic and optimistic about school, though empirically speaking, they are the most disadvantaged.[112] Grasping the subtleties of racism, Turkish teens expect lower grades, yet desire more education. The gap is larger among females, causing them to favor apprenticeships over academic degrees although girls like studying more. Over half want to attend university but anticipate discrimination at work (63 percent males, 46 percent females); perceived hurdles based on gender (46 percent) move girls toward dead-end occupational trajectories.

Although more sensitive to environmental decay and physical insecurity, Kreuzberg youth were satisfied with their neighborhood or *Kiez*. Due to the presence of alcoholics, graffiti, drug-addicts, and litter, Turkish females avoid hanging out in public spaces; it is not "culture" that precipitates their isolation but threats posed by disadvantageous surroundings. So-called honor killings do occur, directed against women who try to live "the German way," (six cases in 2005), but these are no more representative of Turkish culture than domestic violence is among German households: the number of registered domestic abuse cases rose from 7,500 in 2002, to 10, 371 in 2003, to more than 12,800 in 2004.[113] Both are criminal offenses and should be punished accordingly. Strong identification with the *Kiez* turns it into a psychological safe haven, *kleines Istanbul*, infused with Turkish cultural outlets, especially for working-class males.[114] Newcomers from the Middle East, the former Soviet Union, and the Balkans are the ones they perceive as foreigners, precipitating occasional turf wars in Kreuzberg and Neukölln. These conflicts sooner derive from economic disadvantage, boredom, and testosterone than from ethnocultural factors. Berlin is where third-generation youth feel at home; it is really the only homeland they have ever known.[115]

Claims-Making and EU Citizenship: Rights without Representation

As this chapter proves, Germany's ethnic minorities are far from politically passive, irrespective of formal citizenship status. Civic participation within smaller communities can do as much to foster social capital, organizational expertise, and systemic connections among minorities as among indigenous groups, provided local engagement is effectively channeled. Strong migrant organizations and active subcultures can positively shape the political integration of minorities in majority society. Five citizens of Turkish origin now sit in the Berlin House of Representatives. Two, Dilek Kolat and Özcan Mutlu, became active by way of local educational concerns and the Turkish Parents' Organization; Kolat, along with Evrim Baba, belonged to the Lette Union (tied to vocational education). Gyasettin Sayan was active in the Kurdish community; Jasenka Villbrandt (born in Croatia) worked as a teacher and served a local women's organization. They represent their constituencies by way of three different political parties. Two Turkish-Germans have served in the Bundestag, Cem Özdemir and Lale Akgün; Özdemir won a seat in the European Parliament in 2004. Over 100 serve in city councils.

Migrant organizations remain weak in those countries where access channels to state institutions and decision-making apply a one-size-fits-all model to incorporation. Without formal political rights, minorities are easily ignored or instrumentalized. A strong emphasis on cultural-qua-religious rights in the Netherlands presumes self-organization skills that may not inhere in all ethnic groups. The British emphasis on race relations overlooks competing and conflicting national-qua-religious traditions. Legalistic/regulatory emphases in Germany throw the (qualified) baby out with the (certification) bathwater, resulting in a tremendous waste of human capital. German and Swiss citizenship regimes reproduce strong homeland identifications via their rigid legal barriers to political participation: they seem alienated partly because the receiving society defines them as foreigners and offers them few political rights and opportunities, partly—and as a consequence of the former—because migrants in these countries continue to identify themselves with the national and ethnic categories of their homelands. . . . The restrictive citizenship regime in these two countries produces exactly the ethnic "parallel societies" that the proponents of such exclusive policies say they seek to avoid. . . . How the receiving society defines itself in terms of citizenship and national identity, and the opportunities and constraints it offers migrants through its integration policies are crucial determinants of how migration changes the receiving society, for better or worse. Even if it is difficult to steer an optimal course, the results . . . are perfectly clear about the kind of approach that does not work.[116]

While I share Koopmans's concerns about the exclusive nature of FRG citizenship policies, I find little evidence of "parallel societies" among Turkish residents outside the fundamentalist Islamic community—which is sooner Arabic or Southeast-Asian in origin.

Ironically, the groups that do prefer a segregated, apolitical existence are those possessing voting rights: *Spätaussiedler* and the EU-national Italians! Over 25 percent of Germany's resident foreigners are EU nationals, with Italians comprising the largest group (33 percent). EU nationals cannot vote for municipal parliaments in city-states like Bremen, Hamburg, Berlin, and Vienna, since they function simultaneously as *Landtage*. While their British, French, Italian, Greek, Portuguese, Irish, and Spanish counterparts can vote in Munich or Paderborn, no foreigners (14 percent of the population) possess real voting rights in the capital city. Add this to "foreign" residents in Frankfurt/Main (28 percent), Stuttgart (24 percent), Munich (22 percent), and Cologne (19 percent) who have no say regarding educational policies, urban renewal, resource allocation, job distribution, or even the regulation of their own behavior in the places they've lived for more than a decade—though they pay the same taxes. More than 65 percent among ten million ethnics inside EU boundaries are "non-nationals" and thus ineligible for voting rights warranted by the Maastricht Treaty (§8). This democratic deficit grows by the year, despite the fact that as many as two-thirds of the disenfranchised were born and educated in Europe.

Germany's exclusionary policies of the last three decades have it riding the horns of a dilemma regarding Turkey's application for EU membership. An increase in German-Turkish voters will favor Turkish membership, given the democratic/human-rights standards the country will have to meet in order to enter.[117] Turkish women have much to gain, at home and abroad, under EU equal-treatment regulations.[118] Germany's 2003 "Multicultural Man of the Year" Cem Özdemir envisions Turkey as a model for democratizing countries in the Gulf region. Germany's deeper fear, reflected in the Central/East European negotiations, is that it will be overrun by a cheap labor supply, despite EU rules mandating fair wages, raising health and safety standards, and outlawing distortions in competition.[119] Neither Polish, nor Czech, nor Hungarian workers have relocated by the millions since their countries joined the EU, however. People abide by their homeland attachments when they have an economic opportunity to do so.

Nor have the EU-national voting rights led to participatory groundswells; only 43 percent of the eligible Germans, even fewer EU nationals, participated in the 2004 European Parliament elections. The latter must personally request and pick up ballots. Elections divorced from state or national legislative contests rarely motivate people with limited experience, irrespective of nationality. The Amsterdam Treaty added new protections against discrimination based on sex, religion, national origin, and sexual orientation; incorporation of the European Charter on Fundamental Freedoms into the Libson Treaty of 2007. takes these rights even further. If Germany's non-enfranchised minorities were to appeal their cases to the European Court of Justice, they could conceivably level the playing field between themselves and ethnic counterparts in other EU states.

The real threat to Germany stems from the fact that (non)integration policies are crucial determinants of how migration changes the receiving society, for better or worse. The FRG has experienced tremendous change across three decades of "non-immigration migration," but it has not effectively managed, much less controlled, the nature of societal change, as the demographic deficit attests. Had politicians not wasted thirty years by shunting minorities into dead-end *Hauptschulen*, they might have avoided the current shortage of technology-savvy workers. They could have embraced the brain gain implicit in Russian/Jewish migration, and modernized the skilled trades through alternative certification processes. The feudal nature of university hiring practices has fueled an FRG brain drain in the sciences—multiple German Nobel Prize winners live in California! If the civil service and church-affiliated welfare organizations do not start hiring professionals of migrant origin soon, Baby Boomers–turned-Establishment will lack elder-care services by 2020—unless, of course, conscientious objection among Bundeswehr conscripts rises to 100 percent.

Had lawmakers actively promoted language instruction by funding kindergartens and keeping kids in school all day, they could have spared the country a decade of dropouts and delinquents. The Program for International Student Assessment (PISA) results show that Germans lag behind most EU countries in literacy, math, and science proficiency, yet state educational ministers worry more about Muslim headscarves in classrooms. Politicians who are serious about strengthening civil society should spend weekends with *their* kids volunteering at neighborhood functions, instead of using "more time with family" as a convenient excuse to resign whenever a scandal pops up. (For the record: there isn't a criticism in these pages that I would not to apply to the United States.)

Were the number of eligible ethnic voters to double in time for the next election, the Federal Republic would not witness radical policy change. Naturally minorities "would be accorded different weight" as voters, and electioneering slogans would certainly change. As one ethnic activist opined, politicians who claim that Germany's problems are caused by fake asylum seekers or foreign welfare cheats would have to stop their scapegoating: "The societal climate would change a great deal, if out of one and a half million Turks in Germany, suddenly 7–800,000 were eligible to vote. All of the parties, from the *Republikaner* to the PDS would have to adapt to that."[120] Most migrants deeply appreciate the quality of life, freedom of movement, and human-rights protection afforded by postwar German democracy. That is why they stay, and that is why they want to participate. Potential terrorist groups who want to overthrow the system are not limited to foreigners: the Baader-Meinhof Gang of the 1960s, the Defense-Sport Group Hoffmann of the 1970s, the June 2nd Movement of the 1980s, and the neo-Nazis of the new millennium have all been homegrown.

A representative survey sponsored by Barbara John in 2001 asked youth of migrant background to identify rights they view as "absolutely indispensable" for democracy in Germany. Heading the list were universal suffrage (95 percent); freedom of expression/press (92 percent); religious freedom (90 percent); minority protection (88 percent); the right to work (87 percent); respect for religious/cultural differences (83 percent); separation of powers (82 percent); the social-market economy (80 percent); artistic freedom (75 percent); and citizen referenda (71 percent). Curiously, response options did not include "equality between women and men"—though it is constitutionally mandated (referenda are not).[121] Like their same-age counterparts, most (93 percent) like living in the capital city; a strong majority feel like Berliners and have no intention of leaving. The time to start their political incorporation is now. Let us turn, finally, to the changing faces of citizenship in other conurbations, and reflect on the future of Germany's democratic deficit.

Notes

1. James Coleman, "Social Capital in the Creation of Human Capital," *American Journal of Sociology* 94 (1988): 98.
2. Marieluise Beck and Renate Schmidt, eds. *Migranten sind aktiv: Zum gesellschaftlichen Engagement von Migrantinnen und Migranten*, documentation for the expert meeting, 11 June 2002 (Bonn/Berlin), 32.
3. *Das Ehrenamt: Verantwortung übernehmen—Zukunft gestalten.* CDU/CSU Fraktion in Deutschen Bundestag: Bonn, 1997. In 1953, 53 percent of Western adults were affiliated with one or more organizations, only 17 percent in 1997.

4. Robert D. Putnam, "Bowling Alone: America's Declining Social Capital," *Journal of Democracy* 6, no. 1 (1995): 65–78; also, Robert Putnam, Robert Leonardi, and Raffaella Y. Nanetti, *Making Democracy Work: Civic Traditions in Modern Italy* (Princeton, NJ: Princeton University Press, 1993).

5. Kenneth Newton, "Social Capital and Democracy," *American Behavioral Scientist* 40, no. 5 (1997): 575–586.

6. Beck and Schmidt, *Migranten sind aktiv*, 8.

7. Ruud Koopmans, "Migrant Participation, Citizenship and Democracy: National and Local Perspectives" (workshop on Strategies of Integration: The Multiethnic Society and Local Government, Essen, 24–25 September 2001); Meindert Fennema and Jean Tillie, "Ethnic associations, political trust and political participation," Working Paper 3A UNESCO-MPMC Project, Multicultural Policies and Modes of Citizenship in European Cities.

8. Gabriel Almond and Sidney Verba, *The Civic Culture* (Boston: Little, Brown & Co., 1965), 245; cf. Carole Pateman, "The Civic Culture: A Philosophical Critique," in Gabriel A. Almond and Sidney Verba, eds., *The Civic Culture Revisited* (Boston/Toronto: Little, Brown & Co., 1980): 57–102.

9. Meindert Fennema and Jean Tillie, "Political participation and political trust in Amsterdam: Civic communities and ethnic networks," *Journal of Ethnic and Migration Studies* 25, no. 4 (1999): 712–713.

10. Fennema and Tillie, "Ethnic associations," 4.

11. Ulrike Schöneberg, "Participation in ethnic associations: The Case of Immigrants in West Germany," *International Migration Review* 19, no. 3 (1985): 432.

12. Steve Vertovec, "Minority associations, networks and public policies: Re-assessing relationships," *Journal of Ethnic and Migration Studies* 25, no. 1 (1999): 21–42.

13. Ben Koolen, "Integrationspolitik der niederländischen Regierung," *Integration und Integrationsförderung in der Einwanderungsgesellschaft* (Bonn: Forschungsinstitut der Friedrich Ebert Stiftung, 1999), 5–6.

14. Fennema and Tillie, "Political participation and political trust," 705

15. Anita Böcker, "Paving the way to a better future: Turks in the Netherlands," in Hans Vermeulen and Rinus Pennix, eds., *Immigrant Integration: The Dutch Case* (Amsterdam: Het Spinhuis, 2003), 153–177.

16. Vermeulen and Pennix, "Introduction," in *Immigrant Integration*.

17. Dirk Jacobs, "Discourse, Politics and Policy: The Dutch Parliamentary Debate about Voting Rights for Foreign Residents," *International Migration Review* 32, no. 2 (1998): 350–373.

18. Vermeulen and Pennix, *Immigrant Integration*, 23.

19. Ibid., 9.

20. Ronald Van Kempen and Gideon S. Bolt, "Turks in the Netherlands: Urban Segregation and Neighborhood Choice," *American Behavioral Scientist* 41, no. 3 (1997): 382.

21. Fennema and Tillie, "Political participation and political trust," 723.

22. Ruben Gowricharn, "Integration and social cohesion: The case of the Netherlands," *Journal of Ethnic and Migration Studies* 28, no. 2 (April 2002): 262.

23. Ibid., 262–265.

24. Ibid., 268–269.

25. Anja van Heelsum and Rinus Pennix, "Evaluating integration and participation policies for immigrants and minorities in an Amsterdam district: 'Oost,'" UNESCO MOST Report, MPMC, 38–44.

26. Fennema and Tillie, "Political participation and political trust," 705.

27. Ibid., 713.

28. Ibid., 713–714.

29. Fennema and Tillie, "Ethnic associations," 15.
30. Vermeulen and Pennix, *Immigrant Integration*, 14, 16; further, Mies Van Niekerk, "Paradoxes in paradise: Integration and social mobility of the Surinamese in the Netherlands," in ibid., 64–92; Hans Van Hulst, "A continuing construction of crisis: Antilleans, especially Curaçaoans, in the Netherlands," in ibid., 93–122.
31. Robert Kloosterman, Joanne van der Leun, and Jan Rath, "Mixed Embeddedness: Informal Economic Activities and Immigrant Businesses in the Netherlands," *International Journal of Urban and Regional Research* 23, no. 2 (1999): 253–267; Jan Rath, "A Dutch Bargain: The remarkable Absence of Immigrant Entrepreneurs in Construction" (paper presented at the twelfth Conference of Europeanists, Chicago, 30 March–1 April 2000.
32. Jean Tillie, Meindert Fennema, and Karen Kraal, "Creating Networks within the Turkish Community," Working Paper 3B UNESCO-MPMC Project, 32.
33. Fennema and Tillie, "Ethnic associations," 5.
34. Fennema and Tillie, "Political participation and political trust," 712.
35. Meindert Fennema and Jean Tillie, "'Civic Community', politische Partizipation und politisches Vertrauen: Ethnische Minderheiten in den Niederlanden," *Forschungsjournal NSB* 14, no. 1 (2001): 43.
36. Ibid., 44.
37. Fennema and Tillie, "Ethnic Associations," 5.
38. David McEnvoy, "Greater London in Britain's First Ethnic Census," in Curtis C. Roseman, Hans Dieter Laux, and Günther Thieme, eds., *Ethnicities: Geographic Perspectives on Ethnic Change in Modern Cities* (Boston: Rowman & Littlefield, 1996), 97–120.
39. Giles A. Barrett, Trevor P. Jones, and David McEnvoy, "United Kingdom: Severely Constrained Entrepreneurialism," in Robert Kloosterman and Jan Rath, eds., *Immigrant Entrepreneurs: Venturing Abroad in the Age of Globalization* (Oxford/New York: Berg, 2003), 101–122.
40. Muhammad Anwar, "The participation of ethnic minorities in British politics," *Journal of Ethnic and Migration Studies* 27, no. 3 (2001): 534, 537.
41. Ibid., 537.
42. Ibid., 542.
43. Ibid., 544, 546.
44. Paul Statham, "Political mobilization by minorities in Britain: Negative feedback of 'race relations'?" *Journal of Ethnic and Migration Studies* 25, no. 4 (1999): 597–626.
45. I relied on the draft manuscript, chapter 8, 8, of a book subsequently published by Ruud Koopmans, Paul Statham, Marco Giugni and Florence Passy, *Contested Citizenship: Immigration and Cultural Diversity in Europe* (Minneapolis MN: University of Minnesota Press, 2005).
46. Birgitta Ornbrant, "Sweden," in Steffen Angenendt, ed., *Asylum and Migration Policies in the European Union* (Berlin: Europa Union Verlag, 1999), 311.
47. Maritta Soininen, "The 'Swedish Model' as an institutional framework for immigrant membership rights," *Journal of Ethnic and Migration Studies* 25, no. 4 (1999): 686.
48. Jane Kramer, writing on "the Invandrare," in *Unsettling Europe* (New York: Random House, 1980), 88.
49. Ornbrant, "Sweden," 311.
50. Soininen, "The 'Swedish Model,'" 691.
51. Ibid., 695.
52. Ibid., 698.
53. Ibid., 690–692.
54. Lise Togeby, "Migrants at the Polls: An analysis of immigrant and refugee participation in Danish local elections," *Journal of Ethnic and Migration Studies* 25, no. 4 (1999): 665–684.
55. Jan Hjarno, "Denmark," in Angenendt, *Asylum and Migration Policies*, 110–111.

56. Togeby, "Migrants at the Polls," 673. The register-based study included 3,548 Lebanese, 5,190 Turks; Togeby surveyed 273 Turks and 264 Lebanese.

57. Ibid., 680.

58. Ibid., 681.

59. Ibid., 669ff.

60. Ibid., 671–672; for a theoretical treatment, see Maria Margarida Marques, Rui Santos, and Tiago Ralha, "Immigrants' Participation in Civil Society in a Suburban Context: Between Top-down Activation and Bottom-up Mobilisation," UNESCO MOST Project (MPMC), (Lisaboa: SociNova, 1999).

61. Richard Bernstein, "Wedding Vows Can Lock Danes Out of Their Homeland," *New York Times*, 10 September 2004.

62. Koopmans et al., *Contested Citizenship*, 5, chap. 3.

63. Yasemin Nuhoglu Soysal, *Limits of Citizenship: Migrants and Postnational Membership in Europe* (Chicago/London: University of Chicago, 1994).

64. Gilad Margalit, "German Citizenship Policy and Sinti Identity Politics," in Daniel Levy and Yfaat Weiss, *Challenging Ethnic Citizenship: German and Israeli Perspectives on Immigration* (New York/Oxford: Berghahn Books, 2002): 107–120. Further, Karl Cordell, ed., *Ethnicity and Democratisation in the New Europe* (New York/London: Routledge, 1999).

65. Koopmans et al. *Contested Citizenship*, 12, chap. 3.

66. Studies sponsored by John included: Judith Kessler, *Von Aizenberg bis Zaidelman: Jüdische Zuwanderer aus Osteuropa in Berlin und die Jüdische Gemeinde heute* (1997); Martina Müller, *Afrikaner in Berlin* (1993); Bettina Böwe and Patricia Cerda P.-Hegert, *Portugiesen und Spanier in Berlin* (2000); Gotfried Müller, *Araber in Berlin* (2000); Diedericke M. Oudesluijis, *Hollander an der Havel* (1994); Susanne Nieder, *Iren und Briten in Berlin* (1994); Bahman Nirumand and Gabriele Yonan, *Iraner in Berlin* (1994); Baber Johansen and Fritz Steppat, *Der Islam und die Muslime* (1995); Mario Tempio, *Italien in Berlin* (2000); Bert Becker, *Japan an der Spree* (1995); Frieder Weisse, *Koreaner in Berlin* (1993); Natache Garay, *Lateinamerikaner in Berlin* (1995); Amory Burchard and Ludmila Duwidowitsch, *Das Russische in Berlin* (1994); Martin Greve and Tülay Çinar, *Das Türkische Berlin* (1998); Tran Trong Khoi and Nguyen-Xuan Vinh, *Vietnamesen in Berlin: Exil und neue Heimat, Zwei Generationen* (1997).

67. *TOP EXTRA: Zwanzig Jahre Ausländerbeauftragte des Senats* (Berlin, 5 December 2001), 112. Also, Ausländerbeauftragte des Senats, *Bericht zur Integrations- und Ausländerpolitik*, 1996–1997 (Berlin, 1998).

68. North Rhine-Westphalia, eds., *Selbstorganisationen von Migrantinnen und Migranten in NRW* (Erkrath: Tonnes, 1999), 135.

69. Jürgen Fijalkowski and Helmut Gillmeister, *Ausländervereine—ein Forschungsbericht* (Berlin: Hitit, 1997), 285.

70. Ibid., 288–289.

71. Ibid., 147.

72. Ibid, 179.

73. Ibid., 193.

74. Ibid., 186.

75. Ibid., 216.

76. Ibid., 294.

77. Ertekin Özcan, *Türkische Immigrantenorganisationen in der Bundesrepublik Deutschland* (Berlin: Hitit, 1992), 23.

78. *10 Jahre Eltern Arbeit (1985–1995): Eine Dokumentation des Türkischen Elternvereins in Berlin-Brandenburg e.V.* (Berlin, 1995).

79. Fijalkowsi and Gillmeister, *Ausländervereine*, 219.

80. TBB, *Jahresbericht 2001–2003* (Berlin, 2003), 8.
81. Ibid., 18–19.
82. TDU website and interview with Bahatkin Kaya, 12 June 2002.
83. *Selbstorganisationen von Migrantinnen und Migranten in NRW,* 110.
84. Ibid., 103–104, 109, 112.
85. Basil Kerski "Chancen der Multikulturalität: Die polnischsprachige Gruppe in Deutschland," in Anna Wolf-Poweska und Dieter Bingen, eds., *Nachbarn auf Distanz: Polen und Deutsche 1998–2004* (Wiesbaden: Harrassowitz Verlag, 2005), 269.
86. Ibid., 272.
87. Ibid.; cf. Gerhard Gauck, in *Polen in Berlin*, chap. 6 nn. 144.
88. Cited in Kerski, "Chancen der Multikulturalität," 273.
89. Kerski, "Chancen der Multikulturalität," 157.
90. Claudia Diehl, and Michael Blohm, "Apathy, adaptation or ethnic mobilisation? On the attitudes of a politically excluded group," *Journal of Ethnic and Migration Studies* 27, no. 3 (July 2001): 410. Further, Andreas Wust, "New Citizens-New Voters? Political Preferences and Voting Intentions of Naturalized Germans: A Case Study in Progress," *International Migration Review* 34 (2000): 560–567.
91. Fijalkowski and Gillmeister, *Ausländervereine,* 258.
92. Diehl and Blohm, "Apathy, adaptation or ethnic mobilization?" 414.
93. Beate Tröster, "Das Netzwerk für Integration in Erfurt," in Friedrich Ebert Stiftung, ed., *Neue Wege der Aussiedlerintegration: vom politischen Konzept zur Praxis* (Bonn: Forschungsinstitut der Friedrich Ebert Stiftung, 2000); Klaus-Dietrich Frank, "Netzwerke für Integration im Erftkreis und in Köln," in ibid.
94. The study polled 750 Turks over age sixteen, coupled with personal interviews, and semi-structured elite interviews in 41 Turkish associations, as reported by Diehl and Blohm, "Apathy, adaptation or ethnic mobilization?" 412ff.
95. Ibid., 418.
96. Ibid., 408.
97. Ibid., 417.
98. Rainer Ohliger and Ulrich Raiser, *Integration und Migration in Berlin: Zahlen—Daten—Fakten* (Berlin: Beauftragte für Integration und Migration, March 2005), 10.
99. Tables available at www.statistik-berlin.de/pms/2a1/1996/96–08–23b.html.
100. In June 2004, I attended one town meeting on "multicultural opening" featuring an administrator who droned on for ninety minutes about legal ordinances behind the opening, much to the frustration of those who had come to ask practical questions or to air grievances.
101. University of Amsterdam and Center for Turkish Studies (Essen) scholars were also involved. See Ruud Koopmans, "Zuwanderer in Berlin unterstützen demokratische Werte: Umfrage zeigt, daß weder Parallelgesellschaft noch Kulturkampf zu befürchten sind," WZB Pressemitteilung (14 January 2002). Further, Maria Berger, Christian Galonska, and Ruud Koopmans, "Not a Zero-Sum Game: Ethnic Communities and Political Integration of Migrants in Berlin" (paper presented at a workshop on Political Participation of Immigrants and their Descendants in Post-War Western Europe, Turin, Italy, 22–27 March 2002).
102. Ibid., 12.
103. Bade cited in ibid., 28.
104. Ibid., 28.
105. Alois Weidacher, ed., *In Deutschland zu Hause: Politische Orientierungen griechischer, italienischer, türkischer und deutscher junger Erwachsener im Vergleich* (Opladen: Leske + Budrich, 2000), 272.

106. Claudia Diehl, "Wer wird Deutsche/r und warum? Bestimmungsfaktoren der Einbürgerung türkish- und italienischstämmiger junger Erwachsener," Bundesinstitut für Bevölkerungsforschung, January 2003, 14.

107. Ibid., 15–16.

108. Weidacher, *In Deutschland zu Hause*, 50.

109. These figures exclude Hamburg. Ibid., 77–78.

110. Ibid., 179, 184.

111. Diehl, "Wer wird Deutsche/r und warum?" 22, 25.

112. Bruce Cohen, "Young People with Turkish Backgrounds: A comparative survey of current lives and future chances in Berlin" (paper presented at Berlin's Humboldt Universität, 6–7 June 2003).

113. "Immer mehr Frauen zeigen Angriffe an Anti-Gewalt—Initiative läuft seit 2002," *Der Tagesspiegel*, 9 March 2004; "Ehre und Emanzipation," *Der Tagesspiegel*, 8 March 2005.

114. Ayhan Kaya, *Sicher in Kreuzberg: Constructing Diasporas: Turkish Hip-Hop Youth in Berlin* (Bielefeld: Transcript Verlag, 2001).

115. Blended identities are beginning to make their mark on the German music scene. See Torsten Wahl, "Stolz in Kreuzberg gefertigt," *Berliner Zeitung*, 25 March 2002; and Ayhan Kaya, "Aesthetics of diaspora: Contemporary minstrels in Turkish Berlin," *Journal of Ethnic and Migration Studies* 28, no. 1 (January 2002): 43–62.

116. Koopmans, "Migrant Participation, Citizenship and Democracy," 10, 12, 19.

117. Bulent Cicekli, "The Rights of Turkish Migrants in Europe under International Law and EU Law," *International Migration Review* 33, no. 2 (1999): 300–353; E. Fuat Keyman and Ahmet Icduygu, "Globalization, Civil Society and Citizenship in Turkey: Actors, Boundaries and Discourses," *Citizenship Studies* 7, no. 2 (2003): 219–234.

118. Susan Sachs, "Adultery a Crime? The Turks Think Again and Say No," *New York Times*, 15 September 2004.

119. Projections ran as high as five million over the next fifteen years. "700,000 Osteuropäer kommen sofort," *Berliner Zeitung*, 25 June 2002; Floyd Noris, "Europe Knows It Needs Lots of Immigrants, But It Also Fears Them," *New York Times*, 11 June 2004.

120. Fijalkowski and Gillmeister, *Ausländervereine*, 252.

121. Barbara John, ed., "Zur Lebenssituation Türkischer Berlinerinnen und Berliner," issued 15 January 2002, 6.

CHAPTER 7

MULTICULTURALISM FOR A NEW MILLENNIUM

Citizenship with a Human Face

In Germany it is easier to build a nuclear energy plant than a mosque.

—Director of a Turkish organization in Berlin (1995)

The answer to the question, how does one spell *integration* with an R for religion, is found above all at the communal level.

—Marieluise Beck (2002)[1]

The function and value of tolerance depend on the equality prevalent in the society in which tolerance is practiced. Tolerance finds itself subject to overriding criteria: its range and limits cannot be defined in terms of the respective society . . . tolerance is an end in itself only when it is truly universal, practiced by rulers as well as by the ruled.

—Herbert Marcuse (1965)

The decade following German unification fundamentally redefined the attitudes of average citizens regarding the age-old question: What does it mean to be German? Three historical breaks with the past have triggered changes

---

in national identity at such a rapid pace that some citizens seek certainty by (re)imagining the nation as an immutable, cultural absolute. Others welcome an opportunity to exchange their Germanness—and the historical burdens it carries—in favor of EU passports. For the youngest cohorts, the reconfiguration of German identity has been breathtakingly normal. The first major break, effected in grand style when the Wall fell in 1989, was geographic in nature. The second seismic force was generational in character, turning former student-movement activists into key players in national government. The third break, rooted in globalization, has been marked by a proliferation of hyphenated identities reflecting a mix of ethnic, cultural, and religious markers.

Previous chapters have explored the status of ethnic minorities in Germany through different lenses of economic, social, and political change, reflecting adaptation processes within such communities as well as within the host country itself. The common lesson deriving from these treatments is that each generation encounters a distinctive set of problems vis-à-vis the dominant culture, requiring new strategies of accommodation. Looking back to the 1960s, one sees that as each set of aliens sought to participate in the host society, German policymakers changed the rules of the game, and then used changes in course to fault migrants for not adequately "integrating themselves." Official reluctance to embrace an expansive concept of FRG citizenship three decades ago resulted in multiple self-fulfilling prophecies. As Ali Akhbar Mahdi writes, "When the concept of 'nation' is usurped by the ruling elite as a community of only 'insiders' and the rest of society are [sic] characterized as 'outsiders' and denied access to political processes, those outsiders have no choice but to develop their own communities/groups of 'insiders' in order to gain a sense of identity and collective presence."[2]

Calling integration "a moving target in its own right," Brett Klopp stresses its nature as a contingent process that proceeds at different paces at various times based on diverse conditions. Thus, "there can be no definitive general law that determines who belongs and who does not, because the criteria and standards are subject to change and redefinition as the composition of society and the citizenry changes over time due to immigration and naturalisation."[3] Riva Kastoryano adds, "each time academics, policy makers and journalists have arrived at a threshold that they thought should not be crossed for fear of social breakdown or national disintegration, the threshold has in fact been surpassed and breakdown did not occur."[4]

Naturalization outcomes, shaped by the timing and sequencing of integration processes, differ not only across national contexts but also across localities. Global cities stretching from New York to Brussels, from Los Angeles to Tokyo, from London to Hong Kong are "no longer territorial subunits within the state territory, but become nodes in transnational flows of money, people and information."[5] Though not typical of all German cities, Berlin shares a host of integration problems facing urban centers throughout Europe. It is the quality of city life, not national citizenship regimes that will attract high-tech workers, multinational corporations, global capital, and scientific research over the next decade. Correspondingly, it is the quality of urban citizenship that will ensure a steady stream of competent service workers willing to make up for Germany's demographic deficit, as Baby Boomers retire.

Confronted with the real costs of "failed integration"—more accurately, lawmakers' failure to embrace active integration policies—cities are taking the lead. We turn, first, to a comparison of integration dynamics in Stuttgart and Frankfurt/Main, along with examples from the Eastern *Länder*, to highlight differences in local approaches. I then examine the phenomenon of Islam in Germany, showing the ways in which migration is changing urban landscapes, physically and otherwise. The Muslim headscarf debate, a misplaced metaphor for national insecurities triggered by "9–11," is not the only rights issue likely to be adjudicated by way of EU directives. French and Dutch rejection of the EU constitution in 2005 has underscored democratic-deficit questions with regard to identity, participation, and social cohesion in a future United States of Europe. Most "foreigner problems," in my judgment, highlight the need for deeper reform processes pertaining to education and employment, especially in Germany. I conclude with final observations on the New Tolerance among younger cohorts.

The Quality of Life in Multicultural Cities: Best Practices

Despite the extraordinary ethnic, religious, and linguistic diversity found between and within migrant groups in Germany, minorities share one perception regarding their political status: "What do all foreigners have in common? Just one thing—that we do not share equal rights with the rest."[6] Berlin is not the only city with a multicultural population taking a proactive stance on integration, underscoring my thesis that local participation and community identification do more to foster citizenship than ethnic roots, religious convictions, or an imagined willingness "to defend the Fatherland."

The sunny, southern city of Stuttgart is best known for its thrifty Swabians, fine wines, high rents, and automotive production extending over 115 years. Thanks to the inventiveness of Gottlieb Daimler, Carl Benz, Wilhelm Maybach, and Ferdinand Porsche, the capital city of Baden-Württemberg nowadays enjoys an export quota of 50 percent. Overall unemployment stands at 5 percent, 10 percent among non-natives, both low by Berlin standards. Despite the high quality of life afforded by the city, the State Office for Constitutional Protection reported a doubling of violent incidents involving right extremists in 2000, long after the sensational post-unification wave had passed. Dependent on international *Standort* concerns, the city overhauled its approach to integration, according it new priority as a communal responsibility. Authorities created an institutional matrix of city agencies, administrative departments, educational and welfare organs, employment offices, unions, and sport, church, media and cultural facilities, citing the Amsterdam Treaty, the "European" pillar on immigration/asylum, as well as two supranational reports linking diversity and social cohesion as a justification for policy change.

In 1998, the city moved to promote cultural exchanges as a mechanism for "spontaneous integration."[7] It created a roof organization, the Forum of Cultures, encompassing 62 organizations from fifty countries of origin. The Forum launched a free monthly magazine, *Interkultur Stuttgart-Encounters among Cultures* (circulation: 18,000), with a regular calendar in 2001; it sponsors a summer Festival of Cultures attracting 35–40,000 participants and forty-two intercultural associations, along with a Workshop for World Cultures. The city provides €67,000 per year, beyond the €320,000 (2003) channeled through the Forum. While official efforts concentrate heavily on culture and education, local activists are expanding political participation through *Immigrün*. Founded at the suggestion of Cem Özdemir, the first naturalized Turk elected to the Bundestag, then European Parliament, this association combines the words *immigrant* and *Greens*, signifying party efforts to embrace the multicultural community, enabling noncitizens to take stands on public policies. The idea quickly spread to Frankfurt/Main and Berlin (interview with Bilkay Öney, June 2002).

Another important step was the decision to transform the commissioner for foreigners into a commissioner for integration, a position held by Gari Pavkovic; he shares responsibility with Deputy Commissioner Isabel Lavadinho and three further staff members in a Department for Integration Policies, accountable to the mayor. They define integration as "the active establishment of a common basis of understanding, . . . a reciprocal process" that assumes the *ability* of individuals to incorporate, given language and orientation courses, as well as their *willingness* to do so, based on dialogue and shared motives. Officials seek to intensify community cohesion amidst a proliferation of cultures: Whereas aliens accounted for 17 percent of local residents in 1986, they represented 24 percent by 2000, stemming from 166 countries. They realize that children born and educated locally are neither foreigners nor migrants but rather "citizens without German passports"; *Aussiedler* with passports also face adaptation problems.

A third step was to rename the Foreigners' Committee, now the International Committee, consisting of thirteen city councilors and twelve experts; chaired by the mayor, the IC meets ten to twelve times per year for consultation. It has established early-warning systems in the districts, new access points, and community data banks to support local politicians. Next came the Pact for Integration, issued in September 2003, outlining eight "milestones" and four areas for community action: fostering language and education; neighborhood integration;

promoting pluralism and diversity across societal domains; and strengthening the city's intercultural self-perception.[8] A Round Table "against discrimination and for peaceful coexistence in the multicultural city" has created an assortment of youth programs collectively labeled the Initiative for Tolerance and Togetherness. There is also an intercultural drug addiction/treatment program.

Heavy residential concentrations in Bad Cannstatt, Feuerbach, Zuffenhausen, Untertürkheim, and Wangen lead to the usual language deficits and low educational attainment. Turks comprise the largest group (24,891), followed by 16,200 Greeks and 15,700 Italians; there are also 28,000 ex-Yugoslavia refugees, divided along ethnic lines. For Commissioner Pavkovic (interviewed 5 July 2002), the biggest problems lie in the educational domain: Comprising nearly 40 percent of the elementary enrollments in 2000, 56 percent of these children were channeled into *Hauptschulen* (20 percent among Germans), while 21 percent went on to *Gymnasium* (55 percent for Germans). Language skills are still inadequate, though 90 percent now attend half or all-day kindergartens. The increase in child placements has been accompanied by "German for Mama" courses. Italians are the second largest group enrolled in special-ed schools. Bosnian/Yugoslav youth who arrived in 1991 were "temporaries" who have run the educational gamut but are not entitled to vocational training or work permits. Given their strong desire to belong, adolescents are drawn to ethnic soccer clubs, or turn to conservative mosques (especially Arabs) for help with homework, since many parents lack advanced educations.

A series of city ordinances introduced a state-level model project to promote free language and civics instruction (fifty hours in each) in four cities, utilizing "bridge personnel" with intercultural competence. Six to eight schools in Stuttgart were singled out for a "language and educational offensive" in 2003, for persons not qualifying for federal integration courses. They have set up district-level dialogues, networking processes, and rely on volunteer or professional associations to seek out best practices. Like Berlin, Stuttgart is committed to an "intercultural opening of the administration," including sensitivity training for bureaucrats. Its Managing Diversity Approach includes gender mainstreaming.

Stuttgart's search for best practices is not confined to its own districts, suggesting that urban officials grasp the impact of global forces on local development faster than national politicians. Several subsidized projects aim to transfer best practices from city to city as well as across national borders.[9] Stuttgart has joined the International Network of Cities on Integration Policy, looking for ways to apply European anti-discrimination regulations at local levels. It hosted a conference on the "Integration and Participation of Foreigners in European Cities," attracting four hundred regional and communal officials from thirty countries in September 2003, as well as the first Network meeting. Topics include negotiating boundaries between religious freedom and civic duties; promoting educational opportunity; multiculturalizing access to health services;

adding diversity management to administrative routines; and promoting conflict resolution at neighborhood levels. Stuttgart was seeking EU funding for its initiatives when I visited in 2002. In 2005, it received the Bertelsmann Prize as Germany's Best Integrated City.[10]

Applications for naturalization rose from 1,928 in 1999 to 3,721 in 2000 under the new law, but the total lags behind expectations, according to Frau Lavadinho (interviewed 5 July 2002). Baden-Württemberg introduced a written language test, along with a "citizenship" test in 2005, making it harder for older residents to pass (the *Länder* agreed to a standardized test, yet to be designed, in 2006). The city needs many facilities for small children, more counseling services for women and girls. Lavadinho stressed the Department's inability to compel city agencies to take positive action; it can only file complaints or take them to court after problems occur. The International Committee lacked real power, leading migrants to seek niches in the political parties. Stuttgart authorities have recognized that the best defense against alienation, unemployment, and social exclusion is a good offense: a holistic, proactive integration policy targeted toward specific groups.

Frankfurt/Main (Hesse) enjoys a reputation as a site of democratic mobilizations. The movement for liberal constitutional reform and national unification was launched from the *Paulskirche* in 1848; in 1968, it gave rise to the student movement, anti-Vietnam protests, *Sponti* initiatives, squatters' occupations, and environmental campaigns (Startbahn West) that ultimately merged into the Green Party. Home to the German Central Bank and the European Central Bank, the city is known by capitalist critics as *Bankfurt* or *Krankfurt*. Frankfurt's desire to serve as a global financial hub renders it sensitive to international clients; it houses the FRG's largest concentration of foreign residents. As in Berlin, local authorities imposed a *Zuzugssperre* in 1972—a ban on new permits in districts where aliens exceeded 12 percent—repealed in 1977; migrants comprised 17 percent of the urban dwellers back then. Its population of 651,000 included 186,000 persons (nearly 29 percent) from 181 nations in the late 1990; the city grew to 655,079 by 2004, but aliens declined to 25.3 percent (163,553), partly explained by the 4,736 who changed citizenship that year. Over 85 percent of the Gallusviertel residents are foreigners, 38 percent of the children under age fifteen do not enjoy citizenship, 46 percent between ages sixteen and forty-six.[11]

A former 1968 protest leader, "Danny the Red" Cohn-Bendit, became the city's first officer for multicultural affairs (AMKA) following a major Red-Green electoral victory. Established as an "honorary" position, the director's staff grew to include eighteen specialists, a number of paid interns and a DM 3 million budget (1996); it draws on EU funds and donations for special projects. Despite state and national constraints, the Frankfurter Way adopted in the mid 1990s offers a multicultural framework with strong practical-communitarian elements. Frankfurt residents of migrant background are "actively engaged in struggles to become politically incorporated in their new places of residence and in their new homes, and this activity is partially driven by the desire for local equality and justice."[12] Although local naturalization rates quadrupled through 1990s (Turks comprised the largest group), they do not capture the breadth and depth of political interest or identification among non-citizens.

On closer inspection, most local conflicts are not ethnic in character but are instead triggered by day-to-day socioeconomic disparities, residential segregation, and overcrowding. Natives and foreigners both rate traffic as the biggest problem facing the city, followed by crime/public safety, unemployment, and housing shortages. When attempts to prevent ethnic concentration using quotas failed, the city revised income thresholds, adopted "socially just" allocation rules, and unified administrative structures in 1994. Officials addressed the affordability problem by purchasing 2,700 housing units (McNair Barracks) from the federal government when US Armed Forces withdrew. Neighborhood stability, the quality of the housing stock, and school resources matter much more than local concentrations.

For multiculturalism to work, the majority must agree to an "equal treatment" framework by extending real participatory opportunities with regard to urban (re)development. EU nationals (1 percent) acquired participatory rights in Frankfurt, starting with the 1997 municipal elections; enlargement raised the EU-national proportion to 8.2 percent. The other 91.8 percent have to settle for pseudo participation. Though grounded in good intentions, the Frankfurt Foreigners' Council (*Kommunale Ausländervertretung* or KVA), like *Ausländerbeiräte* elsewhere, does not ensure migrants effective political voice. The city parliament approved its creation in April 1991; few foreigners helped to draft the statute. Since 1993, every commune with more than one thousand registered aliens must provide an elected assembly. Non-nationals, stateless persons, and dual-nationals age eighteen or older are entitled to vote after six months in residence. Nearly 126,400 from 154 countries registered for the first election but fewer than 20 percent turned out.[13] Lacking a 5 percent threshold, the first 51-seat assembly encompassed over twenty-one parties, making it hard to address city officials in a unified voice. Less than 5 percent (6,353 of 138,358) voted in 2001 for a body reduced to thirty-seven seats.[14]

KVA members have the right to "advise and be heard" but are "simultaneously beholden to AMKA and city administration."[15] Delegates focus on German issues, having gone so far as to debate their shared responsibility for the dark side of FRG history, including National Socialism. By acknowledging responsibility for "never forgetting," they render themselves accountable for and committed to a future devoid of extremism. While non-citizens "do not bear the same burden of German history," they do pay the so-called solidarity tax covering unification, repatriation, victim compensation, and other historical costs, which Klopp labels "reciprocal integration in practice."[16] Assuming power in 2000, the CDU has upheld Green-defined integrationist strategies.

Big cities are not the only ones seeking proactive approaches to local incorporation. The Eastern *Länder* are depicted in the Western-dominated media as particularly hostile to foreigners, although arson attacks in Mölln and Solingen caused more deaths than those in Hoyerswerda and Rostock. Extended discussion among thirty-eight Eastern commissioners regarding xenophobia led to the January 2003 presentation of an "integration-political memorandum." Chaired by Günter Piening (then foreigners' commissioner in Sachsen-Anhalt, now commissioner in Berlin), the group compared the destabilizing influences of unification on unemployment and social (in)security with the "overwhelming immigration experience of the old federal-states." Jobless rates approaching 25 percent lead some to conflate patriotism with (ultra)nationalism, insofar as "those who do not receive any recognition themselves are unable to grant recognition to other cultures."[17] The East faces a special demographic deficit: younger citizens have fled to the West in droves (1.3 million since 1989), meaning that future workplaces in engineering and machine tooling will be hard to fill.[18]

The Memorandum Group stressed that openness to migration is not only an ethical question but a matter of economic survival. The young states are desperate for the innovation, investment, and ability to compete inherent in transnational business. They see diversity management as standard operating procedure among multinational corporations, and "role modeling" as a new responsibility for public administrators, as they network civil-society groups against right extremism. The study detailed thirteen best practices in districts where few foreigners arrived on a voluntary basis (due to federal distributions quotas); only 2 percent in the East are non-citizens, versus 8.8 percent in the old FRG.[19] Mindful that foreign investors account for one-seventh of the jobs in Sachsen-Anhalt, that state initiated an intercultural training program at DOW Chemical/Buna Werke in 2002. The Economics Ministry created an Association for Foreign Relations (Auslandsgesellschaft Sachsen-Anhalt e.V.), linking twenty organizations, and the Magdeburg Model-Project/Intercultural Advising and Networking Center to assist ethnic entrepreneurs. Rostock established IntegrationsFachDienstMigration in the Labor Office to channel migrants into language and occupational training based on individual learning contracts. Other programs transcend national bans on employment among "tolerated" refugees of many years; if they find work for six months in Thuringia (four hundred did), they are granted residency.

Brandenburg recognized in 2002 that a small alien population requires "more structure, not less," since there are few opportunities for building ethnic social capital in rural regions. Leaders see "no alternative" to its Development of Communal Integration Structures (EKIS) initiative.[20] The emphasis on economic advantages underlying Eastern best practices will not automatically generate the civil-society organizations that have evolved in larger cities. East Germans redis-covering the importance of their own voluntary associations may be more eager to share their learning experiences with other latecomers, however.[21] New xeno-phobic violence in 2006 (just before the World Cup) saw the state scrambling to improve its image.

Whether the emphasis falls on cultural-linguistic incorporation (Stuttgart), communal participation (Frankfurt), or economic networking (Branden-burg), each approach falls short of reciprocal integration. Soysal's promotion of post-national membership as a new and stable framework "which makes citizenship less relevant, if not dispensable, for immigrants does not hold true for Germany, . . . one of her primary cases." On the contrary: "national-state citizenship as a mode of practical political incorporation and rights guaran-tees, has not been transcended, despite growing importance of international human rights law and increased speculation about the realization of a trans-national EU citizenship."[22] The modes of civil-society integration witnessed thus far in urban settings "do not represent very stable let alone permanent outcomes. Without political incorporation that is attached to citizenship in a given nation-state (. . . still the only status that allows full political par-ticipation at all levels), social and civil integration will never reach their full-est approximation. The threat of backsliding—the restriction of non-citizens' rights and welfare, especially in economic hard times or in the face of national security threats—will always remain."[23]

Equal access to political rights is by no means a sufficient condition for resolving social conflicts, but it is an absolutely necessary one. Integration is occurring across a variety of urban settings, but as the 1991 Frankfurt Declaration states, there is simply no meaningful substitute for real political inclusion. While national immigration policies have been defensive, reactive, controlling, and fail to achieve their stated goals, local integration practices are multifaceted, proactive, and inclusive, leading to slow but steady success.

Putting the "R" back into Integration: Islam in the City

The 1999 Citizenship Law allows the Federal Republic to shed the histori-cal yoke of ethnonationalism, but it will gain little by shifting to the other extreme, characterized as "difference-blind liberalism."[24] The use of pure ethnicity as a marker for inclusion/exclusion has been replaced by sophisti-cated public discourses emphasizing specific cultural practices that preclude migrant incorporation under civic nationalism or constitutional patriotism. Such practices range from the ritualized slaughter of animals for consump-tion, sex-segregated education, and wearing headscarves, to divorce by Sharia, honor killing, and female genital mutilation. While native citizens insist on differences, migrants emphasize their right to same or equal treatment, e.g., the right to be "taxed" like other faith communities to fund religious instruction and places of worship.

Germans contest religious freedom in some pretty strange places. Consider their peculiar affinity for animal protection (*Tierschutz*). Under US law, a fundamental freedom like religion supersedes secondary issues, such as the public's desire to consume only meat that has been spared "unnecessary pain and suffering" as it moves from the slaughterhouse to the dinner table. The Federal Republic celebrates itself as a land of free-feeding, happy chickens, supported by their own 1999 Constitutional Court ruling that Green Minister Künast labeled "one small step for hens, one giant leap for animal welfare and consumers."[25] In 2002, the Constitutional Court upheld the rights of a Muslim butcher to slaughter animals without anesthetizing them (*halal*) in order to serve the religious needs of his customers. Due to the butcher's "foreigner" status, the Court did not apply Article 12/1 (freedom of occupation) but rather Article 2/1 (free development of personality) in conjunction with Article 4/1 (freedom of religion and conscience—for his customers). Animal protection was deemed secondary, enabling the state to grant an exemption for religious purposes.[26] Opponents immediately pushed through a constitutional animal-rights amendment. New rules regulate laboratory use, restrict animal testing, protect them during transport, and mandate studies on "the causes of leg damage among fattened turkeys." If Germans really believed that farm-, feathered-, and fur-bearing animals do more for democracy than religious freedom, they would all become vegetarians, give up their down comforters, and boycott Italian shoes.

While many conflicts are rooted in contradictory national laws, other integration problems can only be resolved locally, e.g., repositioning toilets in public housing so they do not face Mecca, or educating new arrivals not to flush animal entrails down these toilets, following do-it-yourself *halal* rites. Cultural misunderstandings of this sort are a thing of the past, thanks to learning experiences on both sides. Many new problems lie ahead: as the migrant population ages, city officials need to accommodate dietary restrictions in hospitals, nursing homes and prisons (lots of pork!), as well as to create permanent Muslim cemeteries. Germans can only lease plots for "15 years of peace"; Islamic law prohibits movement after burial.[27]

Although world religions transported themselves across continents and through the centuries "without the aid of federated administrative structures," the domestication of different faiths in an age of globalization has become a curiously complicated process.[28] The secularization of European societies requires, paradoxically, that non-Christians be granted special group rights, to ensure the same religious freedoms historically granted everyone else. Religion no longer correlates with ethnicity: consider the aging '68ers, who experimented with Buddhism, Baghwan, and Feng Shui in search of their own spirituality. Nor does recognizing racial/ethnic differences lead to accommodating religious differences, as seen in Britain, where the Church of England precludes state subsidies to other faith communities. Debates in France and Germany indicate that migrants need real political space to secure their religious place.

Policymakers construe religion as an immutable belief system rather than as an evolving web of shared values and cultural traditions. Connected to history, language, and identity, religion, like the nation, evokes an imagined community, positing an immediate communion with like-minded members, irrespective of distance or diaspora settings. It easily lends itself to transnational practice, however, since many faiths lack a centralized authority, allow for divergent sects, and construct places of worship, along with new rituals, wherever its practitioners land. Yet religion can also be used to sustain or re-establish affective and material bonds to a former homeland. In new settings, shared religious values offer a moral compass and an emotional anchor amidst stormy processes of readjustment. Beyond cultural disorientation and occupational devaluation, migration often leads to a loss of parental authority. Religion may be used to "prop up sagging patriarchal family structures" as well as family honor.[29]

One reason why European religious debates remained dormant for so long was the assumption that "Muslim" guestworkers would return to their countries of origin. The same cannot be said of Bosnian refugees and Iranian asylum seekers fleeing godless or theocratic regimes. Secondly, migrants of the pioneer generation, arriving prior to resurgent fundamentalism, were themselves quite secular. Headscarves were not an issue among recruited workers; Turkish women easily found jobs in the electronics and textile industries. A third explanation rests with the democratic socialization of long-term residents; observing the special treatment accorded recent Jewish immigrants, non-citizens have learned to frame their demands for parity in analogous constitutional and human-rights terms.

What is it about European church-state relations that suddenly projects religious differences as yet another barrier to sociopolitical incorporation? More accommodating than most, due to its history of pillarization, the Dutch parliament opens each new session with Protestant, Catholic, Muslim, and Hindu blessings, despite a 1983 constitutional amendment separating church and state. France, at the opposite end of the spectrum, excludes any religious manifestations or symbols, with a number of curiously Catholic exceptions. Assuming an allegedly neutral posture, despite their state-recognized churches, Britain and Germany push religion to the periphery of political life, hoping to avoid the youth intifada witnessed in French suburbs. The argument that religious identity resists assimilation contradicts the fact that migrants were secular when they arrived four decades ago. It does not explain growing religious identification among younger cohorts, nor clarify why dominant-culture members stressing their Christian roots are more likely to spend Pentecost weekend in Mallorca or Tuscany than attending church in Munich or Tübingen.

As a "lived faith," Islam cannot be confined to an hour of worship on a specific day of the week; devout Muslims pray five times a day, accompanied by ritual washing. Its recognition as a belief system of comparable worth would necessitate host-country adaptation across many institutional domains; it raises hard-to-answer legal, educational, and value questions, in addition to shaping child-rearing, health care–work, and business practices. Gerdien Jonker puts it bluntly: "Those who do best are the ones who have distanced themselves the farthest from Islamic orthodoxy. It includes the laicist Turks and secular Iranians, Afghans and Lebanese who are increasingly finding their way into politics, administration, academics and social professions."[30] Alevis adjust to the German way of life and thus "find allies over and over"; Sunni Muslims, by comparison, are left to their own devices. Ruud Koopmans et al. show that "Islam cannot simply be confined to religious faith but advances into the realm of politics where a state's authority and civic citizenship obligations reign supreme." Muslim groups demand that Islam come to enjoy "an equality of truth" relative to other belief systems, not simply a "parity of tolerance" with long pacified Western religions.[31] The closer to orthodoxy practicing Muslims appear to be, the more barriers to integration governments seek to erect.

In addition to recognizing religion as "power management," Rolf Schieder posits that beliefs secure the right to flourish "under the label of religion" as a result of complex historical negotiation. More complex than most, German history lacks a pluralistic, live-and-let-live tradition: "Americans have a civil religion, Germans have the Frankfurter School and Jürgen Habermas."[32] Rooted in centuries of religious "culture wars," value questions are moreover shaped by the fact that "the Holocaust is a damn big shadow that will follow them into eternity with every step."[33] Hitler, a Catholic, signed a pact with the Vatican; only one branch of Lutherans, the Confessing Church, resisted the Nazis. Under the Weimar Republic, the SPD organized yearly quit-the-church drives; it finally abandoned anti-clericalism after 1945. The "Christian" parties simultaneously stopped requiring that their card holders be "church-members in good standing." Federal presidents Richard von Weizsäcker and Johannes Rau, Protestant synod members, often evoked morality in their speeches but came nowhere close to the open professions of faith or appeals for divine blessing routinely iterated by their US counterparts.

The German state collects and redistributes taxes to "recognized" faith communities, derived from an 8–9 percent surcharge on personal income taxes. Between 1980 and 1992, 1 million Catholics and 1.2 million Protestants officially quit as church members. Based on a 1992 poll, 64 percent wanted the tax abolished in favor of voluntary contributions. After forty years of godless communism, Easterners unwittingly upset the religious balance Westerners thought they had achieved. In 2002, 33 percent classified themselves as Protestant, 33 percent as Catholic, and 34 percent as embracing some other faith, or none at all; 70 percent of the East Germans label themselves atheists or agnostics (84 percent among youth).[34] The remainder left their parishes in droves, once they discovered that religion in "capitalist" Germany is not free.

High courts in each *Land* must accord "corporate status under public law" (*Körperschaftsrecht*) before state authorities can draw up service contracts with religious representatives. This is another case in which German federalism permits administrative discretion, undermining equality before the law. The Lutheran Church is posited as the norm; other faith communities are expected to create parallel structures, e.g., bodies of voting members. Beyond the Prophet Muhammed, Islam does not rely on religious intermediaries (though some Sufis follow charismatic leaders). From the moment of birth, a believer's relationship to Allah is personal and direct. To justify state recognition, believers must demonstrate "self-organization" as well as clear differentiation from other faith groups, though both are antithetical to Islamic tradition. The result is a form of theological entrapment for Muslim communities: "On the one hand, legislature [*sic*] has set up rules for the acceptance of new faith communities. In turn, these set into motion the building of a new center and a new periphery, forcing activist believers and secularized Muslims into two different camps . . . the trap is functioning. German judges and politicians see themselves confronted by Muslim communities of orthodox and engaged believers, which are accused by other Muslims to be [*sic*] in pursuit of extreme political aims. Fear of 'Islam' does the rest."[35] A Bundestag inquiry determined that only 1.2 percent of Germany's estimated 2.8–3.2 million Muslims are members of radical or extremist organizations.[36] Since the Al Qaeda attacks of 2001, however, Islam has been "reified as the primary marker of difference, and demonised, with the help of the media, as fundamentalistic and terroristic. Despite more than thirty years of coexistence with Islamic believers in Frankfurt and other German and European cities, social intolerance based on ignorance is still the rule rather than the exception."[37]

Between the waves of *Übersiedler, Aussiedler,* Russian Jews, Muslim refugees and third generation Turks, migration has pluralized the religious playing-field but has not necessarily stabilized national identity. Opposition to Turkey's EU application offers one example of the ways anti-integrationists use religion to uphold a German identity that is far from unified. Conflating nationality with Islam, they argue that "Turkish" culture is irreconcilable with postwar Judeo-Christian identity, ignoring four hundred years of peaceful coexistence in Andalusia followed by centuries of European anti-Semitism. They insist that since Turkey is a secular state, German-Turks should remain secular—although most people flee their homelands in pursuit of more, not less religious freedom. Furthermore, many Muslims are not Turkish; adherents stem from Bosnia,

Lebanon, Iran, Iraq, Morocco and Algeria, as well as from Southeast Asia. Even Schieder mistakenly refers to Fereshta Ludin (the "headscarf" plaintiff) as Turkish; born in Afghanistan, she came to the FRG via Saudi Arabia.[38]

One should not underestimate the civic potential inherent in religious communities as sites for building social capital and networks; world events nonetheless deny some minorities the chance to use resources found here. Although Turks rejected religion as a source of social capital in the 1960s and 1970s, the specter of "parallel societies" prevails: officials claim that Islamic organizations isolate and mobilize "foreigners" against the host society.

These fears have not been borne out by ethnic associational patterns over time. Indeed, first generation migrants were *more* attracted to orthodox groups when they were "the only game in town." Controlled by the Turkish government, mosques and Qur'an schools focused on homeland developments. In 1961, there were an estimated 6,500 Muslims in the FRG; by 1995, the number had risen to 2.5 million.[39] Quantitative growth has been matched with qualitative differentiation. Over two thousand Islamic organizations reportedly embraced up to half a million members in 1995; this includes many occasional users, so-called Festival Muslims, since there are no dues requirements. The Turkish Islamic Union of the Agency for Religion (DITIB) in Istanbul encompasses 725 entities; in recent years the DITIB has distanced itself from internal national-political conflicts. The Association of Islamic Cultural Centers covers another 299 groups; even the ultraconservative Islamic Society Milli Görüs needs to build consensus among 274 mosque communities. The largest of eight umbrella associations is the Turkish Islamic Association, which has 740 member associations; the second largest is the Association for a New World View in Europe (AMTG), with 262 member organizations; there are also eighty-two Alevi communities. The radical fringe, represented by the Grey Wolves, boasts of 180 groups. Deep religious divisions are sometime compounded by ethnic differences, e.g., Kurds versus Turks versus Arabs.[40]

Limits on social-capital formation by way of Islamic associations existed well before the September 11th attacks. The first barrier is structural in nature. Given its 2–3 million Muslims, 450,000 of whom are citizens, Islam stands as the country's third largest religion; yet state authorities refuse to "recognize" it without a "formal, central authority."[41] Lacking a single leader like the Pope or the Archbishop of Canterbury, Islam cannot qualify as a "corporation of public law." Ironically, Kemal Ataturk secularized Turkey in 1928 by eliminating the position of Caliph, globally recognized as head of the (Sunni) Islamic movement. The lack of a worldwide rabbinical leader denied Judaism administrative recognition in the 1920s, with barbaric results, but it was granted in 1971. Leaderless Alevis have attained *Körperschaft* status in some states.[42] In December 2000, the Constitutional Court even granted corporate status to Jehovah's Witnesses.[43] Besides refusing blood transfusions, Jehovahs denounce military service and abjure voting rights. Denouncing the rule of law as "the work of the devil," believers refuse to dialogue with state officials or other faith communities.

Islam's lack of a transparent organizational structure is one excuse for denying its faithful the right to school instruction. Another is its inability to provide proof of a homogenous membership sharing a doctrinal consensus. Religious instruction in schools is largely denominational (proselytizing) in character, with the exception of Life-and-Ethics Training in Brandenburg. First-generation laborers had neither the time nor the theological expertise demanded by ministerial bureaucrats. Few imported Imams were fluent in German. The second generation, "educational insiders," remained secular. Members of the third generation enjoy some university access, but most are too young to assume leadership positions. Doctrinal differences among Muslims are neither more nor less significant than those among Christians, ranging from Catholics, Episcopalians, Unitarians, and Methodists, to Baptists, Jehovah's Witnesses, Christian Scientists, and Evangelicals.

Durability is a third formal requirement. Without a unified authority figure, there is purportedly no basis for determining whether a religion will "persist" long enough to justify public subsidies, although Islam has survived for nearly two thousand years. Worldwide there are more practicing Muslims than Christians. In exchange for providing a regular tax base, instructional, and construction subsidies, the state requires recognized communities to supply pastoral care in hospitals, prisons, and the armed services (for 1,100 Muslims soldiers in 1999), to manage teacher training and curriculum development, as well as to assume certain welfare responsibilities. As first generation guestworkers age, their desire to "settle debts with Allah" will increase the need for nursing homes, hospice care, and religious facilities. Many are shipped "home" for burial, given a lack of appropriate cemeteries. By 1988, Berlin had two Muslim cemeteries, Columbiadamm/Neukölln and Gatow/Spandau—in contrast to Bavaria, where 250 of the 260 Turkish-nationals who died in 1999 were shipped back for burial (a new ethnic enterprise opportunity!).[44]

Under the myth of return, practicing Muslims had to establish temporary prayer rooms in factories, hostels, and tenements.[45] Beyond funding Qur'an instruction in the 1970s, Saudi Arabia and Iran financed the first real mosques, added to those of Ahmadiyya and Alevi groups in Frankfurt/Main and Hamburg. Mosque construction provoked heated debates and negotiations at the local level, demonstrating that religion has become an urban development issue, as well as an integration concern. Permanent places of worship, perceived as alien intruders on the local landscape, need incorporation into broader urban policy agendas. Tensions first arise in relation to population density, coupled with ethnic concentration in certain districts. Analyzing the spatial politics of religion in the UK, Richard Gale and Simon Naylor suggest that minority efforts to establish houses of worship are equivalent to "negotiating their terms of belonging to Britain" for 1.5 million Muslims, half a million Hindus and another half a million Sikhs. The number of UK-certified worship sites rose from thirteen in 1964 to 614 Muslim mosques, 109 Hindu temples, and 193 Sikh temples by 1998.[46] Germany was home to nearly two thousand mosques by 1995. The largest worship sites include Berlin's Mosque of Martyrs (5,000 seats), the New Center Mosque in Frankfurt/Main (3,000), and the Mannheim Mosque (2,500).[47]

The first complaint usually centers on aesthetic incongruity. Local residents view mid-Eastern architectural features, like cupolas and minarets, as disruptive and out of character with the surroundings, though few complain about the Mercedes star on the Europa Center towering over the bombed-out Wilhelm Memorial Church along the Ku-damm, or grumble that the yellow "pregnant oyster" (former Congress Hall, now the House of Cultures) bears no organic relation to the *Tiergarten* behind it. In Stockton (UK), residents insisted that a seven-foot dome added to the Thornaby Mosque "would be an eyesore leading to road accidents." Locals also declared London's oldest all-purpose mosque in Wandsworth "out of place aesthetically," built before most of the houses surrounding it.[48] Once a mosque is constructed, it often becomes a community center, offering language courses, child-care, and social services.

Another objection is that mosques will "endanger the amenity of the area," attracting bad neighbors who refuse to engage in community activities or increase violence by provoking racist attacks! The problem begins with property acquisition. Jonker describes a crisis that ensued due to one group's lack of knowledge regarding Berlin real-estate and zoning laws. The Islam Vakfi (IV) community, linked to Milli Görüs, paid DM 2.85 million to a private realtor for a site in the Skalitzerstrasse, only worth DM 1.5 million under the city's "renovation ordinance." It commissioned an architect to design a mosque covering 2000 square meters but expanded the layout to 3,500 meters without seeking new approval. It added plans for a mini shopping mall, another zoning violation, declaring it "typical of old-city Islamic structures." City officials withdrew permission, and denied a DM 1 million subsidy, claiming that IV's purchase of five other properties showed it had capital to burn. Both sides walked away feeling betrayed, refusing to communicate further.[49]

A further stumbling block to neighborhood acceptance has more to do with urban density than with doctrinal differences. Natives and foreigners in Frankfurt and Berlin cite traffic as a major problem but part ways when it comes to allocating parking places for mosque visitors. One exasperated British Imam noted: "2000 Muslims—why are we having these problems with the planners when no one complains about the Cathedral?"[50] A more persistent objection centers on amplified calls to prayer, five times a day. Church bells pealing on the hour and every Sunday morning are rarely characterized as "noise pollution."

Outreach to Stuttgart's thirty-five thousand Muslims has taken the form of public dialogues labeled "World Religions in City Hall" and "Discussion Forum City-Religion," including Christian-Jewish dialogues. Commissioner Lavadinho would prefer classes on Ethics, Values and Life Training but, realistically, favors Islamic instruction in schools promoting "respect, recognition of values and mutual knowledge." By 2002, she had undergone a dramatic change of heart concerning Muslim headscarves, however. She initially favored "multicultural acceptance" but now categorically rejects hijab, "having become more acquainted with the scene." Lavadinho stressed Ludin's connections to fundamentalist groups, insisting that Afghan women she knows support the ban.

Educating for Citizenship: Islam in the Classroom

While Muslims have been busy learning the ropes, adapting architectural designs, securing permits, applying for construction loans, and practicing "good neighborly relations," Germans have been queuing up in front of the courts, demanding political remedies that overtax the theological capabilities of the judiciary. Former Chief Justice Ernst-Wolfgang Böckenförde holds that "the freedom-oriented, secularized state operates on the basis of prerequisites that it can itself not guarantee."[51] Article 7/3 GG requires all non-denominational schools to provide religion "as a regular part of the curriculum." The *Länder* regulate the contents in consultation with each faith community; 40 percent of all pupils exempt themselves from participation. Neither Article 6 (protection of marriage/family) nor Article 7 mandates an adherence to Judeo-Christian beliefs on the part of teachers. State neutrality is implicit in these passages, to ensure that no one religion will be granted dominance over others. Yet state educational ministers exercise disproportionate control over curricula, textbook selection, and qualifying exams for teachers. Their bureaucratic minions still enjoy feudal authority over the "calling" of university professors, despite their lack of substantive expertise.[52]

As T. H. Marshall recognized: "The education of children has a direct bearing on citizenship, and when the state guarantees that all children shall be educated, it has the requirements and the nature of citizenship definitely in mind. It is trying to stimulate the growth of citizens in the making."[53] The truth is, "hardly any institution in the Federal Republic has been so poorly prepared for the second and third generation of migrants as the schools."[54] In Frankfurt/Main, 53 percent of all children are of migrant descent, comprising 37 percent of school enrollments. The pattern of dead-end educational placement is disturbingly familiar: their presence in special-ed schools rose from 23 percent in 1980 to 45 percent in 1998, *Hauptschule* enrollments from 41 percent to almost 63 percent, leaving two-thirds stuck in institutions that will not qualify them for high-tech work in a global economy.[55] Minority unemployment (15 percent) is double that of Germans, posing "an integration barrier of the first order."[56] The 4 percent classified as city employees, mostly sanitation workers, maintain proverbial "German cleanliness."[57]

Starting in the mid 1990s, Frankfurt authorities adopted an "Opening of Schools," promoting intercultural pedagogy, along with a handbook for mother-tongue instruction. Still, half of the municipal library's foreign-language holdings are in English or French. Language training at the Volkshochschule has seen big funding cuts, but the Hessian Ministry of Culture allows non-Germans to pursue Italian, Greek, Spanish, Turkish, Portuguese, and Serbo-Croatian as their "first" foreign language. Twelve private associations receive subsidies to provide mother-tongue classes. In 1997, the Ministry worked with the Islamic Faith Community of Hesse, to integrate Muslim groups into religious-curricular and teacher-training processes. A CDU government displaced the Red-Green coalition in 1998, putting that operation on hold.

Analyzing Frankfurt patterns, Klopp asserts that children of migrant background are frequently "torn" between a fundamentalist version of Islamic tradition and German secularism.[58] Had he extended his research to Passau, he might have concluded that school kids there are just as torn between Turkish secularism and Bavarian Über-Catholicism! Bavaria has long used its power to hang fifty thousand crucifixes in public classrooms, declaring "education to honor God" an official learning objective for every pupil. One parent filed suit, arguing that children's constant confrontation with a tortured being hanging in front of their classrooms was "psychologically damaging." In May 1995, the High Court agreed that the state had overstepped the bounds of neutrality, outlawing crucifixes in public schools. Some thirty thousand Bavarians gathered in protest, challenging the competence of the Court, similar to the angry American evangelicals who opposed the forced removal of a multi-ton Ten Commandments monument from Judge Moore's courtroom in Alabama. Bavaria countered with a new law mandating crosses, coupled with procedures for their removal if parents object.

Instead of pillarizing Islam as in the Netherlands, Werner Schiffauer recommends "civil-izing" Islam in Germany by bringing it into the regular curriculum.[59] Through the 1970s, Islamic instruction was provided by teachers trained and paid by non-democratic Turkish and Saudi governments. Imported instructional materials offered few "practical moral choices" concerning the local environment. Ongoing discrimination with regard to housing, education, and employment opportunities through the 1980s enabled imported or self-radicalized "men of God" to create organizations that offered alternative welfare services, a sense of belonging, and regular religious services. About 24 percent (2,000) of all Turkish children were enrolled in Qur'an schools in the mid 1980s. Today there are nearly 700,000 Muslim children in German schools;

locally born, two-thirds are "constitutionally" entitled to seven hundred to one thousand hours of religious instruction.

Federalism accords the states significant educational autonomy, leading to sixteen different approaches; most supply classrooms and salaries. Three basic models emerged by the early 1990s, affording disparate opportunities for citizenship training. The first model (1980s) left voluntary religious instruction up to externally funded Qur'an schools, producing orthodox results and little hope for childhood integration. The second embedded Islamic instruction in Turkish mother-tongue lessons, also intended to prepare children for "homeland" return; rather than consulting with local Muslim leaders, Bavaria relies on syllabi delivered by the Turkish state. The third model, denominational or ecumenical, offers instruction in German, giving children the tools they need to share their beliefs with non-Muslims and to relate their values to daily experiences. Studies show that parents prefer German, which they see as "a clear upgrading" with regard to Islam's curricular standing.[60]

North Rhine-Westphalia made Islamic instruction available to forty elementary school pupils in 1986, extending lessons through the tenth grade by 1991; taught in thirty-seven schools by 1999, it declared this a subject that students must pass to advance to the next grade (pupils can choose mother-tongue classes if at least ten register).[61] Authorities worked with community representatives to define instruction for 240,000 Muslims (9 percent of pupils); consultations included experts from the Education School at the University of Hanover and the Theological Faculty in Ankara. Their aim was to teach Islam in German, affording students a healthier basis for personal religious identities while opening their Christian peers to different faiths. In 1995–1996, state authorities approved a curriculum for grades seven through ten. Materials are produced by the regional Institute for Schools and Further Education. Although the final product was presented to Muslim organizations for comment, the radical Kaplan movement in Cologne, the Central Council of Muslims in Germany, and the Islamic Council objected to the state's "preemptive" action in federal court. No longer employed by the Turkish government, teachers are vetted by educational administrators; lessons are voluntary. North Rhine-Westphalia has fifteen teachers who practice hijab among its regular teaching staff.

In June 1998, the Federal Administrative Court ruled that Article 7/1 GG grants the state "the authority to introduce new and supplementary instructional fields such as the discipline of Ethics" which "based on its inherent qualities, should be taught in a neutral fashion devoid of a particular world view."[62] This verdict has shifted the paradigm for inclusion of Islam in state-mandated classes. A month later, *Die Zeit* featured a series titled "Allah is ready for school." Catholic, Protestant, and Jewish leaders support Muslim demands for equal-opportunity instruction, though their primary interest lies in retaining "confessional" instruction. Circumventing Article 7, Hamburg experimented with an ecumenical model in the mid 1990s, not to be confused with Brandenburg's humanist orientation. Under the motto, "religion for all," representatives from Lutheran, Catholic, Jewish, Greek Orthodox, and other faith communities rotate teaching responsibilities, providing instruction about each religion to mixed groups as an ongoing "moral dialogue." Invited Muslim organizations joined the consortium in 1998.

Baden-Württemberg decided not to wait out final verdicts in four cases, establishing cooperative curriculum development and teacher-training programs. Bavaria announced plans to create a Round Table, pending trial outcomes, but it was never convened. Several schools in Erlangen agreed to participate in a pilot program commencing in September 2001. The government decided to act but ordered Erlangen to put its project on hold "until the rest of the state had 'caught up.'"[63] Hesse's Islamic Taskforce works with the Office of Multicultural Affairs to secure equal footing; as elsewhere, the problem is finding an adequate "negotiation partner." Courses there are taught in German by Muslims. As of 2000, neither Mecklenburg-Vorpommern, Saxony, Saxon-Anhalt, or Brandenburg offered Islamic classes. This owes to the dearth of minorities in the East, as well as to the predominance of atheists/agnostics, after forty years of "godless communism." In the early 1990s, Brandenburg introduced a non-denominational Life-training, Ethics, and Religion (LER) course. Hotly contested at the time, it now leads the pack in *civil-izing* religious instruction.

Berlin's special Four-Power status exempted it from Basic Law provisions through 1989, as did Soviet General Schukow's insistence in 1947 that school law allow parents to decide whether to impart religious education—or not. Schools in Berlin and Bremen set aside two hours each week for voluntary instruction; as of 2000, 52 percent of the elementary pupils, 78 percent of secondary students, and 88 percent of the *Gymnasium* youth opted out of religion or "world view" classes.[64] Only thirty-seven of five hundred schools offer the latter. Home to 140,000 Muslims and more than seventy mosques, Berlin bears witness to deep divisions within the community as a whole. Its largest community, the Islamic Federation (thirteen mosques), had filed multiple suits, seeking a place in schools. A decade of legal battles forced authorities to provide religious instruction for thirty-five thousand Muslim pupils (16.5 percent of 54,537 migrant offspring) as of 1998. Some 70 percent of all pupils in Mitte, Neukölln, and Kreuzberg are non-nationals.

The IFB constitutes a radical-conservative community, one of seventeen roof organizations established by Milli Görüs in 1980. Calling for a Sharia state, its clerics are openly hostile toward the non-Muslim majority; it directs several Arabic, Bosnian, and Albanian mosques as well. Denouncing moral turpitude and persecution in the world around them, its leaders instrumentalize discrimination for internal mobilization purposes. Having followed the group's activities closely, Jonker writes: "Community formation looks as follows: patriarchal, without middle management, internally closed with a swelling generational conflict, lacking any consideration for the abilities of women, presenting a sole partner responsible for dialogue along the border between inside and outside, and adhering to a collective perception that they are not understood, confirmed from time to time by mishaps in external communication."[65]

Mindful of its ultraconservative ties, Berlin judges "repeatedly sent the Federation home again with the task to establish organizational transparency, membership status and continuity," as well as "proof of the validity of its religious consensus." They further stipulated that the IFB had to "build a new organisation embodying its own idea of religious consensus and a marked distance to all other Islamic schools and directions of thought. In other words, to set up a denomination modelled on the Lutheran Church and to forget about the *Umma* as the unity of all Muslims and *Qur'an* and *Sunna* as their common basis."[66] Appearing as an expert witness for the IFB, Jonker insisted, "it is no business of any German court to push a faith community into heresy."[67] Satisfied with its martyr role, the IFB never expected to win; it was subsequently unable to sustain mosque alliances pulled together for the trial, much less to design suitable classroom curricula. It also met with immediate resistance from the Turkish Islamic Union and the Union of Islamic Culture Centers. The secular TBB joined the opposition, supporting inter-faith training in mixed classes. The city's twenty-year commissioner for foreigners, Barbara John, called the choice of organizations "unfortunate" but recognized that "this is the result of our own failure to come up with a different solution earlier."[68]

Since 1999, the Islamic Federation has offered religious instruction to 4,000 children at thirty-seven schools; Berlin covers personnel costs for its twenty-three teachers.[69] Alevis instruct another four hundred; DITIB has not filed for instruction rights, realizing its teachers will not qualify linguistically (interview with Robin Schneider). In June 2005, authorities amended school law, henceforth requiring academic training for Islamic instructors; they must submit to language testing by the Goethe Institute, demonstrating "perfect knowledge of German." Classroom visits revealed that several teachers switch to Turkish for most of the lesson. Berlin Assembly–member Özcan Mutlu (education/migration spokesperson for the Greens) welcomes the requirement as a way to reign in fundamentalist tendencies. The use of German will help pupils communicate their values to peers, and render lessons more relevant to their own surroundings. Education Minister Klaus Bölger (SPD) introduced Islamic Studies as an independent discipline, involving the Free University in a teacher-training program. On 3 June 2005, several hundred Catholics and Protestants demonstrated in front of City Hall, protesting Mayor Klaus Wowereit's decision to expand ethics/world-religions courses as alternatives to denominational instruction. Reluctant to lose a traditional, tax-subsidized bully pulpit in public schools, protestors declared: "God is more powerful than the Senate."[70]

Berlin's anti-discrimination officer, Sabine Kroker-Stille, supports voluntary confessional instruction combined with obligatory, value-neutral ethics training for all grade levels. State-monitored instruction in public schools would recognize and "upgrade" Islam in ways that would compel alienated youth to seek their identities in mainstream society, rather than in isolated, orthodox mosque communities. The real problem is that "politicians demand more value education . . . but at the same time undermine the integrative powers of schools and church through the conscious deregulation of society in the name of economic competitiveness."[71] I add, however, that deregulation is coupled with the belief that persons of migrant descent should continue to function as an easily exploitable service-economy reserve in decades ahead. Germany's ability to compete in the global economy depends on the educational attainments of this group. The lack of Islamic instruction in state schools is but a metaphor for other forms of educational opportunity denied.

The (re)discovery of Muslim identity allows disadvantaged youth to assert themselves as representatives of minority interests, affording alternative sources of recognition. Had authorities taken a proactive stance on religious instruction in the 1990s, they could have undercut "Islamicization" tendencies among youth. Young males are not the only ones now defiantly asserting their Muslim identities and seeking self-ethnicized leadership opportunities through the mosques. Increasingly conflated with religious fundamentalism, gender norms are re-emerging as markers of exclusion across European borders, as demonstrated by the highly sensationalized *Kopftuch* debate.

Religious Veil or Political Smokescreen? The Headscarf Debate

Setting the parameters of the German headscarf debate are five court verdicts challenging traditional notions of religious freedom. The first was the 1995 verdict prohibiting the classroom crucifixes in Bavaria. The second, in 2002, upheld a butcher's right to slaughter animals in accordance with *halal* to satisfy the needs of Muslim consumers. The Constitutional Court (BVerfG) then refused to review a 2001 appeal filed by Interior Minister Schily against the so-called Caliph-State in Cologne, claiming that Metin Kaplan sought to destroy the free-democratic order in favor of Islamic rule. The judges prevented Kaplan's extradition as an indicted terrorist to Turkey in 2003, where torture could have been used to garner evidence for conviction.[72] Karlsruhe also rejected an employer's complaint that customers *might* refuse to buy perfume from a woman wearing a headscarf in a department store; her concrete right to religious freedom outweighed unsubstantiated business claims. In 2003 the Administrative Court in Mainz nonetheless denied Social Assistance to a woman in a burqa, arguing that her clothing rendered her impossible to employ in the German labor market.[73]

The central figure in the FRG headscarf debate is Fereshta Ludin, the daughter of an Afghani diplomat; she was born in 1973. Ludin found religion as a teenager in Saudi Arabia, having already lived in Germany for two years. Her family is not devout, nor does her mother practice hijab; Ludin married a German who converted to Islam and now sports a beard. Ludin found Saudi treatment of women "deplorable," yet donned a headscarf while pursuing her *Abitur* in Baden-Württemberg; she acquired citizenship in 1995, then studied German, English, and social studies to qualify for a career in teaching. In early 1997, the Stuttgart superintendent rejected her student-teaching application; that decision was overturned by the state educational minister, Annette Schavan (CDU), who ruled that Ludin had the right to complete her degree. School authorities then refused to hire her in 1998. Shortly thereafter, the state assembly voted by a substantial majority *not* to adopt a headscarf ban for schools and universities.

Ludin undertook the first of many appeals in August 1998, denied in February 1999. She then sued, claiming her exclusion violated "state neutrality," rejected by Stuttgart's Administrative Court in March 2002. A Federal Administrative Court ruled on 4 July that Baden-Württemberg was not obliged to instate her. Constitutional Court proceedings commenced in July 2003. Voting five to three, the justices (six men, two women) declared on 24 September that Ludin could not be barred from public-school employment, since no state law banned headscarves per se. The verdict did not clarify "what rights [Muslims] actually do possess vis-à-vis majority culture."[74] Politicians jumped into the fray, declaring that they would take legislative action to exclude headscarf wearers from public service.

Ludin insisted that adherence to Islam *and* democratic values are essential to her personality; her headscarf is equated with support for the oppression she left Saudi Arabia to escape. She sought citizenship at a time when officials were free to decide whether an applicant was "committed to German-ness." Ludin now teaches at a private elementary school in Berlin, directed by Milli Görüs (under surveillance by the Office for Constitutional Protection). Denied public employment in her home state, she probably had few alternatives, since Catholic or Lutheran schools are unlikely to hire a Muslim; nor is she qualified for special-ed schools.

Prior to the High Court's "cowardly verdict" (citing Bundestag President Wolfgang Thierse), Justice Winfried Hassemer asked: "Is [a headscarf] just a pure piece of clothing, a sign of religious conviction, or a symbol of integration denied?" It can be one, none, or a combination of all of the above. The *Kopftuch* controversy has become a metaphor for bigger identity debates. Paradoxically, young Muslims with and without headscarves advocate women's self-determination learned in Germany, while feminists side with conservatives. Muslims interpret multiculturalism as the right to develop hyphenated identities; it requires tolerance, sharing, and respecting the "moral uniqueness" of others.

Opponents apply the simplistic formula: headscarf equals female oppression equals Islamicization equals threat to freedom and democracy. This projection mirrors the post–September 11th climate but upholds arcane notions of secularism unbefitting a global age.[75]

From a US perspective, claims based on Article 1 (personal freedom), Article 4 (religious freedom), and Article 12 (educational/occupational choice) should easily outweigh the penumbral rights of parents (Article 6) who choose *not* to expose their children to persons of different faiths in public schools. A blanket exclusion of women with headscarves amounts to a lifetime career ban hardly proportionate to one year of classroom "exposure" for hypothetical pupils. This ban would deny Muslim women, and only women, equal protection before the law, reversing burden-of-proof standards required by the EU in sex discrimination cases.[76] Women are automatically presumed guilty of attempted fundamentalist inculcation; no equivalent identifying feature applies to men. Imagine the outcry if they had banned beards!

Headscarf critics argue that "the state . . . identifies itself with an affected religion as soon as it allows the instruction for which it is responsible to take place in a certain kind of clothing. This occurs independently of whether or not the pupils themselves perceive the clothing in question as 'missionary' in nature."[77] Permitting hijab in one domain would open a Pandora's box, evoking demands "that even police women be permitted to wear scarves on duty." Aye, there's the rub: Grant minorities equal treatment in one workplace, and they will demand an end to discrimination in all walks of life! If the aim is to prevent terrorism, wouldn't officers fluent in Turkish or Arabic make better undercover agents?[78]

Bavaria finances several schools for nuns garbed in their own version of the black chador; Hesse, however, banned Baghwan clothing, monks' frocks, and nuns' habits from schools in the 1960s. Robert Leicht, president of the Evangelical Academy in Berlin, notes: "no one would ever think of denying nuns in public schools the right to voluntarily wear habits, merely because Catholic men forbid women from becoming priests, and thereby question their equality."[79] Strict Catholics, orthodox Jews, and fundamentalist Christians likewise reject the equality of men and women. The Taliban are as representative of Islam as the Spanish Inquisition leaders were of Catholicism. Forty years of terrorist activity among Catholics and Protestants in Northern Ireland has never been deemed "typical" of those religions.

It's a Generational Thing!

Leading the state since 1998, the '68ers have forgotten the vehemence with which they once blamed "the system" for the world's ills. Recalling parents who functioned as Nazi perpetrators, they underestimate family as a source of positive affirmation. Nor do today's sixty-somethings understand teenagers: Over 40 percent of my generational counterparts are childless; anyone with a teenager at home knows that the worst way to stop her from self-destructive behaviors is to declare things *verboten*! Muslim youth who feel unaccepted by mainstream society, female or male, construct positive identities for themselves based on the very symbols used to exclude them. One only needs to recall the "Black is beautiful" movement of the late 1960s.

The High Court declared in 2003: "A headscarf worn by a teacher for religious reasons can indeed have an especially intense effect on pupils because pupils are confronted by a teacher who stands at the center of instructional activity for the entire period of their school attendance, from which they cannot deflect their attention." As the mother of a fourth grader who attended school in Berlin in 2002, I have to ask: When was the last time either the justices or the *Kopftuch* critics spent a day in a German classroom, or more accurately, *half* a day, since regular public schools send kids home by noon? PISA test scores infer that FRG schools fall quite short of "intensive learning" regarding math, language arts, etc. Why presume that pupils pay more attention to a teacher's religious beliefs? If the instruction is really that intense, then why do so many kids lack fluency in German even if they make it as far as the ninth grade?

Headscarf opponents are evading the real issues of residential segregation, outdated teacher training, and little economic opportunity for minority youth. Many turn to mosques for acceptance, where they are exposed to fundamentalist teachings. Girls who wear headscarves find friends and even leadership roles denied them in classrooms where their attire provokes exclusion.[80] Those who possess higher educations stand poised to conquer that last bastion of historical male domination: the State. Access to lucrative, secure public employment would enable them to transcend second-class citizenship *and* help to civil-ize Islam. Instead they face a new glass ceiling.

"Islam ist jung, schic, cool!" Religious dress has become fashionable. Tekbir Inc., Turkey's largest manufacturer of Muslim clothing, markets modesty with a twist, as stressed by CEO Mustafa Karadurman: "Women thought that they had to drape a bag over themselves in order to practice Islam. We're breaking with that image. Many media outlets have had to admit that 'Islamic attire' can be beautiful. What preachers are unable to achieve with their sermons, we have been able to communicate with our shops and fashion shows."[81]

One woman's oppression can become another woman's liberation: "While many of their mothers and grandmothers have thrown off the veil as a sign of female subordination, the new 'Islamic covering' is donned nowadays by young, educated women, including academics and students from the modern middle strata, as a matter of personal choice."[82] Veiling is infused with new meaning:

while the practice was construed as rural/backward/ignorant in the past, it is now associated with urban/modern/educated identity choices.

It's a Gender Thing!

An uncovered head is no sooner a bona fide occupational qualification for professional employment than maleness used to be.[83] Thirty years ago, the hijab was a non-topic, although many guestworkers came from conservative Anatolian villages—what mattered was their manual dexterity for assembly work at Siemens. Even now, few Germans find it oppressive when Muslim women wear headscarves while scrubbing public toilets or mopping school hallways at night. In the 1980s, Western feminists hailed a scarf-draped Benazir Bhutto as a politician/mother who triumphed over macho-militaristic Muslims.[84] A 1924 ban in secular Turkey forces devout women to wear wigs *over* their headscarves, to avoid expulsion from universities. Besides suffering through extreme heat, young women must deliberately break the law in order to exercise religious freedom.

Like their conservative counterparts, feminist Cassandras see an unbroken progression from hijab to chador to burqa. In real life, Afghan women subjected to burqa were *first* kicked out of the professions, then denied education. Marriageable age was lowered from sixteen to thirteen to nine for girls; thereafter females were denied freedom of movement, refused medical treatment, re-subjected to genital mutilation, and required to paint their home windows black. "Barefoot and pregnant" was all that remained. The 1979 Khomeini revolution in Iran overthrew the very Shah, Reza Pahlavi, Berlin students denounced in 1967. Iranian women are making a comeback, however: by the late 1990s, over 50 percent of all university students were female, chadors notwithstanding, rising to 62 percent at the University of Teheran by 2003.[85]

In September 2003, seventy prominent women from Berlin-Brandenburg appealed to lawmakers *not* to bar headscarves from the workplace.[86] They were immediately challenged by autonomous feminists claiming to be the real defenders of women's rights. "We note with amazement," the Anti-Manifesto group declared,

> those now coming forward in vehement support of a basic right to headscarves in the classroom. We have pushed for years for an intercultural opening of the civil service, for equal opportunity in the labor market, the right to vote, for independent residency rights for migrating wives, for the recognition of sex-specific persecution regarding asylum, against racism and discrimination. We wished then that the *Promi-Women* who now want to raise public consciousness for a right to headscarves would have engaged themselves with equal vigor for the equal opportunity of migrant women who don't wear headscarves.[87]

In fact, they did, albeit not by way of the autonomous feminist movement. Since 1998, female politicians, using the legislative process, have reversed the burden of proof with regard to employment discrimination, and amended domestic abuse laws to read: "the batterer goes, the victim stays." The Red-Green government adopted new immigration laws, supported by CDU-femocrats Rita Süssmuth and Barbara John. Citizenship will guarantee minority women greater equality, independent residency rights and access to civil service jobs—a great leap forward—provided they don't have to sacrifice religious freedom in order to access opportunity.

Renouncing hijab will not end domestic violence: Homes for battered women were created in the early 1970s to assist natives, not foreigners; Eastern shelters opened in 1989 rapidly filled to capacity. Even Sweden reports mounting abuse, 22,400 cases in 2003, up from 14,000 in 1990.[88] Nor will it eliminate heinous practices like forced marriage or "honor killing." According to Foreign Ministry data, 21,447 Turkish citizens entered Germany under family unification in 2001. There are no reliable statistics on forced marriages, characterized as "a modern form of slavery"; the number of brides exported back to Turkey is also unknown. A 2002 survey led the Berlin Senate to "guestimate" forced marriages at 230 among local 16–22 year olds (interview with Kroker-Stille, 1 July 2005). According to a 2003 Family Ministry study, half of the 150 women interviewed admitted their parents had chosen their partners; a quarter had not met their spouses prior to marriage, twelve were married against their wills.[89] Exporting parents "un-register" (*abmelden*) daughters under age eighteen to preclude their return—§44 of the Aliens Act automatically cancels residency permits for persons who do not re-enter within six months; only citizenship can ensure unlimited return, should women choose to flee.

The solution lies in educating young women about their rights, sensitizing personnel at schools and consulates, and prosecuting family collaborators, as recently happened in Denmark.[90] Baden-Württemberg took the first step toward countering forced marriage in 2004. Berlin Justice Minister Karin Schubert introduced a Bundesrat proposal in June 2005, subsequent to expert hearings in Berlin and North Rhine-Westphalia (draft documents 15/3544 and 15/3274). Rather than relying on implicit protection against *Nötigung* (holding someone against her will under §240 Federal Criminal Code), forced marriage merits "a law of its own," imposing criminal sanctions on all who profit from such unions through dowries, cash, or work permits. Schubert advocates amending the Civil Code, allowing nullification of such unions up to three years (instead of one); modifying residency rules to allow for a later return (three months after dissolution); granting residency rights to imported brides even if the marriage lasts less than two years—to meliorate the consequences they face as "damaged goods" if forced to return to home villages; and terminating inheritance rights for parents and other relatives.

One solution would be to raise the minimum age for family unification; spouses must be twenty-four to enter Denmark, twenty-one in the Netherlands. Partners should be required to provide full support, including a separate dwelling, to prevent routine exploitation by in-laws. In addition to outlawing entry for multiple wives—accepted if married outside the FRG!—Necla Kelek (a controversial figure) would prohibit marriages among first cousins and other close relatives. One investigation among Berlin gynecologists discovered fourteen fetuses with serious genetic anomalies (8.5 percent) among 160 pairs of cousins who sought prenatal care in 2002.[91]

One of seventy Manifesto signatories, Birgit Rommelspacher links new patterns of racism and diversity problems among contemporary feminists with an identity complex vis-à-vis the national past.[92] Feminist rhetoric has been touched by far-right discourses reinvoking ethnonationalism; some now label themselves "white German Christian feminists" vis-à-vis religious Muslim women. They could learn a great deal by exploring the role of female honor and virtue in a comparative migration context. Gloria Gonzales-Lopez discovered that as newly arrived Mexican mothers in the US "replace marriage with career goals for their daughters, their ideas about appropriate sexual behavior also change. Virginity depreciates as a form of social capital. Education and employment opportunities emerge as new goods."[93] Yen Le Espiritu argues that racialized minorities often denounce the morality of white women as a strategy of resistance, turning "a morally superior public face to the dominant society."[94] Asserting German fashion preferences as a criterion for emancipation leads the migrant community "to exert its moral superiority over the dominant Western culture and to reaffirm its self-worth in the face of economic, social political, and legal subordination. . . . The immigrant community uses restrictions on women's lives as one form of resistance to racism. This form of cultural resistance, however, severely restricts the lives of women, particularly those of the second generation, and it casts the family as a potential site of intense conflict and oppressive demands in immigrant lives."[95]

Women's attire has always been a battleground for repression. Consider the extraordinary sums spent outfitting US brides! Scarves were even an issue in Nazi concentration camps, after women's heads had been shaved: "In spite of regulations against this, [French women] wore their kerchiefs in a hundred different ways," not only to preserve their personal identities but as a form of symbolic resistance.[96] Members of the '68 generation imagined themselves a revolutionary force every time they donned Palestinian scarves en route to university classes or demonstrations. Odd that they would now require Palestinian women to throw *off* their scarves in order to appear liberated. Headscarves need not serve as proof of repression; they also signal a demand for self-determination. Muslim women report that their scarves give them a sense of security in public, whether they work as computer experts, postal employees, physicians, or police officers. One woman who began wearing the hijab in Britain after September 11th describes it "as an act of solidarity with Muslim women all around the world. . . . I have found a great deal of strength through wearing the *hijab*, and now every day is a good hair day as far as I am concerned!"[97]

Many Germans think nothing of sun-bathing nude on public beaches in conservative vacation spots like Greece or Turkey. This feminist mother would rather see her teenage son sitting next to a diligent girl in a headscarf than surrounded by Britney-Spears wannabes flaunting belly-button piercings, tattoos, and cleavage. Pregnancy rates among Germans under age fifteen have risen dramatically, as have abortion rates (most Muslims endorse sex education in the schools).[98] Rather than regulating what goes *on* the heads of Muslim girls, authorities should address things taking place *in* the heads of these girls: worrying about role conflicts, unemployed parents, macho brothers, etc. One Frankfurt teacher admitted "that girls need extra support and that the social workers 'must take other cultures' feelings of honor seriously', because they do in fact 'get internalized', even by those trying to rebel against such cultural constraints."[99]

I concur with Marieluise Beck: "Forced emancipation through exclusion cannot be the answer. It hits girls and women, not the male oppressors who stand behind it all."[100] Muslim girls face a double bind: They are eager to take on new roles, yet ethnic socialization provides females few opportunities to "act out" through sports or gang activities. Yes, devout parents refuse daughters the right to participate in field trips or physical-education classes. Jehovah's Witnessess and other Christian sects deny *their* children medical treatment, blood transfusions, and attendance at school dances. I do not doubt that forced marriages or "honor killings" occur; Berlin registered six cases in 2005. Involving women who reject hijab and pursue German lifestyles, these cases are rare, sensationalized, and erroneously projected onto an entire ethnic group.[101] If headscarves afford protection against the unwanted looks of lascivious males, then our first priority ought to be changing the "sinful and satanic behavior" of men, rather than denying women the one freedom they have been granted by fathers, husbands, and brothers: the right to educate themselves and to receive decent wages for their labor. United Nations and World Bank studies show that women's biggest enemy is ignorance.[102] Schools should provide the ultimate refuge for women and girls who face subjugation at home or in their religious communities.

It's a German-Identity Thing!

The headscarf is clearly a symbol, but who is qualified to decide *what* it symbolizes? Is "the veil of women the flag of the Islamic crusaders" á la Alice Schwarzer, an indicator of anti-Semitic sympathies, or a symbol of religious solidarity?

CDU Culture Minister Karin Wolff insists that "wearing headscarves hinders integration," clearly confusing cause with effect.[103] It is the lack of serious integration policies over a span of several decades that has led to an exponential increase in headscarf use. Indeed, the public debate is loaded with subjunctives: should, would, could, and might.

Denying women education in the name of preserving Judeo-Christian culture is a perversion of rights. In countries where Islamic extremists "have targeted women's bodies as an ideological battle ground for control," women are peeling off the layers.[104] In Germany, where women are routinely stripped naked and commodified by way of newspaper kiosks, television commercials, and posters at public bus stops, some control their bodies by covering themselves. Ban females with headscarves from public schools, and this is what you get: In September 2003, the Averroes Lycée, France's first Muslim high school, opened its doors to twelve boys and six girls. Privately funded (tuition is $1,000 per year), the school is owned by the Islamic League of the North, linked to the extremist Union of Islamic Organizations of France and the Egyptian Muslim Brotherhood. The König-Fahd-Akademie in Bonn, funded by Saudi Arabia, also preaches radical Islam. Founded in 1994, it has 460 pupils (200 are German citizens); one of its teachers has called for a "holy war" against the west.[105] Boys educated in schools supported by fundamentalist groups are more inclined to interact with terrorist circles than girls, as we know from madrasas in Pakistan that fed the Taliban ranks in Afghanistan.

An *Inländer*'s decision to distance herself from some traditional practices may be accompanied by a desire to strengthen other connections to her religious community. While German and French pundits focus on the radical fringe, Euro-Muslims, with and without head coverings, see themselves as the antithesis of a darkly imagined Islamicized Europe. The career goals of young Muslims prove that they do not reject "assimilating" forces, only the one-size-fits-all formula dictated by the host culture: they choose to live as Germans by birth, as Muslim-Germans at home, and Muslims in public. Colored headscarves accentuate their makeup and mounted hairdos, long coats offer temporary cover for tight pants, platform shoes, and fashion T-shirts underneath.

The *Kopftuch* controversy triggered a transnational citizen mobilization heretofore unseen among Euro-Muslims, beyond Kurdish protests of the 1990s. Demonstrations in January 2004—attracting 5,000 protesters in Paris, 3,500 in Lille, 2,400 in London, and 2,000 in Berlin—should have triggered fond memories among the '68 generation. One Berlin banner boasted "Mein Kopf gehört mir," reminding German feminists of their own emancipatory mantra, "Mein Bauch gehört mir."[106] German-Muslims need to dialogue their own way through this issue. For many, the headscarf is a profession of faith, for some a symbol of resistance, for the rest a political fashion accessory. Young Muslim women *are* challenging the legitimacy of "universal" religious codes restricting the rights of women—even if they are following the Sinatra Doctrine, doing it "their way."

My experiences with educational institutions in Hamburg, Erfurt, Stuttgart, and Berlin revealed that the entire system needs an "extreme makeover." Underachievement among ethnic minorities is only the tip of the iceberg. Comparative testing (PISA I and II) proves that German educational outcomes fall shockingly below international averages. In 2002, Berlin instituted a language test in four central districts for children entering school. The Bärenstark ("Strong as a Bear") study tested 9,874 children in Mitte, Friedrichshain-Kreuzberg, Schöneberg-Templehof, and Neukölln; 51 percent were natives, 49 percent had different mother tongues. Only 10 percent of the latter could participate in school without language tutoring; 60 percent needed "intensive training." Among native speakers, only 55 percent were ready for school; 13 percent required a six-month intensive prep course, the rest an intermediate course. One school in a well-tended section of Charlottenburg recently failed 15 of 22 eighth graders![107] Over 12,100 failed in 2005: 1,288 in elementary schools, 1,929 in *Hauptschulen*, 2, 346 in *Realschulen*, and 2,703 in *Gymnasien*, and 3,441 in comprehensive schools.

In 2004, twice as many minority children left Berlin schools without certification (24 percent) as qualified for university admission (12 percent). Ethnic females are the real losers of educational opportunity: comprising 28 percent of *Hauptschule* dropouts, they account for only 36 percent of the *Abitur*-earners. The rest, shunted into *Realschulen*, add up to a serious waste of brain power—lacking active career counseling and "new-economy" apprenticeships; 43 percent of the *Inlander* in higher education are female, yet only 8 percent of Berlin's minorities completed degrees in 2003–2004. College graduation rates among Germans are equally abysmal at 25 percent. The Urban Renaissance Study highlighted the material costs this holds for the city's future.[108] Women are crucial integration agents. As the African proverb attests, "Educate the girl, and you educate the village." All women need access to language and civics courses, irrespective of economic dependence or marital status. Imported brides need special courses defining their rights to physical integrity, self-actualization, freedom of conscience, and family protection under the Basic Law.

Comprehensive school reform in Berlin (2004) has been blocked by the budget crisis. Indeed, I was advised by a member of the integration commissioner's staff in June 2005 *not* to seek a school for my son until "things settle down in 2006." Educational deficits begin with Germans, becoming cumulative disadvantages among ethnic kids in poor neighborhoods; in 2003, 32 percent under age fourteen lived with welfare-dependent families. The Eberhard-Klein-Oberschule in Kreuzberg does not have a single native speaker among its enrollees. Created in response to the industrial needs of the 1800s, the *Hauptschulen* have become a fast track to unemployment; stigmatization is only one reason why

10.7 percent of the German Berliners and 24 percent of the "hyphenated" youth quit school with no certification in 2003–2004. Replacing them with multi-track, modernized comprehensive schools would be my first recommendation.

In 2005, the Berlin Assembly enacted a Neutrality Law, banning headscarves in relation to schools, the legal profession, and police careers. Characterized as "the most liberal option possible" by two interview partners, the law allows headscarf use in kindergartens, provided parents do not object. No one has been "fired" to date; the real problem is that the city is so broke it can't hire new teachers to deal with increasing classroom demands. The 2004 Zuwande-rungsgesetz (Migration and Integration Law) adds to the burden, mandating (unaffordable) language/orientation courses for new migrants and many denied these opportunities in the past.[109]

The only limitations on freedom of movement and the exercise of a chosen profession across EU boundaries are those pertaining directly to certified train-ing or bona fide occupational qualifications. European Council Regulation 1612/68 (1968), as amended by Council Regulation 312/76 (1976), was modi-fied further in 1998 to allow any EU national to seek employment, participate in vocational training, or pursue self-employment in another member state. The Amsterdam Treaty (Article 13) prohibits "all discrimination on the grounds of sex, racial or ethnic origin, religion, belief, disability, age or sexual orientation."

The separate and unequal status accorded Muslim women across EU bound-aries puts Germany and France on a collision course with the European Court of Justice under cover of several equal-treatment directives, revised Treaties, and the European Charter. I believe that anti-discrimination rules will ultimately prevail, despite a Court of Human Rights ruling upholding headscarf bans in Turkey. Paradoxically, religious rights will be imposed in ways that make nation-als feel that their identities are even more threatened by integration and global-ization. French and Dutch citizens rejected the proposed EU constitution in June 2005.[110] Ironically, the (embedded) European Convention on Human Rights and Fundamental Freedoms, added to new national parliamentary controls over Union decision making, would have strengthened a *citizens' Europe*. Minority-rights protection would apply not only to historical populations like the German Sorbs and Sami-Lapplanders, but also to bona fide migrants and aging guest-workers. Berlin has drawn up an "action package," expecting to transpose EU constitutional protections into state practice following ratification.[111]

Conclusion: Beyond Repressive Tolerance

Composer Richard Wagner once observed: "Deutsch-sein heisst die Sache, die man treibt, um ihrer selbst willen treiben" (Being German means doing what-ever one is doing for its own sake). Sixty years have passed since Germany was forced to incorporate over twelve million war refugees. Two-thirds of its 7.3 million non-citizens have made the FRG the focal point of their lives for more than twenty years, accounting for 13 percent of all births, despite claims that it is not "a land of immigration." Citizenship laws of the last four decades have trapped millions of human faces behind exclusionary masks of foreignness. In summer 2005, state officials deported Afghan and Bosnian refugees back to purportedly "stable" homelands. Countless children have learned German, attended local schools for six years and appear "integratable," Minister Otto Schily noted. Still, they are ineligible for citizenship, since their parents are not permanent residents. They will have a hard time adjusting to cultures many no longer remember. Though their own people are aging at a precipitous rate, leaders insisted on expelling a great deal of brain power, entrepreneurial spirit, productive labor, and democratic commitment, "doing whatever it is doing for the sake of being German." The rest of the country was away on vacation.[112]

My participant-observer status over many years has enabled me to pinpoint oddities, asymmetries, and outright contradictions in FRG law that natives accept as normal. Like Norbert Cyrus, I believe that deliberate efforts *not* to integrate foreigners over the last three decades have rendered migration a negative byproduct of uncoordinated policy choices in other domains. The Federal Republic offers a clear case in which social reality has overtaken the structural connection between law and identity, between culture and politics. Politicians kept hoping the "foreigner problem" would go away—literally. Instead, the *Outlanders* multiplied, as did the problems created by Germany's exclusionary citizenship laws.

According to Margarete and Alexander Mitscherlich, what rendered Germans susceptible to Nazi barbarity and left them with an historical "inability to mourn" is a much deeper inability to empathize.[113] I see striking parallels between German skinheads and alienated Muslims. Lacking direct experience with the Nazi period, or with life in a distant homeland, most teens take their ties to a democratic Federal Republic for granted. Natives and *Inlanders* evince an instrumental relationship with the state, not a sentimental one rooted in organic or *völkish* traditions. Most find positive sources of identity in educational attainment, travel opportunities, hobbies, and language skills; they thus feel at home in a variety of contexts. Like neo-Nazi skinheads who have fallen between the cracks, ethnic gangs and Islamicist *Fundis* seek their identities at the extremes insofar as their marginalized position in society leaves them with no other place to look. Both groups turn to re-ethnicization ("Germany for the Germans!"), hyper-masculinity, and provocative behavior to defend what little turf they have.

Reluctant to articulate "love for the *Vaterland*," Germans cannot empathize with what Mahdi labels the "paradoxical nature of biculturalism."[114] Until the Germans themselves can admit to positive feelings about their own country, or identify values and lifestyles that set them apart from others, how can they expect foreigners to do likewise? Even the insistence that migrants learn "proper German" is undermined by the barrage of billboards, TV ads, and political talk shows using English phrases for cosmopolitan flair.[115] As Ulrich Gutmaier observes, "If Germany continues to present itself as a *Volksgemeinschaft* of paranoid petty citizens, then we will really have a problem."[116]

What lessons can we derive from this complexly interwoven story of Germany as a land of active immigration and thwarted integration? For starters, none of the standard migration theories apply to the German citizenship paradigm when it is analyzed as more than a sum of its parts. Most scholarly works concentrate either on a single "ethnicity" (Russians, Turks, Italians), or on groups sharing a particular legal status (guestworkers, repatriates, asylum seekers), or on communities evincing allegedly monocultural traits like religion (Muslims, Jews). A focus on any one category may lead to definitive conclusions, but these are only valid for one section of a bigger societal puzzle. Theories "affirmed" at the macro level quickly lose their explanatory power at the micro level; in short, the devil is in the detail, as we discovered regarding four broad ideational frameworks.

The liberal-individual orientation, focusing on legal barriers to political participation, is unlikely to emerge as a national solution to migration management. The conservative-organic approach, institutionalized under *jus sanguinis*, acquired mythical standing and legitimation. However, historical conflicts between Prussians and Bavarians, Catholics and Protestants, *Ossis* and *Wessis*, not to mention among "repatriates" from Poland, Russia, and Kazakhstan, prove that Germany was never ethnically homogeneous. Generational, geographic, and global change have laid this imagined community to rest. Alternatively, migration theories emphasizing mobile-transnational patterns are "high on inflationary rhetoric" but "low on critical theoretical reflection and systematic empirical evidence."[117] Italian and Polish migrant workers are sooner ignored than integrated; their offspring are trapped in-between. Temporary laborers have little in common with the jet-setting managers and IT professionals who benefit from such theories. Though still evolving, the practical-communitarian approach works best in fostering migrant integration, irrespective of national political context. Social capital and its structural correlate, civil society, is absolutely essential in sustaining the trust, reciprocity, and connectedness needed to "make democracy work." Substantive rights to participation make more sense when they derive from sharing a stake in day-to-day community outcomes, as opposed to pseudo-organic identities grounded in ethnic descent.

I have also shown that motley waves of migrants encountered distinctive problems in relation to the host society, compelling them to develop new strategies of accommodation across time. As each generation sought to participate in the host society, policy makers "switched codes," compelling migrants to carve out their own paths. The citizenship-equals-ethnicity paradigm (chapter 3) failed to explain successes of repatriate groups through the 1980s, compared to the failures of their co-ethnic counterparts after 1990; the latter score poorly in terms of economic, social, *and* political integration. Nor does the citizenship-equals-legal-status paradigm (chapters 2, 5, 6) offer a clear explanation for the effective (self-)integration of Berlin's non-national Turks versus the poor economic and political integration record of its EU-national Italians, and now Poles. The citizenship-equals-religion paradigm (chapters 4, 7) is even more tenuous. Muslims and Jews are being pushed back into identities many never actively embraced, rendering the former "unintegratable" and the latter privileged in its access to integration services and accelerated naturalization.

My cross-national comparisons of the Netherlands, UK, Sweden, and Denmark show that laws and structures do shape political integration. As the horse-trough-water dilemma suggests, however, groups have to cultivate their own sources of political trust and social capital, achieved through ethnic mobilization and networking. Ethnic networking can nonetheless produce "mobility traps" with respect to educational and occupational progress, necessary for sustainable economic integration. Urban comparisons (Berlin, Frankfurt, Stuttgart) illustrate that local leaders can raise or lower barriers to legal integration but often lack the power resources needed to remedy problems resulting from national "non-policies."

The demands of seven million *Inlanders* are finally yielding to dialogues over citizenship, multiculturalism, and the role of minorities in the "leading culture." Ethnonationalism fails to recognize that each person can embody a variety of sentimental and instrumental allegiances. As one Frankfurt activist declared: "We want to have German citizenship, but not German-ness."[118] Like District Commissioner Doris Nahawandi (Friedrichshain-Kreuzberg), I have yet to receive a satisfactory answer to the question: who or what is an *integrated German*?[119] It is time to replace a negative, reactive emphasis on the "deficiencies" of minorities with proactive "diversity management" on the part of the majority culture. This study further shows that the integration failures of the last thirty years owe, first, to a lack of political will and, secondly, to arcane German policy structures responsible for overarching socioeconomic stagnation. The Red-Green government undercut its own reform initiatives by ignoring the recommendations of its Independent Commission on Immigration (ICI), and then by disbanding a new Integration Council in December 2004.

Mosque construction, school curricula, and the regulation of women's attire all testify to the socially constructed nature of religious recognition in Germany. All three have the dubious distinction of rendering Islam physically visible in urban settings, confirming the permanent nature of migration—and the need for a broader value consensus in a would-be global city. Metropolitan officials do recognize that integration is a reciprocal process, requiring a comprehensive, proactive "package" of rights, regulations, and programs. However, neither cities nor districts control the policies that render them pockets of blocked opportunity, e.g., school curricula, apprentice programs, housing, or welfare policy. Integration is occurring across urban settings employing numerous strategic approaches, but all point in the same direction: though not a sufficient condition for mediating sociocultural conflicts, equal access to participatory rights is an absolutely necessary one. There is no substitute for genuine political inclusion.

Rosa Luxemburg said it best: "Freedom is always and exclusively freedom for the one who thinks differently. Not because of any fanatical concept of 'justice' but because all that is instructive, wholesome and purifying in political freedom depends on this essential characteristic, and its effectiveness vanishes when 'freedom' becomes a special privilege."[120] FRG policymakers need to stop attributing "failed integration" to cultural differences and recognize that structural factors hold enormous consequences for societal incorporation. Under the 1999 Citizenship Law, third-generation "migrants" can finally access political rights denied their parents and grandparents on the basis of bureaucratic discretion. Ethnic youth face qualitatively different problems in forging their national identities, caught between parental "homelands" experienced only during vacations, and local landscapes devoid of social mobility.

Herbert Marcuse, a literary favorite of the Baby Boom activists, recognized that "law and order are always and everywhere the law and order which protect the established hierarchy; it is nonsensical to invoke the absolute authority of this law and this order against those who suffer from it and struggle against it—not for personal advantages and revenge, but for their share of humanity."[121] Do *Bundesrepublikaner* still have so little faith in their own democratic institutions that they can't withstand new forms of religious freedom among 3 percent of the population? Attitudes toward immigration tell us more about German fears of European integration than about foreigners; claims that they will "lose" their national identity tell us more about globalization-*Angst* than about how Germans define themselves. Complaints that migrants take German jobs are expressions of frustration over leaders refusing to address economic problems really tearing at the social fabric.

Germany's aging '68ers have lost their radical-emancipatory edge, a consequence of moving through the lifecycle. Decades of protest, and eight years of Red-Green government, have left the nation a lot more tolerant than they found it, but they find it hard to move beyond their own paradigm. Marcuse's logic regarding "repressive tolerance" still holds, even if the cohorts comprising The Establishment have changed:

> Within the affluent society, the affluent discussion prevails, and within the established framework, it is tolerant to a large extent. All points of view can be heard: the

Communist and the Fascist, the Left and the Right, the white and the Negro, the crusaders for armament and disarmament. Moreover, in endlessly dragging debates over the media, the stupid opinion is treated with the same respect as the intelligent one, the misinformed may talk as long as the informed, and propaganda rides along with education. This means that previously neutral, value-free aspects of learning and teaching now become, on their own grounds in their own right, political.[122]

He continues, "When tolerance mainly serves the protection and preservation of a repressive society, when it serves to neutralize opposition and to render men [*sic*] immune against other and better forms of life, then tolerance has been perverted."[123]

Higher crime and delinquency rates are not a function of ethnoreligious differences but rather evidence that youth are denied access to everyday opportunity structures, like quality education and job training. If minorities appear to be more violent, it is because spatial concentration makes their aggression easier to observe, and because they have already experienced more violence by way of parents, police, or other hostile youth. The share of non-German youth (age eight to twenty-one) arrested in Berlin declined from 33 percent to 26 percent in 2003; German males account for over two-thirds of the group violence, even though these adolescents comprise a much smaller segment of the total population.[124] The bigger question is why so many native kids, born into a country as wealthy, orderly, free, and democratic as the Federal Republic, likewise embrace violence as an acceptable form of conflict resolution. When asked whether they could "imagine any personal conflicts that just have to be settled with violence," 27 percent of the *Aussiedler* youth agreed, but so did 20 percent among German teens.[125] The July 2005 attacks on subways and buses in London were executed by males of Pakistani origin born and educated in Britain. Under-educating children of migrant origin will not secure the nation against terrorism; neither will tougher border controls: terrorists are increasingly homegrown. Islamic fundamentalism and misogynist perversions of Sharia can only be prevented through the active engagement of Europe's Muslim community, not by working against it.

A final lesson gleaned from my efforts to put a human face on migration and integration debates is that "diversity is not what it used to be."[126] It is no longer the state but the city that bears primary responsibility for resolving conflicts wrought by structural adjustment, physical dislocation, and privatized membership privileges. Cities hoping to secure their future in the globally competitive market place will have to ensure investors that they can deliver what Richard Florida labels "the Three Ts: Technology, Talent, and Tolerance."[127] High achievers look for political communities that respect their differences.

Full citizenship, along with the responsibilities it brings for promoting the common good, cannot be forced on anyone but should be available to all who want it. For many Turkish residents, post-unification developments resulted in a demotion from co-citizenship to third-class citizenship. This has led entrepreneurs, political activists, and younger cohorts to naturalize at higher rates since the late 1990s, but their identification with Germany is sooner rooted in the local community than in an historical-national territory.

Fostering social, economic, and political integration through citizenship is "neither a policy problem nor a problem of institutional design; it is, instead, a problem of political will."[128] I spent April–July 2006 back at the Humboldt University, within walking distance of the "Fan Mile" that attracted nearly one million World Cup revelers. The stretch between the Brandenburg Gate and the Siegessäule (the Victory Column), commemorating highs and lows in German history, was packed with young people waving/wearing FRG flags, covered in black/red/gold face paint and wigs, offering spontaneous renditions of the national anthem and the official FIFA theme song—"Arriba, Arriba!" composed by Jorge Luis Piloto. Mirroring the 2006 motto, "die Welt zu Gast bei Freunden" (the world as guests among friends), young crowds everywhere resembled "the united faces" used to advertise Benetton clothing. Turkish-German youth headed the car caravans cruising up and down the Ku-damm (where I sat with beer-drinking friends), honking incessantly after the FRG's first two victories. The mood was characterized as the "New Partyotism." Thousands cried, literally, as the party came to an end with the closing ceremony on 10 July. These scenes, and the deep feelings they evoked among all participants, offered compelling visual testimony that Germany has become a land of immigration and integration. All it needs is the political will to accept itself as one.

Notes

1. Beauftragte für Ausländerfragen, eds., *Von Dialog zur Kooperation: Die Integration von Muslimen in der Kommune*, In der Diskussion no. 12 (Berlin/Bonn, May 2002).
2. Ali Akbar Mahdi, "Iranian Women: Between Islamicization and Globalization," in Ali Mohammadi, ed., *Iran Encountering Globalization: Problems and Prospects* (London/New York: Routledge, 2003).
3. Brett Klopp, *German Multiculturalism: Immigrant Integration and the Transformation of Citizenship* (Westport, CN: Praeger, 2002); Klopp, "The political incorporation of EU foreigners before and after Maastricht: The new local politics in Germany," *Journal of Ethnic and Migration Studies* 28, no. 2 (2002): 185.
4. Riva Kastoryano, "Transnational Participation and Citizenship: Immigrants to the European Union," WPTC-98–12 Centre d'etudes et de Recherches Internationales (France), 242.
5. Rainer Bauböck, "Reinventing Urban Citizenship," *Citizenship Studies* 7, no. 2 (2003): 156.

6. Cited in Klopp, *German Multiculturalism*, 19.
7. All figures stem from the *Integrationsbericht 2000*, graciously provided by Isabel Lavadinho, Stabsabteilung für Integrationspolitik, Stuttgart.
8. *A Pact for Integration: The Stuttgart Experience* (September 2003), 13.
9. The "Good Neighbour" project, promoted by the Barcelona City Council, Birmingham, Lyon, Milan, and Rotterdam, exchanges best practices for remedying social exclusion. See Ministry of Refugee, Immigration and Integration Affairs, *General European Experiences and City Examples of Best Practices* (Denmark, April 2003); A. Zolberg and A. J. Clarkin, eds., *Sharing Integration Experiences: Innovative Community Practices on Two Continents* (New York: International Center for Migration, Ethnicity and Citizenship, 2003); Jeroen Doomernik, "The Effectiveness of Integration Policies Towards Immigrants and their Descendants in France, Germany and the Netherlands," #27 (Geneva: International Labor Organization, 1998).
10. Frank Drieschner, "Entwicklungshilfe für Deutschland," *Die Zeit*, 28 April 2005.
11. *Frankfurter Statistik Aktuell*, Nr. 09/2005; Klopp, *German Multiculturalism*, 136, 147.
12. Klopp, *German Multiculturalism*, 18, 161.
13. Ibid., 172.
14. The KAV website can be accessed through the official city page, www.frankfurt.de.
15. Klopp, *German Multiculturalism*, 176.
16. Ibid., 188ff.
17. Redaktionsgruppe Memorandum, eds., *Memorandum: Zuwanderung und Integration in den neuen Bundesländern. Chancen, Risiken, Aufgaben* (Berlin, January 2003), 6.
18. Thomas Kralinski, "Leere oder Lehre: Wie die Bevölkerungsentwicklung im Osten Land und Menschen prägt," in Tanja Busse and Tobias Dür, eds., *Das neue Deutschland: Die Zukunft als Chance* (Berlin: Aufbau Verlag, 2003), 79ff.
19. The Federal Office for Statistics recently "cleaned" its files, indicating that there are 6.7— not 7.3 million—"foreigners" in Germany, *Migration und Bevölkerung* (Berlin, July 2005).
20. Ibid., 17–18.
21. Joyce Marie Mushaben, "*Die Lehrjahre sind vobei!* Re-Forming Democratic Interest Groups in Eastern Germany," *Democratization* 8, no. 4 (Winter 2001): 95–133.
22. Klopp, *German Multiculturalism*, 187.
23. Ibid.
24. Jan Rath et al., "Introduction," in Rath et al., eds., *Western Europe and its Islam* (Leiden/Boston/Cologne: Brill, 2001), 3.
25. Renate Künast, Bundesministerium für Verbraucherschutz, Ernährung und Landwirtschaft press release, "Bundesrat agrees to Hen Husbandry Ordinance: Battery cage systems now only allowed on a transitional basis" (Berlin, 19 October 2001).
26. The Court opined: "If there were no exceptions to *halal* or kosher forms of butchering, then the religious freedom of affected Muslims would be limited to an unacceptable degree, and animal protection interests would enjoy unilateral priority without sufficient constitutional justification." See Reinhard Müller, "Religionsfreiheit und staatliche Neutralität," *Faznet*, 23 September 2003.
27. Alan Cowell, "Islamic Turks Seek Acceptance of Culture in Germany," *New York Times*, 14 December 1995.
28. Peggy Levitt, "Between God, Ethnicity, and Country: An Approach to the Study of Transnational Religion" (WPTC-01-13, Workshop on Transnational Migration: Comparative Perspectives, Princeton University, 30 June–1 July 2001).
29. Dursun Tan and Hans-Peter Waldhoff, "Turkish Everyday Culture in Germany and its Prospects," in David Horrocks and Eva Kolinsky, eds., *Turkish Culture in German Society Today* (Providence/London: Berghahn Books, 1996), 137–156. Further, Werner Schiffauer,

Die Gewalt der Ehre: Erklärung zu einem türkisch-deutschen Sexualkonflikt (Frankfurt/Main: Suhrkamp, 1983).

30. Gerdien Jonker, "Probleme der Kommunikation zwischen Muslimen und der Mehrheitsgesellschaft—Analyse und praktische Beispiele," *Vom Dialog zur Kooperation: Die Integration von Muslimen in der Kommune* (Berlin/Bonn, May 2002), 9.

31. Ruud Koopmans et al., *Contested Citizenship: Immigration and Cultural Diversity in Europe* (Minneapolis: University of Minnesota Press, 2005) 32, chap. 5.

32. Rolf Schieder, *Wieviel Religion verträgt Deutschland?* (Frankfurt/Main: Suhrkamp, 2001), 119. In the US, scientology is seen as a self-help/motivational brand of religion; in Germany it is regulated as a dangerous cult.

33. Ibid., 156.

34. Andreas Meier, *Jugendweihe—Jugendfeier: Ein deutsches nostalgisches Fest vor und nach 1990* (Munich: Deutscher Taschenbuch Verlag, 1998).

35. Gerdien Jonker, "Muslim Emancipation? Germany's Struggle over Religious Pluralism," in W. A. R. Shadid and P. S. van Koningsveld, eds., *Religious Freedom and the Neutrality of the State: The Position of Islam in the European Union* (Leuven: Peeters, 2002), 45.

36. Deutscher Bundestag, *Islam in Deutschland*, Drucksache 14/4530 (8 November 2002), 5.

37. Klopp, *German Multiculturalism*, 120.

38. Schieder, *Wieviel Religion*, 159.

39. Klopp, *German Multiculturalism*, 159; also, Deutscher Bundestag, *Islam in Deutschland*.

40. Yasemin Karakasoglu, "Turkish Cultural Orientations in Germany and the Role of Islam," in Horrocks and Kolinsky, *Turkish Culture*, 157–179.

41. Joyce Marie Mushaben, "More than Just a Bad Hair Day: The Muslim Head-Scarf Debate as a Challenge to European Identities," in Holger Henke, ed., *Crossing Over: Comparing Recent Immigration in Europe and the United States* (Lanham, MD: Lexington Books, 2005), 182–220.

42. Krisztina Kehl-Bodrogi, *"Was du auch suchts, such' es in dir selbst": Aleviten (nicht nur) in Berlin* (Berlin: Concept Verlag, 2002). Regarding recognition problems in France and Italy, see Sara Silvestri, "EU Politics and Muslim Communities in Europe: The creation of national Muslim councils," in Henke, *Crossing Over*, 101–129.

43. "Verfassungsgericht gibt 'Zeugen Jehovahs' recht: Religionsgemeinschaften müssen keine positive Grundeinstellung zum Staat haben," *Frankfurter Allgemeine Zeitung*, 20 December 2000.

44. Gottfried Müller and Ute Bublitz, *Araber in Berlin* (Berlin: Verwaltungsdrückerei Berlin, 1992); *Türkische Berliner: Eine Minderheite stellt sich vor* (Berlin: Verwaltungsdrückerei Berlin, 1987). Deutscher Bundestag, *Islam in Deutschland*, 21.

45. Gerdien Jonker and Andreas Kapphan, eds., *Moscheen und islamischen Leben in Berlin* (Berlin: Verwaltungsdrückerei Berlin, 1999); Deutscher Bundestag, *Islam in Deutschland*, 21.

46. Richard Gale and Simon Naylor, "Religion, Planning and the City: The Spatial Politics of Ethnic Minority Expression in British Cities and Towns," *Ethnicities* 2, no. 3 (2002): 387–388.

47. Deutscher Bundestag, *Islam in Deutschland*.

48. Ibid., 394.

49. Gerdien Jonker, "Ahnungslosigkeit und Zerrbilder. Zum Verhältnis von Islamischen Organisationen und Deutscher öffentlichkeit" (paper presented at Evangelische Akademie Loccum, 7–9 January 2002).

50. Ibid., 392.

51. Schieder, *Wieviel Religion*, 188.

52. They exercise so much control that top quality professors, fed up with the interminable academic hiring practices, have taken jobs in the US, the UK, and Canada. See Heiko

Schwarzburger, "Warum Berufungen so lange dauern. System ist unsozial," *Deutsche Universitätszeitung*, no. 18 (26 September 2003): 10–12.

53. T. H. Marshall and Tom Bottomore, *Citizenship and Social Class* (London: Pluto Press, 1992), 16.

54. Klopp, *German Multiculturalism*, 103.

55. Ibid., 102.

56. Ibid., 19.

57. Ibid., 20.

58. Ibid., 103.

59. Werner Schiffauer, *Fremde in der Stadt. Zehn Essays über Kulture und Differenz* (Frankfurt/Main: Suhrkamp, 1997); Schiffauer, *Die Gottesmänner. Türkische Islamisten in Deutschland* (Frankfurt/Main: Suhrkamp, 2000).

60. Ulrich Pfaff, "Islamische Unterweisung in Nordrhein-Westfalen," in *Islamischer Religionsunterricht an staatlichen Schulen in Deutschland* (Berlin/Bonn, September 2000), 16; also Dokumentation: *Wie verändert der Islam die Schule im Kiez*, forum sponsored by Berlin's Integrations- und Migrationsbeauftragte, 8 March 2004.

61. Ibid., 10.

62. Schieder, *Wieviel Religion*, 168.

63. Jonker, "Muslim Emancipation?" 47.

64. Angelina Knubbertz, "Das 'Berliner Modell' oder: Die andere Art, Religionsunterricht zu organisieren," in *Islamischer Religionsunterricht an staatlichen Schulen*, 17.

65. Jonker, "Probleme der Kommunikation," 13.

66. Ibid., 46.

67. Ibid.

68. Cited in Roger Cohen, "Long Dispute Ends as Berlin Court Backs Islamic School Lessons," *New York Times*, 6 November 1998.

69. Susanne Vieth-Entus, "Deutschstunden für Islamlehrer," *Der Tagespiegel*, 3 June 2005.

70. Reported in *Berliner Zeitung*, 3 June 2005.

71. Schieder, *Wieviel Religion*, 191.

72. After Turkey eliminated the death penalty and approved sanctions against torture, Kaplan was deported, tried, and sentenced to life imprisonment for a terrorist plot (*Tagesschau*, 21 June 2005).

73. Regarding crucifixes, the Court declared in May 1995 (BverfGE 93,1): "Die Anbringung eines Kreuzes oder Kruzifixes in den Unterrichtsräumen einer staatlichen Pflichtschule, die keine Bekenntnisschule ist, verstößt gegen Art 4, Abs 1 GG. 2." On slaughter rites, see the *Schächtenurteil* of 15 January 2002 (Az: 1BvR 1783/99). The Ludin verdict of 24 September 2003 is cited as 2 BvR 1436/02; for details, see Jost Müller-Neuhof, "Mit Kopfschütteln," *Der Tagespiegel*, 25 September 2003; Helmut Kerscher, "Karlsruhe verlangt klare Entscheidung der Politik," *Süddeutsche Zeitung*, 25 September 2003. The organizational ban for the so-called Caliph-State was issued on 2 October 2003 (1 BvR 536/03). The Mainz case is cited as (Az:1 L 98/03.MZ).

74. Mirjam Mohr (Associated Press) cited in *Spiegel* Online, 3 October 2003; also, Arnim Adam, "Die Pluralisierungsfalle: Das Kopftuch–Urteil eröffnet eine längst fällige Debatte," *Süddeutsche Zeitung*, 29 September 2003; *Das Prinzip Kopftuch: Muslime in Deutschland*, "Das Kreuz mit dem Koran," *Der Spiegel* 40 (29 September 2003): 82–96;. Alexander Schwabe, "Kruzifix runter, Kopftuch auf," *Spiegel* Online, 24 September 2003; Heike Schmoll, "Karlsruhe stellt das Beamtenrecht auf den Kopf," *Frankfurter Allgemeine Zeitung*, 25 September 2003.

75. Martin Klingst, "Feige Richter," *Die Zeit*, 25 September 2003; cf. Kerstin Krupp, "Deutsche Muslime bekennen sich zum Grundgesetz," *Berliner Zeitung*, 21 February

2002; also, Ulrich Preuss, "Citizenship and the German Nation," *Citizenship Studies* 7, no. 1 (2003): 37–55; and Edwige Liliane Lefebvre, "Republicanism and Universalism: Factors of Inclusion or Exclusion in the French Concept of Citizenship," *Citizenship Studies* 7, no. 1 (2003): 15–36.

76. Council Directive 97/80/EC of 15 December 1997 on the burden of proof in cases based on sex (Brussels).

77. R. Müller, "Religionsfreiheit und staatliche Neutralität," FAZ-Net, 23 September 2003.

78. Sabine Beikler, "Kein Kopftuch zur Uniform," *Der Tagesspiegel*, 19 November 2003; Patrick Goldstein, "Deckname 'Heidi,'" *Berliner Morgenpost*, 2002.

79. Robert Leicht, "Mit dem Fremden leben lernen," *Der Tagesspiegel*, 9 September 2003.

80. Asiye Kaya, "Migration aus der Türkei in die Bundesrepublik" (paper presented at the IFADE Workshop, Humboldt University, Berlin, 6–7 June 2003).

81. Renate Kreile, "Markt, Moral and Kopftuch—politischer Islam and Frauenfrage in der Türkei," *Peripherie* 24, no. 95 (2004): 311.

82. Ibid., 306.

83. Joyce Marie Mushaben, "Separate and Unequal: Bona fide Employment Qualifications and the Not-so-great Muslim Headscarf Debate in the US and Europe" (forthcoming 2008).

84. Pakistanis claim that General Musharraf did more for women than Bhutto, introducing female quotas in parliament and town councils (BBC Online forum, 20 January 2004).

85. Ali Akbar Mahdi, "Iranian Women," 15ff.

86. "Religiöse Vielfalt statt Zwangsemanzipation! Aufruf wider ein Lex Koptuch": appeal of seventy prominent women in front of the Brandenburg Gate. Also, "Prominente Frauen starten Aufruf gegen Kopftuchverbot," *Der Tagesspiegel*, 2 December 2003.

87. "Die Debatte um das Kopftuch: Für ein Verbot per Gesetz?" Heartfelt thanks to Gabi Abels, editor of *femina politica*, for supplying this and countless other documents. Migrant women first responded five months later with an open letter to *die tageszeitung* "against the paternalist standpoint of Marieluise Beck" on 14 February 2004.

88. Lizette Alvarez, "Sweden Boldly Exposes a Secret Side of Women's Lives," *New York Times*, 6 April 2005.

89. Necla Kelek, *Die fremde Braut* (Cologne: Kiepenheuer & Witsch, 2005), 218; further, Y. Inci, *Erstickt an Euren Lügen: Eine Türkin in Deutschland erzählt* (Munich: Piper, 2005). Amnesty International reports that 46 percent of the women living in Turkey's eastern/southeastern provinces are not asked to consent before engagement; 51 percent are married without their consent, violating Islamic law.

90. Peter Lueber, "So sollte es sein: Dänisches Gericht verurteilt erstmals Familie wegen Ehrenmord," *Die Zeit*, 30 June 2006.

91. Kelek's "fictional work" is marked by Islam bashing, while her "scholarly work" suggests little outright oppression, *Die fremde Braut*, 232, 229–230. Similar concerns have arisen in Afghanistan and Saudi Arabia; see N. C. Aizenman, "Taking a Genetic Gamble," *Washington Post National Weekly*, 25 April–1 May 2005.

92. Birgit Rommelspacher, *Dominanzkultur, Texte zu Fremdheit und Macht* (Berlin: Orlanda Frauenverlag, 1995).

93. Gloria Gonzales-Lopez, "*De Madres a Hijas*: Gendered Lessons on Virginity across Generations of Mexican Immigrant Women," in Pierrette Hondagneu-Sotelo, ed., *Gender and US Immigration: Contemporary Trends* (Berkeley: University of California Press, 2003), 233.

94. Yen Le Espiritu, "'We Don't Sleep Around Like White Girls Do': Family, Culture, and Gender in Filipina American Lives," in Hondagneu-Sotelo, *Gender and US Immigration*, 279.

95. Ibid., 279–280.

96. Jack G. Morrison, *Ravensbrück: Everyday Life in a Women's Concentration Camp, 1939–45* (Princeton, NJ: Markus Wiener Publishers, 2000), 118.

97. Shaista Aziz, BBC Newsvote forum, 20 January 2004 transcript, 2.
98. "Mehr Mädchen Schwanger," *Die Tageszeitung*, 1 January 2004; "Türkische Gemeinde lobt Pflicht zu Sexualkunde," *Frankfurter Rundschau* online, 20 January 2004.
99. Klopp, *German Multiculturalism*, 117.
100. Interview with Marieluise Beck and Özcan Mutlu, "Das Stück Stoff und die Staatsgewalt," *Der Tagesspiegel*, 28 November 2003.
101. Werner Schiffauer, "Schlachtfeld Frau," *Süddeutsche Zeitung*, February 2005; Schiffauer, *Migration und kulturelle Differenz* (Berlin: Ausländerbeauftragte, 2002), 29ff.
102. *Engendering Development: Through Gender Equality in Rights, Resources, and Voice* (World Bank/New York: Oxford University Press, 2001).
103. Stefan Töpfer, "Tragen von Kopftücher behindert Integration," *Frankfurter Allgemeine Zeitung*, 25 September 2003.
104. Azadeh Moaveni, *Lipstick Jihad: A Memoir of Growing up Iranian in America and American in Iran* (New York: Public Affairs, 2005).
105. Elaine Ganley, "France's first Muslim high school opens," Associated Press (US), 2 September 2003; "König-Fahd-Akademie wird doch nicht geschlossen," *Süddeutsche Zeitung*, 28 October 2003.
106. "Jugendliche: Bekenntnis und Modeaccessoire," *BerlinOnline*, 19 January 2004.
107. J. Haak and A. Vorbringer, "Durchgefallen," *Berliner Zeitung*, 25–26 June 2005.
108. Rainer Ohliger and Ulrich Raiser, *Integration und Migration in Berlin: Zahlen—Daten—Fakten* (Berlin: Beauftragte für Integration und Migration, 2005), 26ff.
109. Joachim Fahrun, "Integrationskurse versinken in Bürokratie," *Berliner Morgenpost*, 18 July 2005.
110. Ian Bickerton, "Dutch find 20 reasons to reject EU treaty," *Financial Times*, 2 June 2005; and George Parker, "Europe in Turmoil as the Dutch vote NO," ibid.; Thomas Gack, "Suche nach einer Therapie," *Der Tagesspiegel*, 3 June 2005.
111. Interview with Robin Schneider, 23 June 2005. The draft proposal, registered as Drucksache 15/3929, runs over 150 pages.
112. Peter Kirnich, "Alles ausgebucht," *Berliner Zeitung*, 25–26 June 2005.
113. Alexander and Margarete Mitscherlich, *Die Unfähigkeit zu trauern*: *Grundlagen Kollektiven Verhaltens* (Munich: Piper, 1967).
114. Ali Akbar Mahdi, "Iranian Women," 16; Mahdi, "Ethnic Identity among Second-Generation Iranians in the United States," *Iranian Studies* 32, no. 1 (Winter 1998); Mahdi, "Trading Places: Changes in Gender Roles within the Iranian Immigrant Family," *Critique*, no. 15 (Fall 1999).
115. Enno von Lowenstern, "English über alles," *Die Welt*, reprinted in the *New York Times*, 11 September 1990.
116. Ulrich Gutmaier, "Deutschland braucht das Kopftuch," *NETZEITUNG.DE*, 3 December 2003.
117. Ruud Koopmans and Paul Statham, "How national citizenship shapes transnationalism," *Revue Européenne des Migrations Internationales* 17, no. 2 (2001): 63–100.
118. Klopp, *German Multiculturalism*, 20.
119. Doris Nahawandi, *Diversity Leitlinien für eine Kultur der Vielfalt im Einwanderungsbezirk Friedrichshain-Kreuzberg von Berlin* (Berlin, December 2004), 4.
120. Rosa Luxemburg, "The Russian Revolution" (1918).
121. For those who can no longer find their personal dog-eared copy, Herbert Marcuse's 1965 essay, "Repressive Tolerance," appears online (academic.evergreen.edu/curricular/fopa/marcuse/tolerance.pdf). Page references here derive from this online version, 13.
122. Ibid., 9.
123. Ibid.

124. Frank Gesemann, *Junge Zuwanderer und Kriminalität in Berlin* (Berlin: Beauftragte für Integration und Migration, 2004), 32, 42.

125. Barbara Dietz and Heike Roll, *Jugendliche Aussiedler—Porträt einer Zuwanderergeneration* (Frankfurt/Main: Campus, 1998.) Also, Dirk Enzmann and Peter Wetzels, "Gewaltkriminalität junger Deutscher und Ausländer: Brisante Befunde, die irritieren," *Kölner Zeitschrift für Soziologie und Sozialpsychologie* 52 (2000): 142–176.

126. Clifford Geertz cited in Klopp, *German Multiculturalism*, 31.

127. My thanks to Reinhard Maiworm, Goethe Institut-Berlin, for sharing this thought. See Richard Florida, *The Rise of the Creative Class: And How It's Transforming Work, Leisure, Community and Everyday Life* (New York: Basic Books, 2002).

128. Theodora Kostakopoulou, "European Citizenship and Immigration after Amsterdam: Openings, Silences, Paradoxes," *Journal of Ethnic and Migration Studies* 24, no. 4 (1998): 639–656.

INTERVIEW PARTNERS

Individual	Institutional Affiliation	Discussion Date
Dr. Steffen Angenendt	German Council on Foreign Relations; Office of the Independent Commission on Migration (DGAP); Office of the Federal Immigration Council	Berlin: May 2002, 4 June 2003, 8 June 2004
Saim Aygun	Co-owner of six Hasir Restaurants	Berlin: 21 June 2004
Jan Cyankiewicz	Polnischer Sozialrat/ZAPO	Berlin: 23 July 2002
Dr. Eduard Ditschek	Director Volkshochschule Wedding Berlin (now VHS Berlin-Mitte)	Berlin: 2002, 2003, 2005 (multiple discussions)
Tatjana Forner	Club Dialog e. V.	Berlin: 10 July 2002
Stojan Gugutschkow	Commissioner for Foreigner and Refugee Affairs, Leipzig	Leipzig: June 1991
Dr. Barbara John	Ausländerbeauftragte des Berliner Senats	Berlin: 23 September 1983, June 1993, June 1998, 14 June 2002
Bahattin Kaya	Executive Director, Turkish-Deutsch Unternehmer vereinigung (TDU); CEO of Kaya Travel	Berlin: 16 June 2002
Basil Kerski	Editor-in-Chief, *Dialogue, Deutsch-Polnisches Magazin*	Berlin: 15 June 2004
Gülay Kizilocak	Zentrum für Türkeistudien	Berlin: July 2002

(continued)

Individual	*Institutional Affiliation*	*Discussion Date*
Kenan Kolat	Executive Director, Turkischer Bund Berlin-Brandenburg	Berlin: 12 July 2002
Karin Korte	Commissioner for Migration/ Integration-Neuköolln	Berlin: 10 June 2003
Sabine Kroker-Stille	Anti-Discrimination Director for Berlin	Berlin: 1 July 2005, 9 July 2007
Isabel Lavadihno	Deputy Commissioner for Integration	Stuttgart: 5 July 2002
Joanna Matuszak	Student, Collegium Polonicum and Europa Universität Viadrina	Frankfurt/Oder: June 2002
Özcan Mutlu (Greens)	Member of the Berlin House of Representatives	Berlin: June 2004 (multiple discussions)
Doris Nahawandi	District Commissioner for Migration, Friedrichshain-Kreuzberg; Chair, State Council for Integration-/Migration Questions	Berlin: 22 June 2004, 28 June 2005
Bilkay Öney	Speaker for Immigrün Berlin; producer for a Berlin-Turkish TV station	Berlin: June 2002
Dr. Ertekin Özcan	President, Federal Turkish Parents Association; cofounder, Berlin Turkish Parents Association	Berlin: 11 June 2003
Cem Özdemir	(Greens) Former Member of the Bundestag, now Member of the European Parliament; cofounder of Immigrün	St. Louis, MO: April 2003
Gari Pavkovic	Commissioner for Integration, Suttgart	Stuttgart: 6 July 2002
Klaus-Henning Rosen	Ministerialrat, Federal Ministry of the Interior	Berlin: summer 2000–2003 (multiple discussions)
Sabahattin Sari	CEO of Manolya/Medianess	Berlin: 14 June 2004
Dr. Robin Schneider	Parliamentary Affairs Counsel for the Berlin Commissioner for Migration and Integration	Berlin: 23 June 2005
Ana Skrobat	Russian Aussiedlerin; community organizer	Berlin: 16 June 2003
Dr. Ingrid von Stumm	Federal Interior Ministry and Office of the Independent Commission on Migration	Berlin: May 2002, June 2002

BIBLIOGRAPHY

Abell, Nazare Albuquerque. 1997. "Safe Country Provisions in Canada and in the European Union: A Critical Assessment," *International Migration Review* 31, no. 3: 570–590.

Akgündüz, Ahmet. 1998. "Migration to and from Turkey, 1783–1960: Types, numbers and ethno-religious dimensions," *Journal of Ethnic and Migration Studies* 24, no. 1: 97–120.

Alba, Richard, and Victor Nee. 1997. "Rethinking assimilation theory for a new era of immigration," *International Migration Review* 31, no. 4: 826–874.

Almond, Gabriel, and Sidney Verba. 1980. *The Civic Culture Revisited.* Boston/Toronto: Little, Brown & Co.

———. 1965. *The Civic Culture.* Boston: Little, Brown & Co.

Al Syyad, Nezar, and Manuel Castells, eds. 2002. *Muslim Europe or Euro-Islam: Politics, Culture and Citizenship in the Age of Globalization.* Lanham, MD: Lexington Books.

Anderson, Benedict. 1991. *Imagined Communities: Reflections on the Origin and Spread of Nationalism.* London/New York: Verso.

Angenendt, Steffen, ed. 1999. *Gibt es ein europäisches Asyl- und Migrationsproblem?* Bonn: Europa Union Verlag.

———. 1997. *Migration und Flucht.* Bd. 342. Bonn: Bundeszentrale für politische Bildung.

Anwar, Muhammad. 2001. "The participation of ethnic minorities in British politics," *Journal of Ethnic and Migration Studies* 27, no. 3: 533–549.

Ausländerbeauftragte des Berliner Senats. 2002. "Zur Lebenssituation Türkischer Berlinerinnen und Berliner" (January 15).

———. 2001. *TOP: Zwanzig Jahre Auslanderbeauftragte des Senats* (December).

————. 1998. *Bericht zur Integrations- und Ausländerpolitik, 1996/1997.*

————. 1997. *Berliner Jugendliche türkischer Herkunft* (December).

————. 1995. *Polen in Berlin* (January).

————. 1993. "Berlin geschlossen gegen Ausländer-raus-Parolen" (February).

————. 1989. "Zur Lage der jungen Ausländergeneration: Berlin" (April).

————. 1982. *Miteinander leben: Ausländerpolitik in Berlin* (October).

Bade, Klaus J. 2001. *Konzeptionsentwurf zur institutionellen Strukturierung des Migrations wesens unter besonderer Berücksichtigung der Organisation der Migrationsforschung in Deutschland.* Gutachten für die Unabhängige Kommission "Zuwanderung" Osnabrück.

————, ed. 1996. *Migration, Ethnizität, Konflikt: Systemfragen und Fallstudien*, IMIS Bd. 1. Osnabrück: Universitätsverlag Rasch.

————, ed. 1992. *Ausländer, Aussiedler, Asyl in der Bundesrepublik Deutschland.* Niedersächsische Landeszentrale für politische Bildung.

Bade, Klaus J., and Rainer Münz, eds. 2002. *Migrationsreport 2002: Fakten—Analysen—Perspektiven.* Frankfurt/Main: Campus Verlag.

————. 2000. *Migrationsreport 2000: Fakten—Analysen—Perspektiven.* Bonn: Bundeszentrale für politische Bildung.

Bade, Klaus J., and Dieter Oberndörfer, eds. 2002. *Integration und Illegalität in Deutschland.* Osnabrück: IMIS/Rat für Migrationsfragen.

Bade, Klaus J., and Jochen Oltmer, eds. 1999. *Aussiedler: deutsche Einwanderer aus Osteuropa.* IMIS, Bd. 8. Osnabrück: Universitätsverlag Rasch.

Bade, Klaus J., and Myron Weiner, eds. 1997. *Migration Past, Migration Future: Germany and the United States.* Providence/Oxford: Berghahn Books.

Bafekr, Sigrid, and Johan Leman. 1995. "Highly-qualified Iranian immigrants in Germany: The role of ethnicity and culture," *Journal of Ethnic and Migration Studies* 25: 95–112.

Bauböck, Rainer. 2003. "Reinventing Urban Citizenship," *Citizenship Studies* 7, no. 2: 139–160.

Baumgartner-Karabak, Andrea, and Gisela Landesberger. 1983. *Die verkauften Bräute: Türkische Frauen zwischen Kreuzberg und Anatolien.* Reinbek: Rowohlt.

Baur, Rita, with Heli Aurich, Heidrun Czock, and Thomas Schulze-Roebbecke. 1980. *Untersuchung der Determinanten der beruflichen Ausbildungsbeteiligung von ausländischen Jugendlichen in Berlin (West).* Berlin: Senatskanzlei.

Bayes, Jayne H., and Nayereh Tohidi. 2001. *Globalization, Gender and Religion: The Politics of Women's Rights in Catholic and Muslim Contexts*. New York: Palgrave.

Beck, Marieluise, Bundesbeauftragte für Ausländer, eds. 2003. *Islamischer Religionsunterricht an staatlichen Schulen in Deutschland: Praxis—Konzepte—Perspektiven*. In der Discussion, #8. Berlin/Bonn.

———. 2002. *Vom Dialog zur Kooperation: Die Integration von Muslimen in der Kommune*. In der Diskussion, #12. Berlin/Bonn.

———. 2000. *Migrationsbericht der Ausländer im Auftrag der Bundesregierung*. Berlin.

Beck, Marieluise, and Renate Schmidt, eds. 2002. *Migranten sind aktiv: Zum gesellschaftlichen Engagement von Migrantinnen und Migranten*. Bonn/Berlin.

Beetz, Stephan, and Tsypylma Darieva. 1997. "'Ich heirate nicht nur den Mann, sondern auch das Land': Heiratsmigrantinnen aus der ehemaligen Sovietunion in Berlin." In *Zuwanderung und Stadtentwicklung*, eds. Hartmut Häussermann and Ingrid Oswald, 386–405. Opladen: Westdeutscher Verlag.

Bemelmans, Yvonne, and Maria José Freitas. 2001. *Situation of Islamic Communities in five European Cities—Examples of local initiatives*. Vienna: European Monitoring Center on Racism and Xenophobia.

Benz, Wolfgang, ed. 1993. *Integration ist machbar: Ausländer in Deutschland*. Munich: Beck'sche Reihe.

Berking, Helmuth. 2000. "'Homes away from Home': Zum Spannungsverhältnis von Diaspora und Nationalstaat," *Berliner Journal für Soziologie*, no. 1: 49–60.

Bommes, Michael. 1999. "Probleme der beruflichen Eingliederung von Zuwanderern—Migranten in Organisationen." In *Integration und Integrationsförderung in der Einwanderungsgesellschaft*. Bonn: Friedrich Ebert Stiftung.

Boos-Nünning, Ursula, and Yasemin Karakasoglu. 2004. *Viele Welten leben: Lebenslagen von Mädchen und jungen Frauen mit griechischem, italienischem, jugoslavischem, türkischem und Aussiedlerhintergrund*. Berlin: BMFSFJ.

Bosswick, Wolfgang, and Veit Bronnenmeyer. 2001. "Integrationsmaßnahmen der Wohlfahrtsverbände." Gutachten für die Unabhängige Kommission "Zuwanderung" Bamberg, March.

Bousetta, Hassan. 2000. "Institutional theories of immigrant ethnic mobilization: Relevance and limitations," *Journal of Ethnic and Migration Studies* 26, no. 2: 229–245.

Böwe, Bettina, and Patricia Cerda P.-Hegerl. 2000. *Portugiesen und Spanier in Berlin*. Berlin: Ausländerbeauftragte des Senats.

Büchel, Felix, Joachim Frick, and Wolfgang Voges. 1999. "Der Sozialhilfebezug von Zuwanderern in Westdeutschland," *Kölner Zeitschrift für Soziologie und Sozialspychologie* 49, no. 2: 272–290.

Bundesministerium des Innern, eds. 2003. *Islamismus*. Berlin (December).

Burchard, Amory. 2000. *Das russische Berlin*. Berlin: Ausländerbeauftragte des Senats.

Conrad, Christoph, and Jürgen Kocka. 2001. *Staatsbürgerschaft in Europa: historische Erfahrungen und aktuelle Debatten*. Hamburg: edition Körber-Stiftung.

Cordell, Karl, ed. 1999. *Ethnicity and Democratisation in the New Europe*. New York/London: Routledge.

Cyrus, Norbert. 2003. "Work-permit decisions in the German labour administration: An exploration of the implementation process," *Journal of Ethnic and Migration Studies* 29, no. 2: 225–255.

———. 2003. " . . . als alleinstehende Mutter habe ich viel geschafft: Lebensführung und Selbstverortung einer illegalen polnischen Arbeitsmigrantin." In *Vom Wandergesellschaften zum 'Green Card' Spezialisten*, ed. Klaus Roth, 227–264. Munich: Waxmann.

———. 2001. "Stereotypen in Aktion: Die praktische Relevanz nationaler Schemata für einen polnischen Transmigranten in Berlin," In *Nachbarschaft. Interkultureller Beziehungen zwischen Deutschen, Polen und Tschechen*, ed. Klaus Roth, 165–196. Munich: Waxmann.

———. 1997. "Grenzkultur und Stigmanagement: Mobile Ethnographie und Situatutionsanalyse eines irregulär beschäftigten polnische Wanderarbeiters in Berlin," *Kea, Zeitschrift für Kulturwissenschaften* (Winter): 83–104.

De Graaf, Nan Dirk, and Hendrick Derk Flap. 1988. "'With a Little Help from My Friends': Social Resources as an Explanation of Occupational Status and Income in West Germany, The Netherlands, and the United States," *Social Forces* 67, no. 2: 452–472.

Delanty, Gerard. 1997. "Models of Citizenship: Defining European Identity and Citizenship," *Citizenship Studies* 1, no. 3: 285–304.

Deutsch, Karl. W. 1996. *Nationalism and Social Communication: An Inquiry into the Foundations of Nationality*. Cambridge, MA: MIT Press.

Deutscher Bundestag. 2002. *Islam in Deutschland*. Drucksache 14/4530 (November).

————. 1999. *Das Ehrenamt: Verantwortung übernehmen—Zukunft gestalten.* CDU/CSU Fraktion in Deutschen Bundestag. Bonn.

Deutsch-Polnische Gesellschaft/Polish Institute in Berlin, eds. 2002. *Polen und Juden: Geschichte, die trennt und verbindet.* Berlin.

DeWind, Josh, and Philip Kasinitz. 1997. "Everything Old is New Again? Processes and Theories of Immigrant Incorporation," *International Migration Review* 31, no. 4: 1096–1111.

Diehl, Claudia. 2001. "Die Partizipationsmuster türkischer Migranten in Deutschland: Ergebnisse einer Gemeindestudie," *Zeitschrift für Ausländerrecht und Ausländerpolitik* 21, no. 1: 29–35.

Diehl, Claudia, and Michael Blohm. 2001. "Apathy, adaptation or ethnic mobilisation? On the attitudes of a politically excluded group," *Journal of Ethnic and Migration Studies* 27, no. 3: 401–420.

Diehl, Claudia, and J. Urbahn. 1998. *Die soziale aund politische Partizipation von Zuwanderern in der Bundesrepublik Deutschland.* Bonn: Forschungsinstitut der Friedrich-Ebert-Stiftung.

Dietz, Barbara. 2000. "German and Jewish Migration from the former Soviet Union to Germany: Background, trends and implications," *Journal of Ethnic and Migration Studies* 26, no. 4: 635–652.

Dietz, Barbara, and Heike Roll. 1998. *Jugendliche Aussiedler—Porträt einer Zuwanderungsgeneration.* Frankfurt: Campus.

Doomernik, Jeroen. 1997. *Going West: Soviet Jewish Immigrants in Berlin since 1990.* Aldershot, UK: Avebury.

Dornis, Christian. 2002. "Zwei Jahre nach der Reform des Staatsangehörigkeitsrechts—Bilanz und Ausblick." In *Migrationsreport 2002: Fakten—Analysen—Perspektiven,* eds. Klaus J. Bade and Rainer Münz, 163–177. Frankfurt/Main: Campus.

Drüke, Luise, and Klaus Weigelt, eds. 1993. *Fluchtziel Europa: Strategien für eine neue Flüchtlingspolitik.* Munich: Verlag Bonn Aktuell.

Esser, Hartmut. 2001. *Integration und ethnische Schichtung.* Gutachten für die Unabhängige Kommission "Zuwanderung." Mannheim.

European Commission. 2003. *More unity and more diversity: The European Union's biggest enlargement.* Brussels.

————. 1997. *The European Institutions in the Fight against Racism: Selected Texts.* Brussels.

Faist, Thomas. 2000. "Soziale Bürgerschaft in der Europäische Union: Verschachtelte Mitgliedschaft," *Kölner Zeitschrift für Soziologie und Sozialpsychologie,* Sonderheft 40: 229–250.

Fassmann, Heinz, und Rainer Münz, eds.,1996. *Migration in Europa: Historische Entwicklung, aktuelle Trends, politische Reaktionen.* Frankfurt/Main/New York: Campus.

Fekete, Erika. 1982. *Eine Chance für Fatma.* Reinbek: Rowohlt.

Fennema, Meindert, and Jean Tillie. 1999. "Political Participation and political trust in Amsterdam: Civic communities and ethnic networks," *Journal of Ethnic and Migration Studies* 25, no. 4: 703–726.

Fijalkowski, Jürgen, and Helmut Gillmeister. 1997. *Ausländervereine—ein Forschungsbericht.* Berlin: Hitit.

Foreigners in Germany. 1991. *Guest Workers, Asylum-Seekers, Refugees, and Ethnic Germans,* German Information Center. New York (November).

Frank, Klaus-Dietrich. 2000. "Netzwerke für Integration im Erftkreis und in Köln." In *Neue Wege der Aussiedlerintegration: vom politischen Konzept zur Praxis.* Bonn: Friedrich Ebert Stiftung.

Freeman, Gary P., and Nedim Ögelman. 1998. "Homeland citizenship policies and the status of third country nationals in the European Union," *Journal of Ethnic and Migration Studies* 24, no. 4: 769–788.

Gale, Richard, and Simon Naylor. "Religion, Planning and the City: The spatial politics of ethnic minority expression in British Cities and Towns," *Ethnicities* 2, no. 3: 387–409.

Galenkamp, Marlies. 1998. "Do We Need Special Collective Rights for Immigrants and Refugees in Western Europe?" *Citizenship Studies* 2, no. 3: 501–517.

Gesemann, Frank, ed. 2004. *Junge Zuwanderer und Kriminalität in Berlin: Bestandsaufnahme—Ursachenanalyse—Präventionsmassnahmen.* Berlin: MercedesDruck.

———. 2001. *Migration und Integration in Berlin: Wissenschaftliche Analysen und politische Perspektiven.* Opladen: Leske + Budrich.

Goldberg, Andreas, and Faruk Sen. 1997. "Türkische Unternehmer in Deutschland: Wirtschaftliche Aktivitäten einer Einwanderungsgesellschaft in einem komplexen Wirtschaftssystem." In *Zuwanderung und Stadtentwicklung,* eds. Hartmut Häussermann and Ingrid Oswald, 63–84. Opladen: Westdeutscher Verlag.

Gowricharn, Ruben. 2002. "Integration and social cohesion: The case of the Netherlands," *Journal of Ethnic and Migration Studies* 28, no. 2: 259–273.

Green, Simon. 2000. "Beyond Ethnoculturalism? Gerrman Citizenship in the New Millennium," *German Politics* 9, no. 3: 105–124.

Greve, Martin, and Tülay Çinar. 1998. *Das Türkische Berlin*. Berlin: Ausländer-beauftragte des Senats.

Guild, Elspeth. 1998. "Competence, discretion and third country nationals: The European Union's legal struggle with migration," *Journal of Ethnic and Migration Studies* 24, no. 4: 613–625.

Halfmann, Jost. 1997. "Two Discourses of Citizenship in Germany: The Difference between Public Debate and Administrative Practice," *Citizenship Studies* 1, no. 3: 305–322.

Häming, Oliver. 2000. *Zwischen zwei Kulturen: Spannungen, Konflikte und ihre Bewältigung bei der zweiten Ausländergeneration*. Opladen: Leske + Budrich.

Hansen, Randall. 1998. "A European Citizenship or a Europe of Citizens? Third country nationals in the EU," *Journal of Ethnic and Migration Studies* 24, no. 4: 751–768.

Harris, Paul. "Russische Juden und Aussiedler: Integrationspolitik und lokale Verantwortung." In *Aussiedler: deutsche Einwanderer aus Osteuropa*, eds., K. J. Bade and J. Oltmer, 247–264. Osnabrück: Universitätsverlag Rasch.

Haug, Sonja. 2000. *Soziales Kapital und Kettenmigration: Italienische Migranten in Deutschland*. Opladen: Leske + Budrich.

Heckmann, Friedrich. 2004. "Illegal Migration: What Can We Know and What Can We Explain? The Case of Germany," *International Migration Review*. 1103–1125.

Heinemann, Karl-Heinz, and Wilfried Schubarth, eds. 1992. *Der antifaschistische Staat entlässt seine Kinder. Jugend und Rechtsextremismus in Ostdeutschland*. Cologne: Papy Rossa.

Hillmann, Felicitas. 1998. *Türkische Unternehmerinnen und Beschäftigte in Berliner ethnischen Gewerbe*. WZB discussion paper FS 198–107 (December).

Hoffmann, Lutz. 1992. *Die unvollendete Republik: Zwischen Einwanderungsland und deutschem Nationalstaat*. 2nd edition. Köln: Papy Rossa.

Hondagneu-Sotelo, Pierrette, ed. 2003. *Gender and US Immigration: Contemporary Trends*. Berkeley: University of California Press.

Horrocks, David, and Eva Kolinsky, eds. 1996. *Turkish Culture in German Society Today*. Providence/London: Berghahn Books.

Hübenthal, Christoph. 2000. "Netzwerk fördern, Selbsthilfepotentiale stärken: Vom Konzept zur Praxis." In *Neue Wege der Aussiedlerintegration: vom politischen Konzept zur Praxis*. Bonn: Friedrich Ebert Stiftung.

Iglicka, Krystyna. 2000. "Mechanisms of migration from Poland before and during the transition period," *Journal of Ethnic and Migration Studies* 26, no. 1: 61–74.

Irek, Malgorzata. 1989. *Der Schmugglerzug: Warschau—Berlin—Warschau.* Berlin: das Arabische Buch.

Jacobs, Dirk. 1998. "Discourse, Politics and Policy: The Dutch Parliamentary Debate about Voting Rights for Foreign Residents," *International Migration Review* 32, no. 2: 350–373.

Johansen, Baber, and Fritz Steppat. 1995. *Der Islam und die Muslime.* Berlin: Ausländerbeauftragte des Senats.

Jones-Correa, Michael. 1998. "Different path: Gender, immigration and political participation," *International Migration Review* 32, no. 2: 326–349.

Jonker, Gerdien. 2002. "Muslim Emancipation? Germany's Struggle over Religious Pluralism." In *Religious Freedom and the Neutrality of the State: The Position of Islam in the European Union,* eds. W. A. R. Shadid and P. S. van Koningsveld, 124–136. Leuven: Peeters.

———. 2002. "Probleme der Kommunikation zwischen Muslimen und der Mehrheitsgesellschaft: Analyse und praktische Beispiele." In *Vom Dialog zur Kooperation: Die Integration von Muslimen in der Kommune* (May), 9–23. Berlin/Bonn.

———. 1997. "Die islamischen Gemeinden in Berlin zwischen Integration und Segregation," *Leviathan, Zuwanderung und Stadtentwicklung,* Sonderheft 17: 347–364.

Jonker, Gerdien, and Andreas Kapphan, eds. 1999. *Moscheen und islamischen Leben in Berlin.* Berlin: Verwaltungsdrückerei Berlin.

Joppke, Christian, and Steven Lukes, eds. 2000. *Multicultural Questions.* Oxford: Oxford University Press.

Kara, Yade. 2005. *Selam Berlin.* Zurich: Diogenes.

Karakasoglu, Yasemin. 1996. "Turkish Cultural Orientations in Germany and the Role of Islam." In *Turkish Culture in German Society Today,* eds. David Horrocks and Eva Kolinsky, 157–179. Providence/London: Berghahn Books.

Kastoryano, Riva. 1998. "Transnational Participation and Citizenship: Immigrants to the European Union." WPTC-98–12 Centre d'etudes et de Recherches Internationales.

Kaya, Ayhan. 2002. "Aesthetics of diaspora: Contemporary minstrels in Turkish Berlin," *Journal of Ethnic and Migration Studies* 28, no. 1: 43–62.

Kecskes, Robert. 2001 "Soziale und identifikative Assimilation türkischer Jugendlicher," *Berliner Journal für Soziologie,* no. 1: 61–78.

Kehl-Bodrogi, Krisztina. 2002. *"Was du auch suchst, such' es in dir selbst": Aleviten (nicht nur) in Berlin.* Berlin: Concept Verlag.

Kehl-Bodrogi, Krisztina, and Ingrid Pflüger. 1997. *Die Ehre in der türkischen Kultur—Ein Wertsystem im Wandel.* Berlin: Die Ausländerbeauftragte des Senats.

Kelek, Necla. 2005. *Die fremde Braut.* Cologne: Kiepenheuer & Witsch.

Kerski, Basil. 2005. "Chancen der Multikulturalität: Die polnischsprachige Gruppe in Deutschland." In *Nachbarn auf Distanz: Polen und Deutsche 1998–2004,* eds. Anna Wolf-Poweska and Dieter Bingen, 267–277. Wiesbaden: Harrassowitz Verlag.

Kessler, Judith. 1997. "Jüdische Immigranten seit 1990," *Zeitschrift für Migration und soziale Arbeit,* no. 1: 40–47.

———. 1997. *Von Aizenberg bis Zaidelman: Jüdische Zuwanderer aus Osteuropa in Berlin und die Jüdische Gemeinde heute.* Berlin: Ausländerbeauftragte des Senats.

Keyman, E. Fuat. 2003. "Globalization, Civil Society and Citizenship in Turkey: Actors, Boundaries and Discourses," *Citizenship Studies* 7, no. 2: 219–234.

Kloosterman, Robert, and Jan Rath. 2003. *Immigrant Entrepreneurs: Venturing Abroad in the Age of Globalization.* Oxford/New York: Berg.

———. 2001. "Immigrant entrepreneurs in advanced economies: Mixed embeddedness further explored," *Journal of Ethnic and Migration Studies* 27, no. 2 (April): 189–201.

Klopp, Brett. 2002. "The political incorporation of EU foreigners before and after Maastricht: The new local politics in Germany," *Journal of Ethnic and Migration Studies* 28, no. 2: 239–257.

———. 2001. *German Multiculturalism: Immigrant Integration and the Transformation of Citizenship.* Westport, CN: Praeger.

Klusmeyer, Douglas. 2001. "A 'guiding culture' for immigrants? Integration and diversity in Germany," *Journal of Ethnic and Migration Studies* 27, no. 3: 519–532.

Kofman, Eleonore. 1999. "Female 'Birds of Passage' a Decade Later: Gender and Immigration in the European Union," *International Migration Review* 33, no. 2: 269–299.

Kolat, Kenan. 1999. "'Gleichstellungspolitik' statt 'Ausländerpolitik.'" In *Integration und Integrationsförderung in der Einwanderungsgesellschaft.* Bonn: Friedrich Ebert Stiftung.

Koolen, Ben. 1999. "Integrationspolitik der niederländischen Regierung." In *Integration und Integrationsförderung in der Einwanderungsgesellschaft.* Bonn: Friedrich Ebert Stiftung.

Koopmans, Ruud. 2001. "Migrant Participation, Citizenship and Democracy: National and Local Perspectives." Workshop on Strategies of Integration: The Multiethnic Society and Local Government. Essen (24–25 September).

Koopmans, Ruud, and Paul Statham. 2001. "How national citizenship shapes transnationalism," *Revue Européenne des Migrations Internationales* 17, no. 2: 63–100.

Koopmans, Ruud, Paul Statham, Marco Giugni, and Florence Passy. 2005. *Contested Citizenship. Immigration and Cultural Diversity in Europe.* Minneapolis: University of Minnesota Press.

Koser, Khalid. 1997. "Social Networks and the Asylum Cycle: The Case of Iranians in the Netherlands," *International Migration Review* 31, no. 3 (Fall): 592–611.

Kostakopoulou, Theodora. 1998. "European Citizenship and Immigration after Amsterdam: Openings, silences, paradoxes," *Journal of Ethnic and Migration Studies* 24, no. 4: 639–656.

Kotter, Ute. 2000. "Interkulturelle Orientierung und Vernetzung der Maßnahmnen zur beruflichen Integration. Das Beispiel Lüneburg." In *Neue Wege der Aussiedlerintegration: vom politischen Konzept zur Praxis.* Bonn: Friedrich Ebert Stiftung.

Kreile, Renate. 2004. "Markt, Moral and Kopftuch—politischer Islam and Frauenfrage in der Türkei," *Peripherie* 24, no. 95: 306–321.

Kühne, Peter. 2001. *Zur Lage der Flüchtlinge in Deutschland.* Bonn: Friedrich Ebert Stiftung.

Lachmann, Günther. 2004. *Tödliche Toleranz: Die Muslime und unsere offene Gesellschaft.* Munich: Piper.

Lambert, Helene. 1995. "Asylum-seekers, refugees and the European Union: Case studies of France and the UK." In *Migration and European Integration*, eds. R. Miles and D. Thränhardt, 112–131. London: Pinter.

Leggewie, Claus, ed. 2004. *Die Türkei und Europa.* Frankfurt/Main: Suhrkamp.

Levy, Daniel, and Yfaat Weiss. 2004. *Challenging Ethnic Citizenship: German and Israeli Perspectives on Immigration.* New York/Oxford: Berghahn Books.

Light, Ivan, and Steven J. Gold. 2000. *Ethnic Economies.* San Diego: Academic Press.

Mahdi, Ali Akbar. 2003. "Iranian Women: Between Islamicization and Globalization." In *Iran Encountering Globalization: Problems and Prospects,* ed. Ali Mohammadi, 47–71. London/New York: Routledge.

Marschang, Bernd. 1998. "Misstrauen, Abschottung, Eigensinn—Entwicklung der europäischen Asylrechts: 'Harmonisierung' bis zum Amsterdamer Vertrag," *Kritische Justiz* 31, no. 1: 69–83.

Marshall, T. H. 1964. *Class, Citizenship and Social Development.* Garden City, NJ: Doubleday.

Marshall, T. H., and Tom Bottomore. 1992. *Citizenship and Social Class.* London: Pluto Press.

Martiniello, Marco. 1995. "European citizenship, European identity and migrants: Towards the post-national state?" In *Migration and European Integration: The Dynamics of Inclusion and Exclusion,* eds. Robert Miles and Dietrich Thränhardt, 37–52. London: Pinter Publishers.

Meehan, Elizabeth. 1993. *Citizenship and the European Union.* London: Sage.

Meinhof, Ulrike H., Heidi Armbruster, and Craig Rollo. 2003. *Border Discourse: Changing Identities, Changing Nations, Changing Stories in European Border Communities.* Final Report SERD-1999–00023. University of South Hampton (March).

Meinhof, Ulrike H., and Dariusz Gallasinski. 2002. "Reconfiguring East-West identities: Cross-generational discourses in German and Polish border communities," *Journal of Ethnic and Migration Studies* 28, no. 1: 63–82.

Miera, Frauke. 1997. "Migration aus Polen: Zwischen nationaler Migrationspolitik und transnationalem sozialen Lebensräumen," *Leviathan, Zuwanderung und Stadtentwicklung,* Sonderheft 17: 232–254.

Minkenberg, Michael, ed. 2004. *Transborder Relations: Going Local in Frankfurt (Oder) and Slubice.* Berlin: Pro BUSINESS.

Mitscherlich, Alexander, and Margarete Mitscherlich. 1997. *Die Unfähigkeit zu trauern: Grundlagen Kollektiven Verhaltens.* Munich: Piper.

Müller, Gotfried. 2000. *Araber in Berlin.* Berlin: Ausländerbeauftragte des Senats.

Müller, Martina. 1993. *Afrikaner in Berlin.* Berlin: Ausländerbeauftragte des Senats.

Münz, Rainer, Wolfgang Seifert, and Ralf Ulrich. 1997. *Zuwanderung nach Deutschland: Strukturen, Wirkungen, Perspektiven.* Frankfurt/Main: Campus.

Münz, Rainer, and Myron Weiner, eds. 1997. *Migrants, Refugees and Foreign Policy. U.S. and German Policies toward Countries of Origin.* Providence/Oxford: Berghahn Books.

Mushaben, Joyce Marie. 2006. "Thinking Globally, Integrating Locally: Gender, Entrepreneurship and Urban Citizenship in Germany," *Citizenship Studies* 10, no. 2: 199–223.

———. 2005. "More than Just a Bad Hair Day: The Muslim Head-Scarf Debate as a Challenge to European Identities." In *Crossing Over: Comparing Recent Immigration in Europe and the United States,* ed. Holger Henke, 182–220. New York: Lexington.

———. 2001. *"Die Lehrjahre sind vobei!* Re-Forming Democratic Interest Groups in Eastern Germany," *Democratization* 8, no. 4: 95–133.

———. 1998. *From Post-War to Post-Wall Generations: Changing Attitudes towards the National Question and NATO in the Federal Republic of Germany.* Boulder, CO: Westview.

———. 1997. *"Auferstanden aus Ruinen:* Social Capital and Democratic Identity in the New Länder," *German Politics and Society* 14, no. 4: 79–101.

———. 1993. *Identity without a Hinterland? Continuity and Change in National Consciousness in the German Democratic Republic, 1949–1989.* Washington, DC: AICGS/Johns Hopkins University.

———. 1985. "A Crisis of Culture: Social Isolation and Integration among Turkish Guestworkers in the German Federal Republic." In *Turkish Workers in Europe: A Multidisciplinary Study,* eds. Ilyan Basgöz and Norman Furniss, 125–150. Bloomington: Indiana University Press.

Nahawandi, Doris. 2004. *Diversity Leitlinien für eine neue Kultur der Vielfalt im Einwanderungsbezirk Friedrichshain-Kreuzberg von Berlin.* Berlin (December).

Nirumand, Bahman, and Gabriele Yonan. 1994. *Iraner in Berlin.* Berlin: Ausländerbeauftragte des Senats.

North Rhine-Westphalia, eds. 1999. *Selbstorganisationen von Migrantinnen und Migranten in NRW.* Erkrath: Tonnes.

Özcan, Ertekin. 1995. *10 Jahre Eltern Arbeit (1985–1995): Eine Dokumentation des Türkischen. Elternvereins in Berlin-Brandenburg e.V.* Berlin.

———. 1992. *Immigrantenorganisationen in Deutschland.* Berlin: Hitit.

Pagenstecher, Cord. 1996. "Die 'Illusion' der Rückkehr: Zur Mentalitätsgeschichte von 'Gastarbeit' und Einwanderung," *Soziale Welt* 47, no. 2: 149–179.

Pfeiffer, Christian, and Peter Wetzels. 2000. "Integrationsprobleme junger Spätaussiedler und die Folgen für ihre Kriminalitätsbelastung." In *Neue Wege der Aussiedlerintegration: vom politischen Konzept zur Praxis.* Bonn: Friedrich Ebert Stiftung.

Pfeiffer, Ulrich. 2001. *Einwanderung: Integration, Arbeitsmarkt, Bildung.* Berlin: Friedrich Ebert Stiftung.

Pichler, Edith. 1997. "Migration und ethnische Ökonomie: das italienische Gewerbe in Berlin," *Leviathan, Zuwanderung und Stadtentwicklung,* Sonderheft 17: 106–137.

Putnam, Robert D. 1998. *Making Democracy Work: Civic Traditions in Modern Italy.* Princeton, NJ: Princeton University Press.

Rada, Uwe. 2001. *Berliner Barbaren: Wie der Osten in den Westen kommt.* Berlin: Basis Druck.

Rath, Jan, Rinus Pennix, Kees Groenedijk, and Astrid Meyer. 2001. *Western Europe and its Islam.* Leiden/Boston/Cologne: Brill.

———. 1999. "The Politics of Recognizing Religious Diversity in Europe: Social Reactions to the Institutionalization of Islam in the Netherlands, Belgium and Great Britain," *Netherlands Journal of Social Sciences* 35, no. 1: 53–68.

Redaktionsgruppe Memorandum. 2003. *Zuwanderung und Integration in den neuen Bundesländern: Chancen, Risiken, Aufgaben* Berlin (January).

Rieker, Yvonne. 2003. *Ein Stuck Heimat findet man immer: Die italienische Einwanderung in die Bundesrepublik.* Essen: Klartext.

Romberg, Otto R., and Susanne Urban-Fahr, eds. 1999. *Juden in Deutschland nach 1945.* Bonn: Bundeszentrale für politische Bildung.

Roseman, Curtis C., Hans Dieter Laux, and Günther Thieme, eds. 1996. *EthniCity: Geographic Perspectives on Ethnic Change in Modern Cities.* Boston: Rowman & Littlefield.

Rosen, Klaus-Henning, ed. 1992. *Die zweite Vertreibung: Fremde in Deutschland.* Bonn: Dietz.

Rotte, Ralph. 2000. "Immigration Control in United Germany: Toward a Broader Scope of National Policies," *International Migration Review* 34, no. 2 (Summer): 357–389.

Rubenstein, Kim. 2003. "The Centrality of Migration to Citizenship," *Citizenship Studies* 7, no. 2: 255–264.

Rubio-Marin, Ruth. 2000, *Immigration and the Democratic Challenge: Citizenship and Inclusion in Germany and the United States.* Cambridge: Cambridge University Press.

Rudolph, Hedwig, und Felicitas Hillmann. 1997. "Döner contra Boulette— Döner und Boulette: Berliner türkischer Herkunft als Arbeitskräfte und Unternehmer im Nahrungsgütersektor," *Leviathan, Zuwanderung und Stadtentwicklung,* Sonderheft 17: 85–105.

Schieder, Rolf. 2001. *Wieviel Religion verträgt Deutschland?* Frankfurt/Main: Suhrkamp.

Schiffauer, Werner. 2000. *Die Gottesmänner: Türkische Islamisten in Deutschland.* Frankfurt/M: Suhrkamp.

———. 2000. *Migration und kulturelle Differenz.* Berlin: Ausländerbeauftragte des Senats.

———. 1997. *Fremde in der Stadt: Zehn Essays über Kultur und Differenz.* Frankfurt/M: Suhrkamp.

———. 1991. *Die Migranten aus Subay: Türken in Deutschland. Eine Ethnographie.* Stuttgart: Klett-Cotta.

———. 1983. *Die Gewalt der Ehre: Erklärung zu einem türkisch-deutschen Sexualkonflikt.* Frankfurt/Main: Suhrkamp.

Schoeps, J. H., W. Jasper, and B.Vogt. 1999. *Ein neues Judentum in Deutschland: Fremd- und Eigenbilder der russischen-jüdischen Einwanderer.* Potsdam: Verlag für Berlin-Brandenburg.

———. 1996. *Russische Juden in Deutschland: Integration und Selbstbehauptung in einem fremden Land.* Weinheim: Beltz.

Schölzel, Christian, ed. 1999. *Vom Balkan nach Berlin: Ein Streifzug durch die Beziehungen zu Jugoslawien und seinen Nachfolgestaaten.* Berlin: Ausländerbeauftragte des Senats.

Schuck, Peter, and Rainer Münz, eds. 1998. *Paths to Inclusion: The Integration of Migrants in the United States and Germany.* Providence/Oxford: Berghahn Books.

Schutze, Yvonne. 2000. "Dauerhafte oder transnationale Migration: Das Beispiel der russischen Juden in Berlin," *Berliner Debatte INITIAL* 11: 104–110.

Seidel-Pielen, Eberhard. 1996. *AUFGESPIESST: Wie der Döner über die Deutschen kam.* Berlin: Rotbuch.

Seifert, Wolfgang. 2002. *Berufliche Integration von Zuwanderern in Deutschland.* Gutachten für die Unabhängige Kommission "Zuwanderung." Düsseldorf (March).

———. 1996a. "Berufliche, ökonomische und soziale Mobilität von Arbeitsmigranten zwischen 1984 und 1993." In *Lebenslagen im Wandel: Sozialberichterstattung im Längsschnitt,* eds. Wolfgang Zapf, Jürgen Schupp, and Roland Habich, 240–263. Frankfurt/Main/New York: Campus.

———. 1996b. "Neue Zuwanderergruppen auf dem westdeutschen Arbeitsmarkt," *Soziale Welt* 47, no. 2: 180–201.

Sen, Faruk, Martina Sauer, and Dirk Halm. 2001. *Intergeneratives Verhalten und (Selbst-) Ethnisierung von türkischen Zuwanderern.* Gutachten für die Unabhängige Kommission "Zuwanderung." Essen (March).

Shadid, W. A. R., and P. S. van Koningsveld, eds. 2002. *Religious Freedom and the Neutrality of the State: The Position of Islam in the European Union.* Leuven: Peeters.

Skapska, Grazyna. 2001. "Zwischen Kollektivismus und Individualismus: Staatsbürgerschaft in der polnischen Verfassungsgeschichte." In *Staatsbürgerschaft in Europa: historische Erfahrungen und aktuelle Debatten,* eds. Christoph Conrad and Jürgen Kocka. 255–278. Hamburg: Körber-Stiftung.

Soininen, Maritta. 1999. "The 'Swedish Model' as an institutional framework for immigrant membership rights," *Journal of Ethnic and Migration Studies* 25, no. 4: 685–702.

Soysal, Yasemin Nuhoglu. 1994. *The Limits of Citizenship: Migrants and Postnational Membership in Europe.* Chicago: University of Chicago Press.

Stach, Andrzej. 1999. *Das polnische Berlin/Polski Berlin.* Berlin: Ausländerbeauftragte.

Süssmuth, Rita, et al. 2001. *Structuring Immigration, Fostering Integration.* Report by the Independent Commission on Migration to Germany (*Zuwanderungsbericht*). Berlin (4 July).

Tan, Dursun, and Hans-Peter Waldhoff. 1996. "Turkish Everyday Culture in Germany and its Prospects." In *Turkish Culture in German Society Today,* eds. David Horrocks and Eva Kolinsky, 137–156. Providence/London: Berghahn Books.

Tempio, Mario. 2000. *Italien in Berlin.* Berlin: Ausländerbeauftragte des Senats.

Tertlit, Hermann. 1996. *Turkish Power Boys: Ethnographie einer Jugendbande.* Frankfurt/Main: Suhrkamp.

Thaler, Peter. 1997. "A Bridge Lost: Interethnicities along the German-Polish Border," *International Migration Review* 31, no. 3: 694–703.

Thränhardt, Dietrich. 1999. "Integrationsprozesse in der Bundesrepublik Deutschland: Institutionelle und soziale Rahmenbedingungen." In *Integration und Integrationsförderung in der Einwanderungsgesellschaft.* Bonn: Friedrich Ebert Stiftung.

———. 1995. "Die Reform der Einbürgerung in Deutschland." In *Einwanderungskonzeptionen für die Bundesrepublik.* Bonn: Friedrich Ebert Stiftung.

Tietze, Nikola. 1997. "Moslemische Handlungsstrategien bei jungen Erwachsenen: Ein Vergleich zwischen einer deutschen und einer französischen Stadt." In *Leviathan, Zuwanderung und Stadtentwicklung,* Sonderheft 17: 365–385.

Togeby, Lise. 1999. "Migrants at the Polls: An analysis of immigrant and refugee participation in Danish local elections," *Journal of Ethnic and Migration Studies* 25, no. 4 (October): 665–684.

Tomlein, Oliver, ed. 2001. *Leitkultur—Besonderes Kennzeichen: D. Wahre Deutsche, Staatsbürger zweiter Klasse und die unsichtbaren Dritten.* Hamburg: Konkret.

Tran Trong, Khoi, and Nguyen-Xuan Vinh. 1997. *Vietnamesen in Berlin: Exil und neue Heimat, Zwei Generationen.* Berlin: Ausländerbeauftragte des Senats.

Tröster, Beate. 2000. "Das Netzwerk für Integration in Erfurt." In *Neue Wege der Aussiedlerintegration: vom politischen Konzept zur Praxis.* Bonn: Friedrich Ebert Stiftung.

Türkischer Bund Berlin-Brandenburg, e.V. 2003. *Bericht des Vorstandes.* Berlin (March).

Ulrich, Ralf E. 2001. *Die zukünftige Bevölkerungsstruktur Deutschlands nach Staatsanghörigkeit, Geburtsort und ethnischer Herkunft: Modellrechnung bis 2050.* Gutachten für die Unabhängige Kommission "Zuwanderung." Berlin/Windhoek (April).

Van Heelsum, Anja, and Rinus Pennix. 1999. "Evaluating integration and participation policies for immigrants and minorities in an Amsterdam District: Oost." UNESCO MOST Report, 38–44. Amsterdam/Liege: MPMC.

Van Kempen, Ronald, and Gideon S. Bolt. 1997. "Turks in the Netherlands, Urban Segregation and Neighborhood Choice." *American Behavioral Scientist* 41, no. 3: 374–395.

Vermeulen, Hans, and Rinnus Pennix, eds. 2000. *Immigrant Integration: The Dutch Case.* Amsterdam: Het Spinhuis.

Vertovec, Steve. 1999. "Minority associations, networks and public policies: Reassessing relationships," *Journal of Ethnic and Migration Studies* 12, no. 1: 21–42.

Wallraff, Gunter. 1985. *Ganz Unten.* Cologne: Kiepenheuer & Witsch.

Weidacher, Alois, ed. 2000. *In Deutschland zu Hause: Politische Orientierungen griechischer, italienischer, türkischer und deutscher junger Erwachsener im Vergleich.* Opladen: Leske + Budrich.

Weisse, Frieder. 1993. *Koreaner in Berlin.* Berlin: Ausländerbeauftragte des Senats.

Welt, Jochen. 2000. "Die Aussiedlerpolitik der Bundesregierung: Zwischenbilanz und Ausblick." In *Neue Wege der Aussiedlerintegration: vom politischen Konzept zur Praxis.* Bonn: Friedrich Ebert Stiftung.

Westphal, Manuela. 1997. *Aussiedlerinnen: Geschlecht, Beruf und Bildung unter Einwanderungsbedingungen.* Bielefeld: Kleine Verlag.

Winkler, Beate. 2003. *Migrants, Minorities and Employment: Exclusion, Discrimination and Anti-Discrimination in the 15 Member-States of the European Union* (October). Vienna: EUMC.

———. 1994. *Was heisst denn hier fremd? Thema Ausländerfeindlichkeit: Macht und Verantwortung der Medien.* Munich: Humboldt.

Wittenberg, Reinhard. 1998. "Antisemitische Einstellungen in Deutschland zwischen 1994 und 1998," *Kölner Zeitschrift für Soziologie und Sozialpsychologie* 52, no. 1: 118–131.

Wobbe, Theresa. 2000. "Die Koexistenz nationaler und supranationaler Bürgerschaft: Neue Formen politischer Inkorporation," *Kölner Zeitschrift für Soziologie und Sozialpsychologie,* Sonderheft 40: 251–274.

Wolf-Poweska, Anna, and Dieter Bingen, eds. 2005. *Nachbarn auf Distanz: Polen und Deutsche 1998–2004.* Wiesbaden: Harrassowitz Verlag.

Y, Inci. 2005. *Erstickt an Euren Lügen: Eine Türkin in Deutschland erzählt.* Munich: Piper.

Zentrum Demokratische Kultur, eds. 2004. *Aspekte der Demokratiegefährdung im Berliner Bezirk Mitte und Möglichkeiten der demokratischen Intervention.* Berlin (March).

———. 2003. *Demokratiegefährdenden Phänomene in Friedrichshain-Kreuzberg und Möglichkeiten der Intervention.* Berlin (February).

Zentrum für Türkeistudien (ZfT). 2001a. *Türkei: Jahrbuch des Zentrums für Türkeistudien 2000/2001.* Münster: LIT Verlag.

———. 2001b. *Die ökonomische Dimension der türkischen Selbständigen in Deutschland und in der Europäische Union.* Essen (June).

———. 2000. *Die Lebenssituation und Partizipation türkischer Migranten in Nordrhein-Westfalen.* Essen (June).

———. 1999a. *Die Regionalen Transferstellen für ausländischer Existenzgründer und Unternehmer in NRW.* Essen (October).

———. 1999b. *Ausbildung in türkischen Betrieben.* ZFT-aktuell no. 75. Essen.

———. 1999c. *Ältere Migranten in Deutschland.* Zft-aktuell no. 76. Essen.

Zaptçıoğlu, Dilek, 2005. *Türken und Deutsche: Nachdenken über eine Freund-schaft.* Frankfurt/Main: Brandes & Apsel.

Zolberg, A., and A. J. Clarkin, eds. 2003. *Sharing Integration Experiences: Inno-vative Community Practices on Two Continents.* New York: International Center for Migration, Ethnicity and Citizenship.

INDEX

Printed in the United Kingdom
by Lightning Source UK Ltd.
134186UK00001B/214-261/P